WOW!

Anthology of B-24 / 8th Air Force / World War II Stories

Over 65 bomber crew narrations on their most memorable
combat mission.
Plus
50 diverse war-related stories
and
Saga of infantryman, Bulge to Russian soldiers
also
18 WWII personalities
and finally
Short autobiog, other life experiences.

by Ralph Welsh

i

ISBN: 978-0-692-00078-6

Library of Congress Cataloging-in-Publication Data:
2009900317

Cover photo:
"Destruction was not all one way. This B-24 was attacked by
Me262 jet fighters, very close to the end of the war. Only one
crew member survived, though that in itself must have been a
miracle."
For this mission's write-up, see Chapter VI, "Mission 23 –
Baumenheim."

Corporate Offices:
Welsh Products, Inc.
P.O. Box 6120
Arnold, CA 95223
800-745-3255
Fax: 866-855-4239
info@welshproducts.com

Author Address:
1525A Golden Gate Ave.
San Francisco, CA 94115
randawelsh@yahoo.com

Table of Contents

This book is dedicated to military men and women—past, present, and future. Their service to our country, unlike some others, is not motivated to achieve influence or personal gain.

Author Biography

Experienced great depression, WWII pilot/commander 33 European bombing missions. College, stockbroker, manager, finder/intermediary sale of 11 companies to H.J. Heinz, Labatt, etc. Founder, owner of a graphic arts supply mail order company 30 years, retired age 87. Married to Ann 53 years, 3 fine boys, one great girl...

ABBREVIATIONS:
Bn, battalion
CAVU, ceiling and visibility unlimited
CW, combat wing
DR, dead reckoning
FG, fighter group
IP, a point above ground from which a straight bomb run was made to a target
Mae West, life preserver
Mickey, radar
OLC, oak leaf cluster (subsequent earning of the same medal)
PFF, pathfinder radar
SQ, squadron
ZI, sone of interior, i.e., US

Prologue

This is a multi-dimensional story, as you can see from the titles of the chapters. The majority of the book is composed of some 100 wartime stories—mostly aerial combat missions—written by those who experienced them. Two chapters are devoted to a condensed version of my, to me, varied and interesting life. Another tells the experiences of an 18-year-old foot soldier, Battle of the Bulge to meeting the Russians at the Elbe, plus his amazing biography, and a compassionate story he wrote for a book introduction. I kept a diary of my 33 missions as pilot/commander of a B-24, recounted word for worried word of a 24-year-old experiencing deadly situations. There's a lot of World War II here written, not mainly by historians, but by the actual participants. It's the #1 raison d'etre of this effort. Should aerial and related war stories grab you, you'll love this book.

I titled this effort "WOW!" because I look for WOWS in my life. The every day, mundane things are fine, but to experience something that automatically makes you exclaim, mouth, or think WOW is a shot of adrenaline. Examples: A couple of years ago I was driving from Hartford to Harrisburg PA and it was a bit past fall color season. But on two, maybe three, occasions, I would round a corner and there would be a beautifully shaped tree still in splendid colors. Without any thought, a WOW came out... We were in an upscale Paris seafood restaurant and the first sip of the suggested wine evoked a, well, you know what. Hear a great solo musician, see an extraordinarily beautiful sunset or a splendid mountain, there are many examples that transcend the ordinary. But the greatest WOWS are us. Frequently I strike up a conversation with strangers and sometimes discover a WOW. Often they have interesting careers and are well traveled. I have many regrets that our paths crossed but once... So—enrich your life by varying your work and living experiences. Go for a WOW! Then you'll more fully appreciate the wonderful thing that is the world and humanity.

I do not mean to suggest that the following pages are full of WOWs. But there are some. For example, in Chapter XI, I think "TAPS" rates one. There are, I believe, many stories you

1

will find compelling. One such is in Chapter I, "Memories of an Interlude in England in 1944." And there are several that make you cringe over the inhumanity war causes. Most readers, I believe, will find stories of interest to them—stories that have not been available to the public at large.

This effort went directly from author to printer. I trust you'll not require the sophisticated product a publisher might produce, and overlook a wart here and there. Oh, and our grandson, Tanner, is responsible for the pictures, plus getting everything in proper order. And our son Brian did most of the laborious transition of getting stories into the computer. And wife Ann did a lot of proof reading. A family project.

I was a kid growing up in the 1920s and 30s in the boonies of northeastern Montana and northwestern North Dakota. The depression, the dust bowl, anemic grain crops ravaged by drought and grasshoppers drove us out in 1936, the day after I graduated from Lignite, ND high school. My parents and I and our dog Terry left with little money and very few belongings in our 1928 Chevrolet. Our route was highway #2 across northern Montana, Idaho, and into Spokane, Washington. We lived by laboring at what we could find. I earned enough working in a logging camp as a lowly brush piler at $4/day to attend Kinman Business University in Spokane, which led to a job—at age 19—as a stenographer in the all male office of Hecla Mining Company in Wallace, Idaho. Here I noted the benefits of higher education, and World War II and the GI bill got me to Gonzaga U and a graduate degree from Stanford. So a 35-month pilot stint in the military literally changed my life. In 1951 I was recalled into the now United States Air Force (different color uniform) and it was a waste of time, and I wasted more. But at age 36 I married, and in a sense that's when the direction of my life began. I enjoyed flying (but not combat), stock brokering in the 1950s and 60s. Management positions led me to my most enjoyable endeavor, acting independently as finder/intermediary in selling companies to the likes of H.J. Heinz, Chef Francisco, a frozen food division of Labatt Breweries, Weedabix, and Shreiber Foods of Green Bay, WI.

We—my great wife Ann and I—sold the San Francisco view home we had built after pretty much raising our 3 boys and a girl in the upscale community of Tiburon in Marin County to start our own business, a graphic arts supply mail order company. Ann grew it, I subsidized the national marketing with my intermediary fees on completed deals, and it has enabled us to travel extensively U.S. and abroad for these last 27 years. In April of 2007 we retired at the ages of 87 and 74 by having one of our sons take over. Long live Welsh Products, Inc.! (WPI to us).

Most of the war stories were gleaned from the 2nd Air Division's "Journal." Should WOW! become a profitable venture, donations are promised. Ray Pytell, the "Journal" editor, suggested the Division's library in Norwich, England, as the appropriate recipient. This to aid them in their worthy and professional task of reminding us the freedoms we enjoy are retained by life giving sacrifices.

ON WITH THE STORY!

Chapter 1: A Sample of What's to Come

The Roar That Gave Them Hope
by James M. Davis (489th)

Our duty as part of the Eighth Air Force during World War II was to drop bombs on German targets such as industry, airfields, transportation, communication facilities, and many other targets as well as to destroy the German Air Force. A terrific price was paid in men and planes.

It was forty-three years later that I discovered that we did much more than we were aware of at the time.

In 1987 Jean and I attended the Second Air Division Association reunion in Norwich, England. After the reunion we flew to Switzerland to visit that country for a week. One day we took an all-day bus tour. About two o'clock in the afternoon we arrived at Bern. The tour director told us that we would have an hour of free time to do what we wanted to. There were about forty people on the bus. They were from all over the world, and I don't believe I heard English spoken. Jean and I decided that we would walk down the street and do some window shopping. We had walked about two blocks and were looking in a window when a gentleman approached and asked if we were on the same tour bus. I had seen him on the bus and told him we were.

He said, "I believe you are Americans." I told him that yes, we were from the United States. He said, "Pardon me, but I would like to visit with you," and suggested we go down the block to a sidewalk café where he would like to buy us a drink. We told him we would be happy to visit with him. We ordered our drinks and he asked what part of the United States we came from.

We told him we were from Texas, and he said he always wanted to visit Texas because he had heard so much about it. He spoke good English with only a slight accent. He asked if we were tourists or on a business trip. We told him we were on vacation and had visited England for about a week to attend a reunion, and since we had never been to Switzerland we decided to make a visit before returning to the States.

4

During our conversation he asked what kind of a reunion we had attended in England. I told him I had been a member of the Eighth Air Force during World War II, and that we returned every four years or so to have a reunion. He asked me what I did during the war. I told him I had been a pilot of a B-24 and flew combat missions over Germany and the occupied countries of Western Europe. He paused for a moment before he arose from his chair, and with tears running down his cheek he put his arms around me and embraced me as I had never been embraced before. For a long time he held me in his arms. Finally, with a broken voice he said, "Excuse me but I owe you so much. I owe you my life." He told me I was the first member of an aircrew that he had had the privilege to meet, and he felt so indebted to me and would like to explain why.

He was a young Jewish boy, sixteen years old, living with his family in Poland when the Germans invaded the country in September, 1939. He was taken prisoner and spent the rest of the war in various slave labor camps. He told me the only way they could survive from day to day was hearing the roar of the airplanes flying overhead. They had no knowledge of what was happening, but as long as they could hear the airplanes they had a ray of hope and it provided them the will to survive another day. The noise of the planes provided their only hope and communication to the free world.

After the war he returned to his home town in Poland. There was no home, no family, no kinfolks or friends. They had all been killed or destroyed during the war. He migrated to Israel and started a meat and sausage processing plant which was very successful. The reason he was in Switzerland was that he had gone to Frankfurt, Germany to attend a display of meat processing equipment by manufacturers from all over the world. He had debated for three years whether he could stand to go back to Germany, and at the last minute he decided to go, even though his family had begged him not to. When he arrived at Frankfurt and stepped off the plane into the terminal, he suddenly realized that he could not emotionally stand it, and rushed over to the airplane ticket desk and asked what was the next plane leaving Frankfurt. It happened to be a flight to Switzerland that was loading and had room. He had a day to lay over before he could get a flight home, so he decided to take the tour that we were on.

He asked us to go with him to Israel, where he had a lot of friends who would be just as happy to meet me. He showed us a picture of his daughter's wedding party. The party was made up of the highest government officials, including the leader of Israel, the defense minister and all of the cabinet members. He assured us that we would get royal treatment and be most welcomed guests. We explained that we could not go at this time because we had to get home, but that some day we planned on visiting his country. I am sure it would be a trip that we would always remember.

He was the most grateful and gracious person that I have ever met.

Somehow all those difficult times I experienced while flying my tour seems to have a different meaning. Until I met this gentleman I never realized that just the sound of an airplane could give a person the will and courage to survive another day. I never regretted the effort and difficulty it took to survive a tour. Now it seems such a small effort compared to the untold millions who suffered so much in Europe during the war.

Ludwigshaven—A Mission to Remember
by Major R. B. Seigh, USAF (Ret.) 389th

January 7, 1944 is a date I shall remember the rest of my life. I was a member of Capt. Jerome M. Kennedy's crew flying the right waist position. We joined the 389th Bomb Group in Sept. of 1943 and were assigned to the 565th Bomb Squadron. On this particular mission our crew was flying deputy lead on the right wing of Capt. Willhite. The mission to the target was uneventful and without too much trouble. As we came off the target for the return to England, my pilot became concerned, as well as Lt. Col. Jack Dieterle, who was flying as Command Pilot, on the route the Group Leader was taking. He elected to leave the main bomber stream and head toward Paris. The flight over France was without trouble until approximately 26 miles from Paris we were hit by fighters. Captain Willhite was hit almost immediately by a head-on attack. I saw the shells hit the right engines and set them on fire. Shells also hit the nose, cockpit area and waist area. Capt. Willhite's B-24 started a bank to the right. My pilot attempted to bank with him but the angle became too steep and we were forced to pull away and level off. In the meantime, Willhite leveled off and flew directly over our aircraft, almost colliding with us. Willhite's plane did a steep turn, nosed down and about 5,000 feet below us the right wing came off and the B-24 cart wheeled toward the ground. Meanwhile, the steep bank had forced us away from the group. Seeing this, Capt. Kennedy increased his speed and took over the lead position of the 389th. At about this time a lone P-47 came by and kept some of the fighters from us but eventually he had to leave the fight and return to England because of low fuel supply. I have no idea where the 445th was, but I can tell you that they were not near the 389th. We lost 8 or 9 B-24s that day. A group of Spitfires picked us up near the French coast and escorted us to England... As a side note, only one man survived from Capt. Willhite's crew and that man was the top turret gunner and I believe his name was T/Sgt. Swetz. We were lucky that day and I guess the Good Lord was with us.

My Comments:

This recount would not have been told if the group leader had done the sensible thing, and that is to follow the main bomber stream. There is strength in numbers! The larger the formation, less likelihood enemy fighters attack you. Maybe he thought it was a short cut, or maybe he wanted to see what Paris looked like. War casualties occur oftentimes because of lack of common sense. I always had a beef with the military's rank consciousness. We would have a mission leader recently from stateside with little or no combat experience, only because of rank, and it would increase the risk. Higher rank didn't always mean better judgment. Experience in combat definitely increases one's odds. Aside from the chance of sheer luck in catching a flak burst in your bomber's belly which could happen on your first or your last mission, the newer the crew the more likely the casualty. This was more true of the ground soldier, where inadequately trained newcomers to the front lines had really high loss rates. Read some of Steven Ambrose's WWII recounts and you will realize that war breeds many mistakes and generals are not exempt.

Ploesti
by Edwin C. Baker, 93rd BG

Orders came down from Command for the raid on Ploesti. Aug. 1, 1943 was to be the day. The evening before we taxied all aircraft out on the field and parked them in a straight line, but cocked at 45 degrees. We were fueled and bomb-loaded from this position, so when we started the engines in the morning, no one would have to eat dust and sand. It would also prevent clogging of engine intakes and other sand related problems. We didn't want any aborts. We were loaded with incendiary bombs and some 500 pounders with delay action fuses from 1-hour to 2-days—the theory being it would prevent their fire crews from entering the area not knowing when another bomb would go off. The final preparation was to have all gas tanks topped off. We were going to need every drop of gas to make this round trip. As operations officer, I went about assigning the crews and aircraft positions. Of course, I assigned myself as Co-Pilot/Plane Commander on my old crew and also assigned Little Lady to the left wing position of the first element of our squadron. In this position, I would fly the aircraft. The squadron and element lead ship (Tupelo Lass) was being flown by Maj. K.O. Dessert (Sqd. C.O.) and Capt. Jake Epting. Lt. Hoover, Wilkie's regular Co-Pilot, begged to go on the mission. Observers were OK'd, so I let him go as extra Co-Pilot and he stood between the seats throughout the flight. We had one other passenger (Observer) 1st Lt. Edward E. Mitchell. I can't remember why he rode with us, or what he did during the mission. I don't remember the positions I assigned for the rest of the aircraft in our squadron. The only reason I remember flying left wing off of Dessert and Epting is because I stared at them for almost 6-hours. I know that the 409th Squadron put up a full compliment of ships—9 aircraft. On August 1, 1943 we had a short briefing at 0700 hours. Breakfast, for those who could eat, and we were in our aircraft awaiting flare signal from the tower for start engines and takeoff. The field was wide enough to permit us to takeoff in our elements of three at a time. This put our Group into the air in short order and we were formed on Colonel Addison Baker (Group C.O.)—no relation—way before other Groups. We finally moved into position behind the 376th Bomb Group and headed out across the Mediterranean toward first land fall—Corfu (on the Ionian Islands, off the coat of Greece). The target approach plan was to fly at tree-top level, passing over two towns before reaching the I.P. The towns were Pitesti, Targoviste, and then the I.P.-Floresti. Each of these towns was nestled in a valley surrounded by rolling hills. At the I.P., we would make a right turn (Southeast) and string out into a single straight line (still in formation, wing tip to wing tip) attacking the refinery on the paths we were trained to follow. K.K. Compton (our 'ole 409th Squadron C.O.) was transferred to the 376th Bomb Group as their C.O. His Group would be the lead Group into the target. We would follow him and be the 2nd over the target. The rest of the Groups would follow in a stair step fashion, each being a little higher than the other. Shortly after we went out over the Mediterranean, one of the ships in the Group ahead of us must have blown up or something. It went straight down into the sea. We didn't see any parachutes or survivors.

We hit Corfu on the money. Turning inland, we were confronted with high mountains, which were covered with cumulus clouds that rose well above them. A cold chill went down my spine. It was obvious we were going to have to fly through these. We loosened up the formation, spread out, noted the compass heading and headed straight in, climbing. At 10,000 ft. we put on our oxygen masks. We finally broke through at about 15,000 ft. and leveled off. It was a great feeling to see the other ships around us and in fairly good order. We quickly squeezed into our 'V' elements of 3 ships as before and crossed the mountains. We felt sure we had been detected now. The plan was to skim across the mountains at a minimum altitude in the hopes of staying below the radar beams. As we crossed the last range, we started a zigzag descent. We leveled off low and continued pressing forward. We stayed at tree top level, only climbing to get over hills and terrain. Still no flak or fighters. Maybe we were actually going to get away with a surprise. Before us lay a basin of beautiful farm land, green with neat cross hatched rows of planting.

Something we hadn't seen in a long time. We began to see our first peasants. Women in gaily-colored dresses with upturned smiling faces waving handkerchiefs at us.Before long we came upon our first town—Pitesti. Then the second town came into view—Targoviste. To the complete shock to all of us, the Group turned south. Hebert called on the intercom, "Where the hell are you going? This isn't Floresti—you've turned too soon." I answered, "I can't help that; we're sticking with the Group." By that time radio silence was broken and I could hear several calls saying, "wrong turn; wrong turn." We moved out to our straight line frontal attack position, wing tip to wing tip. As I looked at K.O. in the lead plane, he shrugged his shoulders and made a motion, indicating he didn't know what was going on. He, too, realized we made a wrong turn. We pressed on. Still no fighters—where were they? Suddenly, the flak started to come. It was bursting above us. Our reaction was to get lower and lower. Our waist gunners were now firing at gun emplacements. I could see men toppling over and doubling up as we passed over them. We came along side of an electrical sub station. The gunners let a blast go into the transformers. The fireworks were spectacular. Colonel Baker broke away from the 376th and started a left turn. I had to pull off power. Since I was so close to the ground, I couldn't drop down. I kept pulling off more power. I was afraid I was going to run over K.O. from my momentum. Finally, we straightened out and I had to really pour the power to the ship in order to keep up. All hell was breaking loose. Anti-aircraft guns, ground fire and the pursuit ships had shown up. We came across a lake area with sun bathers laying around. Some were military and they jumped up and fired rifles at us. A burst from our gunners sent those left standing scurrying for cover. A machine gun turret on a tower in the area fired at us. The gunners raked the tower longer making short bursts; they were going almost steadily. We had to raise our left wing to clear a church steeple with a clock in it. The time was five minutes to 3 o'clock. We leveled off and opened our bomb bay doors. Straight ahead was a row of eucalyptus trees. From underneath anti-aircraft, guns started shooting point blank at us. You could hear the swish and feel the shells go by us. My God, we're sitting ducks! As fast as we were going, I had the feeling we were standing still. The roar of our engines, and noise of guns and flak was unbearable. Planes on both sides of us were being hit. Are we next?

We got two hits, almost simultaneously. One in our #3 engine on the right side and one under the belly of the ship. The hits gave us a reaction of being stopped cold in mid-air. K.O. and Eptings' ship shot ahead of us and out of sight. I never saw them again. Finally, we were at the eucalyptus trees and had to pull up to clear them. Wilkie and I were both on the controls now trying to keep the ship straight and level. Our #3 engine was on fire and gas was pouring out of our belly tank from flak holes. Silverman opened the bomb bay doors as we came into the refinery area. This added to the drag and our airspeed started to drop. Hoover reached down and pulled the fire extinguisher on #3 and I feathered it. Silverman hollered "Bombs Away" and our ship made a lurch upward from the relief of the weight. The gas fumes were getting stronger and it was hard to breathe. Wilkie and I opened our windows for air. The fresh air felt good, but added to the noise. The fire in #3 engine gradually went out after it was feathered and shut down. Why the fire stream from our #3 engine and raw gas from our belly tanks did not get together and blow us up, I'll never know. Everything was happening at once. I saw Colonel Addison Baker (our Group C.O.) take a direct hit. He pulled out his aircraft up and as it fell off on it's right wing, two chutes opened, but they drifted right into the holocaust of fire as their ship went straight into the ground. They didn't have a chance. Silverman called out "bomb bay doors closed." I yelled for him to open the damn things; we were being flooded out with raw gas and fumes from the bomb bay tanks. A storage tank blew up in front of us and we flew just to the right of it. The plane on our left went right through it and I never saw him come out. As we passed the heat of the explosion, it felt like passing a hot iron close to your face. Silverman opened the bomb bay doors. The few seconds those doors were closed is when we passed beside the blown-up storage tank. I'm sure if our bomb bay doors had been opened the raw gas flowing out would have caught fire and blown up. Luck was still with us. We had little fires all over the wings, apparently from gas leaks and debris. They went out on their own, fortunately, before any more serious damage was done. We zigzagged through columns of black smoke and fire. We still were not out of it yet. The other Groups were coming in on their bomb runs above us. We were taking the percussions of their bombs and the debris they blew up. Suddenly, we popped out of the hell hole of fire, flame and smoke into the clear sky and green fields beyond. We were clear and still flying, although badly damaged, but not fatally. Wilkie and I looked at each other and smiled. As I relaxed my grip on the wheel, I realized and felt the pain of numbness in my hands and forearms. My knuckles were white from gripping the wheel. I took a deep breath, leaned back in my seat to relax. I felt as though I had held my breath through the entire bomb run. The thumping in my chest was so hard and fast that I thought my heart was going to pop out.

Hits on our ship not only blew out #3 engine, but damaged our control cables. Wilkie was fighting desperately to keep the ship in the air. I grabbed the wheel again and started helping. Over the intercom the gunners were calling off fighters again and their guns were blazing away. We reduced our power and Hoover periodically called off our airspeed. It was steadily going down, so I had to increase it well above normal. If we could keep this plane in the air, our next goal was to reach the pre-arranged rendezvous for crippled aircraft. I called Rolley (flight engineer) to come to the flight deck from the top turret. He said there were fighters around and he was fighting like mad and swinging the turret from one side to another. I told him to get out of the turret and let Kimtantas (radio operator) take over and do something about the gas in the bomb bay. Rolley switched us over to using the gas from the "Toyko" tanks, which seemed to reduce the flowing from the flak holes. We headed westward and were all alone, easy meat for the pursuit fighters in the area.

We were so close to the ground, coupled with our gunners still firing, that the fighters didn't press too close. Out of nowhere a ship from one of the other Bomb Groups pulled up along side of us and flew formation. The combined firepower of our planes completely discouraged the pursuit planes and they left us for easier pickings. Our companion ship was not damaged and he was finding it difficult to stay with us at such a slow speed. We were indicating about 150, just staying airborne. We reached the rendezvous point and started to circle, waiting for others. None showed up. Finally, the companion ship called on the radio and said he could no longer stay with us. I thanked him and told him to go on his way; we were fairly safe now.

Rolley came on the flight deck and reported that we lost almost all of the gas in our "Tokyo" tanks and couldn't possibly get back to our base. We called Hebert and asked him for the nearest, friendly airfield. He responded with "Our first alternate is a small airfield in Turkey near the town of Edrine, just across the Turkish border. Or possibly the British held island of Cypress, in the Mediterranean, off the coast of Turkey." O.K., that's it—he gave us the heading.

Every time we pulled the nose up in a bid for altitude the airspeed would drop off dangerously close to stalling. We were still having control problems and running on three engines. We kept stair stepping, but we were nowhere near the required altitude to go over the Balkan mountain range. We were at 1500 feet when the mountain range loomed in front of us. Now we had real problems. We didn't have enough altitude to go over them and we were committed too far South to turn back. Damn, after all we had just been through, and now we were hemmed in. As we approached the mountains, we saw a large valley and headed for it. We were about to play the greatest game of chance in our lives. We forged on in.

As we entered the valley, an anti-aircraft gun emplacement was spotted on a mountain top above us. They must have heard us coming and were looking up. When they spotted us below them they couldn't get their guns down to fire at us. They waited until we were well into the valley and then fired. They didn't come close enough to do us any harm. Suddenly, the valley split into a 'Y'.

We went left. The next time we came upon a split, we went right, trying to keep in the general direction and heading Hebert gave us. Each valley produced another 'Y' and another choice. We came into some narrow places where our wing tips just cleared sheer walls. We expected to come upon a dead end every time we made the choice of valleys. We must have picked the only route through those mountains. Finally, to our relief, we broke out into the open country.

Beautiful green trees and some farm land. The pressure was now on Hebert to determine where we had come out. Wilkie cautiously asked Hebert for a new heading. "Hell, I don't know where we are with all that zigzagging through those mountains. Give me a couple minutes to find something to orientate us. Do you see any towns or railroads?" Folley cut in on the intercom and said we had less than an hour's worth of gas left. Wilkie insisted that we try for Cypress. We discussed our options if we ran out of gas trying to make Cypress. A crash landing at sea or at best on a sandy beach on the coast of Turkey. No way! Hebert said we could make the small airport in Turkey and gave us a heading to try. As we crossed the border into Turkey, one last attempt by anti-aircraft was made to shoot us down. Again, we survived. I prayed our luck would hold out a little longer.

We finally spotted the airfield and headed for it. We made a circle to survey the field and soon realized that it was for pursuit ships and the runways were very short. We could see other B24s on the field. If they made it, we could. We picked out the runway that looked the longest and Wilkie started his landing approach. We were still having control cable problems. It was hard to get the ship to respond. I told Wilkie we had only one chance to make it; there would be no going around.

We had no electrical power for lowering the gear and flaps. I went to work hand pumping our landing gear down. The wheels finally came down, but our waist gunners couldn't confirm if they were in locked position. With our landing gear in the air stream, our airspeed started to drop rapidly. Hoover was calling it off for Wilkie. My arm felt like it would break as I pumped harder and faster. Wilkie was hollering for flaps. Wheels down or not, I had to give Wilkie some flaps. I switched the selector switch to flaps and pumped like mad. Wilkie pulled off all power to the remaining three engines.

When I looked up, we were coming in too steep and too fast. I grabbed the wheel and we both pulled with all our strength back, back as far as the column would go and tight against our chest, literally standing on the rudder pedals. We hit nose wheel first, and then the main gear with such force that we ricocheted back into the air. We held the wheel tight to our bellies, as we mushed back onto the runway again with a bang and the sound of scraping metal. The landing gear held together, but there were no brakes. I let go of the wheel and hit all switches to 'OFF'. We rolled off the end of the runway into a dirt field and up a small hill before we came to a sliding halt. Gas fumes, dirt and dust were everywhere. I hollered, "Get out before she blows up." I went out my side window head first. I got hung up a little, but made it. Scrambling, half crawling and running, I headed up the hill until I felt I was far enough away to be safe. The others quickly joined me. We all sat there in complete exhaustion staring at Little Lady. She never caught fire or blew up.

We all sat there in silence and transfixed awe at the ship that brought us through Ploesti unharmed. I thought to myself— My God, what we had been through today and this magnificent aircraft stayed airborne and even held together throughout the most abusive landing I have ever seen or experienced. As the dust settled, I could see the holes in her. It was unbelievable. She looked like a sieve, yet not a man on board was even scratched. The landing gear cracked and slowly lowered the belly of the ship to the ground as the left wing buckled at the fuselage and sagged until its wing tip dug into the soft earth.

Little Lady was dying and never would fly again. I almost expected her to make a final flutter of her wings. I started to choke up and shake inside not knowing whether it was finally realizing I was still alive or that I was seeing an airplane that we had cared for and babied all these months, slowly die.

Nazis Kill 491st BG Crewmen
Reprinted From "Briefing," Fall 1987

The Liberator was named "Wham! Bam! Thank You, Ma'am." It was from the 491st Bomb Group. On 24 August 1944, 8th Air Force Bomber Command attacked many targets in Germany. As "Wham! Bam!" dropped its bombs on an airfield north of Hanover, the aircraft was hit by flak and dropped out of formation.

This was the beginning of what was to be one of the most gruesome, nightmare-like incidents to befall a bomber crew in WWII, as reported in a 20-page lead article in *After the Battle*, published in England.

As the crippled B-24, #42-110107, neared the ground near Greven, some ninety miles southwest of Hanover, the pilot, 2nd Lt. Norman J. Rogers, Jr. gave the order to bail out. First to jump was Sgt. William A. Dumont, ball turret gunner, who injured his ankle on landing. Next was Sgt. Thomas D. Williams, radioman; followed by William M. Adams, nose gunner, who was wounded in the arm; Sgt. Sidney E. Brown, tail gunner; Flight Officer Haigus Tufenkjian, navigator; Sgt. Wilmore J. Austin, waist gunner; and Staff Sgt. Forrest M. Brininstool, engineer, who had a flak wound to his stomach. Last out were 2nd Lt. John N. Sekul, copilot, and Lt. Rogers.

All the crew were taken from Greven to a railway station where they traveled to a Luftwaffe airfield where they were interrogated by German officers. "They treated us decently and asked about our wounds," a crewman related.

Adams and the engineer were taken to a field hospital where Brininstool was operated on to remove a piece of shrapnel from his stomach, after which he was taken to a hospital in Munster. Adams returned to the others.

Next morning the crew was taken by train to Dulag Luft aircrew interrogation center at Oberursel, north of Frankfurt. On the 26th, the train arrived at Russelsheim, fifteen miles southwest of Frankfurt. Here the RAF had hit the town with over 400 Lancasters to knock out the Opel factory, which killed 179 of the residents.

The deaths "did not auger well for the American crewmen who arrived in the aftermath of the attack. The mood in

Russelsheim that morning was ugly, and tempers against the 'terror-fliers' were running high," the article relates.

The article describes what followed:

As the railway line was blocked, the eight Americans, escorted by their three Luftwaffe guards, dismounted from the train... For a while it seems that the guards were unsure of what to do next... for the senior man left the group and they never saw him again... The other two guards... then started to move the group off the station and across the Bahnhofplatz on the northern side of the tracks. Sgt. Dumont with his injured ankle was having difficulty in walking and was being helped along by the other crewmen.

The American airmen soon attracted a hostile audience which very quickly grew to a crowd of 'between 250 and 300 people.' It still appeared that the two Luftwaffe guards had no idea of where they were supposed to be going, and when people began throwing stones, they made no attempt to intervene or try to take the party back to the station.

Reaching Frankfurter Strasse, someone in the crowd threw a piece of iron, hitting Lt. Rogers on the head. This appeared to be the sign for a free-for-all to begin, and a hail of missiles began to bombard the men. As they proceeded east along the road, they passed the Park Hotel where three women came out of their shop shouting to those in the crowd to kill the airmen. The women joined in the general tumult and, and as the Americans stumbled along, they were subjected to a continual rain of blows from bricks, broomsticks, shovels, or whatever came easily to hand.

Sgt. Brown later described how "we were attempting to help Dumont, who had a

broken ankle, along as best we could in the crowd, but as we moved on he soon fell to the ground; he was the first to fall, and the people pounced on him and beat him to death right there in the street."

The article goes on to describe the vicious, continual beating the crew received. After they were beaten to the ground they received additional poundings, then the crowd began to disperse.

A wagon was then used to pick up the bodies of the crew, with Brown and copilot Sekul still alive but pretending to be dead.

Brown testified later, "I saw some person, whom I can't describe, with a club in his hand, come over to the wagon—apparently to finish us off. Sekul's hand was on my shoulder and I could feel him wince as this person beat him on the head. I felt his hand slide from my shoulder as he died. Thomas Williams was also next to me, and I heard him make a sound as he was finished off. I thought that all of the crew had been killed by this time. I could see that the flight officer had his brains beaten out and the pilot, Rogers, had his head beat in on one side..."

The so-called "death-march at Russelsheim" became one of the first war crimes to be investigated after the war. Those townspeople who could be identified with the incident were either hung or jailed.

When an Enemy was a Friend

Air Force Magazine January 1997. Copied from Eighth Air Force Historical Society—Colorado Chapter Newsletter

A remarkable story of a Mission that started off from an airfield at Kimbolton, and ended at Seething airfield 60 years ago, or should we say in America in 1990. Brown's B-17 was perhaps the most heavily damaged bomber to return from combat. It survived because of an enemy's act of chivalry.

December 20th, 1943, was a typical overcast day in Britain as 2nd Lt. Charles L. Brown's B-17F lined up for take off. It was 21-year-old Charlie Brown's first combat mission as an aircraft commander with the 379th Bomb Group at Kimbolton, England. The target was an FW-190 factory at Bremen, Germany. He and his crew of "Ye Old Pub" were to become participants in an event probably unique at that time in the air war over Europe, a mission that would remain shrouded in mystery for many years.

The bombers began their 10-minute bomb run at 27,300 feet, the outside temperature—60 below. Flak was heavy and accurate. Before "Bombs Away," Brown's B-17 took hits that shattered the Plexiglas nose, knocked out the number four, which frequently had to be throttled back to prevent over speeding, and caused undetermined damage to the controls. Coming off target,

Lt. Brown was unable to stay with the formation and became a straggler.

Almost immediately, the lone and limping B-17 came under a series of attacks from 12 to 15 Bf-109s and FW-190s that lasted for more than 10 minutes. The number three engine was hit and would produce only half power. Oxygen, hydraulic, and electrical systems were damaged and the controls were only partially responsive. The bomber's 11 defensive guns were reduced by the extreme cold to only the two top turret guns and one forward firing nose gun. The tail gunner was killed and all but one of the crew in the rear incapacitated by wounds or exposure to the frigid air. Lt. Brown took a bullet fragment in his right shoulder.

Charlie Brown's only chance of surviving this pitifully unequal battle was to go on the offensive. Each time a wave of attackers approached, he turned into them, trying to disrupt their aim with his remaining firepower. The last thing the oxygen-starved Brown remembers was reversing a steep turn, becoming inverted, and looking "up" at the ground. When he regained full consciousness, the B-17 was miraculously level at less than 1,000 feet.

Still partially dazed, Lt. Brown began a slow climb with only one engine at full power. With three seriously injured aboard, he rejected bailing out or crash landing. The alternative was a thin chance of reaching the UK. While nursing the battered bomber toward England, Lt. Brown looked out the right window and saw a Bf-109 flying on his wing. The pilot waved, then flew across the B-17s nose and motioned Lt. Brown to land in Germany, which the aircraft commander refused to do. After escorting them for several miles out over the North Sea, the Luftwaffe pilot saluted, rolled over, and disappeared. Why had he not shot them down? The answer did not emerge for many years.

The B-17 did make it across 250 miles of storm-tossed North Sea and landed at Seething near the English coast, home of the 448th Bomb Group which had not yet flown its first mission. The crew were debriefed on their mission, including the strange encounter with the Bf-109. For unknown reasons, the debriefing was classified "secret" and remained so for many years. Lt. Brown went on to complete a combat tour, finish college, accept a regular commission, and serve in the Office of Special Investigations with the Joint Chiefs of Staff, and in other

Air Force and State Department assignments until his retirement. He now lives in Miami, Fla., where he is a founder and president of an energy and environmental research center.

The image of this strange encounter with the Bf-109 remained firmly embedded in Charlie Brown's memory. In 1986, he began a search for the anonymous pilot. Finally, in 1990, former Oberleutant Franz Stigler, now living in Canada, responded to a notice published in a newsletter for German fighter pilots. By comparing time, place, and aircraft markings, it was determined that Stigler was the chivalrous pilot who had allowed Brown's crew to live. Not surprisingly, Brown and Stigler have become close friends.

On that December day, 1932, there had been two persuasive reasons why Stigler should have shot down the B-17. First, earlier in the day, he had downed two four-engine bombers and needed only one more that day to earn a Knights Cross. Second, his decision to not finish off the aircraft was a court martial offense in Nazi Germany and if revealed could have led to his execution. He considered these alternatives while flying formation with the B-17, "the most heavily damaged aircraft I ever saw that was still flying." He could see the wounded aboard and thought, "I cannot kill these half-dead people. It would be like shooting at a parachute."

Franz Stigler's act of chivalry has been justly, though belatedly, honored by several military organizations in America and abroad. On the other hand, Charles Brown was not decorated for his heroism over Germany, which was never reported by the 448th Bomb Group at Seething to his Commanders. Such are the fortunes of war and its aftermath.

(Author's note: My thought is that the mission briefing was classified "secret" to protect the German pilot. Germany had an excellent intelligence network.)

While Europe Appeased the Barbary Pirates, America Sent in the Navy

by Frederick C. Leiner. Oxford, 239 pages, $28.
Book Review by Jonathan Karl. (From a Wall Street Journal article, April 29-30, 2006)

In 1815, Washington was in ruins: the White House and Capitol building burned and sacked by the British, the national treasury depleted, the U.S. bruised and battered (but not defeated) by the War of 1812. President James Madison called the Congress to its makeshift chamber at the Post Office Building and asked for something extraordinary: a declaration of war against a state thousands of miles away.

What followed was the U.S.'s first war on terror. This little conflict is now largely forgotten, but it had great and lasting consequences, establishing the U.S. as a global naval power and ending more than two centuries of state-sponsored terrorism in the Mediterranean.

"The End of Barbary Terror" by Frederick Leiner recounts Madison's decision and the war that followed against an enemy that had attacked and tormented European powers greater than the U.S. since the 1500s. The Barbary states of Algiers, Tunis, Tripoli and Morocco had run a lucrative kidnapping and slavery racket in the Mediterranean, capturing commercial ships, enslaving thousands of Christians and extorting millions of dollars in ransom and protection money from Europe.

"Slave taking was jihad," writes Mr. Leiner, and the tactics employed by the Islamic leaders of the Barbary states "were a form of terrorism, a method of sea borne violence meant to intimidate the peoples of Europe." It was essentially a system of government-regulated kidnapping. The pirates would capture ships, forcing their passengers to work as slaves onshore until somebody came up with enough ransom money to buy their freedom. Eventually the major European states simply paid protection money, deciding it was easier to appease the pirates than confront them. "Paying the Barbary rulers a 'license' for trade was less expensive than constantly convoying ships or attacking the Barbary powers in their heavily fortified ports', Mr. Leiner explains. America played the game too. In the five years before the war, the U.S. council in Algiers doled out a half million dollars in "gifts" and "tributes" intended to buy safety for American ships.

In August 1812, a 71 foot long American trading ship, the Edwin, sailing off the coast of Spain found itself facing an all too common situation in the Mediterranean. A much larger ship from Algiers armed with two rows of cannons overcame the Edwin, capturing the ship and her 10-man crew. The pirates looted the ship and sold the men off to slavery in Algiers. After the War of 1812, Algiers decided to play hardball with the U.S., demanding a staggering ransom of $1million for the return of Edwin's crew. There was logic to the demand. The rulers of Algiers figured that America, its Navy ravaged by war with Britain, could not afford another fight and decide it would be cheaper to pay the ransom. It was a serious miscalculation. President Madison dispatched an armada of the U.S.'s 10 available fighting ships, headed by Stephen Decatur, to the Mediterranean. Decatur's mission: bring back the American hostages and their ship. Madison ordered him not to pay a single cent in ransom or tribute to Algiers.

"The End of Barbary Terror" may go into a bit too much esoteric detail for most readers, but the book recounts a stunning military success. With a mix of bravery and luck, Decatur defeated two enemy ships on his way to Algiers. Within 48 hours of arriving on the shore of the most powerful Barbary state, Decatur was able to force peace on American terms ("dictated at the mouths of our cannon," as he later said). The U.S.'s infant navy had scored a victory, embarrassed the Europeans, and demonstrated that there was no reason to fear the Barbary pirates. Within months, England battled to free British subjects enslaved in Tripoli and soon the entire system of paying tribute to the pirates came crashing down. The American example gave Europe the backbone to fight the terrorists rather than appease them. (Mr. Karl is the senior national security correspondent for ABC news)

15th Air Force Mission to Brenner Pass
from Bomber Legends, as told by the tail gunner.

December 27, 1944, 1100 hours. We were flying lead for the group, trying once again to destroy the German supply and escape route in the Brenner Pass, northern Italy. We had turned on the IP and started the bomb run. The flak was heavy, intense, and accurate. I saw Dalrymples' plane take a direct hit and explode in a ball of fire. I watched MacGrath's plane fly through that inferno of flaming gasoline and debris and come out with his Liberator completely on fire, one end to the other.

We unloaded our bombs and got he hell out of there.

The following day, Brenner Pass again! Evidently we hadn't hit the tunnel but had started an avalanche that blocked one end of it. I was cursing and praying at the same time when we started the bomb run. I heard and felt a big explosion, and the plane nosed over into a dive with the pilots fighting the controls to get leveled off. As we were going down, I heard the "prepare to bail out" signal, and opened he hatch just in time to see three men bailing out. I didn't know which crew members they were, it could have been the pilot and copilot. The ship was still plummeting to earth. As I started to jump, someone behind me held me back. I told him they were bailing out up front. He just looked me in the eye and kept shaking his head "no." All of a sudden the plane started to level off. Somehow the pilots managed to get back in level flight. We had two navigators and the bombardier, the ones I had seen bail out. Now we had to find our own way back. We were in bad shape, a flying wreck. One engine gone, flak holes everywhere, hydraulics shot out and gasoline leaking and dripping all over. One spark and we would be an inferno. Our plane, "Lady in the Dark," was struggling toward friendly territory. We were losing altitude and gasoline. Spotting an airfield, we were going to try to land, friendly or not. But the wheels would not come down hydraulically or manually. We couldn't make a belly landing. Sparks would set off the gasoline.

Suddenly the engines quit. No more gas, time to bail out. Clear of the ship, I pulled the d-ring. Nothing happened. Pulled it again, still, nothing. I pulled up the flap in front of the chute and dug out the little cable that released the chute. The pilot chute popped out, filled with air

and dragged the main chute out. What a relief!

I landed on top of a small mountain. The other guys who had bailed out ahead of me were still in the air, drifting toward friendly territory, passing over me. I was just sitting there and heard someone walking toward me. It was an Italian soldier in full uniform and a holstered pistol on his belt. I figured I was a "goner," but he asked me for cigarettes. I gave him a pack of Chesterfields. He said "Grazie" and some other words I didn't understand, and walked away. A few minutes later I heard someone speaking Italian, asking if I was English. It was a young girl, fifteen or sixteen. She was hanging back but when I said "Americano" she helped me get on my feet. She took me further up the mountain to an old farmhouse, and the two women and an old man gave me a glass of wine. I gulped it down, and did the same with another. They gave me some kind of soup. They seemed very poor. They had some haystacks to feed the goats, and showed me one with a hole, where the dog slept. They apparently wanted me to hide in case some Germans came around. I crawled in, and slept overnight.

Going back to the farmhouse, they fed me again. I gave them about half of my parachute, the chocolate in my escape kit, and my sheepskin pants to the old man, who thanked me endlessly. I found the British, and they took me back to the American Fifth Army lines. The infantrymen asked me a lot of questions about anti-aircraft fire, fighters, types of targets, and what it was like to go deep in enemy territory. They kept me awake half the night. They took me to an airfield where a C-47 took me back to my base. I then learned the rest of the crew got out of the plane. Frank Visciglia, the engineer, practically rode the plane down before he jumped. He always told me he was deathly afraid of parachuting and wouldn't be able to do it. He apparently pulled his ripcord before he got out of the plane. His chute opened but got on the tailskid, with no time or way to get free. He rode the bomber down knowing he would die on impact.

The three who had bailed out first were taken POW. We were sent to the Isle of Capri to rest up and try to forget what we'd been through. I had to fly ten more missions to complete my fifty. Somehow I managed to live through them and was sent back to the good old USA.

"The Poor 100th"
by Kenneth Kinney
Reprinted from the American Legion Magazine, June 1947

When ex-Army Air Force men get together and talk for more than five minutes at a time, the conversation invariably gets around to the various outfits that flew and fought from England, Italy and points west.

From there the talk will turn to reminiscences of big raids, flak and enemy fighters. Then let one of the former buzz-boys say he was in the 100th Bomb Group, and the respect for this man will fairly permeate the air. For the rest of the men realize that they are conversing with a museum piece—an ex-pilot, bombardier, navigator or gunner who flew a tour with the 100th and lived to tell about it.

When the 100th, a B-17 outfit, joined the Eighth Air Force in England in May 1943, it became just another in the rising tide of groups helping flatten Germany from the air. But it wasn't long before the 100th gained quite a reputation and earned the ingratitude of Goering's fighter pilots.

In October 1943, the 100th was responsible for a stunt, seemingly insignificant at the time, which snowballed into something all out of proportion to its origin.

Nobody seems to know where or how it began, but the word got around that if an American bomber lowered its wheels over German territory, it was a sign that the ship was going to crash-land. Thereupon, enemy fighters would close in, unmolested and unmolesting, to escort the crippled ship down.

It seems that one enterprising pilot of the 100th Bomb Group thought of a way to get a feather in his cap and at the same time give his gunners some good practice. Undoubtedly self-preservation was a major factor too, for this pilot was flying his B-17 back over France after hitting a target in Germany. His ship was shot up some, enough that he'd had to drop out of formation.

Two FW-190s spotted the crippled '17 and closed in. The pilot lowered his wheels and the German fighters came in, one on each wing tip, to escort the big plane down. Whereupon the '17's gunners opened fire, and being in a position where they couldn't miss, quickly downed the two '190s.

The story later got out. The B-17 was crippled and losing precious altitude, so the pilot ordered the crew out, and out they bailed. Most of the crew later reached England with the help of the French underground. The pilot just managed to reach England's shores before he crash-landed safely.

But it seems the Luftwaffe got wind of the incident, too, for almost immediately the German fighters, trying to intercept American formations, began to single out the planes of the 100th for special attention, identifying them by the "Square D" insignia on their tails. One gunner, a member of a group in the same wing as the 100th, has related how the FW-109s and ME-109s would barrel perilously through his formation without firing a burst to get at the ships of the 100th.

It certainly wasn't coincidence that caused the 100th to have 100 percent losses in the short space of two days. On

October 10, a short time after the incident, the group sent 20 planes, full strength for the group, into the air. Eight of the 20 were shot down. The next day, 12 out of the 13 that left England failed to come back, making a loss of 20 in two days.

Then during the following February something else happened that zoomed the losses of the 100th. The target was "Big B" (Berlin) for the first time.

It was an all-out attack involving the whole Eighth Air Force. Bad weather, however, forced all but a few groups to turn back before reaching the target. The 100th was one that persisted. Thus it gained the distinction of being one of the first outfits to hit Berlin.

It probably would have waived that distinction, though, for right after that raid the 100th was given more special attention—Luftwaffe style. The "Square D" group lost 82 planes during February and March 1944, 18 of them, almost an entire complement, being downed in one day.

So if the guy tells you he flew with the 100th, be nice to him. He deserves it!... . (It's said this story has been debunked. It's interesting, true or not.)

Memories of an Interlude in England in 1944

by Russell M. Barnes
Reprinted from Gannett Westchester Newspapers, June 6, 1990

Soon it won't mean a thing...

The sleepy hamlet of Hurn, tucked neatly away in southern England and just a few miles from the English Channel won't mean a thing to you, but then why should it. For most parts of the year it doesn't mean much to me and Hurn is only a few miles from where I live.

But once a year I visit Hurn. Every June I make the journey there preparing myself, as I drive over the narrow humpback bridge and under that line of tall trees, for that tiny lump to arrive in my throat—and it never fails.

You see, in June 1944 I was a teenager. The German army was on the other side of the Channel, which meant they were only 80 miles away—or just 20 minutes as the Heinkel 111K bomber flies—and you tried not to think about that.

Me and the other kids had eagerly watched the "dog fights" up in the blue summer skies of 1940 when Spitfire battled it out with Messerschmitt. We tried to sleep under kitchen tables as German heavy bombers overhead made their journeys in black winter nights across the very heart of England to obliterate the centers of Birmingham and Coventry.

But soon the Russians, who by then had lost 6 million people, were at last getting the better of the huge German land forces which had torn their countryside apart and the British "Tommy" was doing OK in North Africa...but little did we know that soon our world would be turned upside down! The GIs were about to invade. Laughing and singing, truckloads of them winding their way down narrow Dorset lanes, winking and grinning at the girls who giggled and thrilled in their delightful embarrassment.

On Sunday the village green had echoed with the sounds of English cricket as young men swung bat against hard ball and proud parents gently clapped and murmured "bravo." Now it was "yippee," and words we dare not mention, as softball struck by baseball bat sped so unbelievably fast across neat gardens and out of sight.

Yes, the Yanks arrived. They shared a drink in our pub and shared a hymn book in our church. Some even shared Sunday lunch with us and sat around our fireside at Christmas. And to some of those fresh-faced lads our mums became their moms.

In the spring of 1944 the lanes and fields of southern England were choked with American, Canadian and British forces and their equipment. It wasn't difficult to see that plans were underway for the Normandy landings—and Dorset was very much in the front line.

On that first day of June 1944 as I walked across that lane and over the humpbacked bridge, I saw a sea of blue or khaki uniforms. Groups of GIs laughing and talking. Some played cards. And others, alone with their thoughts, sat quietly writing letters home—or perhaps their last letters home.

Within a week it was the Omaha and Utah beachheads. For all it was a nightmare journey to hell and back. And sadly for many—far too many—the soft and gentle down lands of Dorset would be he last thing felt under foot.;

26

Throughout the weeks that followed, aircraft and ships brought the wounded back to Dorset—young men now made older. In the market town of Blandford, the 22nd U.S. Military Hospital, with a devoted staff working day and night, tended wounds and mended bones.

A mile away a Dorset mum carefully placed a GI's personal belongings in a tin box and reverently buried them deep in her garden. He wasn't her son, but he was somebody's son. Only two weeks before he'd been around her home for a cup of tea and a chat. He left a neat assortment of personal things on her table, asking that she look after them and saying, "I'll be back for them when it's all over." He shut the wooden gate behind him and turned to look at her for a second…and was gone.

She had been told that he wouldn't be calling back.

That kind soul, with kids of her own, didn't bury his photograph. Without fail, each June she took it from the drawer and placed it on view. And she did that every year until she died. Now someone else performs that simple but dedicated token of annual remembrance.

When at long last it was all over, GI Joe went back to Los Angeles or Long Island. Tommy Atkins to Liverpool or London. Now there is nothing more across the soft down lands or along the winding lanes of Dorset to tell the generations to come what happened here a lifetime ago. Nothing which even begins to record in history the sacrifice and courage of people, who it seems, may already be forgotten.

Only memories in the minds of those who lived through it all.

The sad fact is that one day—when nobody cares—it won't mean a thing.

B-24 Bashing—The End
by Edward J. Reilly (93rd)

Murray Grainger, you and Bob Chapin may not be in as much disagreement as your three letters would suggest.

Much of what Grainger says is undeniable fact. Our casualties were 30 percent higher than our brother Fort crews in the Eighth. Aside from combat losses, the old Lib was more prone to fatal accidents. I can personally recall two fatal accidents of Libs on takeoff that took twenty lives, one of whom was a dear friend. Experienced flight engineers kept the bomb bay open a crack to reduce risk from fumes of gas leaks. Her glide angle—like a brick. Ditching the bird was almost certain suicide. 17s did it like ducks.

To most of us in our early twenties safety didn't seem to be of much concern to us. Personally, I was disappointed when I wasn't assigned to B-26s, and their safety record was worse than ours. On that score I could have no beef on being assigned to 24s.

I was trained in 17s and knew what they were. They were tough, reliable, sleek, and beautiful. And they came home more often. But if you could stand away from one's feelings and look at facts, the B-24 was a better bomber. It could outrun the 17 by at least 20 knots, carry a ton more bombs 800 miles further and hit targets 400 miles deeper into enemy territory. Her four electric turrets were the ultimate state of the art. Her ten guns were more effective, in my judgment, than the 17s thirteen. But our formations were not as tight as the Forts because of the Libs inherent sloppiness above 18,000 feet. Our optimum altitude was between three and five thousand feet below theirs, making us more vulnerable to flak. Her Pratt and Whitney engines were the most reliable of any built for any aircraft during the war.

I recently heard a leading German fighter ace tell a group of American bomber crews that they would always seek out and attack Libs, passing the Forts by because we were easier to kill. It was not our fire power that failed us. The Lib just could not survive the same level of battle damage as the Fort. And the enemy well knew it. Flak or fighters, in combination, knocked off seven Forts for every ten Libs.

But only the Lib could have hit Ploesti. And it took eight Forts and 80 men to drop the same tonnage of bombs as it took six Libs and 60 men mounted in Libs.

She was a great old bird. Those of us who flew her loved and hated her. We would fight with 17 crews whenever her name was sullied. But deep in our hearts, we know that the 17 was built for the crews and the 24 for the Air Force. If I were underwriting life insurance to bomber crews instead of flying with one, I'd be looking for the Fort crews. If shopping for the weapon that could do the most damage at the lowest cost, I'd be pushing Libs.

The Libs were not as bad as Grainger feels it was. I'm glad he wrote the article. I'm glad Chapin responded as any good loyal Lib crewman should. For most of us who flew Libs and Forts, feelings are deep and facts mean different things to different people. None of us are likely to change feelings that run as deeply as we all feel about an argument that can never be settled... (I think the B-24 bashing has run its course and the above article puts it in proper perspective. Thanks—Editor, 2nd Air Division Journal)

How the Spitfire Stole the Thunder from the Hurricane
by Tom Dix—Reprinted from the 8AF Badger News

(This article is taken from the September 2005 issue of the Framlingham Times, edited by Ian Hawkins of Suffolk, England. It was written by Tom Dix of Suffolk and appeared in the east Anglican Daily Times on 5 July, 2005. In August of 2005, Britain celebrated the 65th anniversary of the Battle of Britain, whom the English people consider to be the most important contribution to the survival of the British empire made by men and women of the Royal Air Force.)

There is no merit in the glorification of war, but there are times in our lives when we feel the need to reflect on circumstances which, had they been different, would have changed our lives completely. Shortly, 65 years will have passed since the Battle of Britain in which RAF Hornchurch, Essex, played a major role.

Adolph Hitler had his Panzer divisions lined up for an invasion of our country, having conquered the whole of Europe. However, Hermann Goering, commanding the German Air Force, convinced Hitler that a successful invasion should be preceded by knocking out the RAF completely which, with vastly superior numbers of aircraft, he felt he could easily do. He code-named this very costly venture "Eagle Day," which was 15 August 1940.

The Spitfire was glamorized as having played the major role in the battle, but here are figures that prove that the Hawker Hurricane, designed by Sidney Camm, emerged as the major factor in the outcome. The strategy employed was that the Spitfires would deal with the German fighters, while the Hurricanes, which could out-maneuver the Messerschmitts, took on the bombers. It was the bombers that could have caused complete destruction of our cities. Of the 67 squadrons involved in the Battle of Britain, 13 flew Bristol Blenheims, Boulton Paul Defiants and Gloster Gladiators, 19 flew Spitfires, and 25 flew Hawker Hurricanes. A total of 1,700 Hurricanes were deployed in the battle—more than all other types put together—with 80% of the victories being claimed by Hurricane pilots. There were 242 Hurricane pilots killed in action, compared to 149 Spitfire pilots.

We must not forget that the success of the RAF was due in part to the back-up of the ground personnel. Aircraft were refueled and returned much faster than the Germans, so the pilots could get back in the air to re-engage the enemy. Young people of today find it difficult to envisage the "old codgers" to have been the gallant swashbucklers that they were—and why not, when the mass media shows the survivors in their mid-80s. During the battle, pilots were in their late teens and early 20s. The aging process does not respect a person's appearance.

Incident On Kiel Mission

The following comments regarding a mission to Kiel were printed in the June, 1984 Second Air Division Journal Association's "The Journal," its official publication. In that I have misplaced that issue, only Roger Freeman's comments are presented here. In researching for the mission in Mr. Freeman's "Mighty Eighth War Diary" I'm quite certain this was a 14 May 1943 mission flown by five B-17 groups and the one B-24 group, the 44th. The toll was the loss of 8 bombers, 5-24s and 3-17s, 36 damaged, 3 killed in action, 17 wounded, and 81 missing, per Freeman. He included an addendum entitled "INCIDENT," partially, as follows:

One bomber was lost through an unusual accident. Shortly after takeoff a B-17 was critically damaged by a runaway machine gun. The weapon was in the left waist internally stowed and was being checked by the gunner when accidentally discharged. Bullets went through the side of the fuselage and shot away half the right horizontal stabilizer and severed the

30

control cables on that side of the bomber. The waist gunner was injured and the tail gunner seriously wounded by the burst. Pilot, Capt. Derrol Rogers, managed to keep control but found he could only fly the aircraft in a gradual turn. Coming back to the vicinity of the base the wounded tail gunner and the other five men in the rear of the bomber were ordered to bail out, after which Rogers continued in a wide circle towards the Wash and the bombs jettisoned. Believing that the damage to the aircraft would make a safe landing impossible, Rogers had the bombardier and navigator parachute, and when the orbit brought the bomber back over the Wash he and the co-pilot followed. It was an hour and a half before 2nd Lt. Norville Gorse, the co-pilot, by then suffering from exposure, was found and rescued from the water. The search continued for Rogers and when eventually located he was found to be dead. This tragic accident brought a directive that in future, guns were not to be adjusted or primed while in the stowed position.

Marine pilots flew medium-bomber missions

"WWII unit faced setbacks on, off field, Marine Corps Times, Aug. 23, 2004   Author, Robert F. Dorr

When the United States geared up for World War II, the Marine Corps began for the first time to operate large aircraft with two pilots and a crew. Former Capt. Bill Parks, 82, of San Jose, Calif., had an advantage over some Marine aviators. On the eve of U.S. entry into the war, he earned a pilot's license in a government-sponsored civilian program. He knew that when you fly a big aircraft you usually start out in the right seat as a co-pilot and build your experience before switching to the left seat. "But the Marine Corps didn't have anyone with multi-engine experience to put in the left seat," Parks said. "Those of us who'd received the most training started out as left seat pilots." From his first day as an aviator in a combat squadron, Parks commanded his aircraft and crew. It was a big responsibility, and it grew bigger when Parks arrived in the South Pacific to fly missions against Japanese island bases.

Born in 1922 in North Carolina, Parks "enlisted in the Navy in summer 1942 under a program that would allow me to fly," he said. "I was just a country boy from the mountains. I didn't even know the Marines had aviators."

At Pensacola, Fla., Parks was among cadets who received a pep talk from a Marine major who wanted them in his service. The major told the trainees, "The Marines have row upon row of P-38 Lightnings at Cherry Point, N.C., and no pilots to fly them." The P-38 was the plane that captivated every youngster of the era. After earning his wings and Marine commission in March 1943, Parks was dismayed to learn the recruiting pitch wasn't true. The Marines didn't possess a single P-38. Instead, Parks became a pilot of the PBJ, the Marines' version of the twin-engine B-25 Mitchell medium bomber. It was the plane Army Lt. Col. James "Jimmy" Doolittle had flown on his famous raid on Japan in April, 1942.

Parks flew with Marine Bomber Squadron 433, the "Fork Tailed Devils," first at Green Island and then at Emirau Island in the South Pacific. "My logbook shows that our first mission from Green was July 21, 1944," Parks said. "It was a full squadron strength daytime raid on Rabaul." By July 1944 the Pacific war was moving to the northwest. Bloody battles for the Solomons island chain had ended. Some Japanese troops remained on Guadalcanal, Munda, and Bougainville. The Japanese base and airfields at Rabaul, New Britain, were less active than previously. Yet 200,000 Japanese troops remained on New Britain and New Ireland and were occasionally reinforced. The job of the four Mitchell squadrons on Emirau, including Parks', was to prevent these forces from impeding the Allied island-hopping advance toward Japan.

Parks squadron suffered both of its combat losses in September 1944. On Sept. 2, a PBJ piloted by lst Lt. Charles Ingals took off on a night mission—and vanished. All six aboard died and were accounted for only after the war. On Sept 11, 1st Lt. Eric E. Terry, Jr., and another Marine were among the lost after being hit by Japanese gunfire. Parks said that a typical mission involved carrying fourteen 100-pound bombs 250 miles from Emirau to Rabaul. That took two to three hours, including about 15 minutes of vulnerability to Japanese fighters and heavy anti-aircraft fire. Parks completed 50 missions and never saw a Japanese fighter but was fired on from the ground often.

Parks worked in postwar years for Lockheed Aircraft. He married Betsy McMillan in 1951. They have a son and daughter. Betsy died in 2002.

A clarification: Parks and other VMB-433 veterans, who held a reunion in Nashville, in October, say that for most of its 25 months in the combat zone the squadron had excellent leadership. They believe a story in this newspaper placed too much emphasis on the squadron's "hard luck" status, which, they say, describes only a brief period in 1945.

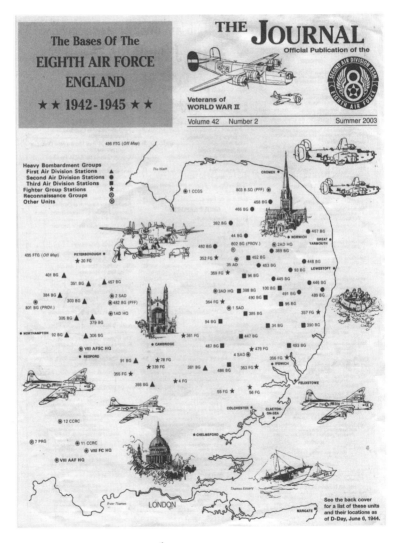

8th Air Force Bases

Chapter 2: Mission Stories

Big-B by Day
by Glenn R. Matson (458th)

It was our third mission and at briefing we were told our target was Berlin, Germany, the capital city of the Third Reich. The date was 6 March 1944 and the Eighth Air Force was about to penetrate the heart of Germany for the first full scale daylight raid on Berlin. The 458th Bomb Group scheduled thirty-three B-24 bombers, thirteen of them aborted or failed to make the mission. The remaining 20 bombers joined up with the 14th and 96th Bomb Wing to form a composite Wing of the 2nd Air Division. The 2nd Bomb Wing would lead with the 14th and 96th composite to follow six miles behind. The 20th Bomb Wing would follow 6 miles behind them, bringing up the rear of the three Bomb Divisions of the B-17s and B-24s to make a bomber stream of over ninety miles long.

The bomber force consisted of 243 B-24s and 567 B-17s. Originally our target was to be the Heinkel Aircraft Factory at Oranienburg, North of Berlin. It was feared that we would have to fly through the heaviest of flak over Berlin to reach our target, so they switched our target Genshagen to hit the Daimler-Benz Motor Works. The bombers had to fly over 1000 miles to the target and back.

Temperatures at altitude were near 60 below zero F. We were to stay below 21,000 feet to prevent contrails and make it harder for the German fighters to spot us. At Horsham St. Faith at take-off, visibility was below 1,800 feet and patches of fog, with complete cloud cover between 3,000 and 6,000 feet.

About 10:30 we departed England and headed for the North Sea and across Holland. We picked up our first fighter escort, the 56th Fighter Group, somewhere over Holland. We were following the 3rd Division B-17s when they got off course between Enschede and Osnabruek. The B-24s and part of the B-17s saw the error and stayed on the planned route.

Our Bomb Group took a course Southeast after passing between Brandenburg and Magdebury to the IP, then swung north into the wind to the target. The worst flak hit us as we approached Oranienburg. There may have been kids firing in those 88mm flak guns, but they were good. It was bad enough riding that flak road in and out of Berlin, but as we arrived at the IP (Initial Point to start bomb run), we were on a collision course with a B-17 Group on their bomb run. Our Group leader who was a Lt. Col. had to abort our bomb run, change course and close bomb bay doors and set up for another run. Again we were off our target and he turned us 360 over Berlin instead of away from it. That put us in almost constant flak for over thirty minutes. He wasn't satisfied with our other two runs, he wanted to hit the rail station and yards, not just Big-B.

We were flying in the lower left three plain element in the position of Purple Heart corner. The guy leading our element took us under the main Group formation. By now our bomb bay doors were open again and we were in a very precarious situation. We didn't like looking up at those open loaded bomb bays directly above us. Our pilot, 2nd Lt. Charles A. Melton decided to leave the element and slid back up in the formation where we belonged. Our element leader and the other wing man were two of our five losses that day. We feared at the time that our own Groups bombs fell on them. It was on this third bomb run that our navigator, 2nd Lt. Charles C. Weinum stuck his head up in the navigators dome in front of the pilots and thumbed his nose at them. He noticed a dog fight and got down inside to get a better view through the side window. After he had left, a chunk of flak made a hole through the dome about the size of a fist. If his head had been there, Pow! no head. He stuck his head up there again, saw a flak hole and got the surprise of his life.

We had to divert to an alternate target. By then we had heavy cloud cover and ended up dropping our bombs near Potsdam. With the target no longer visible, we had to resort to PFF (Pathfinder Forces Radar) and the results were very poor.

Shortly after leaving the target area, we were attacked by two FW-190s without causing any damage. Our Group had been badly shot up by flak, one aircraft lost over the target. This was 2nd Lt. G. Clifford's crew on B-24 42-52515. It crashed West of Berlin, eight men were killed, two bailed out when the plane exploded. Three men of our badly shot up B-24s made it to Holland.

The next to go down was Captain J. Bogusch's crew on 41-29286. Four men were killed and six survived the crash and were taken prisoner. Then 2nd Lt. T. Hopkins' crew on 41-29299 crashed. All ten men survived and were taken prisoner.

Next to crash was Crew #52 of 2nd Lt. Beverly Ballard's on 42-52450. Three were killed and nine men taken prisoner. The Ball Turret Gunner, Sgt. Victor W. Kruger evaded capture for fourteen months when the Dutch Resistance found him and hid him out until the British troops rescued him in April 1945. 2nd Lt. J. McMains crew was shot down by a ME-110 and crashed near Ueltzen, Germany. Two were killed and eight taken prisoner.

As for our crew #67 on the B-24 41-28719Q *Paddlefoot* experienced a bit of flak damage, but no one on the crew was injured and our return to England was uneventful.

This was a very costly mission for the Eighth Air Force as well as the 458th Bomb Group, which alone lost five bombers and three returned with minor battle damage—the most ever for one mission throughout the remainder of the war.

Of the 702 bombers and 832 fighters that reached enemy territory, 69 heavy bombers and crews were lost. Eleven of the 832 fighters were lost to enemy flak or fighters. Of the 69 bombers lost, 53 were B-17s and 16 were B-24s that failed to return. 701 men were lost in action of which 229 were killed or missing. 345 German civilians were killed or wounded and 36 German Airmen were killed and 25 wounded, with a loss of 66 aircraft. Approximately one out of every ten bombers were lost on this mission, the greatest on any separate mission for the Eighth Air Force. We knew we had been on a big one. Yes it was a big one—"BIG-B."

The First Time I Saw Paris, June 2, 1944
by John W. Crowe (491ˢᵗ)

We hadn't flown the "Renegade" since May 23, 1944. The weather began to improve and we were briefed for a practice mission early in the morning of June 2 and told to stand by. Just before noon the practice mission was canceled and we were told to report to the briefing room again. This time it was the real thing, our first mission. The briefing officer, Lt. Col. Goldenberg, told us our target was an enemy airfield just south of Paris. The map showed our flight path in to France, to the target, and the route out, carefully plotted to avoid the many red dots which were known locations of enemy flak guns. The area around Paris looked like the face of a kid with the measles, nothing but red pockmarks. We were assured that the target, some eighteen miles to the south, was out of range of the Paris flak guns and the mission, as planned, ought to be a "milk run"—no problem at all!

Thirty-six planes from the 491st and forty-one from the 489th. The 489th would lead with the 491st following. The 489th had been in England a short time and had flown their first mission on May 30. They were leading the 95th Combat Wing into battle. It would be a very interesting afternoon with the blind leading the blind.

Our escorts were P-51s, and P-38 fighters. The "Renegade" as the other planes of the 491st, had her belly full of five hundred pound bombs.

With a briefing for a real mission and a reloading of the planes with bombs, it must have been 1730 or 1800 hours before we taxied out, like thirty-six pregnant elephants, one behind the other, waiting to take off.

Lt. Col. Merrel, group leader, was the first to take off, followed by the other 491st planes at thirty-second intervals. We climbed at five hundred feet per minute, some forty minutes later we reached the forming altitude of 20,000 feet. Twenty minutes later the group was formed. It was 1930 before we departed the English coast at Selsy-Bill. We arrived over enemy territory just after eight o'clock and continued southeast to the I.P. some six miles southwest of Paris. We had some inaccurate, sporadic flak but the "milk run" mission was going as advertised. At eight-thirty we crossed the I.P. and headed for the target at Bretigny. Then all hell broke loose and the sky around us suddenly turned black with intense accurate flak from enemy flak guns below, thick enough to walk on and close enough to hear the muffled explosion with the familiar R-U-M-M-M-P-H sound that we were soon to know so well.

We didn't know it at the time, but the 489th had failed to take a short zig-zag left turn off the I.P. to the north, then back to the right toward the target. In doing so, we were directly over the heavy concentration of flak guns just to the south of the target. The sky was filled with the black mushroom explosions of 88mm shells.

We continued straight for the target. Lt. Getz, nineteen year old pilot of the "Renegade," with instructions from the bombardier, Chuck Voyles, prepared for bombs away.

Everything except the exploding flak looked normal and then in the blink of an eye it happened. The plane slightly ahead and to our left, Lt. Bill Evans' crew, close enough that I could have hit him with a rock, one of the two engines on the right wing simply disappeared. There was only jagged metal, twisted pipes, and a gaping hole where the engine had been only a minute before. The right wing dropped gently downward and the wounded plane began to drift over and down to the right directly toward the "Renegade." It seemed like an eternity but it probably was no more than two or three seconds. I hit the control wheel with both hands, forcing the yoke all the way forward. The "Renegade" responded, her nose went down, and everything not fastened down went up. I had not taken my eyes off Evans' plane, headed toward us on a collision course, and in response to Lt. Getz's silent stare, I pointed above us with my left thumb. As Getz looked up, Evans' burning plane slid gently across the top of the "Renegade," just above the Plexiglas canopy covering our heads. It couldn't have cleared us by more than a few feet and that may be a conservative opinion. Sgt. Turnipseed (TTG), who was closer than most, said, "I looked up and it was right on top of me. I let out a scream because I was sure it was my last." It was over as quick as it happened. Lt. Getz pulled back into the formation and continued our bomb run toward Bretigny.

Things continued to deteriorate as the 489th approached the target and they found it largely covered by clouds. Only one squadron of the 489th managed to drop on Bretigny, thus a decision was made to go for the secondary target at Creil. The 489th plowed straight north, via the Eiffel Tower and Paris. The 491st lead bombardier managed to see the target at Bretigny and unloaded there, but unwisely the 491st followed the 489th over Paris.

The evening and the land below had given way to the late darkness of the long summer day. The view below was spectacular as we crossed Paris, with the hundreds of bright flashes from the muzzles of flak guns surrounding the blacked-out city. It looked like the Fourth of July on the ground and in the sky around us, which was now blackened with intense flak. It lasted all the way to Creil and beyond.

If the 489th had tried they couldn't have flown the route to be avoided any better. We exited Paris and took the most direct and dangerous route home. It was well after ten o'clock and we landed at Metfield and to add insult to injury, the engines of the "Renegade" began sputtering and cut out as we taxied to our hardstand. We were no longer virgins; the "Renegade" had a great number of holes in her fuselage and wings, all reparable.

The 95th Combat Wing had paid a high price for the mistakes in navigation from the route as briefed. Of the seventy-seven B-24s dispatched on the June 2 mission, five were lost, three crash landed in England, fifty-eight suffered reparable flak damage and one had major damage.

The next day I came to the conclusion that if this was a "milk run" then there was no way short of a miracle that we could survive thirty missions with the 8th Air Force. I therefore decided from that day forward that I was living on borrowed time and that it would be prudent to enjoy to the fullest extent whatever time I had remaining. I never asked others how they wrestled with the problem of survival; perhaps they, too, came to the same conclusion. The first time I saw Paris had been one hell of an experience, never to be forgotten.

Two months later, in early August 1944, Bill Evans showed up back at Metfield, a little lean and haggard but none the worse for being shot down over Paris. He told me that his plane had taken a direct hit in one of the engines in the right wing. The debris from the explosion shattered the cockpit canopy, throwing slivers of Plexiglas into his and the co-pilot's faces. Neither Bill nor his co-pilot could see enough to fly or control their wounded plane. He was unaware of his plane's near mid-air collision with the "Renegade." After more flak and more hits he lost another engine. Realizing the hopelessness of the situation, he ordered the crew to bail out. All exited the plane safely but were subjected to enemy ground fire—rifles and machine guns. The tail gunner, Pvt. Le-May, was cut in half in his chute before he came to earth. The navigator, Lt. Blue, was killed when tracer bullets from machine gun fire ignited his chute and he plunged to earth. Four other members of Evans' crew were taken prisoner. Evans and three others were picked up by the French Underground. He told of working on several night sabotage missions with them.

His benefactors decided the safest place to hide him during the days he was in France would be in the numerous houses of prostitution. Thus Evans was gradually moved from one whore house to another, town to town, between Paris and the English Channel. He smiled when he told me he literally "worked" his way out of occupied Europe to freedom. What a way to fight a war! For Evans the war was over after just one fateful mission. Evaders were not allowed to return to combat duty.

Jinx Ship
by John White

In the summer of 1944 John White was a 448th airplane commander whose crew by June 22 had put thirteen missions of their mandatory number behind them. Now one of the dreads of any crew seasoned in combat was to be assigned an aircraft with a "jinx" reputation. B-24 (last three numbers 758) was one such machine and the following account by John displays how she lived up to that reputation:

We had an experience these last two days [June 22-24] that I shall never forget to my dying day. It was extremely interesting and terrifying at the same time. We were briefed for an afternoon raid on one of the airfields south of Paris, and the ship we were assigned to fly was #758, one of the "jinx" ships on the field [Seething]. Today a couple of the boys remarked how glad they were we got rid of it!

There was a good deal of flak at the target but we managed to drop the bombs OK after having a great deal of trouble with the #1 and #4 superchargers. I don't think we received many hits at all over Paris from the flak. About five minutes after we left the targets we really hit it; we flew over some batteries and they opened up with perfect tracking fire. The fellows in the crew later said they counted 10-12 bursts that hit right under us. We could hear them very plainly and feel them rocking the ship.

I knew right away that we must have suffered some severe battle damage, so I called the boys to look her over. In the waist and tail they reported holes torn all over the thing, while Paladino said the engines were hit. Bush said that the tail looked like a sieve and that a piece had hit him on the foot. Part of the interphone was shot out and we had what Vic said amounted to about 50 holes in the bomb bay. He also told me gas was leaking in there, so I had him open the doors and when I looked around, I just about fainted—gas was just pouring from the wing-tanks into the bomb bay and waist. About this time our control cables

40

broke and I had to set up the A-5 to fly the aircraft. The servo-units in the tail had been hit as well so the A-5 wasn't working very well. Dick knew we were in deep trouble, so he gave me a heading to the beach-head, our original intentions being to land there on an ALG. However, fire broke out in #1, and we had very poor control of the ship, so I decided it was time to leave it. It was just a question of whether we should bail out over enemy territory or wait and take a chance on making the beach-head. There was not any question in my mind that she was going to blow. Looms gave me a position so I called some P-47s who came over and gave us excellent cover all through the experience. I called all the turrets out of their positions and told the entire crew to stand by to bail out. Bob was flying and working his head off to keep the plane on an even keel. Everybody was anxious to leave, but I was amazed at how calm they were—our training had obviously stood us in good stead.

All this time gas was pouring out, so Vic took a big piece of cloth, walked out onto the catwalk and tried to plug the hole. We were at 21,000 feet and despite this, he went out there without gloves or oxygen! He froze his hands, which did not do him any good whatsoever. It took a lot of guts to do that and I am going to recommend him for a decoration for that. We started losing height and we were just about to bail out when more 'Ack Ack' opened up on us. We found out later that it was British but at the time thought it might be Jerries, so we went on a little further. Only when we were sure we were over our own lines did I tell the boys to leave. Dick said he would let me know when the last man left the ship and then he would go; he duly did so and jumped, and then I told Bob to go. We shook hands and I witnessed his safe departure. Just before I jumped I headed the ship out to sea and then I pulled the A-5 release, thinking that the ship would nose down and hit it in the channel. However it blew up a few minutes after I jumped and struck the ground about 200 yards from where some 9th Air Force Engineers were cutting out a landing strip for their fighters. (The next day, a medical Capt. took us around to the spot and the ship was really a mess, all we saw being very small pieces. We could not identify wings, engines, fuselage or anything.)

I delayed my jump for a few seconds—possibly as long as a minute—and found the sensation of falling was very pleasant. I tried to control my body, but it was quite hard. When I finally pulled the rip-cord, the chute opened with a severe jolt and the first thing I remember is looking up and seeing the canopy. A few seconds later I noticed that I still had the rip-cord and I was very surprised at that. I remember thinking how I would razz the boys who dropped theirs.

Another thing that surprised me was how clearly my mind functioned through the ordeal. It seemed to work perfectly with absolutely no excitement or fear; it must be the training that does it. After the chute opened, it seemed as if I would never reach the ground. The only way I knew I was falling was the fact that I had to keep clearing my ears. I also noticed that it was very quiet all the way down. In fact, it was the most intense lack of noise that I had ever experienced and was very pleasant and delightful.

As I neared the ground I heard rifle and machine-gun fire and later on I found out it was directed at me and the crew! I hit the ground with a severe jolt while facing the wrong direction: my head contacted the ground and I was knocked out cold. In fact, I hit so hard that I can still feel the effects two days later. I haven't any idea how long I was out, but when I woke up I was bleeding and was surrounded by American soldiers. I do remember my first words were, "Thank God you're Yanks." We hit within 4 miles of the front line, and I was afraid the Jerries would get me. The fellows who picked me up were from an artillery outfit and it so happened that some of them were at Camp Shelby at the same time I was two years before. They sent me up to a Clearing unit of the Medical Corps and there I met Bob and Bush. The former said he had counted 10 chutes, which was a tremendous load off my mind. I had heard a few minutes before that one of the officers had sprained his ankle, and I'm pretty sure now that it was Looms. We've tried to find out where he was taken, but so far without success. Everybody treated us wonderfully. When Bob and I met, there was a news-reel camera-man there to take our picture and I can assure everybody that the smiles on our faces were genuine.

The Medics were from the 104th Medic Bn attached to the 29th Division, and acted as a clearing unit while operating near the front line. The Division had seen fighting since D-Day and these boys had been through hell. The Bn is commanded by Lt. Col. Arthur N. Erickson and they treated us as if we were kings; they have the highest respect for the boys in the Air Forces.

Of course everybody wanted to hear our story and we had hundreds of questions to ask them in turn. They were in a good position to give us a clear picture of the fighting, and seemed awfully eager to tell it to us. They've treated a lot of Germans, Poles, Czechs, Russians, and even Japs! I was surprised by the fact that the Germans have so many other nationalities fighting for them. They told the Russian boys that Russia had surrendered, and the way they made them fight was to stand over them with a gun and make them. The Bn has had a great deal of trouble with snipers all through the campaign: I guess the Japs have been teaching them this.

The next day one of the Captains took us on a tour of the beach-head and it was a tremendously impressive sight. I could never hope to put into words what we saw. How the boys landed is to me a miracle. We saw the flooded fields, hills with tremendous pill-boxes and tunnels with catacombs all through them. The captain said they were a mile deep. We saw boats sunk on the beach, and graves of men killed on the landings. We saw landing strips literally hewn out of the woods, roads being cut where there had been nothing but trees and rocks. To see how completely organized the entire operation seemed to be gave one a feeling of absolute confidence in our Army, for a change.

In contrast, we saw the beautiful French countryside with its large hedge-rows along every road and highway and large herds of dairy cattle grazing in the fields as if there was no war. The expression on the French people's faces as we drove by seemed that of a liberated population. Overall it was an impressive sight, one which I will never forget.

We took a C-47 back to England and there was an NBC broadcaster at the field. When he found out who we were he had us talk over the radio a bit. It seems everybody on the beach had seen us fall out, and in fact one person made a broadcast of it as we left the ship: this had been heard back at Seething. This, very crudely put, but expressing the facts of the story, is what will probably be my most unforgettable experience.

Nazi Hell Under My Blue Heaven

by Nathaniel "Bud" Glickman (93rd and 44th)
(Same mission as "Men of Gallantry" in Chapter I, different crew member's version)

Twenty-four of my thirty lead or deputy-lead missions resulted in flak damage to the aircraft I flew in.

The first target I was to bomb as a member of the 93rd BG on April 8, 1944 was the ME-110 aircraft plant at Brunswick, Germany. The mission would take us over Dummer Lake, "Flak Alley" en route to the target. In addition the largest number of enemy air bases protected Brunswick. Our group following the 44th watched as enemy fighters hit them repeatedly. Within minutes I counted five bombers spinning in and then saw one ship take a direct flak hit in a bomb bay and explode in a bright red flash.

After dropping my bombs and turning off the target, we were again under attack. Another 44th bomber was hit and we counted ten chutes getting out. That day our 2nd Division lost 34 bombers and 24 fighters. My first mission was over, but I would return to Brunswick two more times.

Upon completing my seventh mission with the 93rd, I was assigned to a "mickey" crew and transferred to the 66th Squadron of the 44th BG. My first mission with them was to Brunswick, recalling memories of my first flight. As we approached the target we were jumped by FW-190s and I was lucky enough to shoot one down as he made a pass at us.

The morning of June 5, the day before the invasion of Europe, my crew was to lead a three-plane javelin formation to bomb a rocket site in the Pas de Calais area. This would be my eleventh mission and was referred to as a "milk run." I lost my first roommate on his 35th mission on a "milk run," and so failed to find this amusing. The two bombers we would lead were from the 489th BG, whose deputy C. O. was Lt. Col. Leon Vance Jr., who would fly with us as the command pilot. He missed the briefing and arrived at our plane with takeoff being delayed awaiting his appearance. I now believe he was aware of D-Day and our flight was a diversionary tactic to draw attention to the Pas de Calais area. Our pilot informed him of the briefing instructions, including the fact that we were to make one run on the target. If there was a mishap the bombs were to be dropped in the Channel. After his acknowledgment we took off on the mission. I flew as the pilotage navigator in the nose turret with a series of photographs to aid the bombardier in spotting the target.

The only danger was the flak batteries situated on the French coast. The mickey crew consisted of Capt. Lou Mazure, the pilot; Lt. Earl Carper, copilot; Col. Vance, command pilot; a navigator, a radio operator, a bombardier, a bombardier/navigator, a radio man, an engineer, and three gunners.

As we crossed the English coast it was evident that the invasion of Europe was imminent, and that every harbor along the coast was filled with boats and landing craft.

We climbed to our bombing altitude and headed towards the target. Approaching the IP the aircraft was turned over to the bombardier. Light flak arose off to our right. I indicated the target and the bomb bays were opened. The bombardier called out "Bombs Away." Nothing happened. Every bomb was still hanging in the bays. Either there had been a malfunction in the bombsight or the arming release switch in the bombardier's panel had not been activated.

We turned off the target and I notified Mazure to head over the Channel and jettison the bomb loads according to the briefing instructions. Colonel Vance countermanded my request and ordered a second run, informing us that he was in command of the flight. We turned south of the target at the same altitude and speed, flying parallel to the coastline and giving the enemy gunners an opportunity to zero in on us. We were sitting ducks.

The second run became hell. The first flak burst exploded off our port wing, killing the pilot. The copilot then took over the controls as we continued the bomb run.

Colonel Vance was standing between the pilots when the next blast hit and tore through the flight deck, hitting him. Flak had raked his right foot so that it hung by a shred. At the same time my nose turret took a series of bursts that shattered the plexiglass and cut open my forehead, and ricocheting, hit the base of my spine. Meanwhile the radar operator applied a tourniquet to the Colonel's shattered leg. Flak continued to explode as we continued on the bomb run. My immediate concern was having the bomb bays hit before the bombs were released. The starboard outer engine shaft was snapped with the blade drooping downwards. The top turret was shattered plus part of the right rudder and elevator had been hit. Nearing the previous release point I called out that I would drop the bombs using my turret toggle switch. This would bypass the bombardier's and release the bombs. After the release my turret took another hit, cutting my left hand and blasting off the remaining plexiglass, leaving me sitting in the open air.

Checking my pilotage map I advised the copilot of our position and gave him the return heading to England, since the radar operator was working on the Colonel's leg and the navigator in checking found his maps and table damaged. The radio room had been hit, with the radio operator sustaining wounds. As we headed towards England the plane was hit again, cutting the gas lines and forcing the copilot to cut the switches to prevent a fire, which also stopped the power to the three remaining engines as well as my turret controls.

We started gliding towards England without a prop turning over, when I heard "Bail out!" Then the bail out bell rang. My turret was turned half around to the port side, with me being buffeted by the air currents. I could feel my hand bleeding in my glove as well as seeing my flight suit stained from the blood dripping down from my forehead. With no power to turn the turret, I called on my throat mike that I was trapped, and as I turned to try to force the turret around, my throat mike wires which had been frayed, separated.

Turning in my seat I watched the bombardier snapping on his chute. Waving to him to turn my turret so that I could fall out into the well was an exercise in frustration and futility. He looked at me, turned and crept through the wheel tunnel toward the bomb bays to bail out. Perhaps he believed my waving had another meaning. Wiping the blood from my face, I tore all my connecting wires free and tried to turn the turret manually without success. It was impossible to get my fingers into the space between the turret opening and my present position. I then disengaged one of the 50-calibre machine gun charge handles, inserted it in the opening and using it as a lever, turned the turret and fell out into the well where my chest chute was lying and I snapped it on to the harness.

Discovering I was paralyzed struck home as I inched towards the bomb bays while we were still dropping in altitude. Leaving the tunnel and unable to stand, all I could see was the dead pilot and what I believed to be another body next to his seat. I continued crawling to the bomb bay and noticed a 500-pound bomb hanging in the forward port bay. Standing on the catwalk was one of the crew, evidently frozen with fear, holding onto a metal strut blocking my exit to bail out. I shoved him out and then rolled off the catwalk, hoping that I wouldn't hit anything as I left the plane.

The ripcord being on the right side of the chute allowed me to use my good hand. After my chute opened, I spotted an RAF air-sea rescue launch circling under me, which gave me some comfort since I couldn't swim at the time. With the blood running into my eyes, trying to see was a problem. I still worried that when I hit the water the chute canopy would drift over me and I would drown.

Meanwhile the wind was blowing me towards shore, and when over the cliffs of Dover I blacked out. Fortunately I hit the ground in a relaxed state to find that I had landed on the lawn of the Royal Marine Hospital at Deal. Standing over me was a Marine in battle dress, with a rifle pointed at me and asking if I was a Jerry. My response was less than polite, at which time he replied that I was too fresh and must be a Yank.

Believing I was the last man alive to leave the plane, I later learned that Colonel Vance had stayed to pilot the bomber into the Channel, at which time the 500-pound bomb exploded, blowing him clear of the cockpit. He was rescued by the RAF launch.

There were more injuries as a result of bailing out. The radio operator was not only wounded by flak but also shattered his ankle on landing. The engineer broke his ankle on landing, and I was to learn that the navigator breaking his leg in two places as he landed probably saved his life. He had put down in a British mine field and was unable to move. The pilot, Captain Louis Mazure, is resting at the bottom of the English Channel.

Visiting Col. Vance at his hospital, I learned that he believed that the radio operator had been trapped, not knowing two gunners had freed him.

Colonel Vance was evacuated to the States via a medivac plane which disappeared in the North Atlantic. He received the Medal of Honor posthumously. The airfield at Enid, Oklahoma was named in his honor.

On July 6th I returned to flying combat. The target was the submarine pens at Kiel and I would be the lead bombardier on a PFF bomber. It would be my 12th mission and a long way to my final mission, No. 30.

North Sea Bailout—May 29, 1944

by Charles M. Trout (492nd)

We were doing fine until we ran into flak over the target. We were hit pretty bad. The co-pilot was hit, but his flak suit prevented injury.

The #4 engine started throwing oil at about 2 gallons per minute. The engine was still putting out power, when the oil pressure reached 20 PSI it was feathered by the co-pilot. I checked the gasoline and it was very low. I transferred the remaining fuel from #4 tank and we were still low on fuel. We thought we could make it to the English coast, but we weren't sure.

The radio operator started to send S.O.S. signals as we knew we were lower on fuel and couldn't make it. We started throwing out everything that was loose or that could be taken loose. While we're doing that, two of the planes from our squadron stayed with us but we were flying too slow for them to stay behind, so they left. Radio operator was still sending S.O.S. signals but couldn't tell if he was being heard, for his receiver was shot out and also the trailing wire, antenna knocked off by flak. Then two P-38's started circling us and stayed with us til they saw there was no hope for us and left.

We knew we would have to ditch or bail out, for our fuel was awful low—about 3 minutes. The crew decided to bail instead of crash. Water was rough with big breakers. Then the pilot heard "Boat in area" when he called "Mayday—Mayday." The rescue boat was below us. We all said a prayer, and I was first to jump. I tried two ways to jump but neither was satisfactory, so I stood up and dove out like diving into water.

When the propeller and slip stream hit me it took my breath and threw me around pretty rough. When I was down low enough for clearance and everything got so quiet, I pulled the rip cord but nothing happened. The chute didn't open. I reached in and pulled the pilot chute out. Everything came out of the pack and I stopped with a sudden jerk, looked up and was very pleased to see that nice white parachute above me. Looking around and saw more chutes, but didn't count them.

Then I saw the plane circle, which made me get a funny feeling for I thought it was going to spin down among us. But the pilot was just getting closer to the rescue boat before leaving the plane and he was the last man out. The plane started to descend slowly on a straight course and #2 went out when the pilot left.

I looked down and seemed to be about 100 feet above water but hit very quickly, a second or two. Don't know how far I went under but came up immediately. When the cold water got through my clothes it took my breath. I struggled for about 10 minutes before I finally got enough breath but breathing was almost impossible due to breaking waves right over the top of me. I unbuckled my chute harness and thought I was rid of it until it started pulling me under. I said another prayer and something made me think of a knife I had in my pocket. I cut everything I could get free, but could not get down far enough to cut it off my feet as my strength was gone. I gave up hope when I couldn't see the rescue boat, but it came to me in about 35 or more minutes. Boy, was I glad to see the boat! They threw me a rope and I hung on and was pulled into a rope ladder. Three Air Sea Rescue men tried to pull me up but couldn't; had to use a hoist. The rescue team told me to save my strength as I didn't have much left, laid me on deck and told me to go below. I had to crawl so they carried me, cut my clothes off and gave me dry ones, but had to dress me. I couldn't help myself at all, shaking like a leaf in a hail storm. I was given a hearty welcome by the survivors already picked up. One handed me a cigarette, which took the salt water taste out of my mouth. When everybody was picked up that could be found, they gave us hot tea and brandy to drink so we would get warmed up, and later hot soup and bread and butter. It sure tasted good. We hadn't eaten for a long time. Headed for shore and when we got there we were led in prayer for the missing crewman by the chaplain. We felt bad about losing him, for he was a great guy.

We stayed there for a few days and were treated like kings. When we finally got back to our home base, most of the clothes were gone, divided out, but we got them all back. The best news was that we would all get a week's rest at a Red Cross sponsored rehab center. I thank God I am alive today.

P.S. A great big thanks to the British Air-Sea rescue. They deserve a lot of credit. This story was written two weeks after bailout and had to be censored. That is the reason for no names.

A Bit of Trouble Over Norwich
by Fred Becchetti (445th)

July 31, 1944, and the 445th Bomb Group was headed for Ludwigshaven, our B-24 bomb bays loaded with unarmed fragmentation bombs.

Pilot Keith Palmer lifts off from Tibenham at 9 a.m. and takes her over the 500 ft. ceiling for the assembly of the group formation over the Wash.

At 16,000 feet and climbing, our No. 4 prop runs away. Palmer feathers it, calls in an aborted mission and reports an altitude loss of 300 feet per minute.

There's no returning to base with the unarmed fragmentation bombs, so I give Palmer a heading to a point over the Channel where we are to jettison the frags.

We dump the bombs, but the ship continues to lose altitude. Then a second engine begins to act up, and our rate of altitude loss increases.

To lighten the ship, Palmer gives the order to toss out everything that is loose. We wrestle with guns, ammo, flak suits and even the generator and send them whistling through the 500 ft. layer of clouds to whatever lies below. At one point, I jokingly grabbed waist gunner McGovern by the leg as though to toss him out. Lots of laughs later about that!

At 2000 ft. and still losing altitude at a dangerous rate, Palmer polls the crew and we vote to bail out in the hopes of saving the ship by lightening it even more.

Over the Norfolk region but unable to see the land because of the clouds, we line up at the rear hatch and bail out one at a time into the unknown beneath the cloud cover: first, waist gunner Gregory McGovern (who fractured his leg on landing); then tail gunner Robert Sherrick; waist gunner Lawrence Sladovnik (who broke his leg); ball turret gunner John M. Smith (who sprained an ankle landing in a British WAAF base, where the women took care of him splendidly); radio gunner Carl McHenry (who sprained an ankle); engineer Bernard Goldstein; and finally myself.

Bailing out at about 1000 feet, I counted quickly to three and yanked the ripcord, while the noisy B-24 flew off, leaving me in the dead silence of the sky as I drifted downward through the clouds into who knows what. I whistle to myself to break the eerie silence.

In the clouds I begin to hear sounds from below. People talking, vehicles. I burst through the cloud cover. I am coming down in a residential area of Norwich. There is only the slightest wind, so I am coming straight down with a little lateral movement.

To my right, a large tree and a house. To my left, a row of small trees and a house. And directly in front of me, there is a small, newly-spaded garden, an 8 ft. high hedge and beyond the hedge, a house.

Delicately, I maneuver toward the center of the garden. I land without a roll, both feet together and falling forward comfortably, with my face slightly pushed into the soft soil of the garden.

Slightly dazed, I lie there and monitor my body, feeling a slight twinge in my left ankle, but otherwise feeling good and thankful, though somewhat reluctant to move.

I hear a rustle of branches in the hedge in front of me. The hedge parts and a ruddy-faced man peeks through, catches my eye and with a twinkle and a smile asks me, "Having a bit of trouble, Yank?"

And I laugh, reviewing in my mind all that has happened since 9:00 in the morning.

Mr. Morris pushes through the hedge while I unhook the harness of my chute entangled in the tree. He helps me into the house and serves me a scotch and soda. After a while, two Bobbies pedal up, eye my Italian name with some suspicion, until the MPs show up to take me back to the base, where I learn that pilot Palmer and co-pilot Cliff Bolton were able to land the ship after the bail-out.

As for my parachute entangled in the tree, we never found it.

They say that several little girls in the neighborhood had new dresses for school the next year.

Tondelayo's Last Mission—Target: Politz
by Jim Blanco (392nd)
(My 14th, and I failed to write it up upon returning, and after going to Berlin the next day, didn't remember much of this tough mission)

Lt. C.L. Bell was last seen heading…

That partial sentence covers nine different experiences which could add pages in terms of experiences. As a member of Bell's crew I remember quite vividly the experience of *that* day.

The mission started about 2300 hours of 19 June, when the C.Q. came to roust us out of our sacks with the usual info of breakfast and briefing times. After breakfast, briefing. I still recall the feeling in the pit of my stomach, because the excess trace line of our route in and out of the target area was not visible on the floor. This meant a long haul. The first two missions, or maybe five, it's still an adventurous experience. After that you start to sober. This was our twenty-fifth. After briefing it was the usual jokes and horseplay to buoy up our spirits as we made our way to the locker room to don our heated suits.

After dressing I locked my locker and discovered I had not put my sidearm away. At that time AAF Regs ordered no side arms to be taken on missions. Being a little late, I decided to check it in to Tech Supply. I told the Sarge, "I'll pick it up, *if* I don't come back." The Sarge remarked, "Don't worry. Bell's crew always comes back." At day's end it was certain that a seer he was not.

As we rode to the dispersal area, I felt apprehensive. This was my first mission without Joe Knight. He was grounded with a bad cold. Group superstition was when one man stayed down, the odds were the crew doesn't return, or the man doesn't on a make-up mission.

Joe and I had a ritual we did before take-off. We ate our caramels from the high carbohydrates box because we didn't want the Luftwaffe to get them, and chewed gum. As we prepared for take-off, we'd stick our gum wads on the tail fin of a bomb and say, "Remember when you're up there your soul belongs to God, your heart belongs to the girl back home, and your a-- is strictly the Luftwaffe's."

Take-off and forming were normal and I prepared my duties transferring gas from the wing tip tanks to the main tanks and leveling the tanks. Then the tensions started with the call, "Enemy coast ahead." Somewhere over Denmark our first fighter escorts dropped off and there was the usual wait of five to ten minutes before the next pick-up. Sometimes these minutes seemed like an eternity. This was one of those times.

Flying on, and always on the alert for enemy fighters, I noted and alerted the crew of a group of forty to fifty fighters flying level and at five o'clock. Someone remarked that it was the second group of our escorts. I was reluctant to accept it, and kept watching them. They were too bunched up to be our escorts. As they approached three o'clock, they were a mile and a half to two miles from our formation. One fighter did a slip maneuver. I noted tail booms—P38?—hardly! How long I watched I do not know. The 492nd was leading the Wing and was starting to turn on the I.P. I thought they were spreading out too wide. It was then when the fighters hit. They definitely were not our escorts! I was fascinated, appalled and scared stiff as the fighters took their toll.

As we turned on the I.P., they turned on us. I can still remember rocket streamers and the machine gun fire. Fortunately, I think they had used their Sunday punch earlier, but what was left was still terrifying. We sustained some minor damage. After they broke the attack, I had the impression those fighter pilots must have been totally without experience or training. The couple that had pressed their attack on us were a JU88 and an ME210. They attacked us flying with the formation. The JU88 started the attack at five o'clock and about two hundred feet above us. I saw the stitch marks my fifties were making on his fuselage before he broke away. The ME210 came in at the same height from six o'clock, and I put the same stitches in his wing.

As we approached the target area someone remarked on the intercom, "Those flak-boys are really checked out." I turned my turret to twelve o'clock to check. I will affirm they certainly were "checked out." It seems they were shooting in a perfect rectangular pattern of about 400 X 600 feet. What seemed worse was, our line of flight would put us right through the center of the barrage. I observed the element leader moving ever so slightly to the left, and mentally I was telling Bell to move it over, out of center.

My next actions are burned deeply in memory. I looked at the flak and knew we would not see any enemy fighters; so I started to think of other targets with heavy flak—Berlin, Brunswick and Fredichshaven. I didn't recall flak coming either from the pilot's compartment or the bomb-bay. I did experience it coming from the sides. My turret had one-half inch armor in front and I had put flak vests at the back and under the jewels. My sides were unprotected. I rotated the turret to nine-o'clock so that my right side was toward the cockpit and my left to the bomb-bay. Next I thought of the plexiglass dome. Shrapnel can and does pierce and shatter if a burst comes close to it. So I reached down and put my helmet on. At this point my guns were elevated, so for added protection, I lowered the guns so that the receivers were on each side of my head. In this cocoon I went I went into the "Valley of Death" with a prayer to the Almighty and the usual promises to reform. I was scared! Not caring to lift my head to see anything that wasn't in my line of sight, I watched the blossoms of flak and felt several bumps indicating hits in the aircraft. Then came the relieving signal: "Bombs away, let's get the hell out of here."

After leaving the flak field, I climbed down from the turret to survey battle damage. Up front, flak had hit our radio and it was a mess. There were numerous holes in the skin, letting in daylight, and one piece of flak severed a run of wires—some of which were for the #3 and #4 engine instruments.

I started to go aft and I will attest to the fact that the combination of rubber flight boots and hydraulic oil make very slippery cat-walks. Fortunately, the bomb-bay doors were closed when the flak hit the hydraulic system. As I entered the waist section, gunners Asch and Seymour were doing a jig trying to avoid being hit by VERY pistol flares set off by a piece of flak.

Returning to flight deck, I was surprised to see we had left the formation. The #3 and #4 engines were running smoothly, but without a tachometer and manifold pressure gauges we did not know how much power to pull back or advance. It was decided to leave the settings as they were for awhile and use #1 and #2 for flight changes. By this time we had hit the deck. Time had lost its magnitude as I busied myself leveling gas tanks and watching #3 and #4 engines for the slightest malfunction.

Decision time came when Bell announced we had three options:

1. Land in Germany
2. Ditch in the North or Baltic Sea
3. Land in Sweden

Personally, I did not like the idea of being a POW, nor did I care to ditch. As for Sweden, it was an unknown, and I thought it the best of what was available. It must have been, in spite of the last few hours, my lucky day. We headed for Sweden.

We limped along nursing that "gawky angel" every mile to Malmo, Sweden. As we approached Sweden, two fighters appeared high at seven o'clock. I turned my turret to meet them and thought, "Here we go again." For some unknown reason we all held our fire. This was unusual because we were all pretty jumpy. The planes were unusual. They did not have the lines of either the FW'S or ME's. Someone identified them as Italian. As they approached closer, we were all tense waiting for them to flash their recognition lights (guns), but none flashed. They were fighters from the Swedish Air Force coming to escort us to Malmo.

What confronted me on landing was that I would have to crank the gear down and kick-out the nose wheel. Not knowing the field in which we would set down, I was more than concerned because we had only enough hydraulic pressure for one application of brakes. With the gear cranked down and locked, the nose wheel kicked-out. Our landing pattern was normal. As we turned in for our final approach, another wounded B-24 cut us out. Luck was with us as we applied power to #3 and #4 engines and they responded. We nursed our angel around again to the base leg. The B-24 that cut us off had touched down, ground looped and burst into flames.

Under the conditions we had flown, our landing was normal. As we passed the burning B-24, the ammo aboard was exploding. Then came our moment of truth. Our one application of brakes brought us within three feet of the end of the runway. Later, after conversations with Swedish friends, we learned that on that day the Swedes thought the entire 8th Air Force was going to land there. Twenty bombers had landed. I never could verify it, but my Swedish friends say the plane that blew up on landing was the 13th to land.

For Bell's crew it was a very long haul that lasted for five months. Bell and I stayed behind for a total of ten months. Through all the years and future years I always say, "Tack a mika for Sverige"—literally translated, "Thanks a million for Sweden!"

Wings Of Memory
by Mary Lou Wilson
Reprinted from the Vacaville Reporter, July 22, 1991
Submitted by W.H. "Bill" Beasley (492nd)

Navigator Berl Robinson grabbed frantically at the maps blowing about the bullet-riddled turret of the B-24 Liberator. Flames were streaming from the plane's No. 4 engines, hit by flak just after bombardier Jesse Briggs dropped his load of bombs on the Stettin Oil Refinery in Politz, Germany.

There were gas leaks everywhere. The fuel gauges in the cockpit were broken and the bomb bay was full of fuel mist. No one knew how much gas was left or which tank it was in.

Certain that the crippled bomber was doomed, one crewman had already bailed out through the nose wheel door. Eleven of the planes flying with them had dropped into the Baltic Sea, but pilot Joe Harris decided there was a chance the "Silver Witch" could reach neutral Sweden.

It was up to Robinson to set the course to safety. He corralled the maps and directed the pilot to a small airfield at Malmo on the Swedish coast.

That day—June 20, 1944—is a part of World War II history, the time when "the air war over Western Europe reached a new peak of fury," the International News Service reported.

That day was also the reason for a quiet reunion in a Davis restaurant a few weeks ago when Robinson, now 78, and Briggs, 72, saw each other for the first time since their internment in Sweden.

Forty-seven years had passed, but in memory they were still the snappy-looking captain and lieutenant who shared that heart-stopping flight across the Baltic.

"It's great, we can't describe it," said Robinson when a friend asked how it felt to be together again.

Robinson has lived in Vacaville since 1949; unknown to him, Briggs has been in Rancho Cordova for 25 years. They got in touch by phone after each received a letter forwarded by the Veterans Administration from tail gunner Willis Beasley who was trying to contact all crew members of the "Silver Witch." It took a while to set up a reunion. But finally—joined by a few relatives and friends, including Robinson's wife, Adele, and Briggs' wife, Christine—the two met again.

They had already caught up on the years that followed that mission. Robinson left the service in 1945, was recalled in 1948 and sent to Japan to replace personnel flying the Berlin Airlift. From Japan, he returned to the then Fairfield-Suisun Air Force Base and became a public information officer for Brig. Gen. Robert Falligant Travis for whom Travis Air Force Base was named. Out of the service, he earned his teaching credential and taught at Vacaville Union High School for several years. After that, he owned a toy and hobby shop in Vacaville called Robby Hobby and later operated Vaca Welcome, a greeting service. He also worked in real estate.

Briggs was recalled by the Air Force in both the Korean and Vietnam wars. After serving in Vietnam, he stayed in. His last assignment was at Mather Air Force Base where he retired in 1970 as a lieutenant colonel.

But those were years spent apart. What they wanted to talk about was the harrowing flight and the four months together in Sweden.

Their memories fit together like pieces of a jigsaw puzzle. One would start a story, the other would finish it; when "Robby" Robinson hesitated over a name, "Snuffy" Briggs supplied it.

Briggs had a few precious snapshots with him. Another member of the group had newsletters from the 492nd Bomb Group which had sent 35 bombers, including the "Silver Witch," on the June 20 run. The newsletter noted that there were 3,500 to 4,000 planes in the air that day—at the time it was the greatest concentration of American heavy bombers ever sent into action.

Robinson and Briggs said they could still picture the chaos: smoke filling the plane; the nose turret being punctured by their own machine gun bullets set off by anti-aircraft fire; crew members inching through the unpressurized plane wearing heated suits and shoes and oxygen masks.

As they headed for Sweden, Briggs jettisoned the ultra-secret Norden bombsight into the sea. When they entered Swedish air space, they found German planes, flown by Swedes, on their wingtips.

They were directed to a grassy field where they landed. They learned later that 21 planes from the 8th Air Force had found their way to Malmo that same day.

"It was lucky the 'Silver Witch' made it," said Robinson. "Despite the maps, I was guessing at where I had been and where I was going. I just told the pilot to head in the general direction of Sweden."

The Swedes treated the internees well, agreed Robinson and Briggs. When given passes, they could bicycle about, visit Stockholm and enjoy the beaches.

But they were anxious to get home. In October, under cover of bad weather, Robinson flew to England with 100 other men in a converted B-24 bomber. Briggs followed in November. So both were back in the States with their families.

On the June 20th 1944 mission to Politz, Colonel Gerry Mason (448th CO) and Major Chester B. Hackett, Jr. (CO of the 715th Squadron) flew with 389th Pathfinder crews. Col. Mason was Command Pilot leading the 20th Combat Wing, while Major Hackett flew as his deputy off his right wing.

Major Hackett remembers the mission:

"Just before midnight on the evening before my 24th mission, Col. Mason and I were driven to Hethel airfield to fly with 389th crews on a mission to bomb the oil fields at Politz.

The mission was uneventful en route to the target with the usual flak and German fighters. We had escort fighters for the entire trip to Stettin and over the target. The weather was clearing as we proceeded across Germany and by the time we changed course just north of Stettin the sky was absolutely clear.

We could look over to the south and watch each twelve-ship formation make their bomb runs on Politz. We were flying at 30,000 feet and the anti-aircraft fire over the target was heavy. Before turning south to the IP, I called Col. Mason and asked him to consider changing our altitude to avoid some of the flak. This was my 24th mission and Col. Mason had only recently joined our Group. He called me back having decided that we would not change altitude. So we made our run at the same altitude as the formations ahead of us.

Just after we dropped our bombs the aircraft seemed to stop in mid-air. We had taken flak hits in the nose section, bomb bay, fuel tanks and waist compartment.

Dropping out of formation, I called Col. Mason and told him I was going to try to reach Sweden.

Power on all four engines was about nil, so I called the crew and directed them to bail out. As it turned out ten men jumped, one of the waist gunners called and informed me that Lt. Rose had been hit and was hurt badly. I instructed him to attach a static line to Rose's parachute, help him out of the waist window and pull his ripcord for him.

58

After this, I unbuckled as a faint odor of smoke began filling the cockpit. I was about to jump out the open bomb bay when I saw Capt. East walking back from the rear of the plane up the cat walk into the bomb bay. I asked him why he had not jumped. He told me he had no parachute. He was wearing a harness but no parachute pack. The bombardier uses a chest-type parachute. He just keeps the harness on and places his chest pack in back of him. This enables him to operate the bomb sight. A piece of flak had hit a walk-around oxygen bottle which had exploded, ripping his chest pack.

He had gone back to the rear of the aircraft looking for another chute. There was none to be found and he said Lt. Rose was dead in the waist section. He also stated that fuel was running all over the rear bomb bay.

With Capt. East missing his parachute and Lt. Rose dead, I really had only one course of action. I told East to climb into the co-pilot's seat and I got back into the pilots seat.

East and I proceeded to shut down everything—all power and electrical equipment to lessen the chance of a fire. After everything was shut down the smoke in the cockpit subsided.

All this took only a few minutes and I told him I intended to crash land. He said for me to go ahead and bail out, he would take the aircraft down. There was no way I would allow this, so we proceeded to descend. Our altitude was now down to about 15,000 feet. As we continued our glide, two ME-109s attacked us from left side. The only think I could think to do was dive, pick up speed and turn into them closing the distance between us as quickly as possible. That was the last I saw of the fighters until we were about to land in a grain field. When we got down to about 2,000 feet I started looking for a field and circled the one I had picked out.

There was very little wind at about 300 feet. We lined up on the field and lowered the landing gear. However, I touched down too fast. After rolling about 2,000 feet we hit a ditch and snapped the nose wheel. The aircraft came up on its nose, but did not flip over. As the plane slowed, the tail section settled back down and we slowly came to a stop. Capt. East immediately went down into the bombardier's compartment and detonated the explosives on the Norden bomb sight and H2S radar system, destroying them both.

During the landing approach, I had seen a ME-109 crash a short distance away. When East and I got out of the aircraft, two P-51 Mustangs flew over, turned and climbed for their flight back to England. It was a great feeling to witness the dedication and bravery of our fighter friends.

We had crashed a few miles northwest of Stettin and were immediately surrounded by the German populace. They had watched our approach and landing, converging on us very quickly. They took us to the local village and eventually turned us over to the Luftwaffe. After being interrogated, we were sent to Stalag Luft 3 near Sagan, Germany."

Lt. Col. Hackett was a POW until May 1945 when they were liberated from Mooseburg by General Patton and remained in the USAF until 1962.

The following is a quote from Al Ciurzack's diary:

"September 11, 1943: Took off at 8 o'clock for Paramushira. Trip was uneventful on the way out, but after the bombs dropped on the target our flight was attacked by a flock of Zeros. We all headed for the deck, and when we got there we stayed at about 50 feet. Major Gash's ship on our right wing crashed in the water not over a hundred feet from us due to enemy fighter action (Feuer was the photographer on that ship.) It sure was a shock to see them hit the water, for I knew the crew well since I flew with them on prior missions, especially Walter Feuer who I have known since I first joined the Army. The Zeros kept coming. We got hit above the bomb bays. All our radios were knocked out and another shell put a big hole in our de-icer tanks and hydraulic system, it's lucky we didn't blow up. I went up to the flight deck to tell Lambe (our engineer) about the de-icer tanks. Just as I stuck my head in the door, two 20mm shells hit the top hatch and went off when they hit the armor plate of the top turret. The place was filled with smoke. When it cleared a bit I climbed in to talk to Lambe, who was standing behind the pilot and co-pilot. Just then a shell hit the front windshield, hitting the co-pilot in the face. Lambe and I got the co-pilot out of his seat, sat him in the corner and Lambe got into the co-pilot seat. I took care of the co-pilot. He was bleeding like a stuck pig. I ripped open all the first aid kits I could find and put on all the bandages, but the blood kept on coming. I then ripped off my winter underwear for it was the cleanest thing I could think of and wrapped it around his head and face leaving an opening near his mouth so he could breathe. The blood slowed up so I gave him some sulfanilamide tablets. He was sure taking it well, didn't squawk one bit, even when I gave him a shot of morphine in the leg to ease the pain. A shell hit alongside me, just above the radio table and the felt lining of the plane caught fire. I put it out by pulling the felt loose. The Zeros finally left and was I glad, so was the rest of the crew, especially the pilot for it was a hard job flying the plane with one hand (the shell that came through the front windshield had also hit him in the right arm.) It's a good thing Lambe, our engineer, knew a lot about flying and he really helped the pilot. When we were sure the Zeros had gone for good, Lt. Lemons, our bombardier, came up to the flight deck and we cleared the empty shells from the top turret and made a place for the co-pilot to lie down. We had a few blankets and bed rolls in the plane so we wrapped them around him to keep him warm.

"Then I left the flight deck and went to the back of the ship where the gunners were talking about the Zeros they had shot down. Rodd, the top turret gunner, found a hole made by a 30 caliber bullet in the bill off his hat (he wore it with the bill turned up.) There were lots of happy gunners, four Zeros to the ship's credit. (Top turret—one; fixed nose guns—one; tail gunner—one; left waist gun—one.) Our happy spell didn't last long for when the engineer tried to transfer fuel from the bomb bay tank to the wing tanks, he found that the pump wouldn't work. That meant that we had about one chance in ten of making it back to Attu. The pilot gave the order to toss everything out of the plane that was loose. Everything went out the bottom hatch; machine guns, cameras, radio equipment, and we even chopped the armor plate out alongside the gunner's position and tossed that out the bottom hatch. We all put on our life vests and went up forward so the ship would fly better. I don't know about the others, but that's when I started to pray and think. I guess this was the hardest I ever prayed in my life. The thought that kept running through my mind was not being able to see Kitty, my wife, again. The engineer and I climbed into the bomb bay and tried to fix the fuel pump. No use, we didn't have the tools. All we could do was pray. According to the gas gauge, we had enough fuel left in our wing tanks to fly until 6 o'clock. The navigator told us we would hit land at 5:55. I relaxed a little for I knew if the weather was clear we could find the field. At 5:15 we were told to go to the back and prepare for a crash landing. We packed our sleeping bags against the rear bulkhead. While this was going on the radio operator was helping the pilot fly the ship. We all stuck our noses to the windows to look for signs of land. At 5:55 we spotted land and our hopes went up. Fog was rolling in, no sign of the airstrip. The ship banked sharply and headed away from shore. We didn't know what was going on but found out later that the pilot couldn't find the Attu landing strip and headed for Shemya, 16 miles away. It was 6 o'clock and our gas gauges read empty. We were flying on borrowed time. Landing gear went down. We heard the wheels hit the end of the strip and we all jumped out and hailed a jeep, sending the driver for an ambulance. We all helped the co-pilot out of the ship and waited for the ambulance. The mission was over. Looking the ship over later, we found it was full of holes and it's a wonder it didn't fall apart."

"I'll always remember the co-pilot as we helped him out of the ship at the end of the flight. His head was covered with my bloody underwear. He was standing and he wanted to pee. Someone said, 'Pee in your pants.' He said, 'Are you kidding?' The ambulance came after he relieved himself near the nose wheel and climbed on the stretcher. They slid him in and away they went. Although I had tossed out the cameras when we got the word to lighten the load, I kept the exposed film magazines and headed to the base photo lab. Great pictures. Wasn't able to keep a set—'Classified.'

"I will always remember September 11, 1943."

Crew: Pilot: Lt. Jerome J. Jones, Top Turret: S/Sgt. Walter E. Rodd, Co-pilot: Lt. Raymond K. Underwood, Radar Operator: S/Sgt. Vale W. Wright, Navigator: Lt. James S. Elliott, Tail Gunner: S/Sgt. Jack Leffler, Bombardier: Lt. Roy L. Lemons, Gunner: S/Sgt. Charles Beech, Engineer: T/Sgt. Dwight C. Lambe, Radio man: T/Sgt. John Stroo, Photographer: T/Sgt. Alexander D. Ciurczak

Retired U. S. Air Force Captain Al Ciurczak received two DFC's during his Aleutian Island tour.

Mission to Zwichau

As told to Dave Patterson by Mike Ciano (445th Bomb Group)

After a number of missions, and a ten day rest period, I was assigned on return as tail gunner on a newly formed crew. The following is an account of my first mission with this crew.

April 14, 1944: The much dreaded sound of the Jeep halting at our Quonset Hut; the hut door opened, and the driver calls out our new pilot's name. Before we knew it, we were eating chow and off to briefing prior to takeoff time. After briefing, we made our usual preparations: checking out personal equipment; preflight preparations, start engines, and taxi out. We took off one at a time and slowly gained altitude. We joined formation in our assigned rear slot spot, and we were on our way to Zwichau, Germany.

As soon as we crossed the Channel and were over Belgium, all hell broke loose. Flack hit our far left engine and black smoke started pouring out of it. A hole the size of a basketball opened up at the feet of our waist gunner. Another direct hit in the waist ripped open the floor. As we gathered our wits and resumed our gun positions we were informed over the intercom that the nose also was badly hit. Bullets began ricocheting around my tail turret; a ME-109 was coming in at eye level. I opened up fire when I felt he was in proper range, and was rewarded by the Messerschmidt disintegrating in a ball of fire, almost hitting the tail turret as it exploded. By now the ship was too crippled, and we lost altitude and dropped out of formation, becoming a "sitting duck" for the rest of the enemy fighters. We tried to keep our guns firing to discourage the fighters from getting in close enough for a clean kill. But the handwriting was on the wall by this time. The intercom ceased to function; then a crew member from up front crawled back to tell us to bail out. Bail out! Those were words we gunners heard in training lectures, saw demonstrated in training films; but to each of us it was always going to happen to "the other guy," not to me! I quickly put out the fire (luckily it was superficial) and put on the chute. There were four of us in the rear section by this time; S/Sgt. Wayne Luce, badly wounded by our first blast; S/Sgt. Pete Clark; our radio operator "Chet"; and myself. We got Luce's chute on, carried him into the waist window and released him, pulling his ripcord at the last possible minute. The chute opened clear of the plane and we looked at each other and smiled. The rest of us decided to jump out the camera hatch as our exhausted condition and the urgency made any other exit impossible. I gave a last look down, jumped, pulled the cord, and looked up to see the ship moving away. Everything then became a blur until I hit Terra Firma; the stinging pain ran from my ankles up to my head as I buckled over and passed out.

I opened my eyes some time later, to see German soldiers looking down at me and mumbling, and civilians in the background gawking at me. I was carried to what looked like our American-type police wagon, driven through the city to a school hall, stayed there overnight, and then by bus (with three of our crew members who also had survived) to a ward in a walled-in hospital in Brussels. There we stayed for two weeks. The patients were wounded Luftwaffe, plus about five American flyers. I was treated for splintered ankles, and a gashing forehead wound from a fragment that hit me just prior to when I jumped. All during this time we were forbidden to speak or in any way communicate with the others; in fact our own policy was to act as if we were complete strangers to each other, to minimize security leaks. Every morning a Luftwaffe Colonel doctor would enter our ward, a German nurse would shout "Achtung" and, regardless of our physical condition and pain, we were expected to come to a rigid attention, and say "Good morning, doctor."

April 20th came, and I remember it especially because the guards and hospital staff celebrated with much champagne and booze, as it was Hitler's birthday.

After a week of recuperating, I was allowed to go out into the walled courtyard and sit in the sun and watch our bombers and fighters fly over. It was an odd feeling to look up and realize they were free, even though in enemy skies, while I was so close to them, yet captive.

It didn't seem logical in the least. Many times I would wait anxiously for their return flights and take note of the formation pattern to see if they had had a rough mission.

One morning, the nurse came in, re-bandaged and re-splinted both ankles, and issued me a pair of wooden shoes, pants too big for my small frame, and an old shirt. Then struggling, I was escorted by two Gestapo agents to a rail station and a train headed for Germany. I was warned not to talk to anyone for they didn't want to provoke trouble as they were responsible for my safe arrival at Dalag Luft, my next stop.

The Frankfurt Station was the rail terminus, and I must say the 8th A.A.F. had done a beautiful job of destruction. The station and the city was just rubble piled on rubble. Everyone wore black, and death was all around us. As we were herded to a trolley for our short trip to Dalag Luft, civilians shook their fists at us, spat on us, and made threatening gestures and remarks.

Dalag Luft was comprised of long, wide hallways and appeared to have been built during World War I. Hallways were flanked with endless doors that opened up into 5 x 7 rooms for prisoners. Each room had a small glass window near the ceiling, a cut-out section at the bottom of the door to slide food plates through, and it was furnished with a cot and improvised urinal. There was no sink, other plumbing, nor electricity. The prisoners consisted of flight crews: some British, but mostly American. Every day a Gestapo agent with a satchel and a large dog would visit me in my cell. He would open the satchel and bring out all sorts of forms for me to read and confirm. Most had to do with military installations in England and the United States (PS: He knew lots more than I did!) He would then bring out American cigarettes, light one and let the smoke drift my way. Then he would try to con me into denouncing America and embracing Naziism, and give him Allied information. He would start out very friendly, offering me a smoke, and chatting. But when he would offer me a pen to sign his forms, and all I would respond with was my name, rank, and serial number, he would become very angry, slap me across the face, gather up his items and leave the room. This procedure went on for ten days, but instead of offering cigarettes, he would try different offers to get me to cooperate, such as the promise of good living quarters, fine food, women, etc.

Eventually I was released and joined hundreds of airmen ready to be transferred to Stalag 17. We were put in closed box cars which proved to be a nightmare all the way to the Stalag 17 area near Krems, Austria. We were overcrowded and with very little food. We could not see out, and how horrifying it was when the train would stop suddenly, ack-ack guns would fire nearby, and the cars would shake from the vibration of nearby exploding bombs. I heard much cussing and banging on the sides of the cars just because of terrible fright. A steady diet of this would crack a person up in a very short time.

How happy we were to arrive at our destination and imprisonment. You have no idea how great a feeling it is to be let out into an unrestricted atmosphere from a totally restricted one. Then, you walk through the main gate of the prison camp, and you begin to feel different and wonder if you'll ever walk back out free again. The first building we entered was a large washroom and resembled something that was used 50 years before. We all were deloused and our heads shaven clean. Then, with large searchlights on watchtowers lighting our way through the dead of night, and with barbed wire and guard towers ringing our periphery, we walked into the first barrack building, and got our first view of how it was going to be for us for a long time. The boys were sleeping 2 together set up in 3 tiers and attached one to another. The tiers were about 2 feet apart.

The guards began the talk of awakening the men and telling them to make room for "your new comrades." New P.O.W.'s meant up-to-date news on how the war was progressing. No one slept the remainder of that night as question after question was asked.

Stalag 17's living quarters consisted of long wooden barracks with a washroom separating the next. The lighting was very dim, and the floorboards thin and drafty. Mattresses were made of burlap filled with straw about 2" thick. The springs were wooden slats about 3" apart. We were each issued one thin blanket. Occasionally, odd noises would come from the mattresses, which upon investigation would reveal a new nest of mice or other vermin. While sleeping, it was common for large mice to run across your body during the night. Our diet consisted of hot water to make coffee for breakfast. For lunch we had hot water, dehydrated cabbage, or boiled carrots, and a piece of black bread which contained sawdust to give it body. Supper was hot water, boiled beets, potatoes, and what looked like horse meat. (Hell, what more would one expect of P.O.W. food when all of Europe was hard up for food?!).

In accordance with the Geneva Convention, all P.O.W.'s of convention member nations were to be assured of food quantity of at least 6% above starvation level. This was barely met by the Germans and so the U. S. government, via the Red Cross in Geneva, had food parcels made up of a can of beef, powdered coffee "D" bar, blades, and 5 packs of cigarettes. These parcels were to be rationed out 2 a month, but unfortunately the Germans handed them out according to how they felt and how we behaved. Many times they would tell us that our bombers destroyed the train load of parcels, etc. There were times we wouldn't see a parcel for as long as two months.

When the camp Commandant was upset about something, he would order us out of the barracks about 5 a.m. and line us up for roll call. We then had to greet him with a loud "Gut morgen Herr Commandant," followed by a "Heil Hitler." (The latter never occurred). He kept us standing for hours and dismissed us when he pleased.

When the RAF was in the area, their chandeliers would light up the valley in yellow, and then they would unload their bombs. Punishment for us would invariably follow the next day: elimination of rations, "roll calls" for hours on end, etc.

The 5th USAAF came over with their medium bombers many times to bomb the huge fuel tank storage facilities just down the valley from us. To hit the tanks, the bombers had to release the bombs just before flying over the camp, and by heck you would see the bombs dropping right at you. In seconds the bombs were falling right past you with the odd sound bombs make when falling. Then the explosions, the black smoke, the earth shaking. Of course, all this was preceded by the camp air raid alarm, shouts of "Achtung! Achtung! Flieger alarm! North American bombers approaching!" We would all make a wild dash for the trenches, body on top of body. Then the all clear, and we would drag back to the barracks in silence, and all contemplating the ordeal of punishment that would face us shortly in retaliation.

I certainly will never forget about the endless attempts at tunneling and what great efforts were made to keep them a secret. Just about the time the diggers were ready to break through to the top, the guards would be waiting with spotlights on the break-through spot. It was always a surprise how accurate they were in picking the spot; but it soon dawned on us that the Germans had planted a few of their own men in each compound unknown to us to monitor our actions. I recall that from time to time a few were suspected, but we were helpless to do anything about it.

We experienced other incidents during our imprisonment brought on by our attempts to aid escape attempts or to resist cooperating with bizarre German directives. Two prisoners escaped on one occasion, but were recaptured soon after. Although none of us were aware of the attempt, punishment, as usual, was meted out to all. In another incident, an American prisoner escaped from another prison camp, was unable to make contact with the underground, and was in desperate condition without food, etc. Our camp prisoners were able to smuggle him into camp, hide him and care for him, and finally deliver him to the underground for safe passage. In almost every incident, the German guards would eventually dig out the story of our disobediences, and punishment in the form of cut-off food or heating supplies, and/or roll call formations in which we stood for hours at attention in the rain and cold, etc. were meted out.

Dead of winter was now upon us and snow covered the valley. The days grew shorter and more time was spent indoors. To fight the devastating cold, many days were spent huddled up in the sack just to keep warm and alive. Coal rations became less and less and we resorted to tearing out the guts of the barracks for fuel to keep warm, only to realize we had thereby created even more drafts and cold. Morale worsened, and our bellies were empty. Our clothes were tattered rags from constant wear. The only good thing we looked forward to was a War news report which was brought around verbally on a frequent basis by a US flyer from Chicago; how he got the up-to-date news (which proved to be very accurate and complete) is still a mystery to us. He would circulate from barracks to barracks, under stiff security cover by his fellow prisoners, letting everyone in on the latest information. He was never caught, to my knowledge.

Soon, spring was near at hand, and the war news began to come alive with action. The guards were becoming less tolerant as the Air Force was turning Germany into a heap of rubble. Rumors of Allied breakthrough all along the Front was indeed promising and liberation was now becoming more real. A rumor swept the camp in March, (1945) that we were all going on a forced march heading westward because the Russians were just east of Vienna. It was all true, as we could hear big guns going off in the east, and the nights brought pink glows in the Vienna area. And sure enough, on April 1, 1945, we prisoners all began to be herded in a westerly direction and into what was to prove to be a frightful travel experience. Our days consisted of marching a good nine hours, with ten minute breaks every two hours. We were out about five days when the rations started to run out. Now, the guards found it too much of a problem to allow us to get water, and so we suffered continually of thirst and dehydration. Two weeks out, and many were now without shoes; more and more were depending on their comrades' shoulders to hang on for dear life. Others, too tired and starving, were falling to the ground, causing many behind them to fall on each other. Many were left to die on the road. It was a sad sight indeed; it has left an indelible memory of how a mass of humans can be made to look undignified by the hands of man.

Into our 3rd week American fighter planes began appearing daily to keep tabs on the P.O.W.'s. The German guards ran scared for cover as the planes came down to buzz us and dip their wings to reassure us. You have no idea how happy it made us feel.

Bombing was taking place just ahead of us at Linz, Austria, causing us to halt for a few hours. Then we resumed our march, and passed through the small town of Braunau, Hitler's birthplace. It was a quaint town, with very narrow sidewalks and streets; stucco houses and iron gates covering the very low first floor windows. I clearly recall the guards pointing to a yellow/beige stucco house and telling us it was the house that Hitler was born in.

Our forced march came to an end on April 29 in the woods of Braunau. We couldn't go further because the G.I.s were about 15 miles beyond. Orders were to settle down and wait to see what happened. Some of the wagon horses were slaughtered and the meat cooked and eaten. We then cut pine branches to make makeshift beds and overhead cover, for by now it was raining. All sorts of rumors were now sweeping the group. Some had it that the Germans had started a heavy offensive. Others had the Germans surrendering unconditionally.

The following day many of us scattered independently to nearby farmhouses to get food. Rifle and machine gun fire by this time were close at hand, so we knew the Front was very close, and liberation near. That night no one slept because of the very increasing roar of guns. Next morning German troops were seen in full retreat; our guards were to be seen no more. Very shortly we began to hear the rumbling of tanks coming up the dirt road, and in a few minutes we saw an American tank come in view. Boy! What a thrilling sight to behold! An officer standing half out of the tank hatch waved at us. G.I.s were now appearing in the area in pursuit of the retreating Germans. We all yelled with maddening joy as more US tanks appeared, and we mobbed them.

We now settled down for the night with smiles on our faces and happiness in our hearts, and all agreed that General Patton's Third Army, 15th Armored Division, was the best fighting unit in the world.

To finish with a happy ending: The next few days brought arrangements to evacuate us first to Stuttgart, then Metz, France, where we were debriefed, got medical assistance, clothes, and etc. Then to Dieppe, and by troop shipped to Hoboken, New Jersey, and the good old USA!!

The Hard Luck 492nd
by Robin C. Janton (From "Bomber Legends")

It was not the "Bloody 100"; nor was it any one of the scores of bomber groups stationed in England, Italy, or the Pacific, which were decimated; it was the "Hard Luck 492nd" at North Pickenham, England, that lost more men and planes in a shorter period of time than any other bombardment group in the history of the US Air Force. This is their story.

The 492nd was one of seven Heavy Bombardment Groups—488th through 494th—activated in the fall of 1943. These were to be the last AAF heavy bomb groups of WWII. The 492nd, on a hurry-up schedule, beat all the others into combat.

In personnel, if not in official lineage, the 492nd could trace its origin to 1920 when the Flying Club of Baltimore was organized for reserve officers of that city. This club became part of the Maryland National Guard on the 104th Observation Squadron. At the outset of WWII the 104th became part of the Anti-submarine Patrol used along the East Coast, operating out of the Atlantic City Municipal Airport. On 17 Oct. 1942 the unit's planes and personnel were transferred to the newly formed 517th Bombardment Squadron, which a month later became the 12th Anti-submarine Squadron under the command of Major Joshua Rome, one of the original Baltimoreans. The Squadron, now based at Langley Field, continued their anti-sub patrols until the fall of 1943 when the Navy took over the anti-sub role from the AAF. (By this time the "sub menace" had basically passed.)

On 24 Sept 1943 the Squadron was transferred to Blythe Army Air Field and became the 859th Bombardment Squadron. It

70

was designated as the cadre source for the new 492nd Bombardment Group that was to be formed at Alamogordo, NM. The other 492nd squadrons were the 856th, 857th, and 858th.

In early March 1944 an Operational Readiness Inspection proved that 32 crews were "not sufficiently advanced" to fit in with the rest of the group. The CO, Lt. Col. Snavely was then able to arrange that they be exchanged for a like number of crews from Biggs Field, TX. These replacement crews had pilots who had been instructors in the B-24 transitional training schools. They were Captains and 1st Lts. with many hundreds of hours flying B-24s. Together with the original cadre pilots , who had built up similar B-24 flight time in the anti-sub squadrons, the 492nd was able to complete its training ahead of schedule and fly the southern route to England without serious incident or loss (a record).

The 492nd was based at a newly constructed airfield near North Pickenham, with the required 6000 ft. runway. Experienced ground crews, drawn from other groups already in England, were assigned to the 492nd. Practice missions were conducted on May 4, 7, and 8 and a full dress rehearsal on May 10 that assembled 40 aircraft. Now it was time for the real thing.

The first operational mission was flown the next day against the marshalling yards at Mulhouse, France. Due to a target recognition problem, they made multiple runs over the area and never did drop, for fear of hitting French, or worse yet, Swiss civilians. As a result of this excessive time-over-target, two B-24s ran out of fuel and were written off in crash landings. It was not an auspicious start for the Group. However, the next three missions went well and were without loss.

Then came the mission to Brunswick on May 19. Nearing the target, German fighters fell on the 14th Wing with a vengeance, bringing down three of the 392nd ` B-24s. But it was the 492nd that paid more of the bill, losing eight ships—five of them from the 858th Squadron. War was real; (the wreckage and remains of one of the Group's planes was not discovered and identified until 1998.)

During the first week of June the 492nd attacked airfields and V-weapon launching sites in France. On D-Day, they bombed coastal defenses in Normandy, and continued attacking bridges, railroads, and other interdiction targets in France until the middle of the month. By June 19 a total of 33 group missions had been flown to strategic targets in France and Germany.

It must also be noted that beginning in June 1944 and for every month thereafter until VE Day flak, rather than fighters, was the number one enemy of the heavy bombers over Europe. While the 492nd lost its share to anti-aircraft fire, it was the Luftwaffe fighter pilots who remained the Group's chief nemesis. This was the case on 20 June when the 8th Air Force attacked oil installations at Politz. In thirty minutes of concentrated attacks, mostly by Bf410 twin-engine fighters, fourteen of the Group-s B-24s were shot out of the sky. (Some of them managed to make it to nearby Sweden.) Every plane and crew in the 856th Squadron that participated in the mission was lost. When the following day's mission was announced, it was a maximum effort to Berlin! The force the 492nd was finally able to put up was pitifully small—only eleven aircraft. But they went, of course, including three crews that had flown the Politz mission the day before. (My mission notes, in Chapter III, show that my crew also flew these two very tough missions.)

Each month seemed to bring another 'black day'. On July 7 when the 14th Wing attacked Bernberg, the 492nd could put up only 23 planes, so the third squadron of their formation was provided by the 392nd Group. The 492nd lost 12, and the 392nd, 5, all to fighters. This time it was the 859th Squadron that was wiped out, losing every plane on the mission, 9 total.

By the first week of August, mission losses had reached 58 Liberators and 578 airmen, (KIA, MIA, POW, interned or returned.)

During the first week of August sweeping changes were made by the 8th Air Force. The 492nd would take over the Carpetbagger Operation, the dropping of agents and supplies behind enemy lines, at night. The 491st was chosen as the group that would continue to bomb Germany. The 489th was scheduled for redeployment to the U.S. to be equipped with B-29s for the Pacific Campaign

There is much speculation as to the cause of the 492nd terrible losses. No paint silver airplanes—loose formations—lousy position—vendetta for their former anti-sub activities through the 859th Squadron—bad luck; whatever it was, as a comparison, the US Marines in WWII lost a total of 29 per thousand combatants. The 492nd lost 442 per 1000! (As an extra note, I believe that if you took Marine losses at two or three of the Pacific Islands you would find losses considerably in excess of the 29 mentioned in this article.)

Second Time Around—August 16, 1944
by Charles M. Trout (492nd)

After 22 combat missions we were shot down again over the North Sea by friendly fire or so we were told. We were supposed to have a high officer (General) fly with our crew and we were to fly high in back of formation, filling in the diamond so he could see how the group looked on a mission. Why over the North Sea? No bombs on board and no targets to shoot at but the orders were changed at the last minute.

I was sitting in the top turret when I heard a thud and the plane shuddered. I looked all around and saw no other planes as they were all below us. Then I smelled rubber burning and no voices on intercom, so I got down on the flight deck, looked in to the bomb bay, and it was full of swirling fire. I tried to use the fire extinguisher, but only a short burst and it was empty. Just at that time there was an explosion and fire flew all over things, setting fire to everything it stuck to, even on me.

I went up on the flight deck and told the pilot we had to abandon the plane immediately. Co-pilot and radio man, Ed Foss, were also told as I went by them. So I had trouble getting my chute harness hooked, turned my back to the fire for it was awful hot and I had to go. Opened bomb bay doors and there was a plane right under us 60-70 yards, so I had to wait a while for it to move over out of the way. The fire extinguisher fell when the doors opened and just missed #3 & #4 engines on that plane. I couldn't wait any longer, so I jumped and passed out from the heat but the plane moved enough and I cleared it. Bob Mattson had the same problem.

On the way down, after I came to and pulled the ripcord, everything was quiet but pieces of the plane were falling close to me. I heard a noise and here comes a P-47 right at me. Scared me almost to death. He made a few passes by me and dropped one-man life rafts for us to get into, but most of them burst when they hit the water and I saw two crewmen in the water approximately a mile from me so I finally got to them in an hour or so. Two in raft and I hung on. Water was warmer than the first time. The fog had started to move in just before dark. The chance of getting picked up wasn't too good, but I looked up over Ed Foss and there was the Air-Sea Rescue boat. As I reached to the fellow who extended his hand, he looked at me and said, "I know you. I picked you up a few months ago. You cut my finger the other time." We had a reunion right there. (Would like to see him again.) Headed for shore and the rescue boys worked on us; clean clothes, hot drinks, soup, and I suppose dope to stop the pain from burns. Ed Foss was the worst off. Landed on shore and our C.O. met us. That showed us he really cared about the fighting men in his unit. Went to a makeshift hospital for a week to rest and start healing. In about three weeks we were on our way home. My final trip to the U.S.A. was with a boat load of German prisoners—all officers. We stood guard night and day with riot guns—12 gauge 00 buck shot. Ten days later I saw the Statue of Liberty. What a feeling to be home on our own soil!

To sum it all up at the end of my tour of duty, I say this: Would not have missed it for anything; sorry for the crews and men who lost their lives. I forgive those who made mistakes, and I thank God it was over. I will never get in the Hall of Fame or be nominated for an Oscar, but my name is pasted to a brick on a brick wall someplace. Hope to hear from all my buddies.

May the good Lord take a likin' to you, one and all.

The Thirteenth Mission
by Wesley Sheffield (492nd)

It was August 1, 1944, and we were set to fly our thirteenth mission. We were a Liberator crew—four-engine heavy bombers—attached to the 857th Squadron, 492nd Bomb Group, Eighth Air Force. Before this day was over we would find an engine afire from a flak hit, ourselves out of gas and still over enemy-occupied France, losing three engines over the English Channel, getting them back only to lose two on the final approach.

The target was Anizy, about 50 miles northeast of Paris, and we were to bomb from 26,000 feet, each carrying a maximum bomb load of 8,000 pounds.

August 1 was a hot summer day—a surprise for England!—and our two Lib crews parked on adjoining hardstands were whiling away the few minutes prior to takeoff by casually ribbing one another about the coming mission. Bill Foster, pilot of Pregnant Angel, kept reminding me that this was my thirteenth mission and that old, battered Sweat Box probably wouldn't make it. I wasn't superstitious then, so I took his digs with good humor, telling him that my crew could come through anything. We took some snapshots of both crews, looked at our watches and climbed aboard our respective ships. In a few minutes, we were airborne.

As the formation approached the enemy coast, it soon became evident that bad weather ahead was either going to seriously hamper the mission or going to cause us to turn back entirely. Then came my first stroke of bad luck, and Bill's words began to take on an ominous sound in my ears. A burst of flak hit my number 4 engine as we crossed the coast. Smoke poured out.

I called to Evan Jones, my co-pilot, to feather the engine—but it wouldn't feather. it ran away and could only be controlled by the throttle. If I cut off its gas supply, it would act like a huge airbrake and I couldn't keep up with the formation. If I didn't, it might well blow us sky high any second. I opted to keep it running, keep up with the formation and hope for the best. That meant I was forced to pull extra power on the three good engines, thus burning extra gas. It was always possible to abort, but I decided to stick it out.

True enough, the weather got worse and worse, and though the formation strained higher and higher, it was no good. We had to turn back—still carrying full bomb loads.

When the coastline again hove into sight, I called "Butch" Carlson, my engineer, on interphone and asked him to check the gas supply. I knew that, due to the bad engine, I had been burning a lot of fuel. Carlson wasn't long answering. "We'd better get the hell out of here, because we're out of gas!" When you check B-24 gas gauges, first you get air bubbles and then a tube filled—or partly filled—with gas. Now, nothing.

My mind raced. Carlson could be wrong. It was just about the same distance to England as it was to the Cherbourg peninsula—where our troops had a widening beachhead and where a crippled bomber could crash land, under an extreme emergency. Number four was now smoking in a steady black stream. I felt as though we were sitting inside a bomb about ready to go off. Stubbornly I didn't want to bail out, yet the thought of ditching a 24 in the Channel was enough to make me turn very, very pale.

I told the crew we were going to try to make England, giving the choice of bailing out over water or ditching if Carlson was right about the gas. We now moved fast. I left the formation, salvoed my bombs in water beneath, throttled back as far as I could, called Harry Abrams, my navigator, for a heading to the nearest air field in England.

When I left the formation, Bill Foster did too and flew off my wing for a few minutes as if to say, "I'm sorry for being such a wise guy." I was too busy to do anything except fly my plane. I couldn't talk to Bill, or anyone else for that matter, since our radio had been knocked out by flak.

When the 492nd was disbanded a few weeks later due to heavy losses—we lost one entire squadron on one mission alone—Bill was assigned to fly unmarked B-24s at night to Sweden to repatriate air crews that took their disabled planes there. I went to the 93rd Bomb Group and completed 30 missions as a lead pilot and Assistant Operations officer.

New trouble soon developed. Harry had no good maps of air bases in southern England, and I couldn't contact any other ship without our radio. Our luck hadn't run out altogether, however. A lone P-47 spotted us by the trail of smoke pouring out of the bad engine, came up alongside and motioned with his hands that he would guide us to the nearest field.

The worst was yet to come. At 10,000 feet, Sweat Box abruptly nosed down and headed for the chill waters below. The three good engines had cooled off during the the long descent, probably developed carburetor ice and conked out before I could move to cover up my error. I frantically pushed turbos, props, throttles full forward—to no avail. Meanwhile I had to crank in full trim to hold the controls against engine number 4 which was still roaring away. And I pushed the "abandon ship" bell. I later learned that the only reason I didn't lose my crew into the Channel was because they were back at the waist gunner windows, arguing over who was going to jump first.

At six thousand feet, I made the last possible move—I pulled the mixture controls back into emergency rich. And I remembered the old adage about no atheists in fox holes and took time to mutter to myself, "No praying around here!" Never before or since have I felt so impotent in face of impending disaster—when I found out that that last move did it! Engines roared anew and the ship promptly went into a steep turning climb—because all the trim was set against number 4 engine. For the one and only time in combat, I yelled for help. "Jonesy, get on that rudder!" We got the plane under control and back on course for England. We were safe at least for the moment.

England now came into sight, but a low cloud cover prevented me from spotting a field from a safe altitude. The P-47 ducked down through the clouds and I could do little but follow, expecting my engines to quit at any moment. We had now been airborne for almost six hours and for the last hour of flight the gas gauges had been bone dry.

Hurrah, it's a field! The P-47 swooped low over it, then hovered above as I made a straight-in approach for landing. With only a few hundred feet to go, engines 1 & 4 quit—out of gas—but by hitting the other two throttles to the wide open position, I made the end of the runway with number 4 still streaming black smoke. We had made it!

All the way in, while taxiing, I urged Jonesy to keep trying to start the dead engines. I just couldn't comprehend what a close call that had been.

When the ground made their check, they found that we had landed with about 50 gallons (we took off with 2800 gallons) in the tanks of 2 and 3, and just enough oil in number 4 to wet the end of a stick. The flak had hit an oil line, which then dripped oil on the hot engine all the way home.

Unlucky thirteen had almost found its mark. And the ten men riding in Sweat Box that day have been religiously superstitious ever since. A later ground check indicated that the oil filters on all four engines were badly clogged, which had led to unusually high fuel consumption aside from the flak damage. A certain crew chief, nameless, got a great chewing out and not a few demerits for that kind of maintenance.

A postscript. When we landed, I congratulated myself for keeping cool through that long ride. Somehow, though, I guess I wasn't so cool. About an hour after landing, I found myself in the tower of that Polish fighter base, wondering where all my gear was. I took a jeep back to the plane—and found all my personal gear strewn haphazardly beneath the plane. I obviously got out in a hurry.

Ed. Note: After WWII, Sheffield went on to become 1) a tabloid news editor, 2) a minister, 3) a college president, 4) a fundraising consultant. He and his wife, Luise, live at Beebe Lake in Vermont.

The "Unforgettable Second"—That Was a Rough Mission!
by George A. Heropoulos (448th)

On December 31, 1943 we were to attack a German air base at La Rochelle, France
near the Spanish border. After a long haul, our formation of B-24s finally reached our target. As our bomb bays opened, we caught holy hell. I don't know why, but I had to toggle our bomb load from my nose turret. Fighters and heavy flak hit us. A burst of flak exploded in front of the nose of our B-24. The flak wounded Lt. Harmon, our bombardier, and me. The lieutenant lost an eye. We were banking to the right when our wingman received a direct hit to the gas tanks. It blew up like a big puff of smoke. I knew no one survived the explosion. My friends from Ohio, Sgt.Holesa and Sgt. Ball, from Canton, my hometown, and Sgt. Indorf from Massillon, were members of that crew.

Messerschmitts jumped us as we hit the target. We had to get out of there fast. On our way home we were forced to land at a Royal Air Force base in Southern England. We had been in the air for nine hours and forty-five minutes and had to refuel. We spent the night there, and the next day, New Year's Day, we had dinner at a U.S. Army base. Although we had been wearing the same clothes for two days, they treated us royally. After refueling we flew back to our base.

After finishing my thirtieth mission on June 22, 1944, we went home. I immediately went back to Canton. After a few days, Sgt. Holesa's sister called and asked me to stop by the house. I hesitated about going, but knew I had to go. I knocked on the door. When his sister opened the door, Mrs. Holesa burst into tears. I froze.

His sister took her mother to another room. We sat and talked. She told me that the War Department sent them a telegram—her brother was missing in action. I was speechless and didn't know what to do. Should I tell her what really happened? I knew I had to tell her the truth, that there was no way he or his crewmates could have survived that blast. I told her I was very sorry. Miss Holesa thanked me for telling her what happened. Our crew was lucky—we came home. More than fifty years later, I still remember that second mission.

I flew with the 448th BG, arriving at our base at Seething on December 20, 1943. Two days later we left on our first mission, a raid on Osnabruck, Germany. You would think this would be my most memorable mission, but it was the second one that I would never forget!

The Second Time Was a Charm!
By Luther S. Bird (93rd)

The 93rd Bomb Group completed its formation and headed across the North Sea for Norway.

There was a low lead section and a high section on the right of the lead. I was the pilot of "El Toro," and we were the co-lead ship in the high section. As I recall, our route and bombing altitude was 12,000 feet. It was extremely cold with the cockpit centigrade thermometer registering below minus 50. Periodically the group had to pass through scattered clouds and on these occasions some ships left the formation to return to base. About halfway to Norway, we passed through clouds, and more ships, including the lead, aborted. At this point, the remaining ships formed on "El Toro," and we became the group lead. Except for seeing a Stuka dive bomber off towards Denmark, the flight to the IP was uneventful. But then our problems began.

My Form 5 listed the November 18, 1943 target as Oslo and nine and one-half hours flying time. According to Roger Freeman's Mighty Eighth War Diary (page 139) the 93rd's November 18 target was Oslo--Kjeller with 20 planes dispatched, 15 bombing and one with 10 men MIA. According to Cal Stewart (*Ted's Traveling Circus*, page 258), on the November 18, 1943 mission to Kjeller repair base "the Circus made two bomb runs, commencing at 11:43." Mention of the two bomb runs stimulated me to write this account.

At the IP we turned on the bomb run. Immediately the bombardier (we had a substitute that day) called notifying that the bomb sight was frozen—a disturbing message meaning we were useless in contributing to a successful mission. There wasn't time for the radio or flares. I rocked the wing tips a few times and went into a left turn to circle and return to the bomb run. About halfway around, another ship cut inside and took the lead. All ships formed on the new lead and the run from the IP to the target continued. No flak or fighters were encountered in the target area. The new lead bombardier did a good job and all ships released on his bomb drop. The men in the back reported that the bombs were all on target. The target, a hangar, literally disappeared from the earth! A mission that could have been a failure became very outstanding for the Circus. (Regrettably I cannot recall the ship or crew that made the day for the 93rd!).

After leaving the target area and heading for the North Sea, our armorer-gunner called with the news that we had a bomb hanging by one latch in the right rear compartment. The decision was made to leave the bomb alone until we were over the North Sea. However, the bomb didn't wait as it dropped knocking the right rear bomb bay door off its tracks. The door was hanging down for the flight back. This did not interfere with the flight characteristics of the plane, flopping in the breeze. But we were concerned about our "stray" hitting civilians.

Despite our flapping bomb bay door, we made a successful landing, and when we reported to interrogation, the Norwegian underground had already reported the success of the mission. The report indicated that high level Germans were involved in a military review and an open house ceremony, and that our aircraft overhead were thought to be a part of the review! Needless to say, we surprised them at a very opportune moment.

The Norwegians did also report that some stray bombs caused some minor damage to their civilians. We immediately reviewed and estimated that our stray bomb would have hit in unpopulated country. It was good to be back at the home base with the warm feeling that another successful mission was completed, even though this time we had to make two bomb runs!

Yanks in Britain

By Cpl. Edmund Antrobus
Reprinted from Wartime "Yank" The Army Weekly

On January 16, 1945, 1st Lt. Albert J. Novik of Tarrytown, N.Y., dived from the flight deck of his fuel-less Liberator headfirst through the bomb bay and saved his life. His leap gave him enough speed to clear the plane while it was still gliding.

On February 16, a month later to the day, he had to bail out again and tried to maneuver a second time. But the plane nose-dived before he could make it, throwing him up against the ceiling, where he stuck, looking down at a fire sweeping through the fuselage and thinking that at any moment he would be dead.

This was the climax of four and a half bad hours for Lt. Novik. He had been flying with a squadron in the 392nd Bomb Group when, a few seconds after dropping his bombs, another Liberator in a higher formation had moved in on top to obtain a more compact bomb pattern. It came too close and dropped six bombs through Novik's left rudder.

Minus a huge chunk of its tail assembly, Novik's Liberator dropped 500 feet, becoming so nose-heavy that it took all of Novik's strength at the wheel to keep it from diving.

Novik, however, decided to continue over the target so that he could stay with the formation as protection against enemy fighters. In this way he managed to struggle back to England, but was unable to land because clouds had closed in over the home base and emergency landing fields. Together with the rest of his group, Novik was ordered to go back and land in France. Realizing that his ship would never make it, he decided to land in England if he could.

It was getting harder and harder to hold the ship in the air. Novik was under a tremendous strain, and the back of his neck was ridged like a weight-lifters. "It was a good thing," says the navigator, F/O Wade Hampton of Toronto, Ont., "that we had a strong, as well as a good, pilot."

For two hours they looked for a suitable field but all were fogged in, and at last they decided to head towards The Wash and bail out.

It was a painful decision. The ship had flown 70 missions without an abort. Everyone knew it was in fine mechanical condition; the fact that it could fly without a left rudder was proof of that. Someone recalled that the crew chief, S/Sgt. Eugene S. Goldsby of Los Angeles, was up for an award for the way he'd taken care of his ship.

The gunners bailed out first, then the navigator, radio operator and engineer.

After that, Novik climbed out of his seat while the copilot, 1st Lt. Jack H. Graves of Birmingham, Ala., hung on the controls. Then, standing, Novik took over, holding the plane steady while Graves jumped. The elevator trim tabs, which normally keep the plane in level flight, were not working, and the automatic pilot could not be used because the slight shake it would cause when it went into control would probably be enough to crash the plane. Novik found that even a 10-degree turn made the ship shudder as if its tail was breaking.

When the copilot hit the silk, Novik gave him thirty seconds to clear the ship and then prepared to jump from the flight deck through the bomb bay, as he had done a month previously. But the second he let go of the wheel, the plane dived like a Thunderbolt. Novik was thrown against the ceiling and pinned there while the plane dived 7,000 feet.

"My first impulse," Novik said, "was to try and beat my way out through the fuselage. I thumped with the sides of my fists, but the air pressure was so strong it was an effort even to move my arms. It was the sensation you have in a dream when you are running from something and your feet get bogged down in quicksand."

Dying did not occur to him—just then. "And yet," he says, "just about this time a guy gets very religious. You start praying to something super-human because you know nothing human can help you."

It was fire that made Novik give up hope. Spread-eagled against the ceiling, he saw flames sucked in from a burning engine, spread through the fuselage, and fan up towards him as if he were on a spit, being grilled alive. At that moment he lost his fear because he no longer thought he was going to live. He smelt his hair being singed. He felt, as he now put it, "eccentric and carefree." He was not delirious or suffering pain.

Then, suddenly, he was dropped from the ceiling, as a wing, or something, came off, changing the direction of the plane. He began to claw his way through the fire up to the bomb bay. He says he didn't feel that he was escaping from death, but from death in a particularly violent form.

Somehow he dragged himself to the bomb bay and fell through, and just as he cleared the bomber it exploded over his head. He pulled his ripcord but only two feet of chute came out. He pulled again, this time with both hands, and the chute opened. He was now about 700 feet from the ground.

Looking up, Novik saw burning pieces of the plane floating down like enormous flaming leaves. He put a hand to one eye and when he took it away it was covered with blood. He thought he had lost the eye, but that did not seem important. All around him burning debris was falling, great chunks of it catching up with him and passing within a few feet of his parachute. But, looking down, Novik saw that the real danger was on the ground, for parts of the burning plane had landed on the spot he was headed for. Only by luck he landed in a tree, which saved him being roasted in the wreckage of the plane.

Men have been hurt more turning over in bed than Novik was during his seemingly interminable brush with death. His face had been burned and his hair singed, and it was the hand he put to his eye, and not the eye itself, that had been cut. As a matter of fact, his fingers hurt more than anything else; they were numb for three days from straining on the wheel during the four and a half hours he had struggled to keep his plane in the air.

All in all, it had been a happier landing than the one Novik had made a month before. On that occasion, two of his men had jumped through the nose-wheel hatch, hit something, and been killed. This time they all landed safely and were in good condition to stand by when the colonel presented Novik with the DFC.

Chapter 3: About Me

First 24 Years

My first sixteen years were spent in the very northeastern county of Montana, and northwestern North Dakota, in small towns located on the branch Soo Line Railroad. My father was an elevator operator; i.e., he purchased the farmers' production of wheat, rye, barley, and flax. This was stored until shipped to grain companies, usually in Minneapolis. This came to an end in the drought of the 1930s, accompanied by depression and sandstorms. My parents and I left the day after I graduated from high school in Lignite, ND, May, 1936, in our 1928 Chevrolet, for western Washington.

My oldest sister, Florence, was teaching in Heron, MT, and was instrumental in getting us work. First, picking huckleberries, living in a tent on a mountain. What a contrast, now there were all kinds of trees, rivers, mountains. I loved it. Next, my parents got a job as domestics on a small estate near Newport, WA, which was the source of the little Spokane River. I had nothing better to do than take a post-graduate year at Newport High School, and learned typing and Gregg shorthand. The next summer, pile brush for a logging company in Clarkia, ID, $4 a day, room and board. The savings sent me to Kinman Business School in Spokane, WA, which resulted in a stenographer job with Hecla Mining Company in Wallace, ID. It was an all-male office of approximately 16 clerks, accountants, plus the three officers of the company. It was a great learning experience and we younger office employees were good friends. I still communicate with three of my fellow survivors. Here, I could see the benefits of the higher education I did not have, and World War II ultimately gave me that opportunity.

By this time, I am 22 years of age, subject to the draft. I took the intelligence and physical tests for pilot training, and became the roughly one in four who passed. Finally, the call came to board a train in Spokane, which had picked up other future cadets on its route through Montana and Idaho. One such was Donald Nutter, who became the governor of Montana, only to die in a plane crash en route to a speaking commitment. This, after surviving as a bomber pilot. The train trip culminated at Santa Ana Army Air Base, our indoctrination into the army as air corps cadets. Here it was ground school, physical ed, marching. I enjoyed it. Just a great bunch of guys and I remember many of them. Our cadet captain was Tim Holt, son of the actor. He had attended a military school and thus was chosen for that position.

Southern California in 1943 was much different from today. No freeways, lots of oranges, no smog. Intersections would have a hollow for winter storm drainage. We would hire a limo to take us to L.A. to look for female companionship, Biltmore Hotel or Wilshire Blvd. Dance at the Palladium in Hollywood, big bands. All this ended upon assignment to Cal Aero, a private flying school some 40 miles east of Los Angeles, near, or at, Chino. We would use the Puente Hills for a reference for slow rolls. Our Stearman biplane, 165 hp radial engine, great for aerobatics. I loved doing spins, looking straight down to the ground. If you let go of the controls, it would come out of the spin. By ground looping and dragging a wing, I almost washed out of primary. I hadn't recognized drift. But when I got to basic, a 450 hp low wing monoplane, non-retractable gear, my instructor, Lt. Phipps taught me so much in the first 20 hours of dual and solo that the remainder of flying school was easy. Thank you, Lt. Phipps, wherever you are. And in advanced we flew a nothing plane, I don't remember the designation, twin engine, almost impossible to stall out on landing in the hot Stockton summer. It was a big thrill to get pilot wings, the golden bar of a 2nd Lt., and much better looking clothes. We traded the lackluster brown for good-looking greens and pinks. With leave, headed home to Spokane, I had met a WASP (Women's Air Service Pilot) that I was anxious to see. One of many female associations that did not amount to anything in retrospect, but I guess important at the time. Off to Kirtland Field in Albuquerque to earn my first pilot position in a B-24. I enjoyed the desert, the Sandia Mountains, learning to fly a much larger and sophisticated aircraft. Two pilots, Harley Watt from Steubenville, OH, and myself, were assigned to an instructor, in this case, Lt. Ruiz. A toughie. He had ditched his B-17 in the Pacific, and survived many days in a rubber raft before being rescued. And on a stormy night, he got us back on the ground in high winds, a feat Harley and I were not yet up to. The first time in the pilot's seat of a B-24 I looked around at the dozens of instruments, toggle switches, buttons, levers, all around the cockpit, and thought I'll never learn where all these things are.

Two weeks later we were able to reach for the proper items, many times without looking to see where they were. It was fun flying this big boxcar. It had marvelous Pratt & Whitney 1200 engines, four of them. I remember one moonlit night Harley, our engineer, and I flew west to the 12,633 feet high Humphreys Peak, circling it before returning. Beautiful. Another time, early in our training acting as co-pilot for Ruiz, taking off from Denver and its 5,000 foot elevation, with considerably less lift than at sea level, after we had climbed a few hundred feet Ruiz said "flaps up." I had forgotten to put them down. I did have the presence of mind to push the flap handle to make the sound which indicated "flaps up." If Ruiz had realized my error, well, I'd never have forgotten what he would have said. Graduating from Albuquerque, it's off to Fresno at Christmas time, 1943, to pick up copilot Al Bacon, Ceres, CA, navigator Frank Erbacher, Ohio, bombardier Phil Goplin, MN, engineer Issy Buechner, Cross Plains, WI, and radio operator, name forgotten. I later replaced him as I felt he didn't seem to fit in a combat crew. We were assigned to Muroc Army Air Base (now Edwards) in the Mojave Desert, a stellar training area that became the Air Force's premier testing base. Chuck Yeager made his epic sound barrier flight from here. And we were assigned the remainder of our crew, Bob and Ken Snyder, brothers from Baltimore, together at the request of their parents, Bob a waist gunner, Ken the tail; Vince Torfin, from MN, assistant engineer and the other waist; and Chuck Barrier, TX, ball turret gunner. The replacement radio operator was Alfred Carrington, from Virginia.

We pilots did a lot of sweating during the learning period of flying formation. Being able to keep your airplane in a proper position was doubly important, one for an effective bombing pattern and secondly, for defensive strength against enemy fighters.

Four officer crews were closely quartered—pilots Red Bassett, CT, Harold Wright, ID, Joe Shogan, PA, and myself. We called ourselves "The Big Four." It was our first experience at flying formation, and the crews would confer as to the difficulties of their pilot in keeping in position. We pilots did a lot of sweating in this learning period. Being able to keep your airplane in a proper position was doubly important, one for an effective bombing pattern, and secondly, for defensive strength against enemy fighters. We did a lot of practice bombing, with duds, for bombardier training. Gunners had some training shooting at sleeves towed by an aircraft. On one of our navigation night missions we flew east for a few hours, on a heading something like 90 degrees. Returning to base, the three of us—pilot, copilot, and navigator—all had, in army parlance, our head up our you-know-what, and set a course for 290 degrees. Well, after a couple of hours we were quite a bit off course and didn't catch it until the bombardier loudly exclaimed, "there's a big hole down there!" It was the Grand Canyon, some hundred miles north of where we would have been if flying the proper 270 degrees.

After 8 days of flying we would get two days off. Generally my pal, Joe Shogan, the pilot from Monessen, PA and I would head off to Los Angeles. The object was to find a female companion. I spent a lot of nights dancing at the huge Palladium ballroom in Hollywood.

On one 2 day pass Joe and I stayed at the upscale Miramar in Santa Monica. We noted that one of the bungalows on the grounds had a number of military police, probably for high rank. The next morning at breakfast a colonel come over and asked Joe and me if we would like to meet the general. We agreed, and here it was #1, and the only 5 star general in the Air Force, Hap Arnold. He inquired where we were stationed. We told him he probably wouldn't recognize our isolated base. "WHERE ARE YOU STATIONED?" When we told him Muroc, he said "HELL, I BUILT THE PLACE!" And this forward looking man recognized the need for an isolated testing ground for future aircraft development, now known as Edwards AFB. (Some 20 years later after the general's death Ann and I and our 6 year old Clark met his widow. From that, she would send him greetings when she attended graduation ceremonies at the Air Force Academy in Colorado Springs. She also gave him one of the general's insignia and a leather patch for a flying jacket, with the general 's name. We still have those. (See photos)

Finishing our training at Muroc the four crews were sent to Hamilton Field, just north of San Francisco in Marin County for further assignment. Bassett and Wright were issued mosquito netting and tropical gear, and Shogan's and my crew, heavy flying suits. It was obvious they were headed for the South Pacific, and we to either Italy or England. In that the loss rate was much lower in the Pacific than in Europe we told them they would probably survive, but we would have a more civilized life, i.e., access to girls, cities, restaurants. Contrary to odds, we heard that their crews were lost, and Joe and I both finished our allotted missions

As pilot/commander it was my duty to sign for this new airplane we were to fly to wherever. I was told, "Lt., do you know you are signing for $160,000 worth of aircraft?" Talk about inflation—that would hardly buy the landing gear today. But it was a lot of $ in 1944.

We flew across the country in four days, ending up at Morrison Field, West Palm Beach, FL. We were there a couple of days, and then given sealed orders not to opened until we reached Puerto Rico, and it was the Eighth Air Force, England. I landed in Santa Lucia to get a bit more fuel from a British base there, and on to Port of Spain, Trinidad for the night. I remember almost nothing of that field in that I believe we arrived after dark, and early next morning set off for Belem, Brazil. It is boring to fly level with the engines droning on and on, especially if the terrain doesn't offer much contrast. If you are on autopilot, check your instruments once in a while, and watch for other aircraft, always. Getting close to Belem, there was flat grassland with cattle. To break the monotony, down we go on the deck for the exciting sensation of speed, whizzing over the pampas grass and the cattle. We heard, whether true or not, some crews allowed the gunners to shoot at the cattle. We did not. However, we did encounter a buzzard. He—or she—hit our leading edge on the left wing between the # 1 and 2 engine, and being tough birds, made quite an impression on this wing boot section. It did not noticeably affect the flying characteristics, but it needed repair.

It took the Portugese several days to repair this, first trying to construct the part with no success, and then remembering a crashed B-24 in the area that supplied the proper part. So we spent time in this fairly large city. On to Fortaleza, Brazil for the hop across the Atlantic to Dakar, Senegal, at night for celestial navigation. Only land on the way were something called St. Pauls Rocks. I thought we blew a tire upon landing, and cussed. But the runway was steel matting on sand, and made a loud and unfamiliar sound upon touchdown. The only thing I remember about Dakar was that the blacks were blacker blacks than I had ever seen before.

Off to Marrakesh, Morocco, in the foothills of the Atlas Mountains. Here we caught up with crews who had gone ahead when we were getting repaired in Belem. Weather had kept them here. Although I have, in later years, spent several days in western Morocco, I feel I have missed out by not visiting interesting Marrakesh again.

The difficulties of the next trip were basically three. First, shortly after taking off in the dead of night, there were some big mountains ahead. Escape that, and the Bay of Biscay was an area that the German fighters could reach, so we had ammunition aboard. Third, it's not easy to find a specific airfield in the south of Wales in the ever-present visibility problems. The Irish had painted numbers on rocks along their southern peninsulas to identify the position, so you wouldn't land in this neutral country. If you did, they'd give you some gas and point toward Wales. Making radio contact we knew we were close to our landing field, we saw it, and that small peek was all we got. I made estimates of flying the pattern, and at something like 200 feet elevation we break out with the runway dead ahead. I was proud of myself. We relinquish our B-24.

From Wales we go to Northern Ireland just outside of Belfast to a base on Lough Neagh for a couple of weeks pre-combat training. I don't remember what we did, except visit Belfast, which was off limits. Then off to our assigned base, the 448th Bomb Group, 20th Wing, 2nd Air Division, Eighth Air Force, some 10 miles south southeast of East Anglia's capital city of Norwich, village of Seething. We learned the plane we flew over had been shot down in the ensuing time. I believe we gave it a name and a painted picture, as was the custom, but memory fails me any details.

The four officers were assigned to a barracks with two other crews, so 12 in all. The enlisted personnel were assigned to another area, but kept together. Bicycles were issued to the pilot and the bombardier. Now, it's time to start flying missions. After each mission I kept a diary describing it in a little notebook. I had originally intended to delete passages that expressed my emotions and fears, bit if I had, it wouldn't be a revealing and true story.

My 33 Missions:

Mission #l, May 19, 1944 (my mother's birthday) Target: plane engine factory, Brunswick. Support: P 38s and 47s. Opposition: Thousands of fighters! Acres of flak! Load: l2 500lb. M-17 incendiaries (hell to carry).

Took off at 0900 as copilot with an experienced copilot as pilot-commander. As we crossed the enemy coast I had a funny feeling. At last, I'm in the war, dammit! Went over the Zuyder Zee. Germany was pretty. Had a few flak bursts on the way to the target. Not many friendly fighters about, it seemed. As we got closer to the target we spotted swarms of enemy fighters. Made one kind of think. Then came the flak! We had about 30 flak holes when we got back. The ship will take a week to fix. Flak went into one of the fuel cells, and it will have to be replaced. Part of our oxygen system was knocked out. Our rudder and waist were full of holes. One of the waist windows had a hole in it. Luckily, no one was hit in our plane. Fighters give you a hell of a scare when they start coming in, nose toward you, spouting cannon and machine gun fire.

Our gunners saw 4 enemy fighters go down. Our group lost one plane, by a Me 109. He was in the bucket of our 4-plane element. Too close! ... We go at it again tomorrow. Now, 29 to go. (Experienced crews say this was one of the tougher missions, if not the toughest, and they wouldn't expect to live in 5 missions like that, so we had a good initiation. Having nothing to compare it to, didn't know if it was normal, or not.)

May 20: Mission scrubbed. Aroused at 0230 for a 0400 briefing, and were briefed on 2 targets. Ground haze kept us from taking off. We were called back at 0900, only to find out it was again scrubbed.

A few minutes ago when I went to shave, 3 Lts. came up and asked if I knew anything about their friend, Silver, who was shot down yesterday. They were from another group and came over to see him tonight. And the crew chief reported we had 38 holes from our Brunswick raid.

May 21: Mission scrubbed.

May 22, Mission #2: St. Pol, France, rocket installation and synthetic factory. 8 1000 lb. GPs (general purpose).

Took off, a supercharger was out, but being an easy Nobal target, decided to go. When at 8,000' #3 caught fire, so we feathered it and came back and landed with a full load (after the mission, the Sqd. CO told us what a good landing it was). Anyway, we got another ship quick-quick and caught the formation half way to the target. As we did, #4 supercharger went out but on we went. Came out between Ostend and Dunkirk. No losses, only 4 flak bursts. Got some Link time, p.m.

May 23: A rest. Censored mail, Link (Link trainers, simulated instrument flying), screwed around.

May 24, #3: Airfield and 2, 400' long hangars, 5 miles SE of Paris. Lots of inaccurate flak, only one hole, went through glass by bombsight and missed the navigator—good! 58 100 lb. M47 jelly/gasoline bombs, no fun! Wiped out the target. Earlier GP bombs left nothing but girders, and our fire bombs burned out the wreckage. Saw Paris—darn good-looking city. France very pretty, farms look good, patches of woods here and there. Airfields and woods where there were guns and installations are darn well wrecked. Our fighters have shot up 303 trains the last couple of days. (Not in notes, but getting ready for D-Day>)

May 25, #4: 12 500 lb. GPs. Nobal, Fecamp, France, on coast. Mission # 1 for Phil Goplen, our bombardier. Over enemy territory 5 minutes, no flak, fighter support didn't show up, no matter.

May 27, #5: 12 500 pounders—Marshalling yards, Trier, Germany. Good hits, blew to hell. No close flak, no enemy fighters, had 38s, 47s, and 51s escort. Long mission, at 23,000' for a while. Our #4 shook so badly across the channel we were afraid we might have to turn back, kept on, it got better... Yesterday I met a Tom Skeffington from Spokane, and used to come to Wallace and knows Herman Brass, Hoban, Doc Fitzgerald, Jim McCarthy, the Murphy boys, and Joe and Donny

Codd. Damn nice to talk to him. He went to Gonzaga and U of WN, and sang with the Bob Crosby band.

May 28: Sunday, day of rest, went to church and communion, and went for a pleasure ride in a 24 to another field, and logged 1 hr. 20 minutes flying time.

May 29, #6: Air Medal day FW 190 assembly plant, Tutow, Germany. 52 100 lb. M47s, (jelly/gasoline) No enemy fighters, some flak, quite thick, though missed us. Entered Germany near Kiel, and came way up near Denmark on the way home. Grounded tomorrow. Hooray!

June 5: 5 easy missions gone to the devil, didn't fly all week (not scheduled) Calibrated airspeed yesterday and buzzed a P-51 and a Mosquito base and hedge-hopped home. Tonight at 2000 we went to a pre-briefing. Know what's going to happen tomorrow—this is it! Read a field order on it. Of course it's all very secret at this hour... Frank Gibson (Hoot to us, from Long Beach, CA) finished his missions today. He'll miss the big show. Sport (his copilot) is through, but Little Olo and Connole (bomb. and nav.) aren't through yet. Gotta hit the sack, briefing is at 2300 and have to eat, so little sleep, if any, tonight.

June 7: at 1710 hrs. June 6 #6 and #7. First, to the invasion coast of France near Caen, pre-dawn takeoff at 0300. Flew around England in the dark along with a couple thousand more aircraft in a big mess, finally got in a formation and bombed the coast minutes before the troops landed. We were repeatedly warned not to drop our bombs on our troops. Couldn't see the coast, flying at 16,000', above a complete overcast. Before reaching the coast we could see ships shelling the coast. Our heavies were the only ones above the clouds. Had a little flak over the channel islands—Jersey and Gurnsey, since then taken by allies. Got to sleep a couple of hours—first time in over 36—and went out again amid all the clouds, and bombed a bridge inland, visually. Ducked under the clouds before hitting England and saw a lot of ships, and made a 4th of July celebration out of it by firing the colors of the day, quite often, and the ships would answer. Came over Portsmouth, which was pretty with the sun shining through the clouds at different angles and hitting the ship-studded water.

Came back in formation, getting dark, the ceiling barely 500 feet, arriving at field all the ships dove into the funnel. Luckily, no collisions. Flew 12:45 hrs. yesterday. Bad weather keeping us down.

June 8, 2045: Did not fly today, but almost took off 3 times, and had two briefings. Weather, terrible. Ceiling from 1000' to over 25000', with icing, so we hoped the missions would be scrubbed. Sqd. CO, Major Glassel S. Stringfellow, got up in the soup, recalled, when salvoed the fragmentation bombs a couple went off in the bomb bay, knocking out hydraulics and wounding the tail gunner. Landed on one wheel, wrecked the plane.

June 10, #9: Evereux, France, airfield. Formed at 26,000', dense contrails at 24,000', undercast below that. Lucky no collisions, had a number of close calls. Big mess trying to form. Tired—had to do almost all of the weather flying today, though Al (Bacon, copilot, Ceres, CA), changed seats (we were flying off a right wing) after we got out of enemy territory. Lost 1 ship today—Tooles, a lead crew. A couple of bombs collided as they were released and the plane caught fire. Our tail gunner saw 8 chutes, and from 4 to 10 were reported. The plane broke in two just after one fellow jumped right at station 6, just aft of the bomb bays. Those who saw it said it was the darndest sight and not pleasant to see, so my restricted visibility from the cockpit spared me from the sight. Had a burst we could feel and hear under the fuselage, but no holes.

Unexplainable, maybe it was a rocket, a shell, or something else.

June 11: Recalled on a mission to Redon, France. Used 57" Hg. on takeoff and used all but 75' of runway (ship had reputation as a bad one) and got off with good speed. Hit some prop wash soon after our wheels were off and I thought we'd lost an engine and I hollered to Al to fix it. All he could do was help push in the rudder. Lots of clouds. Flew over London on way back. Went to church. Am really tired, and hope we don't fly tomorrow.

June 13, 21:30: Just got back from pass in London. Very good city. Couple of little air raids. Guns make a lot of noise, and shoot fast. By accident met friend Van Hersett and he showed me around, stage show, dance at Hammersmith, Picadilly

Commandoes, St. Pauls, #10 Downing, Buckingham Palace, The Admiralty, House of Parliament, etc. Returned and heard that Bailey, in ship #710, didn't come back from a raid Sunday. Hope they're okay, but it sounds bad as they don't know much if anything about it.

NOTE—October 9, 1944: After 53 days in France, waiting for the army to come up, Bailey did come out. He lost 1 or 2 of his crew. Saw him back here a couple of months ago.

June 14, #10: 52 100 lb GPs—(actually, 130 lb) Airfield 10 miles northwest of Orleans, France. Really hit the target today. There were a lot of rack malfunctions today, single bombs being kicked out all the way home. No enemy or friendly fighters. Quite a few ships had bad flak hits, but no one in our group went down.

June 15, #11: 12 500 lb GPs Railroad bridge 10 miles west of Tours, France. Moderate, accurate flak on the way out. No fighters, but a fellow who aborted got jumped by 4 fighters, but 38s came in at the opportune moment and saved him... Think we bombed the wrong bridge... (We did, but the lead section got the right one.)

June 16, #12: 10 500 lb GPs Nobal—Rocket plane supply depot 5 mi. ESE St. Omer, France. Flew up through clouds and formed at 20,000'. No flak or fighters, made instrument letdown.

June 18, #13: 52 100lb M47 gasoline/jelly. Hamburg. More and closer flak than I have seen before, and again, I hope. 4 ships lost in group. Beckman, from our barracks was one, and we ghouled (okay if you save personal items for them, later, or relatives). The flak was thicker than air, and it was damn close. We could hear it go BANG, not just puff, and see the flashes of light as it burst. The air was thick with smoke from the bursts, and we were in light clouds and contrails. Good fighter support from 51s and 38s. We could have been murdered by fighters over the target as we were spread out and confusion was high, not bombing the proper target, a nice mission to have behind you. NOTE—The history of my group was assembled by Jeffrey E. Brett in "The 448th Bomb Group (H). Following is his write up on this mission. Information on the purchase of this complete history, formation at Gowen Field, Idaho to preparations to close the base. Full crew rosters, original and replacement, and more, are included. For purchase info, patricia.everson@lineone.net..."A Lutwaffe Control Center offered a less friendly target for the group the following day, 18 June. A one hour delay before takeoff provided the bombers the luxury of a daylight assembly. The briefed route over the Danish peninsula skirted the known flak areas but unfavorable weather over the target forced the bombers to switch targets. Turning away from Fassberg, the PFF aircraft led the formation directly over the heavily defended city of Hamburg. Flak thick enough to walk on surrounded the bombers as they passed over the city. At 0954, just six minutes from the coast, flak crippled the aircraft flown by Lt. Leland Beckman. The first burst ruptured the number four oil tank resulting in the engine becoming uncontrollable. More bursts did additional damage and tail number 42-52119 succumbed to the dreaded flak. All ten members, on their fifth mission, bailed out... Sgt. George Copeland exited the plane through the camera hatch. After hitting his back on the plane as he jumped, he pulled the ripcord almost immediately fearing he might pass out from pain. Sgt. Dewy Conn suffered a flak wound in the leg before jumping, and Sgt. Michael J. Eannone jumped with his silk parachute in his hand. Somehow it had deployed in the plane prior to jumping. Despite those near disasters everyone survived the exit. As Sgt. Copeland floated earthward, he heard gunshots. Assuming they were aimed at him, he plotted his escape. Spotting a forest near his landing area, he planned to hide in the woods. However, after narrowly missing power lines, he landed only to find 'a pistol in my face in very nervous hands'. He spent the remainder of the war as a POW. Less fortunate was Sgt. Dan Waais. Angry civilians killed him after he landed... While the downed crew tried to evade in Germany, the remainder of the group bombed an airfield near Hamburg as a target of opportunity. After a seven hour flight planes landed at Seething where awaiting medics in meat wagons tended to the wounded aboard 42-51079." (Pages 114-119 in this book describes, in detail, my roughest three missions—Hamburg, Politz, Berlin— all in a 4 day period.)

June 20, #14: 40 100 lb GPs. Oil refinery, Politz, Germany (was in Poland before 1939!) Went up over the North Sea and into Germany east of Stettin. Before we got to the target we could see a lot of flak smoke, and there was plenty of close flak. 21 ships went to Sweden, and our group lost 3, 1 from our squadron Smoke billowed up to 20,000'. We could see smoke screens at some towns, and Hamburg was still smoking from our raid 2 days before... I'm writing this a day late so I don't remember too much about it—except that it was a tough, high loss ratio, mission—because today's (6/21) raid overshadows it, especially for our crew. Read on for Big B

June 21, #15: 10 500 lb GPs. BERLIN. This was really hell. Went up the North Sea and into Germany and until we reached the target. The trip was rather uneventful but then saw a lot of flak smoke from shooting at earlier groups, and they had our altitude down to the inch. They opened up on us with big guns—bigger bursts than we had ever seen before—probably 105s and 155s, and maybe 240s. Anyway, we could really hear those bursts explode. Practically deafening and we almost had to fly on instruments through the smoke. Then we got a hit in our best engine, #1, and the oil leaked and down went the pressure. Before I feathered it we got a close burst on my side and a piece of flak tore through both panes of the thick bullet proof glass at an angle that also took it through the steel separation between the two windows, and hit me in the back. Broken glass was all over the cockpit, and Al, my copilot, was very busy flying off a left wing and thought I was a goner. I could feel my shoulder hurting so asked the radio operator to see if my clothing and back pack parachute was torn, and he said no, so I felt relieved. All I have is a big black and blue mark... Just as we dropped our bombs I feathered #1 and we dropped below our squadron and sweat out flak for a few more minutes—12 minutes of it over Berlin. Saw a ship get hit and flip over on its back with the bomb bay doors open and the bombs still in the racks. Saw a couple more get hits in the engines and go peeling off.

We couldn't catch our group again and our engines had a lot of time on them so we didn't dare pull too much power. I called for fighter assistance and we fired some green-green flares. Then, #3 looked very, very bad. Cylinder head temperature high, oil temp high, oil pressure low, and fuel pressure low with oil all over the cowling. About that time I wasn't so sure. A few minutes before we had discussed Switzerland, Sweden, liberated France (not much of it yet), or home to England. Unanimous—England. So we struggled along, alone, praying for no enemy fighters, and when the 14th wing was passing us we increased a bit more power so we could fly with them to the coast. In the meantime we are tossing out everything we could. The ball gunner was excited enough to toss out 3 maybe needed, light first aid packets. But the heavy ball turret was unleashed, so were heavy flak suits and most of our ammunition. Called air sea rescue for a heading to the nearest English shore. Got back after much sweating and our good luck held out because we found a big enough hole in the 900 foot overcast, needed because our flight indicator was out. All in all, we're damn lucky to be back, and I especially so for the thick glass. Thank God we didn't have the normal plate glass or I don't think I'd be sitting here. The path of the flak would have taken it through me at the location of my heart. (I still have the piece of flak with glass embedded, and a photo of me, next day, holding the two sections of shattered glass.)... We were scheduled to fly again tomorrow, but I saw the doc and got grounded for a rest after the last three missions, and it grounds the whole crew. Had a few drinks and cleaned up and went to church—that one made a Christian out of me. Guess I'll go down and have a bite to eat with Little Olo.

June 22: Grounded today. Censored mail this morning, show this afternoon on the Nazis treatment of the Poles. Tally is 43 bombers lost over and around Berlin yesterday. Darn nice record from nothing much but flak. Heinies are getting pretty darn good shots.

June 24, #16: 10 250 lb GPs. Hote Cote, France. Didn't drop our bombs. Not much flak but got a burst that blew out a hydraulic line. The radio operator called and I finally squeezed it out of him that it was "red stuff," so there was no danger. We got instructions to drop our bombs in the channel, circled our field to let down the nose gear and crank down the flaps. They sure had a lot of meat wagons waiting for us. Landed without incident... George Van Hersett was waiting for me in our hardstand so we went to the party and got damn tite and related 'pushed down the nose wheel and cranked down the flaps' He stayed overnight and left Sunday noon, and is sweating going home now after finishing his missions.

June 25, #17: 20 250 lb GPs. Airfield 12 miles south of Paris (Orly now?) quite a bit of flak, 4 holes in ship. Sweated it out, and have since Berlin. Had trouble getting the nose wheel up. Went through a front—more damn clouds. Hit the wrong target, 10 miles north of where we were supposed to go, and so ran into more flak to sweat out. Am trying to get a pass now, and then a 6 day leave. Payday is needed first, though.

June 26: Stand Down. We almost went to Munich today but it was scrubbed just before takeoff. The clouds run up to 22,000' so we'll surely not fly this afternoon. Will clean up my corner and piddle around.

June 28, #18: 12 500 lb GPs. Rail marshalling yards, Saarbrucken, Germany. Partly cloudy, PFF bombing. Quite a bit of flak, but inaccurate. Was coming home over Belgium and I thought of Amsterdam and The Hague that weren't far off course. Went close to Brussels... Lost two crews in our squadron on yesterday's mission. We didn't go. 3 lost from the group. Was an airfield north of Paris... As we were in the pilot's briefing this morning at 0130 a Jerry, probably a JU88, dropped a couple of bombs on our base. Made quite an explosion, and I certainly wondered what it was at the time.

June 29, #19: Airfield SE of Magdeburg, Germany. 52 100 lb M47 fire bombs. What a horrible day. The leader of the first section aborted, so we went into the third section. Didn't drop our bombs on the primary for some unknown reason, though we made a run on it. Dropped them on some inconsequential field. Came back all alone, 10 little ships, and flew darn near over Magdeburg and got flak we shouldn't and wouldn't if we stayed on course. I called the lead and told him but got no answer. After sweating out his leading us crazily all over Germany we came over the coast at 15,000', off course, and got the hell shot out of us. The formation split up all over. The copilot slammed my helmet on my head and I gave it the gun, doing 30-degree banks at short timed intervals. Could see the fire in the exploding flak and hear and feel it. Luckily we got untouched. Issie in the top turret said shortly after we made a turn, there was the flak where we would have been. The guns were the 30-mm. Bofors guns that shoot very fast but can't reach the higher altitudes. Lost Warke and another crew today. Go on pass tomorrow and am sure glad as I know I'll live 2 more days anyway. (On a couple of occasions the lead navigator would come to Frank Erbacher, our excellent navigator, and say, "Frank, where the hell were we today?" The above is an example of terrible navigation.)

July 6, #20: 3 2000 lb 489-H (These are BIG babies. We have he room to carry 4 of them.) Didn't hit briefed bridge. Big front in the way, so hit an airfield somewhere in France. Good mission, little flak. That stuff's got the hell scared out of me now. Guess the Jerries came up on the boys who went to Leipzig. Glad we weren't there.

July 7: What a delay! Had a 2-day pass spent in Norwich. Shot the old .45 the night of the 4th and they shot flares and running lights, a nice try, but a poor substitute for being back home.

July 9, #21: Weather brought us back as we were over Belgium. Were supposed to go somewhere in France. The weather was so bad we lost the formation as we were returning.

July 11, #22: 5 1000 lb GPs. Munich (home and birth of the Nazi party). Were supposed to bomb an airfield east of town if visual, but it wasn't, so we hit the industrial area of Munich. Glad it was PFF or the flak would have been terrific. Were in flak for 8 minutes but it wasn't too accurate. A piece of flak got the bombardier in the chest area but the flak suit stopped it. Never saw so many planes on one mission before. Sky was full of Libs and Forts. German radio said bombs fell in town for over a half-hour steady, and I believe it. They reported extensive damage. I feel like we shortened the war a bit today... Am very tired, was on oxygen 7 hours today. We were the first ship to land. Left the formation over the channel and came back under the clouds. Tried to pass 4 P38s and was going 270 once but couldn't do I, darnit, but it would have been fun. Navigation was excellent—all pathfinder. Only saw the ground a very few times. Were only 10 minutes from Switzerland. First time I brought a pipe along, but I couldn't see spending a year or so without one, though I wasn't pessimistic. However, I was more afraid this morning at briefing than I've been before a mission, but it wasn't bad in the air, thankfully. That's a nuff.

July 12, #23: 6 500 lb GPs and 4 500 lb fire bombs. Where—MUNICH AGAIN! This time rougher, as expected. Flak was much more accurate and I flew in low-left section and we caught hell. Flew right wing in bucket and saw Kuchwara's #4 engine get shot completely off. I moved up and took his place in deputy lead then. Blanton went to Switzerland. Another of our ships crashed at Hardwick. Anyway, he made it back to England... Just heard Kuchwara got back to England. Sounds unbelievable because after he got out of formation they really started working on him, just like they did to us at Berlin.

We go on a 6 day pass tomorrow. Am going to Scotland, out of Edinburgh, to a small town, Dollar. (When I purchased he train ticket at Edinburgh to go to dollar, the male ticket seller said "to Dollar for a dollar." At that time I think there were 5 shillings for an American dollar.)... We were originally going to Berlin today. Glad we didn't, because we are back. Sure getting rough now, though. Sure hope we can make it. I pray enough for it, I just pray a lot in the air. I don't see how we've gotten by this far without getting it. I'm sure God had more to do with it than anyone else. (I no longer believe the almighty interferes with our life. But under the same stress, if it helps, great.)

Hope we don't have to do over 30 missions too, but they could make us do 35... Well, gotta take a bath and get ready for the big pass. (Kuchwara did not get back.)

July 23, #24: 40 100 lb GPs. Airfield, Leon, France. GH (radar) mission. Good navigation, good escort, P51s all the way. Little flak at target... After an eleven day layoff we flew again. Loved the Highlands, and Edinburgh. I'll remember it so won't write it down here. Joe Shogan, my buddy, is up there now.

We've had a lot of wrecks at the field lately. About a half dozen planes smashed up in a week right on the field. Gears have been giving away.

July 25, #25: 40 100 lb GPs. Support of ground troops at St. Lo. We were to saturate the German area in preparation for an American ground offensive. We were to bomb at 16000', but due to weather we went in at 11200. That's too darn low for a Lib. Our troops moved back 1500 yards and their offensive was to start at H plus 55, or 10:55. We dropped at 10:10. The whole 8th and 9th Air Forces were there. Must have raised hell with the Jerries on the ground. The flak wasn't too thick, but accurate. We had the closest burst ever, right in front of our nose. I ducked as I saw it burst—no safety glass today. It was very audible, the whole crew heard it, and loud. The copilot thought it knocked the nose turret and the bombardier off. I thought it burst between the nose and the flight deck, but it couldn't have unless it went through the ship, but it was too close! ... We certainly have a lot of airstrips on the beachhead... Our artillery shot a red smoke screen to mark the bomb line and also to cover the withdrawal of our troops 1500 yards. However, as each succeeding group dropped he bombs, the line kept moving back toward the troops. The result was the death of 102 and 380 wounded, including the death of General Leslie J. McNair. Apparently there was no communication between ground and air. (It was a pretty unsophisticated war in comparison to the 21st century)... Quite a day, the only time I brought my 45 along as going down amid enemy troops being bombed wouldn't end as a POW.

July 27: No flying last couple of days, only by stand-downs or scrubs did we miss Kiel, and today, close to Friedrichshafen. Got up for briefing at 12:30 a.m. Mission was scrubbed just 15 minutes before takeoff.... Shogan should be back tonight from his leave.

July 29, #26: Oil refinery at Bremen. PFF—thanks! (Flak less accurate if the gunners can't visually see where their shells are exploding) Hell of a lot of flak, barrage and predicted concentration, 8 minutes of it. (3 types, barrage they shoot a lot into a box they think you will have to go through. Looks terrible, but the least dangerous. Predicted concentration, a sort of barrage but more specific in area. And tracking, the most dangerous because they are shooting directly at you and gun crews can get pretty good at this. When you get out of formation, you get tracking.)

Was glad to fly after two scrubs last two mornings. Most flak I've seen so far was, I believe, today, and I can't even imagine what would have happened had it been visual, because it was bad enough the way it was. Lost no planes. One ship had the ailerons shot out but it used A-5 (autopilot) and landed, after taking the precaution of having the crew bail out over Buncher #7. Good for the pilots and probably they also kept the engineer... Had a hard time getting started today. First, a stuck prop governor and then a stuck throttle linkage. Glad we went though—now. Stand down until morning at least. (NOTE—You can see that the break in mission flying really helped the nerves.)

August 1: Started out on #27, but had to abort for the first time. #s 2 and 3 were pretty rough and we lost a lot of oil out of #4, and by the time we got to the final approach we only had 10 lbs left, but didn't feather it or they might have made us go out over the ocean and drop them. Three engines and two rough ones is not the time for that. It was a heavy load to land with, but we've had some experience doing it a couple of times before... Everybody came back, but didn't hit some oil dump as intended, but an airfield... Gotta go meet Joe and go to the show, He just got back.

August 2, #27: 24 250 lb.??. St. Dizier, France, target of opportunity. Lead navigator got lost so we took a Cook's tour of France. Our section, led by the Skipper (pilot in our barracks), bombed an airfield with JU88s on it. Sweat out fighters all day, no 38s or 51s showed up as scheduled, and we were in a good enemy fighter airfields area, one little group, and for quite a while, just one section, as we lost the other two when we bombed. The Skipper did a good job of leading, and we flew deputy lead. As we left France by La Havre we saw the RAF Lancasters bombing the port. They would come in at different altitudes and headings. Looked like a big mess to us. They got a lot of flak, but did good accurate bombing, it looked... Madden's crew bailed out on returning. Shot up too bad to land it, I guess. Think he got hit where we saw the red flak. We came down close to Paris on the way out. The other two sections finally attempted to bomb an airfield, but for some reason, just one dropped.

August 3, #28: 12 500 lb GPs. Oil refinery, Leon, France. Had 365 hours on the engines. #2s left magneto dropped too much on four separate checks, but we took it as it was a short mission. #2 ran rougher and rougher, and at the IP we had to turn around and feather it, as #4 was getting bad too. We were at 25000' and had to pull too much to try to keep up. Hope we got credit. We dropped our bombs in the ocean, and landed only minutes before the returning formation, who blew hell out of the oil refinery and all got back. Good! Blanck got his 33rd today. Sure hope he doesn't have to do any more. We go on pass tomorrow.

August 7, #29: 10 250 lb GPs. Brussels oil refinery and storage tanks. Weather was pretty bad and as it was not to be a PFF or GH as it is in occupied territory, we couldn't drop unless it was visual. We hunted for a last resort and sort of went over Rotterdam twice but there were not enough holes in the clouds, so we brought the bombs back.

August 9: Were briefed for Stuttgart but because of dense fog it was scrubbed a half hour after proposed take off time—thanks.

August 10, #30: Oil refinery 30 miles east of Auerre, France. Had quite a time getting started. It was scrubbed once. We left after the 446th and 95th groups, so I sweat being left wing on the lead, but I got some little friends so we were escorted. This is the same target we tried for a week or so ago and didn't find. Today we found it, but all three sections missed it! Good formation, good navigation, a bit of flak coming out. Capt. Haggin lead the group and for him, his 30th and last. (Lead crews should get a break. They are a main target of the opposition.)

August 12, #31: 52 100lb GPs. Airfield NW of Laon, France. Flew over our own battle lines but went too far left of course and got some flak near Avranches where the Germans made a counter-offensive to split our troops, a week or so ago. Our leader's #1 caught fire over England and aborted, so Gibson lead. We really hit the target, and no flak. Had 18 bombs hang up and 1 of them was armed—the vane had spun off. So we closed the bomb bay doors and worried for about 20 minutes while the bombardier went back from his forward position and took out the fuses,. and then he kicked 'em out. Bombardiers have nasty, dangerous jobs at times like this... Think and hope we only have to do one more, though they are still up in the air about giving us credit for our one and only abortion on the 28th mission.

August 13, #32: 52 100 lb GPs. Road junction south of Rouen. We were to bomb roads to keep the Jerries from escaping a trap. Our group had six targets and each section of six ships was to fine two more. All our bombs were dropped on the first target after which we got the hell out of there, not wanting to through all the flak at Rouen. We hit out for the coast and had an unpleasant ten minutes doing evasive action against ack-ack, but got some bursts right under us, with two pieces of shrapnel as souvenirs… Saw the colonels today and found out we get credit for the 28th mission. Our unliked squadron commander seems to foul up every time he leads a mission. He is trying to make us fly a mission tomorrow. I'm fighting it. (Years later our group had a get-together in Harlingen, TX, and our former squadron commander was there, and several crews from the other three squadrons voiced their dislike for this fellow.) Carrington (our radio operator) will get grounded. He's not in very good shape. I'm not either but I could take another or more if I had to, but surely hate to.

August 18, # 33: Well, I fought it for four days, but rank prevailed. 10 500 lb GPs. Oil dump two miles north of Nancy, France. Flew over our liberated territory as much as possible. Had good support from 38s, and had 51s at the target. Bombed from 14000' (too low!), and went right over Nancy for the bomb run, but even though they had 28 guns reported, not one burst of flak did we see. Thanks. Flew over the Felaise gap on the return and sweat that out. Flew with 11 men—only 6 ours—4 are through—the twins, Hank and Vince. Guess we're through, and it feels damn good, but I'm too tired to get tight. We shot flares, red and green, and that's all we did to celebrate. Go on pass tomorrow. Finis.

Well, I trust that you got through the 33 missions along with me. I was fortunate to catch a tour that occurred during the spring and summer months, and the need to bomb undefended targets like bridges. While I have complained about the weather, it was more treacherous during winter months. While there was still plenty of German fighter opposition, nothing like the crews in late 1942 and much of 1943 with little or no fighter escort, and a stronger Luftwaffe. And as the 8th AF grew, more locations could be bombed any one day, requiring more locations to defend. This was somewhat offset by more flak guns as the allies advanced, and more experienced and accurate gun crews. But on any day, I'd rather face a battery of 88s than a determined FW

190 or Me 109, or later on, the German jets. And by this time, you know how I hated and feared flak.

A highly recommended daily operational record of the Eighth Air Force is Roger A. Freeman's "Mighty Eighth War Diary," Jane's Publishing Company, 730 Fifth Ave., New York NY 10019. It includes mission information such as aircraft losses, missing, wounded and killed, the targets, and fighter activity. It is a very complete, valuable historic record.

The Red Cross was wonderful. They had food and lodging centers in Norwich and at least one in London. They served sandwiches after missions, really appreciated, because churning stomachs couldn't handle lightly fried eggs before a mission.

With my missions finished, what to do. I could go back to the U.S. However, I might be assigned to B29s for a Japanese combat tour. One tour was enough for me. I managed to get assigned as Group air-sea rescue officer. I appointed Joe Shogan as my assistant. I took this assignment very seriously because proper procedures in ditching would save lives. Records showed a ditched B-17 crew would lose one man, as opposed to 4 in an B-24. The 17 had the advantage of lower landing speeds with a lighter wing loading, stronger fuselage, tail rather than nose wheel, and simply a better configuration for a water landing. I wrote two pages of instructions entitled "Dingy, dingy, let's ditch" that gave crews pointers for safer water landings.

It was great to be relieved of the pressure of combat missions, to test fly planes after repairs, calibrate air speed, and just have fun flying. Sometimes we would go up and before long a P-38 would join us in formation, and then maybe a British Lancaster, a B-25 or 26, a Mosquito, and we had a great time. We particularly liked the Australian pilots. They attacked life sort of the way we did. We respected the English pilots. They were, it seems, fearless. They would land their big bombers with the gigantic landing gear, just letting them drop in from wherever. I guess their attitude was, airplanes are for activity in the air, and if you are close to the ground, forget it. And the battle of Britain would not be a happy story without the Hurricane and Spitfire guys. Sometimes we would fly over to the coast and dive down on sailboats, pulling up so the prop wash would hit their sails, hoping to give them a bit of a scare. Buzzing—flying low—was exhilarating, but restricted because of accidents. It was kind accepted to buzz your own base at your completed tour.

As time moved toward the holiday season the urge to be home for Christmas prevailed and I left our base in November for the relocation base in Stone, England. From there, embarkation on the Queen Mary in Glasgow, Scotland, for the voyage to New York. It was a wonderful trip. No more than three to a cabin, whereas the other way, probably eighteen. No escort—our ship was faster than German subs. We did zig-zag a bit. I had never had an ocean voyage. After a few days we got into the much warmer gulf stream, and it was pleasant on deck, watching the restless ocean. The Statue of Liberty was a most welcome sight. I do not remember the train trip to Ft. Lewis, Washington. I arrived home several days before Christmas, and did not have to report back to Santa Ana, California until January 17, 1945, for redistribution. I tried to get assigned to the pink palace, name close to " Don Ce Sar", near St. Petersburg, Florida. It was known as a really nice place for airmen who needed some rest from the emotional rigors of combat. However, I didn't qualify which, of course, was a positive. While most of us were a bit jumpy and a bit resentful of those with no combat, it all wore off before long.

I was unneeded surplus. I was sent to my old B-24 training base in Albuquerque. In 26 days I managed to finagle assignment to Marana Army Air Base, some 30 miles north of Tucson. They had AT-6 planes, known in the navy as, I think, SNJs, or "The Texan." It had a 650 hp radial engine, a low wing monoplane, retractable gear, very maneuverable, a joy to fly. (Still flown today at air shows) It was the hottest thing I had flown, but pretty tame compared to P51s and the like. Next, it's off to another B-24 base in Walla Walla, Washington, working my way closer to my home in Spokane. I don't recall doing anything at this base except flying a bit of Link and pushing for a better assignment. And it came on July 8, 1945, being transferred to Geiger Field, Spokane. Home at last! Geiger was a base for some 25,000 engineers. It required just three pilots to serve its purpose. A Capt. Matthews, Lt. Brock, and me. The diversity of planes to fly was great. An AT-6, BT-13, L-5, AT-11, C-45, PT-17, and two Ford Tri motor aircraft, used by the forest service for fighting fires. To this day I regret not flying this relic.

I can't understand why I didn't realize the significance of doing so. I flew the PT-17 only once, probably because of a subconscious recollection I had ground looped it in primary training. However, I was much more experienced but still, I passed up more time in this great aerobatic machine. I flew the BT-13 ten times, the AT-11 eleven times, the C-45 eighteen times—mostly on business for the engineers, often to Hamilton Field outside of San Francisco—and my favorite, the L-5VW, twenty times. Rather than the 95 horsepower engine it had 195, and I could hold it on the runway to build up speed and then pull the stick all the way back to my belly and push the flaps full on so that I could go practically straight up for maybe 150'. It had side panels that could be opened and locked in place, leaving an unobstructed view of the countryside below, even allowing to place the elbow out the window, as in driving an auto. I note hefrom my log I didn't waste any time trying it out, July 9 was either my first or second day at Geiger.

My log says that the next day, July 10, I flew to Boeing Field in Seattle. I had no plan to, but a navy WAVE had been hitching rides across the U.S. upon graduating as an ensign at Hunter College in New York. She was stranded in Spokane, and the captain suggested I fly her home to Seattle. I did. Through her I met a Nancy Noble, sister graduate, a great gal that was engaged to one of their favorite instructors. It was easy to see why he picked this one. I took her flying a few times, and also took up my mother and sister Florence... Dr. Fitzgerald, my doctor when I was with Hecla in Wallace, Idaho, phoned and suggested I buzz Wallace. I did, but it was dangerous in the narrow canyon to get over town and on my second pass I narrowly missed the flagpole on the county court house. What a scare! .... How loose things were. Taking friends or family flying would not be allowed now, and buzzing would incur serious consequences.

A sad and unnecessary accident occurred some few months after I was discharged. The captain had ferried the base general, colonel, Red Cross man, and my flying companion on many trips and crew chief, Sgt. Sheets, of York, PA. He named this C-45 "The Pride of York." On returning from San Francisco, in weather, they crashed into a hill, killing all.

I do not believe the captain ever flew a much safer entry to the field that Lt. Brock and I had practiced several times... Years later in going through York I looked up the name "Sheets." There were about ten of them. First one, no knowledge. Well, I'll try the last one. "He was my brother!" I sent him a number of photos of this great, happy Sgt., who had flown with me many times as engineer.

The army doesn't need me any more. Frankly, they didn't need me after I finished my missions. But the army, at least in those days, was not efficient, working on the level of lowest common denominator. Slowly, within the ability of the lesser, the job gets done. I appreciate and laud the military. If every 18-year-old male had to serve at least a year I believe the discipline and camaraderie that builds self-respect would drastically reduce crime. And then help them with higher education. Never happen, too bad. I do not include mandatory service for females. They don't need it.

I was discharged in September and my employment at the Hecla Mining Company showed me that more life fulfillment would be achieved from higher education. Stanford had already begun their fall quarter, and the VA (Veterans' Administration) suggested I enroll at the locally located Gonzaga, as their fall semester had not begun. So I, along with a goodly number of other discharged, began our higher education, at ages of 25, more or less. Rah rah was a bit immature for us, but not totally. College spirit is great, and it contends for the happiest, fun, fulfilling period of my life.

What happens next, and until retirement at age 87, is covered in the last chapter. Happy reading until your arrival there!

Commercial Pilot License

Col. Judy Presentation of DFC to R. Welsh

This is to certify that

2nd Lt. Ralph T. Welsh
(NAME AND RANK)

ARMY OF THE UNITED STATES

HAS MET THE REQUIREMENTS FOR THE

INSTRUMENT PILOT CERTIFICATE
(WHITE)

AS PRESCRIBED BY AAF REG. 50-3

17 January 1945
(EXPIRATION DATE)

_____ _____
(CHECK PILOT'S SIG.)   (ORG. C. O. SIG.)

Muroc, Calif.   382nd Gp.
(STATION)   (ORGANIZATION)

TOTAL PILOT TIME TO DATE   508:45

PILOT TIME LAST 12 MONTHS   508:45

WAR DEPARTMENT
A. A. F. Form No. 8
(REVISED 10-1-43)   16—37015-1   GPO

My squadron's mud bath celebration upon graduating from Santa Ana
Army Air Base. Now we get to fly!

Wednesday, July 3, 1985

I ATTENDED THIS
8 GRADES, SCHOOL
1st 6 GRADES

FROM THE PAST--The boarded-up former McElroy school is the only reminder left of the former McElroy community in the northeast corner of Sheridan County.

Garneau Jr. attended the 25th Anniv. for Mr. and Mrs. Lloyd Stringer in Med. Lake June 30.

Mr. and Mrs. Leonard Smith attended the Anniv.

McElroy School

OFFICER'S PAY DATA CARD

LAST NAME—FIRST NAME—INITIAL		SERIAL NUMBER	GRADE	ARM OR SERVICE
WELSH, Ralph T.		0755811	1Lt	AC

PAY PERIOD	LENGTH OF SERVICE		DATE YEARS COMPLETED
2nd	OVER 3	YEARS	21 May 1945

PAY AND ALLOWANCES	AMOUNT	TOTAL
Monthly Base Pay and Longevity	$175.00	
Additional Pay for flying	87.50	
Rental Allowances		
Subsistence (30-DAY MONTH)	21.00	
Date 29 May 1945		$283.50

PAY RESERVATIONS		SUBTOTAL	
Allotments, Class E $110	$	$110.00	
Insurance	D	N X	6.60
War Bonds, Class B			
Allotments, Class X			
Other Deductions (SPECIFY)			
SUBSEQUENT CHANGES IN ABOVE DATA WITH DATES			$ 116.60
		NET	$166.90

DEPENDENTS (STATE NAMES AND ADDRESSES)
NONE

W.D., A. G. O. FORM NO. 77 (29 June 1944)   16—40983-1 ☆ GPO
This form supersedes W.D., A. G. O. Form No. 77, 26 March
1942, which will not be used after receipt of this revision.

Me at Muroc AFB (Now Edwards Air Force Base)

RTW in Scotland

INDIVIDUAL FLIGHT RECORD

(1) SERIAL NO. O-755811   (2) NAME WELSH RALPH T.   (3) RANK 1st Lt.   (4) AGE 1920
(5) PERS. CLASS 18   (6) BRANCH Army Air Forces   (7) STATION Geiger Fld., Sub-Base
(8) ORGANIZATION ASSIGNED 4th   317th   423rd AAF BU Sub Base, Geiger Fld., Wn.
(9) ORGANIZATION ATTACHED   321st   423rd AAF BU Geiger Fld., Wash.
(10) PRESENT RATING & DATE Pilot 10-1-43   (11) ORIGINAL RATING & DATE same
(12) TRANSFERRED FROM 423rd AAF BU Walla Walla, Wash.   (13) FLIGHT RESTRICTIONS none
(15) TRANSFERRED TO 423rd AAF BU Sub Base, Geiger Fld, Wn.   (14) TRANSFER DATE 5 July 1945
(17) MONTH July 1945

DAY	AIRCRAFT TYPE, MODEL & SERIES	NO. LANDINGS	FIRST PILOT DAY	FIRST PILOT NIGHT	RATED PERS. NON-PILOT P-AI CP-AI	NON-RATED	INSTRUMENT	INSTRUMENT TRAINER	SPECIAL INFORMATION
9	L-5VW	2	0:35 0:55		Completed flight test and qualified for				
10	L-5VW	1	0:30		Instrument Pilot Certificate AAA Form 8 (White)				
11	BT-13B	1	0:45		11 July 1945: Check Pilot Raphael Semmes Jr.,				
11	L-5VW	1	0:40		1st Lt., Air Corps.				
12	L-5VW	1	0:40						
12	BT-13B	1	0:50						
13	C-45F	2	1:10						
13	BT-13B	1		1:50					
14	BT-13B	1		1:35					
16	C-45F	2	3:00 1:40		0:30 1:50				
17	AT-11BY	4	4:00				1:30		
18	L-5VW	2	1:20						
19	BT-13B	1	1:45						
20	BT-13B	1	1:45						
21	BT-13B	2	0:50						
21	C-45F	3	6:50						
23	C-45F	2	1:20 1:00				0:45		
25	L-5VW	1		0:15					
24	L-5VW	2	3:20						
25	L-5VW	2	0:20		CERTIFIED CORRECT:				
26	BT-13B	1	1:40				1:00		
27	AT-11B	1	4:25		GEORGE E. MATHEWS,				
29	AT-11B	2	4:15		Captain, Air Corps,				
30	BT-13B	2	1:40		Commanding.				
31	AT-11B	3	1:25						
31	L-5VW	2	1:50 0:50						

COLUMN TOTALS: 1:20   44:45   45:50   0:15   0:30 1:50   P-AI   4:30   CP-AI

	(42) TOTAL STUDENT PILOT TIME	(43) TOTAL FIRST PILOT TIME	(44) TOTAL PILOT TIME
(37) THIS MONTH		45:50 0:30	51:25 1:50
(38) PREVIOUS MONTHS THIS F.Y.			
(39) THIS FISCAL YEAR		45:50 0:30	1:50
(40) PREVIOUS FISCAL YEARS		363:10 46:25	
(41) TO DATE	373:35	409:00 46:55	1045:05 1:50

Flight Record

Geiger Field, Spokane, WA

United States Army

Air Corps Training Center

Be it known that Aviation Cadet Ralph T. Welsh,
19033243,
United States Army, has satisfactorily completed the course of
instruction prescribed for Airplane Pilots.

In testimony whereof and by virtue of vested authority I do
confer upon him this

—— DIPLOMA ——

Given at Stockton Field, Calif. this first day
of October in the year of our Lord one thousand
nine hundred and forty-three.

Lloyd H. Tull,
Colonel, Air Corps,
Commanding

Attest:
W. C. May,
Captain, Air Corps,
Adjutant

115

United States Army

Army Air Forces

Be it known that

Second Lieutenant RALPH THOMAS WELSH, O-755811

has satisfactorily completed the course of instruction

prescribed for

FOUR ENGINE PILOT (B-24)

at the ARMY AIR FORCES PILOT *School*

KIRTLAND FIELD, ALBUQUERQUE, NEW MEXICO

In testimony whereof and by virtue of vested authority

I do confer upon him this

DIPLOMA

Given at KIRTLAND FIELD, ALBUQUERQUE, NEW MEXICO

this SEVENTEENTH *day*

of DECEMBER *in the year of our Lord one thousand*

nine hundred and FORTY THREE.

W. B. OFFUTT,
Colonel, Air Corps,
Commandant.

Attest

E. O. WILLEFORD, Major, Air Corps,
Assistant Director of Training.

Thick glass saved me, projectile after my heart!

Pilot's pane glass was replaced with thick protective glass only when major plane repairs were required at the depot

Chapter 4: Mission Stories

"Drama Over Cologne," 14 October 1944
by Scott Nelson (Florida 58th BG)

On 14 October 1944, B-24J, S/N 42-50864, "JOLLY ROGER," with a crew of ten was the lead plane of the 458th Bomb Group, 755th Squadron, to bomb the marshaling yards at Cologne, Germany. Immediately after bombs away, "Jolly Roger" was hit by three bursts of flak, knocking out the number three engine and injuring several crew members; the most severe was MC Miller who was struck by shrapnel in the head and face. Lt. Robert Ferrel and Lt. Ernest Sands pulled Lt. Miller from the nose turret and administered first aid. The "Jolly Roger" was on fire and going down. Pilot Lt. William Klusmeyer ordered everyone to bail out. Sands attached a line to Miller's parachute ripcord and pushed him out the camera hatch, immediately followed by S/Sgt. Joseph Pohler.

Lt. Sands left the ship via the nose wheel doors and pulled his ripcord after passing through several cloud layers. After landing, Lt. Sands hid himself in a depression till after dark, and then started walking west. The nine other crew members had been captured by German soldiers. Lt. Sands evaded capture for seven days but was caught and beaten by German civilians as he was trying to cross a river to get to Belgium. Sands ended up in Stalag Luft III, and on January 27, 1945, was marched west during a blizzard, eventually ending up in Stalag VIIA at Mooseburg in the spring of 1945.

On April 29, 1945, an American tank burst through the front gate at Mooseburg with a force led by General Patton. It was one day before Sands' 24th birthday.

Ernie Sands always wondered what had happened to MC Miller. The last he had seen him was when he had parachuted from the plane. Had he survived? Many years later, after the war, Ernie received a phone call—it was MC Miller. He had tracked Ernie down to thank him for helping save his life. Miller had survived after being treated by German doctors and had fully recovered in a POW camp.

Ernest Sands served as North Dakota's Lieutenant Governor from 1981 to 1984.

"Drama Over Cologne" Part 2
by Scott Nelson (Florida 58th BG)

While doing the story about Ernie Sands ("Drama Over Cologne," Vol. 46, No. 3, Summer 2007 *Journal*) and him being shot down over Germany, I was able to contact MC Miller and get his side of the story.

MC Miller (Millard C. Miller) was chosen to be pilotage navigator with the Klusmeyer crew on October 14, 1944. Target was the marshalling yards at Cologne. MC was the second navigator because the Klusmeyer plane was flying deputy lead and needed another navigator. As it turned out, the lead plane had to be turned back due to mechanical difficulty, so the Klusmeyer plane had to take the lead and Ernie Sands reluctantly became lead bombardier.

As the Klusmeyer plane left the target after bombs away, it was hit by several bursts of flak, the first shattering the nose turret in which MC was sitting. MC was stunned and noticed a lot of blood coming from a wound on the right side of his face and he could barely see. Someone grabbed him under the armpits and pulled him from the turret, and the next thing he remembered was the bombardier (Sands) giving him first aid. MC remembered being dragged back through the bomb bay and remembered seeing the bomb bay doors still partly open (they never got completely closed when they were hit but were not open far enough to bail out through). MC remembered being pulled back to the camera hatch, then being pushed out, and then a terrific jerk! MC doesn't remember much about his ride down (he probably passed out). The next thing MC remembered is being on the ground with one of the other crew members next to him. As luck would have it, the other crew member was Staff Sergeant Joseph G. Pohler. Pohler was a German-born American and was fluent in Deutsche. Sands had sent him out right behind MC in the hope that Pohler could quickly get medical attention for MC. Well, it worked—Pohler called to the German civilians in the area and quickly got him the medical attention he needed. The aid kit that Sands had stuck in MC's jacket was used for his

119

immediate care. Pohler even passed himself off as an officer, thus this also helped get MC quick attention. The Germans respected rank, even from the enemy!! The initial capture report from the German records lists Pohler as an officer! The Luftwaffe medical service took responsibility for MC's care and he ended up in a Luftwaffe hospital in Frankfurt.

MC was in rough shape with his injuries and his eyeball out of its socket. His eye was scheduled to be removed, but a Luftwaffe surgeon with the rank of Lt. Colonel examined MC and thought he could save the eye.

The doctor sewed MC's eye back in the socket and bandaged him up. After a time the bandages were taken off but MC could not see out of his injured eye. The doctor said "let's try something" and they gave MC treatments of short frequency radio waves directed at his eye. After several days of this treatment, MCs eyesight started coming back and he regained it in full.

Miller remembered the doctor was from Hess and his last name was the Germanized form of Miller. He said he and the doctor could have been distant cousins because Miller's family was from Hess, a state outside Munich.

After his recovery at the Frankfurt Hospital, MC was sent to Stalag Luft 3 to spend the rest of the war as a POW.

Another interesting item about the Klusmeyer crew: The waist gunner on this crew was Jewish and was named Raymond Silverstein. To protect himself in case of being shot down and captured, Silverstein changed his name to Sills to throw off the Germans. Raymond's brother belonged to the 82nd Airborne and participated in Operation Market Garden and was wounded at Nijmegen, Holland. He had been sent to a hospital in England. Sills asked the squadron commander if he could stand down on the Cologne mission in order to visit his wounded brother. The Klusmeyer plane flew without one waist gunner that day and the act of visiting his brother saved Sills from being shot down over Germany. The fact that Sills changed his name did not guarantee that the Germans would not have found him out. Visiting his brother could well have saved his life!

A Textbook on Escaping

by Lt./Col. Edward W. Appel (389th)

I was first pilot of a B-24 which we flew from the States around the southern route up to England in Feb. of 1944.

After flying 29 missions, I had one to go before my tour was completed. My original crew had already completed their 30 missions by volunteering to fly with other crews when we were not scheduled to fly, so this time I would be flying as command pilot with Lt. Frazee's crew, a crew I had never met.

It was Sept. 5th, 1944 and the target was Karlsruhe Marshalling yards. We were to fly deputy lead and I remember we were flying on formation instruments nearly all the way.

Just before reaching the IP we broke into the clear. We had just started our bomb run when the 88s hit. We took a monstrous hit in the right wing which knocked out the right two engines. The last two engines were still going strong but we had no turbos and the fuel cells were ruptured. The rudder cables were also cut, so we had no rudders. The windshield had come in with the first blast and with gas flowing around I thought we were going to burn.

We managed to get turned around using the ailerons and headed back, holding direction with ailerons but losing altitude fast. Two engines out on one side, and without turbos and rudders a B-24 is like a falling rock. At this point I was feeling sorry for Capt. Paul Anderson who was a good friend of mine from my hometown of Redfield, S.D., who had elected to fly my last mission with me. He took up a position between us pilots. Being an ordinance officer he wasn't supposed to be on this mission with us and now we were in a position where he, and we, might not make it.

First we salvoed the bombs (must have scared the hell out of some cattle on the ground) and then had the crew throw out anything loose in order to lighten ship. We were at 24,000 feet, but within 25 miles we were down to 10,000. At that point I knew we couldn't make it as our front lines were 100 miles away. Time to bail out, which we all did. When my chute opened it was only seconds until I hit the ground in a plowed field. I found out much later that we had lost four men. The Navigator had jumped before we did and never got his chute open. Also, two of the crew hid out at a French farmhouse (this was in Alsace Lorraine) for about a month but then decided to get out. I understood they got in with the French Underground, put on civilian clothes and tried to make it through the lines. They were caught and shot by the Germans as spies. My friend, Capt. Paul Anderson took up residence in a Stalag Luft.

After landing in the plowed field, I shucked my chute and looking back about a half mile, I could see the last two men running towards each other, but there were farmers running toward them, so I didn't go back there. I hid in a vineyard for a while, but then decided it wasn't a very good hiding place, so I started to get up. I should have looked first.

As I started to get up there was a lot of yelling "HALT!" I looked back and there in line abreast across the fields were German soldiers with rifles. They could have shot me easy, but they kept yelling "HALT!" so I pretended I didn't hear them and kept walking away. I didn't run because then they certainly would have shot. I walked into a clump of trees and then ran like a scared rabbit out the other side and down into a slew where I jumped into the water and hid among the slew rushes. They knew I was in there somewhere because they kept walking around the edge of the water. They would all get together on one side and fire their burp guns through the weeds. Scared the hell out of me!

Finally they all left except for one man. I could see him standing and watching the place. After awhile they all came back and went through the same procedure—shooting and all. Finally they left and I stayed right there until dark when I sneaked out.

I traveled at night toward the west and the front lines and hid in the daytime using any cover I could find. When I got hungry I would feast from a farmer's field. I also had my escape kit with concentrated rations which helped. Drinking water was another matter, but I found if I walked into a village after dark and stomped around as if I belonged there, I could go up to a pump and pump water into a bucket and carry it out of town and nobody paid attention to me.

Finally after about ten days, I started walking across a field in daylight. There was a farmer and his wife picking rutabagas and putting them in a wagon. They asked if I was an American and I said yes, after which they motioned me to get into the wagon. I was so darned cold and hungry but at that time that I didn't figure I had much to lose. I still had to get over the mountains to the west where both sides were dug in and shooting anything in sight. After getting in the wagon they covered me with gunny sacks and took me to their home in a little village. They hid me out with their son in a hayloft (they were French) as the son was also hiding out from the Germans. We stayed right there until the end of November when the Germans were pushed out and our tanks and trucks came down the road. I was out!

Part 2: Col. Appel's Experience as a Fighter Pilot

I went back to England and while orders were being cut to send me back to the ZI, I decided that instead of going home I would stay and try to hook on with a Fighter Group. I guess I was a little flak happy! I took off for the 56th FG and told Col. Dave Schilling I wanted to fly fighters. He said, "Sure. Come on down."

That was quite a kick getting out of bombers and into fighters. Like getting out of a truck on to a motorcycle. After checking out in the P-47 I flew 16 dive bombing, strafing and escort missions. My last, the 16th of April 1945, saw me busily strafing Muldorf Airdrome 50 miles east of Munich.

I came in on the deck and was shooting into ME 109s sitting on the field when I picked up a lot of ground flak and remember seeing holes appear in the wings. Then the engine started running rough and losing power. I started to pull up, which I shouldn't have done over an enemy airfield, and then they really started to get in the hits.

I was soon out of range, but at full throttle I still wasn't getting any power and the airspeed continued to fall off. I tried to get over one last hill before bellying in but as I started to clear the hill the right wing stalled and went under. The plane cartwheeled across the countryside and I thought school was out again. The wings broke off along with the tail, but by some miracle it came down right side up. I cut my knee and elbow a little bouncing around in the cockpit. At first I thought I was all bloody, but it was just hot engine oil from the ruptured oil tank.

I left the Mae West and parachute in the seat and crawled out. Some farmers were watching but they didn't do anything so I took off running. I ran into some trees and beyond there was a little village strung along a road. I had to get past this village as German soldiers were coming from the airfield I had just strafed and were behind me shooting.

As I came to the village two German soldiers came out and drew their guns hollering "HALT!" With all the shooting going on behind me, I thought I'd pretend I was a German running away from the Americans. I yelled back "NICHT HALT, AMERICAN COMEN." They turned and looked back where I came from with wide, startled eyes and I kept on going. Then they swung back towards me again pointing their guns and yelling "HALT!"

I stopped and waved an arm back toward the woods and yelled "NAY, NAY NICHT HALT, AMERICAN COMEN!" They again turned around and watched the other woods for the Americans they thought were coming, and I made tracks. I ran into the woods and actually sat down and laughed, thinking how they would catch hell when the German soldiers came and found out that they had let me get away.

I couldn't find a good place to hide in the woods as the underbrush was all cleaned out, so I climbed to the top of a big tree and just sat there. The Germans soon came a line abreast again, hunting around under the trees with rifles, but they kept right on going. I stayed in the tree until dark, then climbed down and took off northwest toward the front lines.

I walked at night and hid in the daytime, as I had done before. I had a couple of escape kits along with compasses, maps, hacksaw blades and concentrated rations in them. I also had my .45, which was a big consolation even if I didn't fire it.

I would go up to a house right after dark and knock on the door. Usually the man would come to the door and I would tell him straight out that I was an American flyer and that I needed food. Many times they would have me come in and sit at the table and give me bread, meat and coffee. I wouldn't let anybody leave the house while I was there. I would lay my gun on the table and keep everybody at a distance. Then I would leave and make many miles that night so they wouldn't catch me. Actually, some families would give me some food to take along.

I finally got up near the front lines where there was a lot of shooting. I hid under some small, thick evergreens in a hollowed out spot. Looked like an old WWI foxhole, and probably was.

One night, the German Army moved over me and then for two days I was between the two lines that were shooting at each other using mostly artillery. The shells that hit the trees would really blast things around there.

One night the shooting went to the east so the next morning I crept out to the edge of the woods and watched the roads. Finally I spotted weapon carriers and tanks that were definitely ours. I came out of the woods with my hands held high as I didn't want to get shot at by our own army.

I went back through an Artillery outfit that was the same outfit I came through the first time. The same officers, the same Colonel. The Colonel was a little suspicious of me by this time and thought maybe I was spying for the other side. HOME FREE AGAIN!

By the time I got back to Paris the war was over so I rode an LST across the ocean along with a whole load of ex-POWs.

I was home on R&R helping my dad harvest in the summer of '45 when over the hill comes Capt. Paul Anderson. They had just freed him from a POW camp. His first words were "You son of a gun. You take me on a trip over Germany and you dump me out."

That Specially-Remembered Mission for the 445th

by David G. Patterson

From: The History of the 445th Bombardment Group (H), by Rudolph J. Birsic
Thursday, February 24, 1944

To the 445th Bomb Group veteran that date stands out above other dates. The mission was Gotha; the results were a Presidential Citation for the Group, but the cost was a black day in the Group's history in terms of casualties. Total casualties amounted to 123; of these, later reports officially listed 54 men as prisoners of war. The 702nd Squadron lost its Commander, Major Evans, and practically its entire operations staff. The 700th operation officer, Captain Waldher, was also lost... Here follows the official descriptive narration as recorded in the Presidential Citation.

'The 445th Bombardment Group (H) 2nd Air Division, is cited for outstanding performance of duty in action against the enemy. On 24 February 1944 this group participated, with other heavy bombardment groups of the 2nd Bombardment Division, in an attack on the Gothaer Waggonfabrik, A.G. located at Gotha, Germany. On this occasion the attacking bombers met and overcame the fiercest and most determined resistance the enemy was able to muster in defense of this target, so vital to his ability to wage war. Unprotected by friendly fighter cover the 445th was under almost continuous attack from enemy aircraft for a period of 2 hours and 20 minutes. Although antiaircraft fire was hurled at the formation along the route to and from the target as well as at the target itself, the most deadly opposition was given by enemy aircraft. For 1 hour and 20 minutes before "bombs away" savage attacks were made by single and twin engine enemy fighters in a vain attempt to keep the bombers from reaching their target. On the actual bombing run, that critical period of each bombardment mission, fierce and relentless attacks were unable to keep the bombers from accomplishing their task. Of this group's 25 aircraft which penetrated enemy territory, 13 were lost to these fierce fighter attacks, which number is approximately twice the loss suffered by any of the other groups participating in this mission. In addition, 9 of the 12 surviving aircraft returned from the mission with battle damage. With heroic determination the 445th flew its assigned course, destroying 21 enemy attackers, probably destroying 2 more, and damaging 7 during the long running battle. The target was located and bombed with extreme accuracy and devastating results. This target, the most important source of ME 110s, was so well hit that the enemy air force suffered a most telling blow. The courage, zeal, and perseverance shown by the crew members of the 445th Bombardment Group (H), 2nd Air Division, on this occasion were in accordance with the highest traditions of the military service.

The Hamm Raid, April 22, 1944
by Joseph Broder (446th)

We had a late briefing, a late takeoff, and a return to base after dark at 2130 hours (9:30 PM) and Jerry came back with us. Over a dozen B-24 bombers were shot down, destroyed, and strewn about airfields all over East Anglia, not counting standard aerial casualties. Many ships crash-landed. Our 446th

Bomb Group dispatched twenty-four Liberators. Two failed to return, but this does not include miscellaneous casualties.

The objective was Hamm, one of the greatest traffic centers in Western Europe, and the target itself was a complex of railway marshalling yards. While most combat flights are scheduled for the early morning, an exceptional proceeding occurred this day. Within two hours of noon, crews were rounded up from all over the airdrome—mess halls, barracks, flight lines, orderly rooms, officers' and airmen's clubs, and wherever else aviators congregate. At exactly 1200 the 446th (including me) was to be briefed for a major mission. When the target, flight altitude, and ordnance were announced, there were many gasps and groans. It was a surprise, not unlike the late briefing.

Flixton Airfield became a beehive of activity. Vehicles brought personnel from briefings to the aircraft, planes were hurriedly bomb-loaded, ground crews hastened to their specialized assignments, and tarmacs became busy with equipment handling and testing. Cars and jeeps raced back and forth. "Old Hickory" stood at ready, fully war painted and thoroughly inspected by crewmates Elizer and Whaley. Just a few minutes later the pilot's position cackled "thirty minutes delay." It lasted fifty minutes and the mission was not cancelled.

At 1440, mid-afternoon, we accepted the green-green Very pistol signal from the tower, rumbled awkwardly ahead, raced down the runway at full throttle, finally picked up enough air speed, and barely rose at runway's end. Clearing into a shining sky, we were followed by the rest of the 446th, and our adventure began. Only one aircraft in our 707th Squadron, which led on this day, had to feather a prop and it turned home. He was lucky. We cleared to altitude and droned on.

When met by Focke-Wulf fighters stationed fifty miles south of Hamm, we were clearly able to see the swastika-painted planes become engaged by our P-47 Thunderbolts, dogfight our escorts almost to a standstill and yet still manage to attack our columns. These Germans were very determined. Bitter battles filled the skies as our turrets turned and fired, friends and foes clashed, and two bombers exploded—smoke and debris fluttering earthward. The FW-190s caught it, too, cannon fire exterminating some of them as our friendlies exacted a degree of revenge. Of the three dozen to forty Luftwaffe interceptors, not less than one-third of them were downed by our snub-nosed, fat-bellied friends.

At that time I caught a glimpse of an enemy face as he broke off an engagement with one of our nearby bombers. Turning hard and swiftly to his left from what was a ten o'clock high attacking position and then standing on his wing before deliberately hurling himself nose first towards the below, I spotted a dark-haired, squinty-eyed, pale looking youth who hardly looked Teutonic. He looked like me.

As our B-24 formation lumbered on to its target, an avalanche of ground fire exploded in our midst, the black puffs of smoke downing still another Liberator in the wing directly behind us. It was identified by tail gunner Baker as being from the 458th Bomb Group. There was little let-up. Massive bursts of enemy fire continued, chaff drops proved ineffective, and the Ruhr Valley's smoke screen all but obliterated the aiming point and the target. We bombed to unknown results.

Dusk was barely beginning to settle as we land and were hit by Messerschmitt 109s, perhaps seventy predators in all. Luckily, our revolving escort was there. A brilliant defensive effort by an outnumbered group of P-51 Mustangs saved our skins, enabling us to escape with losses of only two bombers in our entire wing... but three more of the giant war birds suffered damage. One aircraft had a section of its right tailfin blown out by a twenty millimeter shell, one had Davis wing damage and was fast losing fuel and altitude, and a third ship had two feathered props. These Libs would barely make it back to base or else ditch in the Channel. They might be rescued by the Royal Navy—they might be rescued by German boats—or they might drown and die. Not an inconsiderable number of our bombers had wounded aboard.

More bad news: I was right... Our ETA to Flixton was almost exact and would take place with darkness falling. But even worse news was yet to come.

Boche ME-410 fighter-bombers, having followed the division's Liberators, beat us back to bases all over East Anglia and wrought enormous damage, confusion, and casualties. The return from Hamm turned into hell. Intruders struck at almost blacked-out airfields, shot down some B-24s in their landing patterns, and caused blazes and bonfires as ships broke up or belly-landed on nearby farms. Pandemonium ruled. Shots were exchanged. One of the 446th's runways was usable; one wasn't. We landed at Seething, a base about a dozen miles away.

When the 446th awoke to Hamm's morning-after, they hadn't the benefit of the reveling, just the hangover. Runways were potholed from foreign bombs and had to be smooth-surfaced quickly or the field temporarily closed. Wreckage was removed from what twisted metal remained of what was once a Liberator that had just given up ten charred bodies to an already overworked mortuary station. Then another three charburned remains were yielded from an enemy ME-410 aircraft that was still embedded in the B-24. It will never be affixed who destroyed whom on those final fatal yards flown by the young aviators.

The Infamous Kassel Raid, September 27, 1944
by George M. Collar (445th)

The 445th Bomb Group was almost wiped out, and I went down on my twenty-ninth mission, during the infamous Kassel raid of September 27, 1944.

It started out uneventfully enough, with 39 planes scheduled to take off from our group. By the time we got into Germany there had been four aborts, so eventually 35 planes dropped their bombs.

The weather over the continent was not very good, with a thick undercast, cloud base about 3,000 feet and tops 6-7000 feet. It was planned to drop the bombs through the clouds using the PFF in the lead ship.

The 445th was leading the 2nd Combat Wing, the other groups in the wing being the 389th and the 453rd. The lead ship was that of Capt. John Chilton, with Maj. Donald McCoy as command pilot. Deputy lead was Capt. Web Uebelhoer, with Capt. Jim Graham as deputy command pilot. I happened to be flying with Lt. James Schaen in the 702nd BS; we were in the high right squadron.

We were approaching the I.P. in a southeasterly direction, where we were supposed to make a slight left turn in an east-southeasterly direction toward Kassel, but for some reason the lead ship turned almost directly east, a mistake which would take us past the target city of Kassel, too far to the north. The only explanation was that the radar man had made a grievous error.

Practically every navigator in our group picked up on this mistake almost instantly, but it was too late for the lead ship to correct to the right, as he would have run into the stream of bombers coming out from the rear.

In hindsight we can say that the correct thing to do would have been to make a 360° turn to the left and come in on the rear of the second division, but major McCoy decided to continue on east and bomb the city of Gottingen, about 50 miles away. As a result we lost our fighter escort, and flew alone to our destruction.

Some of the pilots contacted the lead ship to report the error, but the only signal they received was "Keep in tight—Keep it together."

We carried on east, and finally dropped our bombs at Gottingen. We then made a turn to the south, and in the vicinity of Eisenach, we made a right turn to proceed west. By this time we were probably a hundred miles behind the rest of the division.

Just as we made the turn, we were attacked from the rear by between 100 and 150 German fighters. They attacked us line abreast in three waves. Most of these fighters were specially adapted FW-190s equipped with extra armor, and both 20 and 30mm cannons. They were accompanied by a smaller number of ME-109s.

The battle probably lasted only a few minutes, but it was a horrendous attack, as the FW-190 assault fighters passed through the bomber formations with 20 and 30mm cannons blazing, and the 50 cal. machine guns of the B-24s responding. The skies were full of bright flashes from the exploding shells. Burning and exploding airplanes were plummeting earthward; debris from the planes was spinning through the air. Bomb bay doors floated down like leaves.

In between, many parachutes were blossoming out and carrying flyers toward the under cast and an unknown fate below.

Now I wasn't supposed to be on this raid, and I was due for a three day pass and was scheduled to leave for London that morning, so I was surprised when they arrested me out of bed at

3:00 AM and told me that I was to take the place of Lt. Jim Schaen's bombardier, who had failed to return from London on the evening of the 26th.

We were the lead plane in the low left element of the high right squadron. I was in the nose turret. The first inkling that we were being attacked was the sudden appearance of many small flak bursts just ahead of the plane, and at the same time a sound like sledge hammer blows hitting the plane. The left wing was hit and on fire, and at the same time there was an explosion under the turret. About this time, the FW-190 that was attacking us streaked overhead not more than a few feet above us. I tried to shoot at him, but the turret controls were inoperative. The explosion under the turret had probably severed the hydraulics to the turret.

After the fighter had passed, I glanced down at the lead squadron and watched with horror as the fighters attacked them. At least two of the bombers were on fire, including the lead plane. At about this time the bail-out bell rang and I descended from the turret. As I glanced around, the nose section looked like Swiss cheese. It was a miracle that neither the navigator nor myself had been hit. Lt. Bean, the navigator, opened the nose wheel door and we both bailed out.

When the smoke of this great battle had cleared, 25 of our bombers had crashed into German soil. Two of our planes crash-landed in occupied France. One had crashed near Brussels, Belgium. Two made it across the Channel to make forced landings at the emergency strip at Manston. One crashed near the base in Norfolk. Only four were able to land at Tibenham.

Of the 238 men aboard the 25 bombers which went down in Germany, 115 were KIA or subsequently died of injuries. One was killed in the plane which crashed in Norfolk and one was killed in the crash in Belgium, for a total of 117.

Another American killed that day was Lt. Leo Lamb of the 361st FG, who belatedly came to our rescue. He collided with an FW-190 in mid air.

During the battle, the German air force lost 29 planes, with 18 German pilots KIA. And it is true that five American airmen were murdered that day near the village of Nentershausen. The murdered airmen were second Lt. Newell W. Brainard (Lt. Carrow's crew), T/Sgt. John J. Donohue (Lt. Elder's crew), 2nd Lt. John W. Cowgill, 2nd Lt. Hector V. Scala, and T/Sgt. James T. Fields, all from Lt. Baynham's crew. The perpetrators were civilians, the main culprits being camp bosses at some hard labor camps near a copper mine in the vicinity. The killers were apprehended after the war and brought to justice at a war crimes trial. They were found guilty, and subsequently executed.

One would have thought that with a battle of this magnitude, more would have been written about it. Aside from a paragraph in Roger Freeman's book *The Mighty Eighth* that stated this was the greatest single loss of any group in the Eighth Air Force, it received no other publicity. This is understandable, since this had been a failed raid, and a big defeat for our side. It is possible that everyone was trying to forget it. But it was certainly not forgotten by those who survived it, nor by anyone who happened to be at Tibenham that day, nor by the next of kin of those who perished.

Being Jewish Was An Extra Risk For This Kassel Survivor!
by Larry Hobbs, Staff Writer, Palm Beach Daily News

Editor's Note: This story, slightly modified, first appeared in the Friday, January 19, 1996 issue of the Palm Beach Daily News.

"I stand here and I still get a feeling about seeing that airplane," said Weinstein, who was a bombardier/navigator in a B-24 with the 445th Bomb Group during World War II.

The restored B-24 "All American" serves as a flying museum for the Collings Foundation of Stow, Mass. They fly it to about 150 cities a year. The plane is kept in the air largely through sponsorship contributions that range from $24 to $5,000.

He was not always this nostalgic about his war years. When World War II was won, Weinstein returned to Chicago and did his best to leave the experience in his past, he said. He never talked much about the day his ten member crew was shot down over Germany, or his harrowing ordeal as a Jewish American in a Nazi prisoner of war camp.

It has only been within the last ten years that Weinstein began searching out fellow Air Force veterans to swap war stories.

"Most of us did try to forget it for about 50 years," said Weinstein, who was awarded the Distinguished Flying Cross, the Purple Heart, and the Air Medal. "It's only about the last seven or eight years that I got back to it. It's fun to talk to these guys. We have so much in common, all the guys who flew in these things during the war."

When Weinstein entered the war in 1941, the magic number was 25—that's how many bombing missions you had to survive to complete a tour of duty. (It was increased to 35 missions later in the war.) The odds of not landing safely back in England were 1-in-3 to 1-in-20 every time you took off on a mission—you never knew the odds when you went out.

Weinstein's crew beat the odds until his 25th and final mission on September 27, 1944. Only 5 of 35 bombers returned from that mission, three of which crashed on the way back. Weinstein's B-24 was flying at 20,000 feet when they were shot down over Kassel, Germany.

As the plane nose-dived, Weinstein climbed from his tiny cubbyhole in the front and jumped. But his parachute got snagged by equipment inside, leaving him dangling outside the plane.

"I bailed out, but the straps got caught," Weinstein said. "I had to chin myself back into the airplane and jump again. By that time we were only about 2,500 feet above the ground."

He spent two weeks trying to reach Switzerland before being captured and sent to POW Stalag Luft 1 in Kassel.

"After I bailed out, two weeks later I was captured and taken to a small compound where there were about a dozen other crew members who had also been captured, and we were all being held in a small cell or room. In that group there were two badly wounded airmen who had received no medical attention. One had a badly shot up leg and the other was completely burned down one side of his body. I was the ranking officer in the group, and I asked the guard to take me to see the commandant. Don't ask me where I got the nerve or guts to do that, but I did!

"I was taken to the commandant's office and gave him my name, rank and serial number and told him that there were two badly wounded men who needed medical attention. I said that according to the Geneva Convention, they were entitled to some help.

"The commandant (a major) was a very militant looking and well dressed officer. He got up and came around from his desk and hit me several times on the cheek with a riding crop. It split my cheek open, and why I don't have a 'dueling scar' there today is a miracle. He proceeded to tell me that we, the Jews and the American airmen, were bombing churches, schools and hospitals, and that is how much he cared about the Geneva Convention.

After I picked myself up from the floor, he had the guard take me back to the cell. In a few hours they came and took the two wounded men out, hopefully to a hospital.

"When I bailed out, my flying boots came off. I was only wearing a pair of wool socks under them. When I landed I hid for a few days trying to make my way to Switzerland. I cut a piece of my leather jacket apart and made myself a pair of moccasins. That's the way I was dressed when I was taken into the commandant's office. Several hours after I was back in the cell, the guard came and took me back to the commandant's office. I stood there at attention while I heard him say to the guard in German, "Take him out and *schiessen* (shoot) him." Since German and Yiddish are very much alike and I had a very, very fleeting knowledge of either, I assumed he meant for the guard to take me out and shoot me.

"The guard marched me out of the building. We were in a walled compound, and I thought he was going to line me up against the wall and shoot me. I saw a gate about 100 yards ahead and thought when I got there, I would make a run for it. If he were going to shoot me, he was going to have to shoot me in the back, not up against the wall.

"About 25 yards from the gate, there was a small building. The guard shoved me in there and proceeded to give me a pair of shoes! Another few yards and I wouldn't be here to tell this story.

"Obviously what the commandant had said was something about *schuhe* (shoes), but in my fear it sounded like *schiessen* (shoot).

"The first thing people always ask me is what is was like to be a POW, and the second thing they ask is what it was like to be a Jewish POW in Germany," Weinstein said.

Nazi Gestapo leader Heinrich Himmler visited the camp of 27,000 POWs and issued a death sentence for its 1,100 Jewish prisoners, Weinstein recalls.

"Himmler came to the camp and left word that all Jewish officers were to be separated and shot," Weinstein said. "Our commander said, 'You march one Jewish guy off this camp and we'll riot.'"

The Nazis backed down, Weinstein said. However, Jewish prisoners were segregated from their fellow American soldiers. They were interrogated often, but the Germans never carried out their threats and intimidation. The camp was liberated on May 11, 1945.

Operation Market Garden
by Lt. Col. Robert E. Oberschmid (93rd)

We were flying 20 feet above the ground, engines howling in protest of a power setting far above normal and the engine instruments in the "red" or close to it. We had an indicated air speed of 205/210 with the wind whistling through more holes than anyone would ever count, still taking hits from small arms fire and no effective means of fighting back. I didn't even have my trusty 45. Where and when, you say? OK, follow me where angels fear to tread but where "all those fine young men" would go so many, many times.

We had been briefed for a practice mission with a real twist—a number (18?) of 93rd BG aircraft together with approximately 102 B-24s from other 2nd AD Groups would assemble and fly a loose bomber stream to an area north of London, descend to treetop level and return to our home base on the deck, individually hedge hopping all the way. What a fascinating opportunity that turned out to be. About as much fun as I ever had flying a B-24, and I'm sure there are bovine descendants that still cringe when a plane passes overhead.

Several days later (18 Sept. 44) we were called for another such flight, but this time we were going to Holland. Armhem to be exact, and we would be dropping parachute supplies to our airborne troops who had gone in the day before. It was to be a "no mission credit" kind of trip. No flak vests or steel helmets but they added a load master for some obscure reason. It wasn't going to be as much fun as the practice mission either, because the trip would be at 500 feet instead of on the deck and we would have fifteen P-51s to intercede for us. They wouldn't be necessary of course, but just in case. I was decked out in a pair of oxfords, pink pants, green shirt, A2 jacket and 30

135

mission crush hat. Piece of cake. An early day version of kick the tire, light the fire, every man's a tiger.

We were doing our pre-flight when jeeps began running all over the place, picking up our navigators to re-brief. Somebody somewhere had decided we were going to the wrong place. Seems we were not going to Arnhem after all—now it was Osterbeck. Talk about confusion—if ever the alarm bells in my head had gone off this would have been the time, but no matter, away we went, we were invulnerable, we were good and this was gonna be fun, at least someone said that.

At its best, the North Sea is an ugly, incredibly cold, foreboding body of water. This day it was fairly calm, but the debris of war was scattered from England to Holland. At the top of the list were several Horsa gliders awash in the sea and one of them had at least three British troops sitting on the wing. We reported their plight to "Colgate" (air sea rescue) but the troops were a long way from shore and had already been in the sea at least 24 hours. Poor odds, I'd say.

Landfall was on time, uneventful, on course and at 500 feet, very beautiful. Holland in the fall is truly a poet's inspiration. It was a clear day with the Dutch countryside before us when all hell broke loose. It started with a loud bang from the front of the plane and our nose gunner, Nick Flureas, said he had been hit and the turret was knocked out. Now anyone who flew 25 or 30 missions with the Mighty 8th knows how such an event can focus one's attention. Our bombardier, Al Faulhaber, gave him first aid and said the injury wasn't very bad, but we had lost the turret we would so desperately need. On to Osterbuck—but now we were really on the deck in a very loose gaggle rather than a formation. A number of the planes had been hit and the radio was alive with the concerns of the various crews, to wit; what the hell's going on and didn't they say this was going to be a fun "no mission credit" trip and where and where are our little friends and hey, a guy could get hurt doing stuff like this. I was flying 10 to 15 feet above the ground and was pulling up to cross dikes and roads. I could see some large electrical transmission towers ahead and I made the decision to fly *under* the wires rather than pull up again. Now just sit back and reflect on that maneuver for a few minutes, and you can't help but wonder where you and I and all the rest of us got the courage to make a decision like that. And the courage of my crew was equal to or greater than mine—they knew what I was going to do and no one

136

uttered a peep. Our top turret gunner Glenn Thompson says he still has a tendency to duck his head driving under a high line.

From here on things just got worse. We came to a guard tower at the corner of a large fenced area which turned out to be a Prisoner of War camp. I lifted the left wing over the first guard tower and flew the length of the fence, waving at the prisoners who were really animated at the thought that deliverance was at hand—little did they know. At the end of the fence I lifted the wing again to clear a second guard tower and there, not more than 30 feet from my face and eyeball to eyeball were two German soldiers with a machine gun in full automatic. They stitched our plane from end to end but didn't hit anything vital; however, my navigator Jerry Baughman developed a blister on the back of his neck from a round that passed a bit too close.

From then on things just got worse than worse. We were flying about 30 feet above a canal that ran along one side of a small town. My left wing was over the street and the right wing over green fields. Soldiers of all nations gravitate toward towns, and this idyllic village was no exception; it had German soldiers every place I looked. One guy on a bike going our direction looked over his shoulder when he heard us coming and somersaulted but came up on his feet with a pistol in his hand and put a few more holes in us.

There were soldiers walking, riding in trucks, half tracks and tanks and they were all shooting at us. We passed a church and a priest was in the belfry waving down at us—at least he wasn't shooting.

Approaching Osterbeck we pulled up to 500 feet, formed up, opened the bomb bays and made the drop on target. Two of our bundles did not release and our engineer, Fred Johnson, did his usual circus trick of going into the bomb bay without a parachute to release them. As we made a left turn away from the drop zone I could see that the trees across the river from our drop point were sprinkled with the parachutes of our paratroopers and many of those men were still hanging there.

As we headed home, it was obvious that a disaster of major proportions had been brought down on our heads. We never did see our little friends but were told later that they had been devastated on the way in and the trip out was just an extension of that mess. We were on the deck indicating about 210 when a terrific explosion occurred in the cockpit. A fire broke out in the fuse panel on my left and the cockpit area was full of smoke and debris. It took me a few seconds to realize I was still alive, if somewhat rattled. When I turned to our engineer Fred, who always flew standing between our co-pilot Art Antonio and myself, I saw a picture of total amazement. Fred had been wearing a baseball cap and the visor was gone. The only remnants were a few threads hanging down his forehead. Anyone who believes "close only counts in horseshoes" has never been shot at and missed.

Over the North Sea headed home we watched one of our Group go in the water. Technically it was a perfect ditching, but there were no survivors. Not even a cushion floated after the second impact which also broke the plane in two. We also saw another B-24 and a C-47 go down in the water. Approaching Milfoil (Hardwick) I requested an ambulance for my nose gunner but it proved unnecessary as his injuries were quite minor. So minor that my recommendation for his Purple Heart wasn't even acknowledged. Because of my request for the ambulance we were greeted by a number of staff and medical personnel whose curiosity immediately shifted to questions such as "Where is everybody?" When we informed them that "everybody" was scattered and splattered from Hardwick to Arnhem, Nijmegan, Osterbeck and back, the mood became somber indeed. In the final analysis Montgomery's end run across the Ruhr was an utter disaster. Inadequate planning, ineffective staffing, confusion and timid leadership led to one of our greatest defeats of the war.

After the war I visited the battle area on the ground and flew over the drop zone several times retracing that portion of the mission. It became obvious we and our paratroopers were victims of incredible error. Simply put, our re-supply drop zone was not in an area controlled by our forces.

Operation Market Garden eventually proved to be a military operation based on political considerations and thus doomed from the start.

For an exceptional account of Market Garden, read Corneleous Ryan's "A Bridge Too Far" and Geoffrey Powell's "The Devil's Birthday."

Our crew consisted of myself and co-pilot Art Antonio, navigator Jerry Baughman, radar navigator Elmer Pearson, bombardier Elwood Faulhaber, engineer Fred Johnson, radio operator Eugene Clement, gunners Nick Flueras, Glenn Thompson, James Duprey and Allen Sorenson.

With the exception of our radar navigator who joined our crew on mission #14, we did our phase training, flight over, 30 missions and return to the ZI together. Jerry Baughman and Nick Fleuras are now deceased but the rest of us and Jerry's widow Mary Baughman have a reunion every year.

"Ordeal" in Paris

by Donald F. Baumler (445th BG) Reprinted from the Kassel Mission Chronicles

On September 5, 1944, we flew a mission to Karlsruhe, Germany. It was a nine-hour mission. The weather was bad and the results were very bad because of the flak, fighters, the leader got shot up, and we missed the target and dropped our bombs on an alternate target. So three days later, on September 8, 1944, we had to go back to Karlsruhe.

On September 8, the weather was again bad. We ran into a front that was 27,000 feet high. Our leader decided to climb over it. After passing it, 100 miles from Karlsruhe, we dropped down to 20,000 feet to bomb. Then we turned around and were faced with the same front.

We couldn't possibly climb over it again and have gas to get home, so our brilliant leader decided to go under it. He put the whole group of some forty planes into a very steep dive. I was indicating over 300 mph when my windshield iced up and I couldn't see the plane I was flying on, so I pulled off to the side and leveled off and gradually let down to 500 feet to get under the clouds. I was scraping ice off the windshield. One of my crew in the back reported a line of concrete emplacements (The Siegfried Line).

Right at that very moment a shell (probably 40 mm) hit us mid-ship, just back of the wing and ahead of the side waist window. The force of the blast apparently went to the front and destroyed all our radio equipment and oxygen bottles, and cut the rudder cables completely. It also put the plane into a severe nose down position. I thought the tail was blown off and yelled for Johnny to put on the automatic pilot. He was in such shock that he handed me my steel flak helmet. I knocked it away, pulled the nose up, and tried to make a sharp turn, only to have the rudder pedal clank on the floor with no resistance. I thought we were goners.

So I called on the intercom to "bail out," but realized everything was dead. However, we were in a flat aileron turn and still flying, so I headed for the cloud base. Many more caliber shells hit us, but I finally made it into the clouds and proceeded to fly blind in a southerly direction toward Switzerland. Then the wings iced up and I had to lower our altitude. Eventually, after several hours, we broke out and recognized what could only be the Alps Mountains. We were way too far south.

Harold Parson, our regular navigator, was not with us, and Leon White, the bombardier, offered to try to get a fix on the "G" box. He said he knew where we were and gave me a heading toward Paris. I knew Paris was captured about four days previously, so I took the heading. About an hour later, lo and behold, there was Paris. We circled the Eiffel Tower and then tried to find an airfield. About 10 miles south, at Britigny, we saw an old German airfield with one runway, now a 9th AF fighter base. Unfortunately, the wind was blowing crossways and strong. We shot off red flares (emergency) and made my approach. But without rudders to crab into the wind, I could only hold direction by lowering the wing (up to a point). When we got near the ground, I had to level out and the plane started going sideways. When we hit, the left landing gear partially collapsed. We did a pretty hard ground loop.

Afraid of fire, I went out the top hatch and ran up the wing. When I jumped, it must have been 20 feet off the ground. Fortunately, I suffered only a slightly sprained ankle. They pulled the airplane off the runway, and only then did I see the rudder cables cut in half and hanging down. There was a three-foot diameter hole in the side of the plane, and it was a miracle that the waist gunners were not hit.

I reported to the base commander, and he was supposed to radio my base. The message never got there. He reported my name as "Roger Barton," and sent it to the 8th AF Headquarters.

The next day, the base engineering officer said he could fix the landing gear, and Johnny, my copilot, said he could splice the cables together, since he had worked for the telephone company. The base radio people had the know-how to fix the radio equipment. So, we went into Paris.

When we hit downtown, many people recognized our flying clothes and began to cheer us and follow us down the street. They gave us wine to drink while we saw all the sights, and eventually it turned dark. We were walking down the street when suddenly bullets started ricocheting off a building. We holed up in a doorway and found out there were still die-hard German snipers around.

A civilian in the next doorway (probably an American deserter), offered to take us to a place for drinks. All we had was invasion money. It turned out to be a "House of Pleasure" and the madam was an American from New York City. We filled her in on how the war was going, and she supplied drinks, no charge. Later, we went to General Ike's Hotel HQ, and they let us sleep in the lobby and gave us coffee and toast for breakfast.

Back at the airfield two days later, our plane was ready to fly. I gave the fighter pilots a buzz job and headed for England. I didn't have the "Code of the Day," and English gunners started shooting ahead of us.

When I got over the base and called "Arton Tower," they said that the plane was not listed. Then I identified myself, and when we landed, all the jeeps from Headquarters came out to meet us. We were debriefed and the Engineering Officer told me that a 4" Channel main bulkhead was cut in half, and said if I had put any stress on it, the plane could have broken in half. I didn't tell him about the buzz job when I left France.

When I got to my hut, they had divided up all my clothes and taken my personal positions to Father Quinlan, who was going to send them to Peggy. They didn't officially notify next-of-kin for about two weeks, so Peggy never knew.

Because of our "ordeal," we were given a week's leave. We went to Edinburgh, Scotland, played golf at some course that was like a cow pasture, and kissed all the Scottish lassies at the USO. It was a tough life!

Prisoner of War: Henry Morris' Last Flight

The following condensed account, written by a friend of Henry Morris over a period of several years, was recently forwarded to us by his son. Sergeant Morris was on his 33rd mission, 12 September 1944, to Misburg. His aircraft "LAMBSY DIVEY" (44-40170) exploded just after bombs away. He was the sole survivor and finished the war as a German POW. This is his story as related by a friend.

"Gaining speed rapidly, the LAMBSY DIVEY rolled down the runway and lifted off, flying low over the end of the runway with a load of incendiary bombs destined for an oil refinery at Misburg, Germany. Gradually gaining speed, Lt. Sparrow banked to the left and headed for forming altitude.

"With a sigh of relief, S/Sgt. Henry Morris, waist gunner, felt the tension ease as he listened to the steady drone of the engines. There was always that tight feeling in his stomach on takeoff.

"At 0700, the 852nd Squadron formed with the other Squadrons of the 491st Bomb Group and headed east to join the other Groups of the 14th Combat Wing. A bright sun was glinting off the plexiglass nose of LAMBSY DIVEY as they bored through the cold morning air.

"The 491st headed east toward CP-1 on the coast of France where they would pick up their fighter escort. Lt. Sparrow's voice came over the intercom, 'Clear your guns and keep your eyes peeled for enemy fighters.' The 50 caliber machine guns clattered as they were fired to ascertain if they were working properly.

"The fighter escort picked them up just before the formation entered enemy territory. P-51 Mustang's were flying area cover, the heavy bodied Thunderbolts, flying 3,000 feet above, were giving close support to the 491st. They were a welcome sight.

"Puffs of black clouds suddenly erupted up ahead, marking the spot where the German AA batteries were firing. The propellers clawed through the cold air as the bombers went up to 26,000 feet to get away from the flak. It was cold, but Henry could feel the cold sweat run down his back.

"They had been in the air over four hours now, and Henry was tense as he watched the little black clouds of death move up towards them. 'Just like the others,' he thought. This was his 33rd mission and he had never liked to see those flak bursts reaching for his plane. 'Well, they are putting out the welcome mat again,' said the pilot. Henry thought about an earlier mission he was on with LUCKY BUCK and how they had caught a flak burst in the tail section. So here he was, in another B-24, being bounced around by the concussion of flak bursts.

142

"As they moved deeper into Germany he searched the sky above, seeking to locate the enemy fighters which he knew were there. Without his Polaroid sunglasses he would never be able to look directly into the sun, but they were up there. He saw the P-47s drop their auxiliary gas tanks and go looking for the German fighters.

"He saw an ME-109, but the German pilot made no move toward his plane. Suddenly a hole appeared in the wing of LAMBSY DIVEY. A B-24 went out of control and headed earthward spinning. He saw no parachutes.

"This was the hottest reception they had ever received. AA fire seemed to intensify as they made their run over the target. 'Let's get the hell out of here,' said the bombardier. Lt. Sparrow banked right, put the nose down and headed for the rally point. Just off the target LAMBSY DIVEY took a hit in the #2 engine from a flak burst. The plane began to burn, leaving a trail of black smoke. Flak was tearing holes in the fuselage. Henry had shrapnel wounds in both legs. Then it happened. With a deafening roar, LAMBSY DIVEY exploded.

"When he came to, he was falling through space. His was the only chute in the sky. 'I've had it,' he thought. Then he pulled his ripcord. With a jolt, he found himself drifting slowly toward the ground. As he dropped, he could see an AA battery close to where he was going to land. He could see the men scurrying around with their weapons. He had heard stories of parachutists being machine-gunned as they came down. But, if anyone was shooting at him, they had missed—so far.

"Remembering his air crew training, he hit the ground and rolled. With pain stabbing through his legs, he started to run for cover but he was caught by an angry mob of German civilians. They kicked and beat him to the ground and hit him in the back of the head. When he revived there was a rope around his neck. He was being dragged towards some trees. They were shouting at him, but he did not know what they were saying. He thought of the irony of it all, being shot down and escaping from the burning plane, to end his life at the end of a rope at the hands of a lynch mob.

"At that time a squad of soldiers ran up and rescued him, removing the rope. Cursing both Henry and the soldiers, the civilians followed them until one of the soldiers aimed his rifle at the mob leader.

"The soldiers shoved him into the back of a truck and took him to a bomb-damaged building to be interrogated. Although he could hardly walk, he was interrogated relentlessly. Consistently he gave only his name, rank and serial number; then the two guards would punch, slap and beat him. The interrogators then changed tactics. They offered him better treatment if he would talk. When that failed, the Major jumped up and shouted, 'Dumpkopf, don't you know we will exterminate your Air Force if you continue to bomb us?' The Major nodded to the troops and said, 'Take him away.'

"They half dragged, half carried him to the truck outside. In a few minutes the truck stopped in front of a barbed-wire enclosed stockade. He was put into a half-lighted room where he could see the forms of men sprawled against the walls. The men were also survivors of the air battles of that day.

"Henry didn't sleep much that night. Hunger pains reminded him that he had not eaten for hours, and his wounded legs throbbed painfully.

"In the early morning they were separated into two groups. Men not wounded were marched away. The wounded men were taken to a bomb-scarred building for medical treatment. Some of the German medical personnel evidently disliked the idea of giving medical treatment to enemy airmen. One, who could speak English, told Henry he thought it was a waste of medicine to give it to them when so many civilians were dying as a result of their bombing. They were given food and loaded into trucks, taken to a railroad station and put into a boxcar. After many hours of traveling they came to a stop.

"The sight that met their eyes was none too inviting. The unpainted buildings of the POW compound stood out starkly against the bare earth. This was to be Henry's home from September 1944 until March 1945.

"They had roll call every morning and every night. They didn't stay outside long, as dogs patrolled the compound until morning. They slept on the floor, huddled together to keep warm all through the cold winter. They were guarded by German soldiers, SS troops, and Hitler's Youth Organizations. The Hitler Youth were detested by the prisoners, mostly because of their habit of jabbing the prisoner with bayonets as they guarded them.

"Food was rationed and there was no medical attention. They all suffered from malnutrition with barely enough food to sustain life.

"Early one morning the men were ordered out of their camp and forced to march westward. Rumors were that the Russian armies were near. On the third day they were the target of strafing planes and Russian artillery. A little later they were attacked by Russian tanks. As the guards fell under the Russian fire, the prisoners grabbed their guns and joined the battle to take their revenge on the German guards.

"Now the former prisoners were faced with another problem. They didn't know what the Russians would do with them, so they formed their own unit, equipped with weapons taken from the Germans. They demanded to fight their way to meet up with the American forces advancing in Germany. This was a new way of life as Henry fought along with the ground forces. They learned how to live off the land as the Russians did.

"After the battle of Berlin, Henry made contact with the soldiers of the 101st Airborne Division. After delousing and a bath, Henry was given some clean clothes.

"Once again Henry was on his way, but this time it was en route to home in the USA. Henry was the only member on LAMBSY DIVEY to survive the war."

Regensburg
Submitted By Sammy Schneider, 485th BG
This Mission Write-Up Is from the Publication "Bomber Legends"

After the raid on Regensburg, February 16, 1945, another drama took place through the Brenner Pass. The following is an account as told to Jo Haden Galbraith, daughter of Lt. Robert (Bob) O. Haden, Navigator from the 831st squadron who passed away in 1995. He was on Glenn Hess's crew and they were on the raid to Regensburg. The target was the Obertraubling Messerschmitt assembly plant. It was the largest plant of its kind in Europe and turned out 200-300 ME-109 fighter aircraft each month.

The crew was on a mission to bomb the Messerschmitt Plant at Regensburg, Germany. As they began the bomb run through heavy flak the number one engine took a direct hit, blowing the prop into the sky and causing the plane to buck like a wild bronco. It was immediately thrown into a severe left bank as the pilot, Lt. Hess, struggled to regain control. Unnerved, and now flying with only three engines, they courageously pressed on toward the target. The bomb bay doors were opened, and within seconds the number two engine was hit, blowing off the turbo charger. Fortunately, it did not explode, but the impact caused the plane to bank hard to the right out of control. To make matters worse, it threw them into the prop-wash of another bomber, causing the plane to flip upside down. The order was given to bail out, but the centrifugal force caused by the fierce spinning kept the men pinned to the airplane floor and walls frantically trying to pull themselves out of the hatches and waist windows. Caught in a death trap and unable to budge, the crew began their final prayers when the plane (aided no doubt by a little Divine intervention) miraculously righted itself in enabling the pilot to pull out of the spin and regain control. Now at 10,000 feet and with a limited amount of fuel the crew was forced to make some quick decisions. They had two choices: fly to Switzerland, which was doable, or take their chances and try to make it to the allied border in northern Italy. If they landed in Switzerland, a neutral country, they knew they would be interned there for the rest of the war. This did not sit well with the men, as there was no telling how long that might be, possibly years. They were also concerned that they might be classified as M.I.A. (missing in action), causing undue stress on their families. Unable to maintain an altitude higher than 10,000 feet with only two engines, the navigator, Lt. Haden, searched for a route to Italy that would cut through the 15,000 ft. Alpine mountains. He found it in Brenner Pass, a valley which connects Innsbruck, Austria with Bolzano, Italy.

Brenner Pass is technically at the border between Italy and Austria. The crews always considered it to include the entire valley that snakes through the Alps Mountains with Verona at the South end and Innsbruck at the North end. In places the valley is just wide enough for a river, a road and a railroad. It was a main connection between the Axis. The valley is well over 100 miles long and every foot was heavily defended by 558 large antiaircraft gun installations. Under the best conditions in peacetime a journey through the Alps at that altitude would be considered treacherous. For a crippled bomber low on fuel and being shot at from all sides, it was darn near suicide. To further complicate matters much of northern Italy was still occupied by the Germans. Which meant even if they made it through the Alpine pass in one piece, they would still have a considerable flight over enemy territory.

Fuel was a major concern. Before take off the tanks were topped off at 2750 gallons and the planes were loaded to the hilt with bombs. On the way to the target, the group tried to gain as much altitude as possible, consequently burning about 3/4 of the fuel by the time they reached their mark. This meant there might be as little as 600 gallons of fuel left after the run. However, if they made it over the Alps it would be downhill the rest of the way.

Haden calculated that if the Gods were with them (and if they didn't hit a mountain or get blown out of the sky) they would have just enough fuel to eke across the Allied border into Rimini, a coastal town on the Adriatic with an army base and runway. With no time to ponder the idea a vote was taken, and trusting their navigator, the captain and crew opted to take their chances and go for it.

Needless to say it was a harrowing flight through the snow-covered Alps, (pilot Glenn Hess likened it to guiding an elephant through the eye of the needle under fire). But somehow, against all odds, their badly crippled plane managed to make it through the Pass, cross the allied border on fumes, and hobble to a stop at the tail end of the Rimini runway. Hess checked the fuel gauge—it was empty.

Stunned and badly shaken by their ordeal, the men crawled out to inspect the plane. Hess recalled: "The plane was so badly shot-up that you couldn't lay your hand anywhere on it without touching a flak hole. We hadn't been out of the plane more than two minutes when this General came flying down the runway raising all kinds of Hell about us landing on his airstrip. It was a fighter strip and the General was screaming at me to get my f------ plane off his runway! I stood there and took his insults for awhile until finally exasperated I stopped him by saying 'Sir, would you like to inspect my plane?' We looked at each other for a moment and then I just walked away. Once he got a good look at it we heard him yell, 'Hell this thing ain't worth movin'!' He then ordered a bulldozer to shove it over the nearest embankment, and that's where it stayed."

Our Unforgettable Mission 23 Was Worth Every "Penny" Of It

by Lt. Col. James R. Maris (392nd), with Vickie J. Maris

After assembly, we headed our B-24s to the coastal departure point, making scheduled turns where other squadrons joined the long line of departing bombers. The B-24s tracked out over the North Sea passing Heligoland. Near Kiel we turned to the southeast assuming a heading toward Berlin. This turn was to throw the fighters off course and make them think the target for the day was Berlin. As we were making this turn, the wings changed the formation and split into squadrons in trail—sixteen B-24s per squadron. Soon after this maneuver, we made a turn to the northwest that put our airplanes on course to bomb the oil refineries at Hamburg.

The antiaircraft guns at Hamburg were not firing at individual aircraft, but instead were set up to fire in predetermined grid blocks over the target we were to bomb. They would wait until a complete squadron was overhead and fire into their assigned grid. This type of firing made a large block of smoke and fire over the target. For a moment, an entire squadron would vanish in the thick, black blanket of smoke.

But the moment didn't last long. Planes would disrupt the layer of smoke as they spun out of formation or blew up before us. With each squadron, we anxiously counted the B-24s that would fly free of the smoke on the other side of the target. Ten, eleven, maybe twelve planes from each squadron survived the flak barrage. The sky was filled with parachutes descending airmen into uncertainty. As many as 40 to 60 men per squadron made the jump.

We now approached with a vivid picture of our near-certain destiny. I was so overcome by this skyline display of death and destruction that I vomited into my oxygen mask in the cockpit. My copilot had to take over for a few moments as I cleaned up the mess, repositioned my mask and steadied my nerves for the task ahead.

We entered the flak storm over our target and were immediately tossed by the severe turbulence created by the exploding 88-mm flak. The "Bad Penny" was bathed in brilliant

148

flashes of light and peppered with exploding shells. She rocked and shuttered with the jarring impact of every burst.

The biggest jolt came when the number one engine was blown off. We rolled hard to the right and it was all that my copilot and I could do to right our B-24. Not long after, a second blast stripped the cowling and supercharger off engine number three on our right wing. An engine oil fire created an expanding plume of white smoke that trailed our aircraft.

But even at half-mast, our "Bad Penny" was determined to get us home. As the airmen had been dislodging the bomb and closing our bomb bay doors, Herbie and I had been carefully watching our descent. We had dropped from 22,000 feet to 18,000 in our recovery process. After calculating our ground speed and rate of sink, we estimated that we would probably cross the English coast at about 1,900 feet. This would allow us to go the remaining distance inland to Wendling—home.

There were a lot of "ifs" involved, though. Because of this, we decided to lighten the load and improve our chances. Anything loose was thrown out of the aircraft. Flak vests. Flak helmets. Machine guns. Ammunition. Cameras. Aircraft manuals. The bombardier had a few choice words to say about his binoculars going overboard.

The "Bad Penny" strained to hold altitude while her engines—the two that had survived the attack—were running extremely hot. I continued to be amazed that our number three was hanging in there. She was running, but without cowling and supercharger. Then, out of the blue, she kicked in with enough additional power for us to cross the English coast at 1,400 feet. I had never dreamed of flying a B-24 on two and a half engines and with a full crew across the North Sea.

When we identified our landfall, Herbie gave us a heading for Wendling. We broke out the red flares and were standing by to shoot them off as we neared the base.

Our problems were not over yet, though. Our electrical system and hydraulics were inoperative. This meant we had to manually lower the landing gear. If we lowered it too early, the gear would create too much drag and cause us to fall short of the landing field. So we worked out the timing as best we could and started to crank when the base came into view. Herbie and our bombardier unlatched the nose gear and with the help of Fitz, pushed the nose gear out. It fell in the locked position.

In the bomb bay, the flight engineer organized the gunners into a team to crank down the mains (landing gear). I put the gear handle in the down position and gunners took turns on the crank. Since the bomb bay doors weren't fully closed, they again used the parachute harness lifeline when lowering an airman into the bomb bay to turn the crank. When an airman would slip or be thrown off balance by the force of the wind blowing in through the doors, the others would pull him to safety with the makeshift line. After many more turns than the 71 defined in the manual, the gear locked into place. We were at 500 feet on the downwind side of the runway. The airmen fired our red flares to announce our arrival.

Just when we thought we were home free, Mother Nature dished up one more challenge. Since the "Bad Penny" had been at high altitude for hours, her surfaces were extremely cold. This caused our forward glass on the nose and windshield to ice over during our descent through the moist air near the ground. I had to peer out the open side windows to judge height and direction. With some divine assistance, I was able to hold our aircraft steady as she settled onto the runway. With no hydraulics and consequently, no brakes, we rolled the entire length of the runway before the "Bad Penny" came to a stop.

I had ordered the crew into crash positions before landing. Everyone was somewhat dazed with the realization that we were safely on the ground. I had to shout to them to get them to quickly exit the aircraft and run to a safe distance. The "Bad Penny" was primed to blow at any minute. According to procedure and to prevent imminent fire, the copilot and I shut down the cockpit and then scrambled down, through the front of the bomb bay and out onto the open tarmac under the right wing. There we found our entire crew, ignoring instructions to flee, waiting for us to make sure we could get out. Once again, I had to motivate them to hurry away from the aircraft!

They were off like a shot. The copilot and I were close behind. At a safe distance, we turned and looked at our "Bad Penny." Her tires were flat. Gasoline was dripping from her battered fuselage and wings. Her pain fell to the tarmac with each drop of ice melting from her aluminum skin. Tubes, pipes, broken metal fairings hung down in tangled disarray. Her once overheated engines now crackled and popped as parts began to cool and shrink. This valiant bomber safely brought us home. But she would fly no more.

My crew was checked over at the infirmary and all were unharmed. I, on the other hand, had been wondering what I would find under my flight vest. I had tried to ignore the pain that was wildly spreading across my side during our return trip, but suddenly it seemed to grow more quickly now that we were on the ground.

After removing my flight suit and flight jacket, we found a piece of flak embedded in a steel plate in my flak jacket. It had bent the plate and severely bruised my side, but beyond that, I was uninjured. Today, touching that steel plate with its embedded flak is an instant reminder of all the events that attempted to end Mission 23 that day in August.

The following day, we returned to the "Bad Penny" to tell her goodbye. We counted 85 holes in her fuselage from nose to tail. Her number one engine was somewhere in Germany along with pieces of the number three. The hole in her left wing was large enough to lower a man through.

My crew and I always felt that the "Bad Penny" shed her own blood to save ours. We are certain that she was running with a power far greater than the lift in her wings to carry us safely home.

Let's Not Forget What Happened to Lt. Edwin M. Helton's Crew

Foreword by Walter J. Mundy (467th)

As Group Vice President of the 467th BG, I was asked by the Roll of Honor review committee to verify that a short list of 467th combat crew members were Killed in Action or Killed in the Line of Duty. The names on the list were those crew members who were not verified as deceased in either classification and official verification is necessary to have them named on the Roll of Honor at the Second Air Division Memorial Library.

Through correspondence with the Army Total Personnel Command, I was able to verify that S/Sgt. Rufus C. Davis on Lt. Charles D. Harrison's crew was Killed in Action on May 8, 1944. I have requested verification of eight other 467th crew members and of this date have received verification of one other that I want to pass on to the Roll of Honor committee and to the members of the 467th and the Second Air Division Association.

The story that follows is one that will stir many emotions of those of us who flew in combat and those Americans and English people who will never forget the sacrifices of the men of the Second Air Division. This is a story of a crew that should be here alive with us but instead must remain always in spirit in our hearts.

This story not only answers the requirements of verifying that Lt. Helton and his crew were Killed in Action, it also provides the vital information concerning the mission, the aircraft, the crew, and the history for inclusion in the electronic database of the 467th BG.

These brave men are no longer Missing in Action. They will always be on the Roll of Honor.

THE DATE: 21 June 1944
THE TARGET: Genshagen Industrial Works near Berlin (Mission #60)
THE AIRCRAFT: B-24H # 4252497

THE CREW MEMBERS:
1st Lt. Edwin Helton, pilot, 0687592; 2nd Lt. Maurice R. Nelson, copilot, 0699712; 2nd Lt. Richard J. Ludka, bombardier, 0694919; T/Sgt. Warren G. Rankin, engineer, 35575827; T/Sgt. Frank Borchick, radio operator, 13171042; S/Sgt. Thomas A. Gensert, ball turret gunner, 35766187; S/Sgt. Charles L. Knowles, Jr., gunner, 18189980; S/Sgt. Carmine Margiosso, gunner, 12037871; S/Sgt. Stanley Brzezowski, tail gunner, 32862091.

THE DOCUMENT:
Lt. Helton's B-24 was damaged by flak over the target and was last seen going down under control with one engine on fire and one engine's prop feathered. Reports indicate that the aircraft crashed on the west bank of the Muritz-sea near the village of Klink, Germany. All nine members of the crew were rescued and captured. Seven crew members, except Lt. Helton and Lt. Hudka, were taken into the town of Waren where they were turned over to the Security Police, who executed (MURDERED) them and had them buried in a common grave in Poppentin, Germany. The remains of these seven were subsequently disinterred and sent to the U.S. Cemetery at St. Avold, France where they were identified. German reports indicate that all seven had been shot in the head.

152

Lt. Helton and Lt. Ludka were turned over to SS Police Commissioner Stempel in Fuerstenbert-Mecklenburg where they were similarly executed (MURDERED) and allegedly buried in Droegen/Stargard. The remains of Lts. Helton and Ludka have been determined to be unrecoverable.

This wartime atrocity was investigated and The Gauleiter of Mecklenberg, one Friedrich Hildebrandt, the Nazi criminal who ordered the murders of these airmen, was tried as a war criminal and hanged. Other German SS police and officials who participated in the atrocity are dead by suicide or were detained by the German police and prosecuted as war criminals.

YES, THIS IS A STORY THAT HAD TO BE TOLD!

Chapter 5: People

Dedicated Control Tower Personnel

Dear Bill: Much has been written about the exploits of the Fighter Aces and Combat Crew Heroes, however very little has been written about their friends in the Control Tower who "Kept 'em flying"!

Ours was not a glamorous job, and at times, it was a long, hard grind under conditions that were less than ideal. There were times, too, when it was touch and go, and no two situations were alike. We did just what we had to do, and I'm quite sure most of us would not have traded places with the Air Crews.

Nevertheless, it seems appropriate after all these years to give some recognition to the dedicated men in the Control Tower who were always ready to help and DID help!

We were down at the runway talking them in when our fickle English weather decided to play tricks on us. Always on the lookout for red flares letting us know there were wounded aboard. Giving priority landing to aircraft in distress. Landing 'em with wheels up, out of fuel, shot up and other various and sundry conditions which required delicate handling. We maintained the Airfield with regard to the safety of the planes, examining the runways after a mission and before takeoff to make sure there were no cracks or potholes. Getting the Engineers to make quick repairs. Making sure that all the lights were working properly. Removing obstructions from the runways.

Getting to crashed aircraft with ambulance and fire-fighting equipment. Many times we were called upon to make split-second decisions (and pray that hopefully they were the right ones). We had to contend with rain, cold, fog, sleet and snow, in addition to our planes being shot up when trying to land.

We were on duty 24 hours a day to assist RAF planes diverted to our field after night missions. We arranged transport, billeting and mess for those crews who remained overnight. We answered Darky Calls and Mayday Calls. Well, sometimes it was just one darn thing after another!

(No author listed)

Who Packs Your Parachute?
by Jim H. Reeves, Group Relations Committee

I recently read an interesting article written by Charles Plumb entitled "Who Packs Your Parachute?" Many, many 2nd Air Division personnel wore parachutes while on active duty. This article can reflect upon our active duty days as well as our daily lives since that age and time. The message is simple, yet very thought-provoking. In his article, Charles Plumb tells about his experiences. As a U.S. Naval Academy graduate and a jet fighter pilot in Vietnam, he flew 75 successful combat missions before being shot down by a surface-to-air missile. He spent the next six years in a Communist prison. He survives and now lectures about his experiences.

One day Plumb and his wife were sitting in a restaurant when a man approached him saying "I know you. You're Plumb! You flew from the carrier Kitty Hawk! You were shot down!"

"How in the world do you know that?" asked Plumb.

"I packed your parachute. I guess it worked," the man replied.

Plumb relates that he didn't sleep much that night. He thought about the man who spent hours in the bowels of a ship carefully folding the silks of the chutes. He wondered what the man might have looked like in uniform. Had he seen him? Had he ever noticed him? He wondered how many times he had not offered a smile nor said good morning, for you see, he was an officer and a fighter pilot, and this man was just a sailor.

We all have our parachutes—our physical parachutes, our mental parachutes, our emotional parachutes, and our spiritual parachutes. It's important for us to realize that we don't weather storms by ourselves.

There are others—some we know, some we don't—who help us survive.

155

Jane Windham, Flight Engineer, Killed in Crash

by Jim Russel.
Reprinted from Stars and Stripes, 4/2/45,

PFC Jane B. Windham, who considered flying for Air Transport Command as a flight engineer no more dangerous than crossing the street, was killed in a crash at a U.K. base on March 31, 1945, the first WAC to lose her life on flying duty in a theater of war. PFC Windham, who was 23, was one of a crew of three aboard a B-17 which collided with a C-47 while attempting to land. None of the crew of either ship survived the crash.

Jane Windham's background was strictly flying. She studied aeronautical engineering at the University of California and could fly anything from a Piper Cub to a B-17. She was a licensed pilot, and taught women to fly before joining the WAC 18 months ago.

She came into the army with the MOS of an aircraft maintenance technician and at a Montana ATC base from which she shipped to the ETO five months ago. She earned her wings crewing bombers ferried by ATC to bases in the states and Alaska. On dozens of trips she took over the controls of the big ships, "just to keep her hand in," as she put it.

With ATC's Air Inspector in the ATO, Jane's flight duties were modified by administrative work. She might have stuck to a desk and lived, but she settled this with: "I didn't come overseas to fly a desk."

She was too enthusiastic about flying to be content on the ground. But nothing vexed her more than someone idealizing her for doing a "man's job."

Most reporters, though, had a penchant for plugging this "man's job," a tendency that made her shy about publicity. It promoted too many embarrassing situations. A note scribbled about a "control cable" might not be legible to the reporter come deadline, and most reporters not being flight engineers, the transcription might result in Jane doing something awfully silly with a control tower.

It was the sincerity of this blonde, blue-eyed girl from San Antonio that made her most attractive.

Something she said three months ago, haunting and ironic today, summed up her attitude. 'I can't say that I envy those men who fly combat," she said. "They put their lives out on a limb every time they go up." Then she added: "The flying I do is like walking down the street."

Gen Jimmy Doolittle Dies

Retired Gen. James H. Doolittle, who became a national hero when he lead the first World War II bombing raid on Japan in 1942, died September 27, 1993 at the age of 96. He died at his son's home after suffering a stroke. Doolittle, known as "Jimmy" to virtually everyone, established an unparalleled string of aviation records in the 1920s and 1930s, first as an Army pilot and then as an employee of Shell Oil Co. In 1935 he became one of the first people to earn a doctorate in aeronautics.

But he was remembered above all for leading the April 18, 1942 raid on Japan. The raid on Tokyo inflicted no major damage, and a later Naval War College study could find "no serious strategic reason" for it.

But it stirred American morale just four months after the shock of Pearl Harbor, and it put the Japanese on notice that their cities were within reach of U. S. air power.

When President George Bush gave Doolittle the Presidential Metal of Freedom in July, 1989, he described him as "the master of the calculated risk." General Doolittle also won the Metal of Honor and many other awards.

Shortly after the mid-day raid which stunned the Japanese, Doolittle was promoted from Lt. Colonel to Brigadier General, and by the end of the war he was the youngest Lt. Gen. in the army. He went on to serve in a variety of posts during the war, including commander of the Algeria-based 12th Air Force and later the 8th Air Force, based in Britain, which blasted away Germany's air power.

"I Remember Billy"
by Jack McKenzie

My name is Jack McKenzie and I was a First Pilot in the 735th Squadron of the 453rd Bomb Group. I flew 11 missions from February 25, 1945 to April 10, 1945. I am a ham radio operator, NSMFG, Extra

Class, and have a more-than-passing interest in Morse Code. The attached is about my boyhood friend, Morse Code and the fact that it resulted in his death over Japan—the day after the war was over! Jack McKenzie, Rt. 3, Box 177-B, Cleveland, OK 74020, n5mfg3@juno.com

His name was Billy Smith and we grew up in the little sleepy town of Mesquite, Texas.

After high school, we both went to Texas A&M. This was during World War II and we both hitchhiked to Dallas and volunteered for Aviation Cadet training in the Army Air Forces. We entered service the same day at Shepherd Field, Texas, where we were assigned to different barracks according to our last names. When we left basic training, Billy went to Aviation Cadet Pre Flight at San Antonio, Texas, whereas I was sent to Maxwell Field, Alabama. In Pre Flight we both had to learn to copy five words per minute Morse Code.

I did... he didn't.

After Pre Flight I went to Primary Flight School, followed by Basic Flight School and Advanced Flight School where I received my commission and pilot wings. I then went to the Four Engine School back at Maxwell Field, where I learned to fly B-24 bombers. This was followed by crew training and eventually to the 735th Squadron of the 453rd Bomb Group (Heavy) of the 8th Air Force in England from where I flew missions over Germany.

In the meantime, Billy repeated another two months of Pre Flight whereby this time he had learned to copy Morse code at twenty words per minute or so. And then, for reasons that would only be understood by someone who has served in the military, he did not ship out again and was held back for another onerous two months of Pre Flight! By this time the need for pilots had declined, and as soon as he got to Primary Flight School he washed out. He was sent, where else, to Radio School.

Radio School took a long time and then he was assigned to a B-29 crew. Crew training took a long time, to the end that his crew did not make it to the Pacific Theater of Operations until the war was nearly over.

On V-J Day all combat crews were stood down and further missions were flown by crews like Billy's who had not been in combat. His crew was assigned to a low level mission to drop food parcels to American prisoner-of-war camps in Japan, a mission for which they were not trained. They flew into a mountain, and Billy was killed along with his entire crew.

Thus Billy died the day after the war was over, and all because of Morse Code.

Life sometimes doesn't seem fair.

Major General Andrew S. Low, Jr., USAF—Retired
by A. Edward (Abe) Wilen (453rd)

Andy Low led the 453rd Bomb Group and in turn led the 8th Air Force on May 8, 1944, on a mission to Brunswick, Germany. The 453rd was badly hit by German fighters. Among the planes that went down was Crew #8, Pilot Richard Witton, Co-Pilot Wallace Croxford, Bombardier Walter Conneely and Navigator Abe Wilen. Thirty-nine years later, May 1983, in Indiana, Pennsylvania at Jimmy Stewart's 75th birthday celebration, Andy Low on reuniting with me said, "Wilen, you were badly hit on May 8, 1944, I saw you rammed by a German fighter and then your plane went down."

In mid-May, Witton, Croxford, Conneely and I wound up at the West compound in Stalag Luft III, Sagan, Poland. This is the camp that the movie "The Great Escape" was about. Two months prior, seventy-six men escaped through a tunnel. Only three made it to England. Of those captured, 50 were shot at Hitler's orders.

On July 29, 1944, on a mission to Bremen, Germany, Andy Low was shot down. He was badly hurt and wound up in a hospital for 16 days. He almost lost an arm but was fortunate to have a South African doctor save it for him.

In mid-August, Andy wound up at Stalag Luft III also, but in the North Compound. From that date until the 27th of January, 1945, POW life went on for Andy, myself and the rest of our crew. On January 27th, with the Russians advancing in our direction, we got orders to march.

About six inches of snow had accumulated and the temperatures went down as low as 10 degrees below zero. We were all handed Red Cross parcels and started our march. We in the West Compound left about 11:30 p.m. to midnight. Andy, in the North Compound, left about 3:00 a.m. on the 28th. Snow fell and created blizzard conditions. Men froze, men fell out, some were shot. Andy Low and we marched together, not knowing the other was there.

There are some good books on Stalag Luft III and the march. The important thing was that Low, Witton, Croxford, Conneely and Wilen survived it together.

At this point, Croxford and Conneely went on to Stalag VIIA in Moosburg, Germany. Andy Low, Dick Witton and Abe Wilen wound up at Stalag XIIID in Nurnberg, Germany, a mile away from the marshalling yard.

This target was bombed repeatedly by the 8th A.F. in daylight and the British at night. Late in February our own 453rd bombed us. Many bombs fell near our camp. There was little food, and rats, mice and bugs were everywhere. There were not enough beds, so some slept on the floor. At night during the bombing, we were told that anyone trying to get out of the barracks would be shot. We saw the flashes, counted the seconds and could determine how close the bombs came.

Eventually, on April 4th, as Patton's Third Army was moving toward us, we marched south to wind up at Stalag VIIA in Moosburg. On the way, we were strafed by our own fighters as we marched on the road. We had to tear up anything white and work out the letters POW in the field to warn our fighter planes away.

When we got to Moosburg, Dick Witton and I were in a large tent with many others. Andy Low was in a smaller tent next to ours.

On April 29th, we were liberated together and we in the tents were flown out first on May 3rd. Many years passed until our paths crossed again.

When I think of Andy Low and his relationship to our crew and myself, I feel that the thread that ties us together is best expressed in a quotation from a veteran's magazine:

"I know why men who have been to war yearn to be together. They long to be with men who once acted their best. Men who suffered and sacrificed. Who were stripped raw, right down to their humanity."

Are These the Final Details of Glenn Miller's Death?

by Thomas E. O'Connel (338th BG)

Reprinted from the Torretta Flyer, Summer-Fall 1990

The mystery is solved. We now know quite certainly what happened to Glenn Miller. A Royal Air Force Lancaster Bomber was responsible for his disappearance on a flight from England to Paris in December 1944. The jettisoning of the Lank's bombs after an aborted mission to Germany accidentally caused a small plane flying below to spin into the English Channel. The small plane was carrying Miller, everybody's favorite World War II band leader.

Why in the world did it take forty years for the truth to emerge? The answer lies in the word "aborted." If that RAF bomber squadron had completed its bombing mission to Germany, the crews would have been debriefed after the flight was over. At that debriefing they would have been carefully quizzed by trained intelligence officers to find out everything that occurred during the mission. The Lancaster pilot and navigator who have now come forward to tell of the previously forgotten incident of their 1944 flight, would surely have informed authorities of seeing the small plane going into the Channel if that had been the case.

The particular crew in question took off in England, got in formation and headed for their target, the railway yards at Siegen, Germany. Then the weather deteriorated, and before the planes crossed into Germany they were ordered back to base. Under such circumstances, the procedure in both air forces was to jettison the bombs into the Channel. It would have been dangerous to land back in England with those heavy, volatile bombs aboard.

There was apparently one key procedural difference between the RAF and the USAF: in aborted missions the RAF bombs exploded and ours were dropped unarmed. Ours didn't explode; they dropped to the bottom of the Channel. I don't know why the RAF didn't do it this way.

I was a bombardier on the crew of a USAF bomber and flew missions from England similar to the one the "Lank" was on. I never armed our bombs until it was absolutely clear we were going to drop them on the target. In the event of jettisoning on an aborted mission, the impact on friendly craft below us would have been much less. Apparently, it was the shock waves from the exploding bombs which caused the little Norseman aircraft carrying Glenn Miller to fall into the sea. If the bombs had been from a USAF plane, Miller might be playing his lovely music even now.

Apparently, the weather was really terrible that day, December 15, 1944.

An early inquiry to the RAF about its possible inadvertent involvement in Miller's disappearance elicited the reply that "not even the pigeons were flying that day." But recently the RAF crew's navigator, who now lives in South Africa, caused an article about his suspicion of his plane's involvement in Miller's disappearance to be published in a South African newspaper. He thus set in motion a sequence of events which resulted in a further investigation of the RAF records. It turned out that, true, no RAF bombing missions were officially recorded for that date, but yes, there was one flight of 150 Lancasters which had been sent out but then ordered back.

What prompted the navigator to remember now that his fellow crew members had seen a Norseman D-64 crash in the Channel that day after their jettisoned bombs had exploded? He saw a rerun of the movie *The Glenn Miller Story* in South Africa. As a further irony, he had first seen the movie in 1954, and had realized that his crew's bombs might have been responsible for Miller's death. But when he approached newspaper reporters on the matter, they didn't pay any attention.

Of course, there were lots of airplane accidents over England and the English Channel during that period. Thousands of bomber crews were zipping all over the sky, going to continental Europe and coming back. Most of us had little training compared to today's airline crews, and air control systems were nothing like the sophisticated current ones. My crew got to England about six weeks after Glenn Miller's disappearance. By that time our planes were so numerous that there was more danger to young bomber crews in our chaotic daily pre-dawn rendezvous with planes from our own squadrons than there was from enemy action over Germany. Losing one small Norseman D-64 was no big deal.

What made it important, of course, was that Glenn Miller was on it, and he was everybody's darling. His sweet music stood for peace and for good times past and—if we all made it back—yet to come. I remember his death as a personal loss. It was so to millions of us, somewhat the way John Lennon's death was to my current students and their contemporaries.

Historian Lillian de La Torre once advanced a theory that ran something like this: any historical mystery will eventually be solved if there is sufficient continuing interest in it and curious investigators are prompted to explore it for long enough. Glenn Miller's death was such a long-standing mystery. I'm glad it is solved after forty years.

Hap Arnold: America's First Airman! Army Air Force, WWII

by Jack Stankrauff, Historian of the Yankee Air Force

Reprinted with Permission from Yankee Wings, July-September 1995

On June 20, 1941, the U.S. Army Air Forces officially came into being (replacing the Army Air Corps). Hap Arnold began organizing and staffing an organization which now was much closer to his vision and to those of air power advocates. (Arnold's title was changed to Commanding General six months later, with an added star.)

DECEMBER 7, 1941—WAR!

Arnold inspected two B-17 squadrons at Hamilton Field, California prior to their departure for the Philippines on Saturday, December 6, 1941. These same aircraft arrived over Pearl Harbor in the midst of the Japanese Navy's surprise attack. When Arnold learned of the attack, he exclaimed, "How could the Japs be so stupid?"

As America entered the war, one of Arnold's first major objectives was to bring the AAF up to strength in aircraft, facilities, and doctrine. This job was made easier by the reorganization of the War Department, which he and Spaatz had proposed long ago. Pearl Harbor was the catalyst for this reform. Under the reform completed in March of 1942, the War Department was split into the air forces, ground forces, and supply. Now the AAF was not only equal with the Army ground forces, but was also one step closer to independence.

In the days following Pearl Harbor, Arnold spent many hours poring over maps. He painstakingly noted small details of islands, mountains and peninsulas which would be vital and strategic in the coming war years.

Arnold tried to follow an established office routine during the war. A typical Arnold duty day was described by Geoffrey Perret: "He would arrive for work around 7:30 each morning and tackle the stack of cables that had come in overnight. There would be as many as 1,000 messages from around the world. All would have been reviewed; the most important 40 or 50 were on his deck. There would be a pile of plans, studies, and reports to read, but Arnold insisted that the contents of each be reduced to a half-page summary. He'd read the summary. Occasionally, he'd ask for the original document. The hundreds of letters that arrived each day were reduced to a list of one-sentence summaries. He'd scan the list and decide which letters he wanted to read in full. Reading alone would keep Arnold occupied for much of the day. When he had finished with the cables and correspondence, the briefers would come in and offer a 30 to 45 minute rundown on operations in theaters of war throughout the world during the past 24 hours. They'd offer a statistical breakdown on what the AAF had done and its state of readiness. They'd also provide him with the latest top-secret information from spies or code-breaking that affected the air war. The rest of the day was spent mainly talking to people, in person or on the phone. Arnold was blessed, moreover, with an ability to read an official document while holding a conversation. That enabled him to continue reading as documents flowed non stop across his desk."

Arnold hated staff meetings, committees, and other military routine. He issued informal directives—typically a quick note scrawled on a single sheet of paper and passed to an officer with orders to expedite it. He possessed a brilliant mind, which enabled him to go straight to the heart of a complex matter. He abhorred the red tape of military bureaucracy, with its myriad of time-consuming paperwork. "Hitler won't wait that long," he said, "and neither will I!"

Arnold impulsively drove himself, and as a result, suffered five heart attacks during the war. One historian wrote, "To many, at the time and later, Arnold *was* the Army Air Force.

He threw himself into his work in a way that was both impressive and deplorable. He didn't delegate anything, unlike Marshall, who had freely delegated to mere majors and lieutenant colonels powers that few generals would ever possess. Every day Arnold got involved in decisions large and small, like a man suffering from deprivation. Instead of having deputies with real authority, he had five aides with fancy titles, but they were little more than messenger boys. Marshall, by way of contrast, chose strong, able and decisive staff officers, such as General Joseph McNarney, whom he made deputy chief of staff. Like Marshall, they believed in the power of well-run organizations to get results and he trusted them to make decisions in his name, often without telling him what they'd done. Arnold couldn't bring himself to do that. The pivot of Arnold's management style was his legendary impulsiveness. He would stop people walking past his door and tell them to drop everything they were doing and go across the country or overseas, and tackle some problem that had just landed on his desk. On one famous occasion he ordered the chief air surgeon to head for Wright Field and work the bugs out of a troublesome engine. He'd noticed the brigadier general's stars, but not the medical Corps insignia. The impulsiveness was a form of stress management. A problem was stress, and by dumping it into someone's lap he'd gotten rid of it for now."

THE "CHART TRICK"

As the war went into 1942, the AAF was threatened by superior fighters—the Zero (code-named *Hap* early in the war until Arnold ordered it changed to *Hamp*) and the Messerschmitt ME 109. The press picked up on this, belittling our airplanes as inferior and causing the deaths of young, brave American pilots.

Determined to set the record straight, Arnold had a chart posted in his office showing the performance of the world's fighter planes, although the planes were not identified. "Then he asked one of the country's most outspoken aviation writers to examine the chart and tell him which aircraft the AAF ought to buy. The writer's first choice turned out to be the P-47; second was the P-38; third was the P-51. His newspaper, *The New York Herald-Tribune*, went overnight from being one of the AAF's fiercest critics to being one of its most reliable friends. When Arnold pulled the chart trick on another hostile aviation writer, the man was so thoroughly converted that he gave up his job and joined the AAF."

"SPECIAL AVIATION PROJECT"

In the first six months after Pearl Harbor the Allies sustained a string of defeats which had a significant adverse effect upon the public's will to win. A bold stroke was needed to jolt public opinion and that stroke began as the "Special Aviation Project." Navy Captain Francis Low conceived a plan to attack the Japanese capital with twin-engined bombers launched from an aircraft carrier. Arnold assigned to the project one of his most experienced and innovative staff officers, Lt. Col. Jimmy Doolittle. Although Arnold did not want him to lead the mission, Doolittle took charge of all USAAF support, from the selection of the North American B-25 as the bomber, to the recruiting and training of the crews.

Upon giving the Chief a progress report, Doolittle asked to lead the mission himself. Arnold told him to check with his Chief of Staff, General Millard Harmon. "I smelled a rat," Doolittle recalled later. Expecting that Arnold would phone Harmon and forbid him to lead the mission, Doolittle hurried to the Chief of Staff's office before the call was made. Using all of his persuasive abilities, Doolittle told Harmon that he wanted to lead the Tokyo mission, implying that if it was all right with him, it was all right with Arnold. "Sure, Jimmy, it's all yours," Harmon replied.

While not a great success in terms of a blow to the enemy's war-making potential, the Doolittle Raid was a tremendous boost for Allied morale, as well as exposing the vulnerability of the Japanese homeland to aerial attack. It also forced Japanese Admiral Isoruku Yamamoto to develop a plane to draw out and destroy the American carriers missed by the Pearl Harbor attack. The resulting Battle of Midway in June 1942 severely crippled the Japanese carrier forces, which led in turn to a shift in the balance of power in the Pacific Area. After the raid Doolittle was promoted to brigadier general and awarded the Medal of Honor.

ARNOLD AND "THE MURDERER"

Arnold used Doolittle's piloting skills for another task, too. The Martin B-26 Marauder (variously nicknamed "The Murderer" and "Widow Maker") was causing the AAF problems. Propellers over speeded on takeoff, causing spins into the ground. "One a Day in Tampa Bay" became the ominous slogan at a Marauder training field in Florida. Arnold sent Doolittle to demonstrate the Marauder to trainee pilots, as well as the famous aviatrix, Jacqueline Cochran. After finishing a flight, she said anyone afraid to fly one was a "sissy." (Arnold and Doolittle ensured Marauder crew safety by getting the Martin Company to make wing and engine changes. As a result of these changes, the Marauder became one of the finest aerial weapons of the war.)

MacARTHUR AGAIN

If Arnold thought that after the Mitchell court martial and the Alaskan flight he could avoid further encounters with Douglas MacArthur, he was mistaken. ISAAF General Harold George, who headed air operations in the Southwest pacific, continually fought with MacArthur over tactics, supplies, and practically everything else. The air war suffered because of their bickering, so Arnold proposed that General Frank Andrews replace George. MacArthur wouldn't hear of it—he had given Andrews a written reprimand in 1935 for extolling the B-17. Arnold then nominated Doolittle, which also angered MacArthur because the Navy used an entire carrier task force to position Doolittle's bombers to raid Tokyo, yet couldn't send reinforcements to his beleaguered forces in the Philippines. Arnold then sent General George Kenney, who the imperious MacArtlhur finally accepted.

"ARNOLD LINE"

Arnold was a genius with logistics. With AAF bases scattered over the world needing supplies, he initiated the Air Transport Command to not only carry vital material, but also to ferry planes. (Today's Air Force reflects Arnold's concept of a worldwide logistics system.) To ferry planes to England, routes were carefully surveyed and landing fields built, complete with refueling and weather facilities.

WASPs

Arnold concurred in the formation and support of the Women Air Force Service Pilots (WASP) organization. WASPs performed admirably during the war, ferrying all types of planes—from fighters to bombers and other training missions, including searchlight and radar tracking, gunnery and mock attack missions on ground troops. Arnold lauded their accomplishments: "It is on record that women can fly as well as men. We will not again look upon a women's flying organization as experimental."

Arnold chose his old flying comrades, Carl Spaatz and Ira Eaker, to respectively command the Eighth Air Force and its bomber force. They saw their vision of a strategic bombing force attacking the enemy's industrial heartland in accordance with the Mitchell gospel. Arnold organized the Committee of Operations Analysts to study German and Japanese industry and transport and to recommend targets for attack missions.

MISADVENTURE?

During 1940 and 1941, German operations in Holland, Belgium, and Crete interested Arnold. In February 1941 he ordered Wright Field to develop "a glider that could be towed by an aircraft (capable of) transporting personnel and material and seizing objectives that cannot normally be reached by conventional ground units." Then he sent Col. Michael Murphy to formulate tactics. The USAAF and Army had few gliders available and practically no training programs underway. Furthermore, few military leaders believed in the canvas and wood gliders, which were slow, easy antiaircraft and ground fire targets. One Arnold staffer worried: "The man who sold General Arnold on gliders is Hitler's best friend!" Wright Field designers came up with the CG (Cargo Glider)-4As.

Arnold witnessed an impressive display of the glider's combat capabilities in North Carolina on August 4, 1943—the famous "Pea Patch Show"—orchestrated by Murphy. After briefings and dinner the VIPs were bussed to the demonstration as twilight turned to darkness. They thought they were going to another briefing, but Murphy had planned a demonstration of night glider operations. This was a very touchy subject in view of the debacle at Sicily a few weeks prior, when a breakdown of inter-service coordination had resulted in the destruction of numerous gliders and their tow planes by U.S. Navy anti-aircraft fire.

As Murphy extolled the virtues of gliders, ten CG-4As cut loose from their tow planes in the dark sky several miles away, and headed for a dim light which was concealed from the VIPs. Murphy's booming voice prevented the audience hearing the muffled thumps as the gliders landed and disgorged their loads. On command the field was brightly illuminated, to reveal the gliders and combat-ready troops arrayed practically in the VIPs' laps. Ever the showman, Murphy had saved the best for last. As the audience stared at the scene, a nine-piece band exited, playing the Air Corps' song. Arnold returned to Washington convinced that fully loaded gliders could be effectively employed in darkness.

THE COMBINED BOMBER OFFENSIVE

Early in the war Arnold urged the British to cooperate with the Combined Bomber strategy. Relations were strained with the Royal Air Force, but Arnold mollified them. England's Prime Minister Winston Churchill believed in air power too, but wanted the USAAF to join the RAF in night missions. Due to the urgings of Spaatz and Eaker (as instructed by Arnold) the Prime Minister changed his mind and agreed to the USAAF bombing by day and the RAF by night.

Arnold vehemently disagreed with the British on the grounds of inhumanity when they suggested carpet-bombing German cities. He believed in crippling air strikes on German military and industrial targets. The "Round the Clock" plan was finally agreed to by the British and Americans at the Casablanca Conference in 1943. Now respected on both sides of the Atlantic, and supported by President Roosevelt and the Joint Chiefs of Staff, Arnold received his fourth star in 1943.

Arnold and the entire Eighth Air Force command hierarchy originally believed that heavily armed bombers in massed formations could easily defend themselves without fighter escort, a doctrine from the 1930s, until the Luftwaffe destroyed this fallacy with their cannon. In a letter dated August 24, 1942, Arnold wrote Spaatz that Eighth Air Force bomber operations "...can be extended, as soon as the necessary size force can be built up, into the heart of Germany *without fighter protection* over the whole range of operations." Actually, as late as 1943 USAAF production priorities were bombers first, medium and light bombers second, then reconnaissance planes, transports, and finally, fighters. The USAAF desperately needed a long-range fighter that could accompany the bombers all the way to and from the targets.

To solve the problem, Arnold sent General Barney Giles to North American to find ways to extend the range of the P-51 Mustang. Giles' suggestion to increase the fighter's fuel capacity by 300 gallons was met with healthy skepticism by the Chief Engineer, Dutch Kindelberger, and the company's president, but an attempt was begun. In conjunction with design changes to install the Rolls Royce Merlin engine, additional fuel capacity was added in the wings. The increase in performance was phenomenal, and the Mustang was changed from a cart-horse into a thoroughbred.

"DECLARATION OF INDEPENDENCE"

The use of Eighth AF units to support the North African invasion in November 1942 greatly incensed Arnold, Eaker, and Spaatz. They were further upset by continual command difficulties between the Army ground forces and AAF personnel. With the insistence and support of Arnold, Marshall issued Field Manual FM 100-20 *Command and Employment of Air Powers* on July 21, 1943 which stated that air and land forces were: "...co-equal and interdependent forces, neither is an auxiliary of the other. The gaining of air superiority is the first requirement for the success of any major land operation...Land forces operating without must take such security measures against hostile air attack that their mobility and ability to defeat the enemy land forces are greatly reduced. Therefore, air forces must be employed primarily against the enemy's air forces until air superiority is obtained. The inherent flexibility of air power is its greatest asset. Control of available air power must be centralized and command must be exercised through the air forces commander if this inherent flexibility and ability to deliver a decisive blow are to be fully exploited. Therefore, the command of air and ground forces in a theater of operations will be vested in the superior commander charged with the actual conduct of operations in the theater, who will exercise command of air forces through the air force commander and command of ground forces through the ground force commander." This doctrine worked well for the rest of World War II. Just as important, FM 100-20 signaled a separateness of the USAAF from Army ground forces.

While Arnold gave of himself during his career and especially during the war, he expected the same from both the forces he commanded. He increased bomber crew missions in the European Theater from 25 to 30 and later to 35. Statistics proved that the more experienced crew was more effective and would survive. This was especially true when the Allies gained air superiority in Europe.

General Carl Spaatz always carried bomb strike photos with him to show world leaders and VIP visitors. Arnold picked up this habit. An idea struck Arnold: A magazine for AAF personnel all over the world. In 1943, *Impact* was born, a monthly magazine classified confidential which carried stories and pictures of military aviation, intelligence information, operational data, new aircraft developments, and tactics written by ex-newspapermen and magazine writers with deadline immediacy. *Impact* was a popular morale-builder at AAF facilities all over the globe.

CHENNAULT

While morale was important to Arnold, some personnel were not, including Claire Chennault. The two locked horns in (1933?), when Arnold commanded March Field. Back then Arnold subscribed to the theory that heavily armed bombers "...would always get through." Arnold never forgot Chennault's abrasive challenges of this dogma. "Who is this damned fellow Chennault?" he sarcastically asked.

Frustrated with the generals' hide-bound attitudes toward fighters, Chennault resigned from the service in 1937, after which Madam Chiang Kai Shek hired him to organize and train the Republic of China's air force. Concerned over Japanese advances in China, President Franklin D. Roosevelt intervened on several occasions, and at least twice in matters involving the U.S. Army Air Force. An April 15, 1941 executive order allowed US. military pilots to resign their commissions to fly to China for a year, and then return to their respective rank and service. These pilots manned Chennault's American Volunteer Group (better known to the public as the Flying Tigers); however, the U.S.

military brass regarded them as paid mercenaries. Just as badly needed in China were modern fighter aircraft. After Chennault's appeals for aircraft were turned down by both the Army and Navy, FDR and Navy Secretary Frank Knox intervened to arrange for the transfer to China of 100 Curtiss P-40s. For this Arnold would pay Chennault back later.

Arnold promoted Clayton Bissell, a World War One fighter ace and one of the pilots who bombed the German battleships in 1921 with Mitchell, to major general with a date of rank *one day* prior to Chennault's. Bissell was ordered to command the 10th AF in the China-Burma-India Theater, where he outranked 14th AF Commander Chennault.

Colonel Robert L. Scott was another who felt Arnold's wrath. A combat veteran who stayed on after the Flying Tigers were disbanded in July 1942, Scott performed brilliantly as Commanding Officer of the 23rd Fighter Group. When his tour was over, however, Arnold ordered him back home for a nationwide publicity tour in connection with his book, *God Is My Co-Pilot*. When Scott continued to request a return to China, and aware of his close relations with Chennault, Arnold sternly lectured him: "We are in the military profession. We do not dabble in politics. Go down there and tell those ladies [of the American Legion Women's Auxiliary in Orlando, Florida] about the Air Force. If you talk about political matters, I will send you to South America where there is no war!"

When Scott gave his talk, the nation was immersed in controversy over labor leader John L. Lewis and his United Mine Workers, whose strike was threatening to slow down the war effort. In response to one persistent woman's questions about the strike, Scott finally relented and said it was only his personal opinion, but he'd shoot down the labor union leader for slowing war production. This comment made nationwide headlines the following day. Months later Arnold cornered Scott in a bar, and snapped, "Scott, I damn well thought I'd find you here. I've watched you all evening, but with all the amenities here, there hasn't been time to ask you a question which has been troubling me for almost a year. It's about that talk you gave to those ladies in Orlando. Before I leave I want the un-garbled truth from you. You weren't really stupid enough to shoot down that labor leader with six .50-cal machine guns, were you?"

"Sir, I said it," he replied, "but I explained both before and afterward that it was just my personal opinion and not that of the War Department."

Arnold, now livid, retorted, "Personal opinion hell! Son, as long as you wear that uniform, *you don't have a personal opinion!*"

On the other hand, Arnold could treat his top flyers with paternal humor. When he wanted Major Richard Bong, the highest-scoring AAF fighter ace (40 kills), out of combat, Arnold wired Fifth Air Force commander General George Kenney: "Major Bong's excuses in matter of shooting down three more Nips noted with happy skepticism at this headquarters. Subject officer incorrigible. In Judge Advocate's opinion, he is liable under Article of War 122." (Article 122 referred to a willful or negligent damage to enemy equipment on aircraft.) Bong had been ordered to fight only when attacked, and not to seek out enemy planes to shoot them down. Bong was later awarded the Medal of Honor. Arnold saw to it that Bong was brought home.

Arnold was just as quick with action as with his tongue. When German V-1 and V-2 rocket attacks were terrorizing England in 1944, he came under pressure from British and American military and civilian officials to destroy the launch sites using air power. Arnold first wanted low level attack tests made. Weary of Material Command at Wright Field dictating to him what he could or couldn't do, Arnold had set up his own research and development center at Eglin Field in Florida. Here were created remote-controlled gun turrets, Azon guided bombs, napalm, and other innovative aerial weaponry. He phoned the commander of Eglin Field and ordered him to build test sites: "I want the job done in days—not weeks. It will take a hell of a lot of concrete…give it first priority and complete it in days. Weeks are too long!" The sites were completed and the tests were flown, and they aided in the destruction of the German rocket installations.

BETTER HIS CAREER

As early as November 1939, Arnold wanted a bomber with a 5,000 mile range to replace and be superior to the B-17 and B-24. The first candidate was the Douglas XB-19, but it was underpowered. Boeing's XB-29 Superfortress design was accepted in 1941. Just in case the Boeing bomber didn't work, Consolidated built roles of carrier-based and land-based aircraft. No land or sea campaign could have been won without the command of the air. While air power alone did not defeat the enemy, it was critical to the outcome of the sea and air battles. Thus, Arnold shrewdly wrote the evaluation to disarm the critics of his dream of an independent air force.

The Chief of Staff was ready for retirement, but who would succeed him? The top candidates with four-star rank were George Kenney, Joseph McNarney, and Carl Spaatz. Kenney was experienced in tactical, not strategic, air power. McNarney had served throughout the war as a staff officer. Spaatz was chosen based largely on his wartime strategic experience in the European and Mediterranean Theaters. Arnold retired on February 28, 1946 and moved to Sonoma, California in June. He and his wife Bee raised four children, one girl and three boys (one son died in 1927). Arnold relaxed at his 50-acre ranch, raised prize cattle, and enjoyed his hobbies of furniture making and quail and pheasant hunting. (During a wartime leave, he was accidentally shot in the head and shoulders. He wasn't seriously injured, however, since the shot came from a long distance away and he was protected by his glasses and a heavy hunting coat.)

A DREAM COMES TRUE

Thanks to his pre-war efforts, astute maneuvering during World War II and the USAAF's wartime performance, Arnold's dream of an independent air force came true on July 26, 1947 with president Truman's signature on the National Security Act of 1947.

While Henry Arnold spent billions during his military career, by 1949 his personal financial resources were very low. He appeared in beer advertisements and even tried to get back on active duty. His royalties from *Global Mission* weren't enough. Arnold died of a heart attack on January 15, 1950. His estate was a $20,000 insurance policy. His wife struggled along on a $75 per month widow's pension and supplemented her meager income by selling real estate.

Arnold was unique in aviation history annals. One historian summarized Arnold's significance in aviation history: "Arnold provided firm but often erratic leadership. He was such a strong and singular figure that it is impossible to imagine

174

anyone like him ever leading the Air Force again. Modern military bureaucracies, dominated as they are by committees and staff studies, don't allow men who are so idiosyncratic to rise to the top. For every fault, though, Arnold offered a compensating strong point, such as his belief in and his love of innovation and improvisation."

Over his career, Arnold received many decorations, including two Mackay Trophies (1912 and 1934), the Distinguished Flying Cross (1936), the Collier Trophy (1942), the Distinguished Service Medal (1943) with two Oak Leaf Clusters (awarded later), the Victory Medal, three theater ribbons, plus numerous foreign decorations, awards and medals. He was inducted into the National Aviation Hall of Fame at Dayton, Ohio in 1967.

Note: (Ann and I and our 7 year old son Clark met Mrs. Arnold by chance, and Clark knew of her husband, and she was impressed. Here are the contents of a letter she wrote him July 23, 1965. "Mrs. Henry H. Arnold, El Rancho Feliz, Sonoma, California—Dear Clark:- Thank you for your card from the Air Academy. I wish you could see a parade when the whole regiment is there. It's an inspiring sight. The enclosed is a replica of the tracking ship the USAFS 'General H. H. Arnold' and has taken part in the latest space flights. My boys use these pins as tie pins but you could put it on that wonderful blouse of yours. Please give my regards to the family and thanks again. Sincerely, Sharon P. Arnold. Mrs. "Hap" Arnold."... (Another time she sent Clark a couple of the general's personal insignia—which we still have—with the comment she would have sent more but some Sgt. took most of the items.)

His Bravery Was No Act
by Randolph E. Schmid Associated Press

WASHINGTON—Lots of actors play war heroes on the screen. James Stewart was one in real life. A decorated World War II bomber pilot who returned from battle to star in *It's A Wonderful Life,* Stewart has been commemorated on a 41-cent postage stamp that was recently released. Stewart served in the 445th BG, 453rd BG and 2nd Combat Wing of the 8th Air Force. He flew twenty bombing missions over Germany, including one over Berlin, after wangling combat duty when commanders would have preferred to use a movie star for morale-building work at home. As a squadron commander, Stewart flew many dangerous missions when he could have sent others instead, recalled Robbie Robinson, a sergeant who was an engineer-gunner in Stewart's B-24 squadron. But while Stewart rose to colonel during the war and later retired as a brigadier general in the reserves, he didn't stand on ceremony.

Robinson, of Collierville, Tennessee, recalled one time when a creative tail gunner managed to "liberate" a keg of beer from the officers club. That evening, Stewart wandered into a hut where some men were resting, picked up a cup, walked over to the "hidden" keg, poured himself a beer and sat back and drank it slowly, relaxing in a chair. "We were shaking in our boots," Robinson said. But Stewart merely got up, wiped out the cup, asked the men to keep an eye out for a missing keg of beer, and left.

Another time, Robinson recalled in a telephone interview, his plane landed behind another that was stuck on the end of the runway, nearly clipping its tail. After watching this, Stewart rubbed his chin and commented: "Ye gods, sergeant, somebody's going to get hurt in one of these things." "Once in your lifetime, someone crosses your path that you could never forget, and that was Jimmy Stewart," Robinson concluded.

Dedicated in ceremonies at Universal Studios, Hollywood, California, this was the 13th stamp in the "Legends of Hollywood" series. A separate ceremony was held at the Jimmy Stewart Museum in Indiana, Pennsylvania, the actor's hometown. "It's our privilege to pay tribute to James Stewart, a fantastic actor, a great gentleman, a brave soldier, and an inspirational human being who truly led a wonderful life," Alan C. Kessler, vice chairman of the postal governing board, said in a statement.

Other highlights from Stewart's career include the movies *Rear Window, Vertigo,* and *The Man Who Knew Too Much,* all directed by Alfred Hitchcock.

Stewart played a country lawyer in *Anatomy of a Murder* and played a lawyer again in *The Man Who Shot Liberty Valance,* a western.

He won an Oscar for best actor in *The Philadelphia Story* in 1940.

Stewart died at age 89 on July 2, 1997.

One Day in the Life of Aviation Ordnance
by Ben Hooker (458th)

It is late evening, May 7, 1944, and the second shift of 754th Ordnance is reporting for duty. The 754th is part of the 458th Bomb Group (H) stationed just outside Norwich, England. The ordnance office is a little cubicle located along the side of the big hangar near the control tower. As we enter, the clerk doesn't look up from his typewriter, for he knows that someone will ask the inevitable questions, "Have we been alerted?" or "What is the bomb load?" Most of the time he doesn't know any more than we do, so his answer is usually meant to deceive. If we can find out the type of bomb ordered we can speculate on the target, or at least the type of target.

As the day crew has cleaned up most of the work, a few of us drift down to flak suit storage under the pretext of checking their condition, but actually to goof off more than anything else. Someone decides he is hungry. We ante up the shillings required to send for a few pounds of fish and chips, and he slips out through a hole in the fence and comes back shortly with a bundle wrapped in a London or Norwich newspaper.

Flak suits are just about as popular with the air crews as car seat belts are now. Pilots (particularly new ones) usually sat on them until a heavy barrage ventilated the cockpit—then they had a change of attitude. It is our job to place one for every crew position.

At about 2200 hours the order comes down—the mission is on, and a lot of work by a lot of men is required this night before the big birds can fly. Of course we still don't know where the target is, but we later learn that it is Brunswick. Bomb load is 12 500 lb. GP, with M-103 nose and M-106 tail fuze, instantaneous. All crews mount their bomb service trucks (BST) and race to the bomb storage area. Since all four squadrons are vying to be first to load, there is some confusion and traffic congestion. After a wait that seems interminable, we are finally loaded with bombs, fins, fuses and other accessories required to put together a bang big enough to ruin Herr Hitler's day.

The big birds (B-24s of the 754th) are sitting on the hardstands waiting for the eggs to be loaded. Each bomb is moved by dolly to the bomb bay, hoisted and attached to the shackle, fused, arming wires attached, and safety pins checked and tagged. This is repeated until all aircraft are loaded. My notes indicate that AC #276 is already loaded from a previous mission, probably aborted. Normally if a mission is scrubbed all bombs must be removed and returned to storage, making double work.

Dawn is just breaking as we finish the last plane, and it won't be long until preflight and then the air crews show up for the day's business. We head for the mess hall and some hot chow, and then to the barracks for some "sack time."

I'm just barely asleep when one of the day crew awakens me to inform that one of the planes we just loaded has crashed and burned on takeoff. It is "Belle of Boston," AC #42-52404, and the pilot is Lt. Paul Kingsley, my cousin. I can't get back to sleep, so I sit on the side of my bunk and smoke a cigarette. I have previously witnessed crippled bombers come in and the customary red flare arcing skyward indicating wounded on board, but for the first time I'm really aware that people are being killed in this war.

I attend the military funeral for Lt. Kingsley at the Cambridge Military Cemetery, and later, when his body is brought back to the States I act as pall bearer at a second burial service.

Paul is buried in the same cemetery where my father and mother are laid to rest. When I visit the cemetery I invariably gaze at the 8th AF insignia on his grave marker and I'm transported in memory back to the date also inscribed there, May 8, 1944.

"The Gunner": The passing of an incredible era
by Bud Conder, CMSGT USAF RET Submitted by John J. Logan (467th)

The twilight has slipped away; the sun has set on the career of the Aerial Gunner. The last official flight of the Aerial Gunner has been completed. The Aerial Gunner has flown heroically into the pages of history aboard... a B-52G model Bomber, number 62595. This historic flight took place on 30 September at Castle AFB, CA. The Unit: The 328th Bombardment Squadron, of the 93rd Bombardment Wing, 15th Air Force.

The era of the Aerial Gunner began for the United States in 1917, during WWI.

John L. Cox, a member of the AFGA, wrote: "In the beginning, Man had no need for defense, because Man had no weapons. As time progressed, Man invented weapons and became his own enemy... by World War I, Man had evolved the airplane... Alas, they eventually began to shoot at each other during aerial flight. Thus was born the aerial defensive gunner."

During and since WWI, Aerial Gunners have done their share of flying and fighting for national defense. In air to air combat, through five wars, their aircraft have advanced from the slow open cockpit biplane, to the jet powered B-52.

WWI produced four Aces, all then called "Observers," who manned rear cockpit machine guns, downing twenty-two aircraft.

Gunners were overlooked in most cases and were not credited with aerial kills, because the public was more enamored with the fighter pilot. In the Argonne Offensive during WWI, gunners on observation planes shot down fifty-five aircraft; bombers accounted for thirty-nine.

Gunnery technology improved between WWI and WWII; better sighting devices, better guns and ammo and more guns were added to the bomber aircraft.

One thing didn't change in WWII; the "glory" still went to the fighter pilot. The thousands of enemy fighters downed by gunners were counted as a "team" effort, rather than crediting individual gunners. The Air Force claimed that record keeping was too difficult.

In spite of all the hardships encountered during aerial combat, the gunners gave an admirable account of themselves... Eighth Air Force bombers claimed 6,259 enemy aircraft shot down or destroyed; 1,836 probable, and 3,210 damaged. Their records exceeded that of the fighter pilots. Other theaters show similar results.

Dr. William Wolf, in an article appearing in the Winter 1991 issue of the USAF Museums Friends Journal, tells of the deadly expertise of S/Sgt. Donald B. Crossley, the highest scoring gunner in WWII; next highest was Michael Arooth, also in the ETO. After him, S/Sgt. Benjamin F. Warmer, flying in the MTO. Also discussed were T/Sgt. Arthur Benko, flying in the Pacific theater and S/Sgt. John Quinlan flying in the ETO.

S/Sgt. Donald Crossley, a Virginian and a B-17 tail gunner, flew combat with the 95th Bombardment Group of the 8th Air Force. On 11 May 1943, Don scored his first two "kills" while flying on the LITTLE LADY. On 13 June 1943, he downed two more fighter planes, as a crew member aboard the B-17 EASY ACES. On 25 July 1943, his count climbed again. On 12 August 1943, he added a double over Bonn, to bring his score to eleven victories. His last victory, the twelfth, came on his 22nd mission in September 1943. After his 25th mission he was assigned to instruct, but was killed from injuries suffered in a jeep accident.

Michael Arooth of the 379th Bombardment Group was credited with downing nine enemy aircraft.

T/Sgt. Thomas Dye scored eight "kills" while flying with the 351st Bombardment Group.

On 5 July 1943, S/Sgt. Benjamin F. Warmer (also known as the wild waist gunner), a member of the 99th Bombardment Group serving in the MTO, was credited with shooting down seven German fighter aircraft that single day, while flying over Sicily. Later, he downed two more, for a total of nine.

Johnny Foley, "Johnny Zero" as he was called, while serving in New Guinea during WWII, without ever firing a gun in his life, volunteered to replace an injured turret gunner on a Martin B-26. Johnny downed two Zeros on his first mission. Later he shot down five more enemy aircraft. He survived three crashes and completed thirty-two missions in the Pacific. In Europe, he flew 31 more missions as a bombardier.

T/Sgt. Arthur Benko, an Arizonian flying with the 387th Bombardment Squadron, 308th Bombardment Group, was the top scorer in the Pacific. Arthur, flying as a top turret gunner on a B-25, on 2 October 1943 shot down seven Zeros. Later, he shot down two more aircraft and was credited by 14th Air Force for nine more ground victories. T/Sgt. Benko was lost when shot down over Hankow.

S/Sgt. John Quinlan, the tail gunner on the famous B-17, the MEMPHIS BELLE (now stately displayed in a place of honor on Mud Island in Memphis, TN), downed five German aircraft. John volunteered for further combat and scored three more "kills" against the Japanese, flying on the B-29, the MARIETTA MISS FIT.

During the Korean War, (Police Action??), B-29 gunners were credited with twenty-seven confirmed "kills." An extremely remarkable feat since the crew "prop-job" B-29 was up against the soft MIG fighter.

In Vietnam, the first MIG "kill" was credited to S/Sgt. Samuel O. Turner, a tail gunner aboard B-52D, #60676, flying with the 307th Bombardment Wing, out of UTapao, Thailand.

At sunset, on 18 December 1972, Operation LINEBACKER II was launched, the most intensive bombing campaign since WWII. At 1945 hours, MIG KILLER ONE began its bomb run on Hanoi. The sixth bomber over the target, she was under heavy attack by SAM missiles. The bomb run lasted only 2 minutes; then after leaving the target, Turner's B-52 also came under enemy fighter attack. That night, S/Sgt. Sam Turner entered history books; he was the first bomber gunner to shoot down a MIG-21. His victory was witnessed and confirmed by M/Sgt. Lionel L. LeBlanc (a member of the AFGA).

In all there were five MIG-21 aircraft claimed by B-52 gunners during Operation LINEBACKER II, but only two were confirmed.

Six days later, on Christmas Eve, 24 December 1972, A1C Albert E. Moore, flying as the tail gunner on B-52D #55083, DIAMOND LIL, downed the second MIG-21. His "kill" was also confirmed.

In 1985, M/Sgt. Samuel O. Turner passed away, but his legacy is not forgotten, because B-52D #60676, MIG KILLER with a big red star painted on her side stands guard over the Memorial to Sam in Heritage Park, Fairchild AFB, Washington. Old MIG KILLER was the last B-52D flying and was retired in October 1983.

It is interesting to note that the Call Sign for B-52D #60676 on the flight on 18 December 1972, was called RUBY III.

448th Bomb Group Profiles
by George DuPont

Although Military regulations prohibited keeping animals, there were always a few who managed to find a stray dog or two. As crews passed through places like Belem and

Marrakesh, they also found ways to collect other animals such as the Spider monkey.

One such monkey made it half way across the South Atlantic before a joyful urge compelled him to jump out the waist gunner's window. (He was not seen again.).

Another such monkey with better manners made it to England. "Flak" as he was called was not your ideal house guest. Anything on a shelf or left unattended was at your peril. Among some of his more notable bizarre escapades was jumping onto a red hot stove (much to his chagrin) and eating a whole can of cheese from our "K" rations. The cheese weighed half as much as he did. The results were almost final. Only the love of a friendly medic (who gave him and an enema with an eye dropper) saved him. He was adopted by a radio operator who (using a razor) cut an oxygen mask down to fit him. He carried Flak on his missions, keeping him warm between his heated suit and his sheepskin jacket.

He made quite a sight peeping out of the jacket, only his beady eyes and furry head visible through the open zipper.

As the fates would have it, people were more concerned about Flak than whether the target was hit.

One day Fate terminated his career. Two bombs failed to release and the radio operator (forgetting about Flak) stepped into the bomb bay with a screwdriver and started prying the lower bomb latches loose. At this moment he caught sight of Flak sitting on the fins of the top bomb. Just as he reached up to grab him, both bombs fell away with Flak still attached.

When things got dull around the bar racks someone would remark, "Boy, I'll bet if the Germans saw him they'd think we had guided missiles," or "I wonder if Flak ever let go?" To which another would add, "No way, he was too smart for that."

M/Sgt. Alexander was a hard working dedicated crew chief. I remember the pride he felt when he learned that our base commander Colonel Mason was to fly his aircraft and lead the formation. He and his crew labored all night to fine-tune the engines and then; to complete their task, used buckets of varsol and, mopping away every evidence of crude and mud had the aircraft as shining as a new dime. It actually glowed in the misty dark.

Col. Mason noticed it too and approaching M/Sgt. Alexander asked politely, "Don't you like me sergeant?" Puzzled Alexander replied, "What do you mean?"

"Come with me," he motioned and walking across the perimeter he pointed to all the other dirty, dingy aircraft and said, "Sergeant, if you were a German fighter pilot and you saw this aircraft glistening in your eyes, wouldn't you want to *put out the light*? I want my aircraft to look like every other aircraft!" The sergeant and his crew mixed some mud with varsol and re-washed the aircraft to make it look dirty and dingy.

From Bomber Legends

Reading Bomber Legends rekindles memories of escorting B-17s and B-24s into the territorial belly occupied by Germany.

My stateside training for combat was some 50 hours in the razorback P-47, firing nary a shot. We did get considerable low-level navigation flights which was invigorating to skim at tree top level or below, but likely not amusing to the local residents who endured our devilish tactics.

Debarking at Tripoli, quickly found myself near the viallage of San Severo, westerly of Foggia at the spur of Italy. Displaying my best 2nd Lt salute to the squadron commander, Major Lee Wiseman, I was informed to take a short flight in the P-38. I had never seen a P-38 or been in the cockpit of a twin engine aircraft, so I asked for the Pilot's Operating Manual. He stated there was no manual available and move as I was scheduled for a mission.

Checked out a parachute, oxygen mask and canvas helmet and was jeeped to a P-38 where the crew chief instructed me on the procedure for getting to the cockpit by opening a retractable scissor-like ladder at the trailing end of the gondola fuselage. Settling into the cockpit, the crew chief reached over and started the engines. I felt at home in the cockpit. At the end of the dirt runway, which was the width of a residential street and some 2000 feet long at best, pushed the throttles forward and was impressed by the purr of 1400 horsepower on each side. With no external load, the counter-rotating props thrust me into the air in short order. This was love at first flight.

My first mission was a short strafing run in northern Italy, staying on the deck until reaching the target. The next day was an exposure to our primary mission; escorting long-range bombers, this time to Ploesti. Awoke that morning to the distant sound of bombers herding into formations and heading to the target. After a hefty breakfast – there were no snacks for the next five hours or more – the skies were silent as we were briefed on our role in protecting the bombers; namely, do not get sucked into a battle that would expose the bombers to assault. Briefly, we were to position between the bombers and any enemy aircraft, entering into battle only if the bombers were threatened. The more agile P-51s were responsible for engaging the enemy fighters.

Our flight became airborne some two hours after the bombers set course for the target area. We would rendezvous with the bomber formations about 150-200 miles from the target. Over the bomber formation, reduced RPM and increased the manifold pressure to conserve fuel. My more experienced tent mate instructed me on this procedure, which was passed over from Charles Lindbergh who was flying the P-38 in the Pacific area. We stayed two to three thousand feet above the bomber string in lazy S turns to stay abreast of the bombers and have better sight for enemy fighters.

The temperature inside the cockpit was the same as the outside temperature – damn cold – 50 to 60 degrees below zero. I had traded my leather jacket for British fur-lined boots, but my feet were numb. Looking down on the graceful B-17s I began to absorb the plight of the crews jammed in a tube of thin aluminum at sub zero temperature and sitting on several tons of explosives. Aggravating were the bursts of antiaircraft fire over the target – Ploesti – incessant blasts of fire leaving a thick cloud of black smoke. I agonized for the crews that flew into that pulsating mass of firepower with its attendant shrapnel. It did not seem plausible that any aircraft could survive such compact antiaircraft defense. No words or monuments can adequately portray the skill and courage of those bomber crews.

Nearing the flak area, we broke off coverage. Fighter pilots may not be the most intelligent lot, but neither the allied or German fighters penetrated the flak zone. While skirting the target area I noted a conspicuously large burst of flak which I reported in my intelligence debriefing. Only on a later mission did I realize those bursts were bombers receiving a direct hit in the bomb bay. We would pick the bombers up as they exited, often scattered vertically and horizontally. The German fighters preyed on stragglers or crippled aircraft. It was at this stage that we were more likely to engage the enemy.

Believe it was on my sixth escort mission to Ploesti that I was separated from my flight short of the target area, so maneuvered to the north to pick up any stragglers. Obviously too close to the flak zone, my plane took a hit in the right engine, which I feathered while pushing the throttle forward on the left engine to retain airspeed. The power in the left engine diminished, inadequate to maintain altitude, thus began a slow descent toward home, some 500 plus miles distance. My objective was to reach Yugoslavia, bail out and have the local tribes return me home through a U.S. friendly network.

Heading away from Ploesti, the visibility was unlimited and no other aircraft were in sight; it was like someone flipped a switch and the war was over. It was an eerie sensation being in a war zone of tranquility – and a bit lonely. I grasped the placid beauty of the quilt of farmlands and villages basking in an admixture of midsummer greens and scattered patterns of gray and brown. At about 15,000 feet, I could maintain altitude at a comfortable speed above stalling. However, I felt like a piñata hanging on a heavenly string awaiting someone to swat me.

In that moment of mixed emotions – serene anxiety – observed a crippled B-17 several miles to my left and eased toward it cautiously so as not to be mistaken for a German at the controls. In North Africa there were reports of downed U.S. planes being repaired, and German pilots mischieviously attacking allied planes. Hanging off the right wing of the B-17, the waist gunner waved and I signaled in return, comforted by the protection of their gunners and relaxed knowing some 16 or so other eyes were scanning the skies, allowing me to check my instruments and calculate my fuel and position for the flight home… I wondered how this would look on my fighter pilot resume: "Crippled B-17 escorts fighter to safety." At that juncture, I didn't care.

Am unaware how long I ambled along under the protective wing of that B-17 – seemed like hours. As we approached the mountains of Yugoslavia, I drifted down and away, picking up speed. Shortly, the gleaming Adriatic reflected the sun streams and some small boats were hugging the crusty shore, a scene that made me complacent. That was short lived as some tracers altered my composure, dictating some modest evasive action. I was directly over Spit where the Germans harbored one of the elite antiaircraft units. I assume most of the soldiers had called it quits for the day as I was an easy target. From there it was clear sailing.

I wonder if that B-17 crew made it back okay and are readers of Bomber Legends. I'd like to thank them for their hospitality and security of the escort.

Soldiers, Sailors and Airmen of the Allied Expeditionary Force!
Eisenhower's D-Day Speech

You are about to embark upon the Great Crusade, toward which we have striven these many months. The eyes of the world are upon you. The hopes and prayers of liberty-loving people everywhere march with you. In company with our brave Allies and brothers-in-arms on other Fronts, you will bring about the destruction of the German war machine, the elimination of Nazi tyranny over the oppressed peoples of Europe, and security for ourselves in a free world.

Your task will not be an easy one. Your enemy is well trained, well equipped and battle-hardened. He will fight savagely.

But this is the year 1944! Much has happened since the Nazi triumphs of 1940-41. The United Nations have inflicted upon the Germans great defeats, in open battle, man-to-man. Our air offensive has seriously reduced their strength in the air and their capacity to wage war on the ground. Our Home Fronts have given us an overwhelming superiority in weapons and munitions of war, and placed at our disposal great reserves of trained fighting men. The tide has turned! The free men of the world are marching together to Victory.

I have full confidence in your courage, devotion to duty and skill in battle. We will accept nothing less than full victory!

Good luck! And let us beseech the blessing of Almighty God upon this great and noble undertaking.

–Dwight D. Eisenhower

8th Air Force Nomads

by Sgt. Earl Anderson, Yank Magazine Staff Correspondent

Reprinted from 3D Strategic Air Depot Association Newsletter
(First published in Yank Magazine, circa 1944).

As the men of the Eighth Air Force started to pack for the long trek home or to the Pacific, many of the ground force men are probably reflecting that, being based in England, they really didn't see a lot of country. But there was one group that followed close behind the advancing armies and whose trails crisscrossed every part of four Continental countries, and then led into Germany. Their shop trucks rattled over the transport-cluttered roads of France, Belgium, Holland, Luxembourg and Germany, and often, following their map coordinates, the men left the main highways to come upon secluded regions where the sight of American GIs brought curious natives into the village street to see their "liberators."

These men made up the mobile crews of the Eighth Air Force Service Command on the Continent. In groups of ten, headed by a sergeant, they left their home bases for weeks at a time, either to repair or salvage Eighth Air Force planes that had been forced down on the Continent and were unable to reach any one of three emergency landing fields.

The mobile crews were part of the Continental operations of the 8th AFSC that sent back almost 1,300 bombers and fighters before V-E Day. Summing up the accomplishments, Col. J.M. McCullough, the C.O., said, "Prior to D-Day all planes that could not get back to England were either lost to the enemy or the English Channel. But since the first beachhead was secured, of 1,288 planes, valued at about $300,000,000, which were forced down in repairable condition, all but 67 were returned to England and made airworthy. Critical parts were also recovered from 422 un-repairable planes which crashed on the Continent."

The first man to reach France after D-Day was John R. Campbell. He was then a master sergeant, but later earned a field commission. Campbell flew into the beachhead on D-plus-11 to count the planes that were down and run a quick inspection on them to see if they could be repaired. The first group of men—13 of them landed seven days later with only hand tools, and, of course, field equipment and arms. They tackled the planes with

187

what they had, and with what they could "beg, borrow, steal or invent." One month after D-Day, two B-17s and one P-47 took off from the landing strips in France and headed for the depots in England.

Then began the race to satisfy the insatiable demands from the United Kingdom for planes to keep the divisions at full strength, and for parts that could be used to repair the damaged planes that had made their way home.

The "13 men and a jeep" grew into a full-blown Strategic Air Depot, and three landing fields were established on the Continent, where pilots were briefed in land in an emergency. The mobile crews went after those ships which had to land quickly on any old spot.

The crews were stocked with 10-in-1 rations. Sometimes they lived on those. Sometimes they scrounged. Sometimes they put up with other outfits near the plane they were repairing. Inspectors went ahead of them, finding the planes, putting guards on them, and marking them for "salvage" or for "repair." The crew would pile into their 6 x 6 shop truck as soon as one job was done and head for the next one, maybe miles away. They became the nomads of the Eighth Air Force.

When the pressure was on, as it was for months following D-Day, they started work at the crack of dawn, and finished at night using flashlights. They had to know every plane in the Eighth Air Force. No man could specialize. They took on Lightnings, Thunderbolts, Mustangs, Libs and Forts as they came. Hangars to protect them from the winter blasts were an unknown luxury.

"During those months it seemed like there wasn't anything between us and the North Pole but a bush," one of them said. "We'd keep a five or ten gallon can of oil burning near the plane to de-numb our hands."

As our armies pushed the Germans back, the Service Command men followed in their wake, and their shop trucks were familiar sights to the men in the ground forces.

They tell a story about one crew working on a plane in the Ardennes in the latter part of December. "Where's the front?" they called to a couple of infantry Joes. The men came over and watched the mechanics for a moment, then replied, "The front! If you wait a couple of hours it ought to be right here. Our outfit is regrouping a couple of miles further back."

Rommel: Leader of the Afrika Korps; Master of Mobile Warfare

Reprinted from Lincolnshire Military Preservation Society Magazine, Lincolnshire, England

Field Marshal Erwin Rommel (1891-1944) was one of the great generals of World War II, and his inspired leadership of his armored and mobile formations made him a legend in his lifetime, even among his enemies.

After serving in the First World War, he taught at the new infantry schools and in these inter-war years he caught the attention of Adolf Hitler. When war came in 1939, Rommel was commander of Hitler's personal headquarters. After the defeat of Poland, Hitler granted his request to be given command of a Panzer division.

The division that he took over was the 7th Panzer. As part of Army Group A, it was allotted an important part in the strategy that had been devised to break through the allied defenses in the Ardennes in May of 1940.

After the defeat of France, Rommel was recognized as an outstanding exponent of "Blitzkrieg," but his orders when he took up his next command were to be on the defensive. This command was of the German forces that had been sent to North Africa to shore up the tottering armies of their Italian ally, which were headed for Suez and beyond before being badly mauled and defeated by the British.

In spite of his orders, Rommel decided to take the offensive. This was the first of a long series of attacks, launched on 31 March 1941. The British, however, would not give up the port of Tobruk, which was only taken finally in November. Shortly afterwards, General Claude Auchinlech ordered the newly named British 8th Army against the Germans in Operation Crusader. This time the Allies had more success.

The first six months of 1942 saw Rommel recover from the setback of Crusader and take the offensive again. The initial German victories in this new offensive were stunning. The Gazala battles defeated the 8th Army and then Tobruk fell again to the Axis forces. Rommel decided to push on again to Alexandria, hoping to defeat the British totally in North Africa. He managed to reach El Alamein, but there, stiffening British forces forced him to a halt. He attempted many times to advance further, but failed in his objectives.

189

Under its new commander, Lieutenant-General Bernard Law Montgomery, the 8th Army stood firm.

As the autumn wore on, the Allies in turn prepared their counter-offensive, opened by the Battle of Alamein in October/November 1942. Rommel had supervised the construction of a very effective defensive position, and although numerically superior, the British forces found it hard to break; but eventually they did so, and the Afrika Korps began a long pull back. Meanwhile, the Allies had landed an Anglo-American Army in French North Africa and were soon advancing on Tunisia. The Axis forces in North Africa were soon inevitably squeezed to death, but nevertheless, Rommel fought an inspired retreat as he pulled back, eluding Montgomery's attempts to trap him and his much depleted army and at the same time giving the U.S. forces a bloody nose in Tunisia at the Kassarine pass. Rommel left Africa before the final Axis defeat in May of 1943.

In January of 1944, Rommel was handed the command of Army Group B, in France, preparing to meet the expected Allied landings in northwest Europe. He ordered great effort to be put into improving all beach defenses. After the successful Normandy D-Day beach landings, however, he clearly realized that the German Army would eventually have to retreat in the face of the invading forces. He advised Hitler of this. Hitler refused and Rommel gave some support to the plotters who were planning to assassinate the Fuhrer. When the plot failed and Rommel's name was linked with the plotters, he was given the option of standing trial or taking his own life. He chose the latter. What marks Rommel above most high ranking German officers was his insistence that moral standards must be observed at all times, on and off the battlefield—towards prisoners and civilians especially. This combination is rare in any epoch.

A Viking in the 8th Air Force
by Major Kenneth L. Driscoll (801st "Carpetbaggers")

He was a Norwegian national hero, but most Americans, including Army Air Force veterans, do not even recognize his name. Yet he was both an American and an 8th Air Force B-24 pilot!

Yes, Col. Bernt Balchen was one of the most talented and knowledgeable aviators of the 20th century. He was a superb aircraft mechanic, a precise navigator, and probably the most talented Arctic pilot of his time – and it is time you know the "whole" story!

He was born in 1900 in a small southern Norwegian town named Kristiansand. When he was about 21 years old, he got his wings in the Royal Norwegian Air Force. He spent several years gaining a vast amount of Arctic type flying throughout snowy, rugged, mountainous Norway.

In 1926 he was at Spitzbergen, an island about 500 miles north of the tip of northern Norway. He was there as a member of the expedition of the famous Norwegian polar explorer Capt. Roald Amundsen. They were preparing to be the first to fly across the North Pole (by dirigible, not aircraft).

While they were at Spitzbergen, U.S. Navy Commander Richard Byrd's ship arrived carrying a trimotor aircraft which was to be used by Byrd's expedition to fly across the North Pole. Byrd's pilot was Floyd Bennet.

Members of both expeditions, although rivals, became friendly. Bernt Balchen, since he was an expert in snowy, cold weather flying conditions, improvised and modified the skis on Byrd's aircraft so that it could safely take off under overloaded conditions.

Byrd's aircraft got to the North Pole first and then returned to Spitzbergen. When he returned to the United States by ship, he took Bernt Balchen with him. Balchen then became Byrd's pilot.

In the spring of 1927 there was a race on to see who would be the first to fly across the Atlantic Ocean. While Lindbergh was planning his flight from Roosevelt Field, Byrd was also planning his at the same time from the same airfield. Balchen was one of the two pilots of Byrd's aircraft. Lindbergh made the first successful Atlantic crossing. Byrd's aircraft flew across a month later. Balchen's extensive experience in instrument flying made it possible to safely cross the ocean under very adverse weather conditions.

Although he still loved his native Norway, he took out his first papers to become a citizen of the United States after he returned from France.

From 1920-30 he spent much of his time with Commander Byrd preparing for and successfully completing the first flight of an aircraft across the South Pole.

The crew of the expedition had a tremendous welcome when they returned to New York City in June, 1931. They then went to Washington D.C. where they were honored by President Hoover at a reception at the White House.

Soon thereafter, Balchen was served a subpoena by the U.S. immigration authorities. He had broken his residence requirements, after getting his first papers, by being with the Byrd expedition for two years outside of the United States, and was to be deported!

The story made the headlines that evening in all of the Washington D.C. newspapers. New York State Representative to Congress, Fiorello LaGuardia (later to become mayor of New York City), after discussing the matter with President Hoover, introduced a special bill to Congress the following day to grant Bernt Balchen full citizenship. That bill was passed and signed by President Hoover.

Balchen stayed very active in aviation activities during the rest of the 1930s. Some of his close friends and associates during that time were Charles Lindbergh, Amelia Earhart, Wiley Post, Floyd Bennet, Hap Arnold, Tooey Spaatz, Ira Eaker and Eddie Rickenbacker.

On June 30, 1941, six months before the U.S. entered into World War II, Balchen was in the Philippines delivering a PBY to the RAF when an urgent telegram came from General Hap Arnold, Commanding General of the U.S. Army Air Forces, requesting his immediate return to Washington.

On July 3, 1941, in a meeting with General Arnold, he was asked to join the Army Air Forces for a very special assignment. Balchen agreed, and was granted the rank of Captain.

His first assignment was to plan and supervise the construction of an airfield in southwestern Greenland. This airfield was named Bluie West Eight. It was later used by hundreds of aircraft going to and returning from Europe during WWII.

While there, he led rescue missions to save the crews of two B-17 type aircraft that had crashed hundreds of miles away on the icecap of Greenland after becoming lost.

He was directed by a top secret message from General Marshall, Washington D.C., to seek out and destroy a German weather station that had been secretly set up on the barren northeast coast of Greenland. He successfully accomplished that mission by using four bombers flying from Iceland.

In September 1943, Balchen was still in Iceland when General Arnold stopped over. Arnold asked what type of assignment he would like next. Balchen told him that he would like to assist the Norwegian resistance movement against the Germans occupying Norway.

Back in Washington, he had a meeting with General William (Wild Bill) Donovan, the head of the O.S.S. One of the missions of the O.S.S. in Europe was to train spies, saboteurs and organize resistance forces in German occupied countries. Balchen was briefed by O.S.S. in Europe personnel on some projects and sent to England.

With the backing of Generals Tooey Spaatz and Jimmy Doolittle of the 8th Air Force, and the O.S.S., Balchen was given the top secret project to organize and implement an airlift between Stockholm, Sweden and Scotland using modified, stripped-down B-24s.

There were thousands of military-aged men, Norwegian and others, stranded in Sweden, who could be used in the Allied war effort.

Armament was removed, and the B-24s had seats installed also. The exterior was painted dark green, without any identification. Crews in civilian clothing were issued passports and visas to enter Sweden, Finland and Russia.

The 801st Prov. Bomb Group (code name Carpetbaggers) supplied the B-24s, crews, and support to complete his missions. This group had been flying top secret night missions working with the O.S.S. dropping agents and supplies to resistance groups in German occupied countries, mostly France, at that time.

(Note: Just by chance, I was a pilot in the 801st BG (Carpetbaggers) from May 25, 1944 to August 27, 1944. I had 30 night missions during that three-month period flying from Harrington Air Base.)

Five modified B-24s were prepared at Bovington Air Base, north of London.

Due to its unique nature, this unit was assigned to headquarters, European Air Transport Command.

Although his mission was approved in late January, 1944, Balchen ran into much red tape (primarily from the English) in getting a suitable airfield to set up his operations. Finally, about the end of March, 1944, the King of Norway asked Winston Churchill to intervene, cut the red tape, and provide Balchen with facilities at a Royal Air Force Base for his operations. Within two days, Balchen got permission to operate out of Leuchars RAF base on the east coast of Scotland, north of Edinborough. The code name for his project was "Sonnie."

About 5,000 people were evacuated from Sweden to Scotland. Balchen's aircraft also flew hundreds of people and many tons of war material into Sweden, finding its way across the border to be used by the Norwegians resistance forces.

When the war started in Europe, Sweden stayed neutral. It had close ties with Germany and with its neighbor, Norway. But by early 1944, the Swedish people, and government, became pro-Allies and anti-Nazi.

Early in the summer of 1944, while Col. Balchen was in Stockholm on one of his many flights, he was contacted by an old friend who was pro-Norwegian and held a position very high up in the Swedish government. The Swedes had recovered, almost intact, a top secret experimental German V-2 rocket. Two were launched from the German coast into Sweden. Rather than make a diplomatic protest to the German government and let the Germans know where they landed, the Swedish government decided to turn one of the rockets over to the Allies. Balchen borrowed a C-47 cargo aircraft from his headquarters and his executive officer Lt. Col. Keith Allen picked up the three-piece V-2 rocket in Sweden and flew it back to Leuchars. It was then delivered to the English government at Farnsborough Air base near London.

This same Col. Allen was shot down and killed while on a secret mission (code name "Project Ball") to northern Norway a short while later. His mission was to drop an agent near the great German battleship Tirpitz, which was hiding in a deep narrow fjord. The agent was to spy on the Tirpitz and report back to England via radio any movement of the battleship.

After the agent was dropped, the aircraft developed engine problems over northern Norway. Rather than flying the long over-water flight back to Scotland, he elected to fly on to Murmansk, Russia for an emergency landing. As his aircraft was flying over the heavily defended seaport of Murmansk, it was shot down by Russian naval ships. Ten of the crew bailed out and were returned to Scotland by the British battleship HMS Rodney, which was at Murmansk. Col. Allen went down with the aircraft.

Around May, 1944, it was brought to Col. Balchen's attention that additional war supplies were urgently needed by the resistance forces in Norway. He got direct approval from HQ 8th Air Force to set up a miniature "Carpetbagger" operation to drop military supplies and agents into Norway. The code name for this secret operation was "Project Ball." It was also directly supported by the 801st B.G. (Carpetbaggers) from its base at Harrington, England. Around August 13, 1944 this group became the 492nd B.G. (Carpetbaggers).

Because of its very secret and sensitive nature, little has been published about Project "Where and When." This operation took place in Sweden in early 1945. Its mission was to transport over 1400 Norwegian police troops (trained in Sweden), a field hospital, and supplies from Kalax, Sweden to Kirkenes, Norway and other Norwegian towns when the Germans withdrew from northern Norway. Col. Balchen had ten C-47 cargo planes operating in Sweden before the end of the war in Europe. Prior to the day that the war ended there, he was in the Norwegian town of Kirkenes, which at the time was occupied by the Russians.

After World War II ended, Balchen returned to Norway and was president of Norwegian Airlines (DNL). He was also one of the original directors of Scandinavian Airline System (SAS).

In 1947 I met Col. Balchen a number of times; in fact he was a guest at my wedding in Oslo, April 21, 1948. Here is the background:

In February 1948 I was a captain, USAF, stationed at a training unit at Westover AFB, Massachusetts. I was then assigned to the U.S. Air Attache Office, American Embassy, Oslo, Norway as Assistant Air Attache.

About a week after I got to Oslo, about the end of February, on a Saturday morning as I was walking into the embassy office building in downtown Oslo, I met the U.S. Ambassador to Norway, Charles Ulrick Bay, who was also entering the building at the same time. I recognized him, and since I was in uniform, he recognized me as the new Air Force captain assigned to the embassy. He asked me if I had my family with me, and I told him that I was single but was thinking about getting married to my girlfriend who was back in the States. He said, "If you bring her over, I will give you a wedding." I decided to take him up on his offer. Since I was newly assigned to the embassy, I knew very few people in Oslo. The ambassador and my boss, the Air Attache, Major Dale Jensen, decided who should be invited to my wedding at the ambassador's residence at Five (5) Noblesgate, Oslo (this was a mansion given to the U.S. government by the famed Nobel family). The guests they invited were VIP from the Norwegian Air Force, U.S. Embassy, prominent Norwegians and Col. and Mrs. Balchen. We had a captive audience. I do not know of anybody in Oslo at the time who would not have accepted an invitation from the U.S. Ambassador to attend a function at the ambassador's residence.

Over an eight-month period in 1948, I met Col. Balchen at numerous social events. I really did not get to know him well, however. Our paths never crossed other than at social events. He was about 21 years older than I. He was a bird (full) colonel and I was a captain. He was deeply involved in rebuilding the Norwegian Airline (DNL), and being a director in starting a new international airline, Scandinavian Airline System (SAS). I remember him as being quite stout and speaking with a very distinct Norwegian accent.

Around November 1948 he was recalled by the U.S. Air Force and was assigned as commanding officer of the Tenth Rescue Squadron, Fairbanks, Alaska. He had been recommended to the Army Air Forces many years earlier, and was instrumental in establishing a base at Thule, Greenland. This did become a reality, and that base is part of the DEW LINE now protecting the northern approaches to the United States.

He was an advisor to King Haakon of Norway on aviation matters prior to, during, and after World War II.

He was honored for various achievements by Presidents Coolidge, Hoover, Roosevelt and Eisenhower.

He was the American Viking!

Patricia's Enduring Mission
by Angi Kennedy, from EDP Sunday, November 10, 2007

196

(For Patricia Everson, remembrance isn't only something that only happens every November; it is part of every single day. She tells how a whispered promise on a deserted 448th BG Norfolk airbase helped shape her life.)

The wind rattled the doors of the empty buildings, as Patricia Everson stood silently staring down the distance of the airstrip. Where the B-24 Liberators of the USAAF had once thundered to their takeoffs, now tufts of grass and weeds were insolently breaking a way through. Natural decay was slowly but surely reclaiming this deserted airbase at Seething, southeast of Norwich.

The village teenager had gone there in search of wild cowslips, but instead found herself pledging a promise that, many years later, would set her on a remarkable, life-changing mission. Patricia remembers that April day clearly. "Everything was so charged up with what had happened there. There and then, I swore I would never forget the men who had been based there."

Life and the years rolled on. Soon there would be little clue to the airbase's story left to catch the eye of anyone passing through Seething. Only the other people of the communities around the base would share the frisson of excitement whenever a trans-Atlantic accent was heard from a rare American visitor to the villages.

It was the early 1980s, and moves were afoot to create a memorial in the village and at the airfield to the 400-plus men based at Seething who had lost their lives in the Second World War. Patricia Everson, by then in her mid-40s, offered her help, raising funds for the event at which some of the former airmen and their families would be present.

For her, this would be a chance to fulfill a secret longing that had been burning away at her since childhood.

Patricia was a five- year- old schoolgirl when war was declared. She was one of the generation who can even now summon up the smell of the claustrophobic gas mask and the dank, stale air of the shelter in the garden. She grew up in the days of rationing, of course, of cod liver oil and malt supplements for undernourished youngsters, of sanctioned days off when she and her fellow schoolchildren would pick soft fruit, rose hips to be made into syrup, acorns to feed the pigs, and to collect aluminum foil and metal scrap to help the war effort.

Her father, Fred Knights, had joined up as a driver with the RAF. Patricia and her young brother, Reggie, did their best to help their mother, Jean, grow vegetables for their meals and collect water from the well.

Although she has no memory of hunger in those days of hardship, Patricia certainly recalls a sense of drabness. But that was to change in 1943. America had entered the war, and East Anglia was ideally placed to become its "airbase." Airstrips were being carved into the landscape, accompanied by mess halls, billets, and control towers. A mile outside the little village of Seething, the 58th Station Complement Squadron turned acre after acre of open field into a new airbase, ready for the arrival of the aircraft and flight crews of the 448th Bomb Group of the USAAF.

"I was nine years old when they came," Patricia said. Suddenly we went from the 300 to 400 people in the village to having 3,000 young Americans down the road with these huge B-24 Liberator bombers.

"We had been at war for quite a few years by then and, to some extent, we were still living under that sort of Victorian thing of us children being seen and not heard.

"But now the Americans treated us like equals, and they really endeared themselves to us children, happy to spend a lot of time talking to children like us. They were so friendly to everyone. They made quite an impression on the older girls too!

"They would cycle through the villages, and because all the road signs had been removed to confuse the enemy, they were forever asking where the nearest pub was and if we had got a big sister at home.

"You must remember, many of them were only young boys themselves. Their average age was 19—anyone in their mid-20s was called the old man of the crew!"

Many were astonished by the tough conditions that the English had been living in. "They wrote begging letters home, asking for things to give to the children," said Patricia. "They were extremely generous. When they heard that the Jenny Lind Children's Hospital was running short of supplies, they took things there, and they had a choir that would go singing round the wards.

"One of the Americans said he never realized how bad things had been here. He had an orange in his pocket and decided he would give it to the first child he came across. He gave it to this little boy who'd never seen one before, and he bit into it—he didn't know you had to peel it first.

"Most of the children wanted chewing gum, they called them 'the gum chumers', but I loved the comic strips out of their newspapers the most."

"The highpoint was the Thanksgiving and Christmas parties though, when the children of the surrounding villages, homes and evacuees were invited to the base. For the Thanksgiving party in 1943, they came down to the school in their trucks and I can remember even now the excitement of being lifted over that tailboard.

"When we got there it was the first time I had heard live music outside church, and the food was so different to ours— even the gravy was a different colour.

"I wanted to ask a lot of questions because I didn't know much about America. But I was seated at a long table with all the young Americans and they were firing questions at me. Suddenly I was too shy to ask anything and I just said yes and no and thank you."

The regret at this missed chance stayed with Patricia, and resurfaced all those years later in 1984 as the preparations took shape for the memorial service. This time, she told herself, she would have the courage to talk to the Americans about their lives.

"I was so looking forward to it," she said. "But two and a half weeks before the service my brother and mother were killed outright in a car crash at Kirstead."

For the tight-knit family, who had lived just doors apart at Seething, it was a terrible blow, and a shock for the community too which had been so focused on the memorial that it was about to see put in place for the U.S. airmen of four decades earlier.

"I went to the service, but I wasn't emotionally able to do what I wanted to," said Patricia. "After the Americans had gone home, I really felt I had failed myself for a second time.

"So I managed to get the names of the people in America who had sent contributions for the memorial. I wanted to write to them to ask them about their experiences.

"There was no one more badly equipped than myself. I couldn't type or write letters, but there was a drive inside me pushing me to carry on.

"First in my letters I had to clear the air so that they knew I wasn't an illegitimate child or an ex-girlfriend trying to track them down. Sometimes I would send out fifty letters and not get back a reply.

"Some of the men just weren't ready to look back. But the first time I got a letter with some black and white photos of when the man was at the base, I thought 'Yes, I can do this.' "

And gradually the letters began to arrive through the post, some just a few notes or names, others pouring out wartime memories. Today she has some fifty albums of their writings and hundreds of photographs, from official poses to relaxed off-duty shots of Americans on and around the base. Over the last twenty years, Patricia has gradually pieced together the jigsaw of names, numbers, memories and missions to build a comprehensive picture of life at Seething airbase from November 1943 to June 1945, when the Americans left. And in the process she has brought about reunions of old crewmates, friends, colleagues and, of course, people from the villages around the base.

"I was able to reunite a whole crew of ten and to put them in touch with the young boy from the village whom they sort of adopted while they were here."

For her too there have been many revelations. Although she lived through the war, she saw it with a child's eyes; it was not until many years later that she was able to comprehend the true toll on the men who were at Seething.

"As a child it was exciting. It is only when you are older that you realize how many people had died. There was one particular night when we lost two whole crews, twenty men, including one man who had been shot down just two days earlier and saved by the air-sea rescue.

"How brave they had to be. They were so young and I am sure a lot of them never thought it would happen to them."

Since hearing from Patricia, many of the old airmen have visited Seething to see the base once more and to pay their respects at the memorials to their fallen colleagues. And she has also gone over to America to take part in the large reunions there as the historian of the 448th Bomb Group collection. Her husband, Ron, has also played an important part in the Seething airbase story. He was part of a small group that restored the base's near-derelict control tower which is now a "living memorial," home to a collection of memorabilia, donated uniforms and equipment from its wartime days, as well as being a focus for those making pilgrimage to the airfield.

Opening the latest letter to arrive at Stanmare, her home on The Street at Seething, Patricia never knows what to expect, although more often these days they are the requests of grandchildren and great-grandchildren eager to discover information about their elderly or late relatives' wartime experiences.

"Some of the families say they didn't even know he was in the forces in the war," she said. "I think that quite a lot of the men buried it inside themselves when they returned home. Because so many of them were quite young, a lot had to go back to education and then get themselves a job so that they could start paying for their house and to get their children through their education.

"When they stand on he runway and think of their friends who didn't make it, yes, it is very emotional," she said.

"I have worked hard to get as many records as I can, but I can't get the personal details unless the men tell me them. But they do talk to me because although I was a child then, I knew what it was like for them in some ways.

"Sometimes their families will stand there with their mouths open because they have never heard him tell these stories before. They say "Why didn't you ever say anything?" and the men say 'You never asked.'"

"It's hard now because so many of them have become personal friends and we are losing them fast," she added, "but I feel I was able to share their golden years with them and put them in touch with each other when they hadn't been in contact since they finished their missions."... (Author's note—it was some 20 plus years ago that I received a letter from Pat saying she was a 9 and 10 year old school girl when we were there, and would like anything we had to offer about our Seething days. We have corresponded for years, and met Pat and Ron several times, both in England and the U.S. She has been and is the catalyst for the archives of the 448th Bomb Group.)

Hearty Hilda
by Candice Henderson

My maternal grandmother, Hilda Bertina Hillestad Welsh, was one of a kind. When I was growing up in Spokane during the 1950s I would spend many summer days with my grandparents while my parents were working. Hilda was of Norwegian descent and was as hearty as they come. I remember vividly traveling downtown with her on the bus in the middle of the afternoon. When we arrived we would head straight for Newberry's lunch counter where she would treat me to an ice cream sundae, and Hilda would eat her dinner. She would always be dressed in a shirtwaist dress, complete with hat, decorative combs in her hair, nylons and black dress shoes. After our snack we would wander around the variety store looking at everything and purchasing usually root beer, cakes, and other sweet treats to take home. But after shopping it wasn't home we went. Then it was time for work. Hilda would then start her workday cleaning offices in downtown buildings. She would work at her own pace, never rushing, stopping along the way to enjoy whatever diversion might come her way. After the cleaning was done, usually about 11 or 12 p.m., it was time to catch a bus home. Then walk a mile in the dark to her home on the outskirts of town. When Hilda arrived home her day was still not over for she would settle down at her card table with a root beer and a snack and begin to write letters to her many friends and relatives around the country. I know she had lots of friends for on her birthday she would receive 50 or more greeting cards...

My grandma was a woman who loved life, loved people, loved to dance, play the harmonica, and play like a kid! Her day, aside from cleaning offices, was never structured. If anyone personified the term "joie de vivre" it was my grandma Hilda.

Issy was a Hero

The following was sent to the Madison, WI newspaper somewhere around 1998.

"Whenever our local columnist Herb Caen would write a beautiful column detailing the wonderful things about this just-deceased person, I would privately lament that he should have written it so the subject could have enjoyed it. But here I am guilty of the same thing. Although I am not a writer, I do wish I had sent this to you a year ago. I was the pilot of a B-24 crew that flew 33 missions in the Eighth Air Force in England the

202

summer of 1944. My engineer, who was the top non-com of this ten person crew, was from Cross Plains, Wisconsin. He had a trucking business, and was a very good mechanic. He also had a wife and daughter, but even though his age would have excluded him from service, he joined because he knew he had skills that would contribute. Many years later my wife asked Issy's wife Adeline her reaction to this. Her response, "I was mad." Americans were never so undivided as during WWII. It was a far different general attitude than we have in today's divisive world. We who experienced it are glad for it.

Issy (Isidore) was assigned to my crew in Fresno, California, Christmas time, 1943. We got a full crew at Muroc Air Corps base in the Mojave Desert (now Edwards Air Force base) where we had combat training for 3 months prior to an overseas assignment. While at Muroc—because of his excellent capability—Issy was offered an instructor's position where he could have finished out the war in the safety of a domestic base. I had forgotten this, but years later on one of my trips when I visited him he told me that he came to me with this offer and what about it? I'm happy that I was mature enough to tell him that we would certainly hate to lose him on our crew, but I couldn't stand in his way to accepting such a good offer. True to form, Issy turned it down as he wanted to have more exciting experiences than a training base position. Lucky for us. Although I was the oldest member of the crew save one, Issy, who was 8 years older than I, his mechanical knowledge of engines, his more mature counsel than mine, his position as the top non-com of this young crew (19, 20, 21 year olds) was absolutely invaluable to our successful mission completion. In 1957 my wife and I visited Cross Plains. Issy was in his garage, under an auto, and I peeked in under the open hood. He spied me and I'll never forget his response. "For Christ's sake!" That after a 13 year period, but after that we had several more visits with Issy and Adeline. His business grew and he became a very successful Jeep dealer, which his family continues to operate after Issy's death last year.

One more story. We were on a mission, heading home, and here comes a German fighter coming in at US at about 1 o'clock. I could look right down his gun barrel, winking away at us. Issy is in the top turret and I call to him "Get him, Issy!" And his two 50s open up, shaking our plane. The German decided that this was a good day for both him and us to survive, and broke away before either was damaged.

So that is a short story about a pilot's engineer—a brave, resourceful, intelligent, nice man. And a hero—Isidore Buechner, born, raised, lived, and died in Cross Plains, Wisconsin.

A Post-War Talk with Top Nazi Albert Speer

by the late Lt. Gen. Ira C. Eaker, USAF (Ret.) and Arthur G.B. Metcalf
Reprinted from AIR FORCE Magazine, April 1977

On October 21, 1976, retired Air Force Lt. Gen. Ira C. Eaker, who commanded both VIII Bomber Command and then Eighth Air Force in 1942-43, and Dr. Arthur G.B. Metcalf, Chairman of the Board of the United States Strategic Institute, met with Albert Speer, Hitler's minister of armaments production, at Mr. Speer's home in Heidelberg. These highlights of their discussion concerning the effects of Allied airpower on German production were made available to AIR FORCE Magazine by General Eaker and Dr. Metcalf. The insights that were revealed in the conversations are a significant contribution to understanding the development of strategic airpower and its contribution to victory in World War Two.

EAKER: Mr. Speer, it seems we worked at cross-purposes in the last war. It was your mission to supply the weapons for the Nazi land, sea and air forces. It was my job to prevent your accomplishing that by bombing your munitions factories and their supporting systems—oil, ball bearings, power, and transportation.

If I had had a more accurate estimate of your problems, it would have improved our chances of accomplishing our mission.
Now, more than thirty years after Allied bomber operations began in World War II, there is a renewal of interest in airpower operations in that war. One of the major current interests concerns this question: Which hurt you more, the RAF night bombing or the American daylight bombing? Or was it the combination, called "round-the-clock bombing," the most effective Allied strategy?

SPEER: At first, of course, it was the British night bombing. We had that to deal with a year before the American daylight raids began, and a year and a half before you made significant attacks with a hundred or more of your daylight bombers.

After the British night bombing raids on our industry in the Ruhr, and especially their heavy raids on coastal cities like Bremen and Hamburg, I was directed to concentrate on night fighter production. Eventually, we began to take heavy toll of the British night bomber force as a result of devising tactics and techniques and developing equipment to deal with the night bombing effort.

I often wondered why the RAF Bomber Command did not continue their thousand-plane raids on our cities. Had they been able to do so, the morale of the German population and the German labor force might have been significantly weakened.

Of course, one reason why the burning of Bremen did not hurt the morale of our people more was because they did not know at the time the full measure of that catastrophe. Hitler's Propaganda Ministry had full control over all communications. Naturally they did not play up bad news. I, myself, did not know the full extent of the fire bombing of Bremen, the horrible loss of civilian life, until much later.

Later on, when American bombers came in daylight in ever-increasing numbers, attacking our munitions factories very effectively, our military leaders repeatedly told Hitler that unless the daylight bombers could be stopped, the end of war was clearly in sight. So I was ordered to concentrate on day-fighter production. For a time we held our own, often causing your raids heavy losses, as at Schweinfurt and Regensburg on August 17, 1943, but eventually you overwhelmed us. So I should suppose that it was the combined air effort that destroyed our means to wage war, and eventually the will and resources to continue. You will note that in my book Spandau I pointed out that you in fact had started a second front long before you crossed the Channel with ground forces in June 1944. Air Marshal Milch told me that your combined air effort forced us to keep 900,000 men tied down on the so-called "West Wall" to defend against your bombers. This, of course, included the fighter defenses, the antiaircraft artillery people, and the firefighters, as well as a large number of workmen needed for repairing damaged factories. There was also the large number of artillery pieces required all over Germany because we never knew which of our industrial cities you would attack next. It was your freedom of target choice and our uncertainty that enabled a limited number of bombers to tie down such tremendous numbers of people and equipment in our defense effort.

I suspect that well over a million Germans were ultimately engaged in antiaircraft defenses, as well as 10,000 or more antiaircraft guns. Without this great drain on our manpower, logistics, and weapons, we might well have knocked Russia out of the war before your invasion of France.

EAKER: Your view of the bomber offensive as constituting a second front is one I have never seen advanced elsewhere. Which of the target systems—shipbuilding, fighter plane and engine factories, oil, ball bearings, or transportation—was most decisive?

SPEER: It was the combination. At first I was most worried about ball bearings. If you had repeated your bombing attacks and destroyed our ball bearing industry, the war would have been over a year earlier. Your failure to do so enabled us to get bearings from Sweden and other sources and to move our damaged ball bearing machines to dispersed localities.

EAKER: There were several reasons why we did not repeat our attacks on Schweinfurt immediately. In the first place, the strike photos showed great damage. Secondly, we sent out 376 bombers that day against Schweinfurt and Regensburg and lost sixty. No air force can sustain that loss rate. We always tried to hold our operational losses below the programmed number of replacement bombers and crews. I was determined that our bomber force should always be a growing force.

In addition, we had other target systems of high priority, such as aircraft production, oil, transportation, etc. If we had continued all our effort against one of these systems, you would have concentrated your defenses around that system, and our resulting losses would have been unacceptable. Further, we always endeavored to send our daylight bombers against a high-priority target, which was for that particular day free of cloud cover. All these conditions naturally diversified our bombing attacks.

SPEER: You are quite right. Ball bearings were not our only critical weapons production system. Your attacks on our petroleum supply, for example, were also decisive in our pilot training program. After your successive raids had severely damaged Romanian oil sources, you followed up by mining the Danube and by constant attacks on locks and barges so that eventually our supply of gasoline and oil from natural sources was greatly diminished. Then you turned, quite logically, to our synthetic oil production. By that time you had such overwhelming air superiority that your long-range fighters were not all required to protect your bombers, but began very disastrous attacks on fighter planes on our airdromes.

Your air attacks on our transportation system were also very effective. They not only interfered with transport of troops and their equipment, but also disrupted my weapons production system. We often were producing engines and planes in required numbers, but we could not get them together from our dispersed factory sites. This was particularly true with respect to rail and barge transportation throughout Germany, especially in critical locations like the steel making Ruhr, which also supplied coal and coke to other critical industries.

The Allied attacks on our shipping did much more damage than you apparently realized at the time—not only the destruction of the shipbuilding facilities in our coastal cities, but the attacks on our submarine pens in the occupied Channel ports as well. And, of course, it was your long-range air reconnaissance over the Atlantic sea lanes that eventually reduced our submarine effectiveness and enabled the Americans adequately to supply those vast invasion forces. Sir Arthur Harris undoubtedly was correct in his contention that the so-called Combined Bomber Offensive was critical, perhaps decisive, in the three campaigns he described: land, sea and air.

EAKER: Aside from the bombing of German industry, a very high priority with the Allies was the destruction of the Luftwaffe. Since the Luftwaffe did not show on June 6, 1944, when that great naval armada appeared off the three French invasion beaches, we thought we had positive evidence that our Allied air offensive had largely destroyed the Luftwaffe.

SPEER: I think your surmise was essentially correct. I was still turning out the required number of fighter planes, but by that time we were out of experienced pilots. We were so short of fuel that we could give the incoming pilots in our flying schools only

3 ½ hours flying training per week. These poorly trained and inexperienced Luftwaffe pilots, by that time, were suffering heavy losses. A pilot only survived for a maximum of seven missions against your bombers and their accompanying long-range fighters in 1944 and '45. This was very discouraging to German pilots. It represented an attrition of fourteen percent for each mission. I do remember Hitler had ordered that 1,000 fighters take to the air on the day of the invasion. I do not know the reason for their not showing up. Perhaps General Galland [chief of German fighters] could tell you.

METCALF: Do you believe, as some do, that the Luftwaffe was misused?

SPEER: Yes, I do. First of all, the performance of our fighters and bombers, which had been developed well before the war, was inferior to your military aircraft. Hitler insisted that the Me-262, the twin-jet fighter we developed, be converted to a bomber, since Hitler was interested only in offensive weapons. It was a great mistake. I believe that as a fighter, it would have offered much more serious opposition to your bombers than the fighters we did use. When we removed the guns, ammunition, and other fighter armament from the Me-262, it was capable of carrying only a single 500 pound bomb, which was hardly worthwhile. Also, the shift of our aircraft industry from the production of bombers to the production of fighters and then back to the production of bombers was a nightmare. This disruption was hardly conducive to producing the aircraft we needed with which to fight the war.

METCALF: Was Goering's leadership of the Luftwaffe bad?

SPEER: One would have to say yes. After all, he spent most of his time at Karinhall, his country estate, dressed in long, exotic robes, heavily bejeweled, etc. As you know, he was on drugs for a long time. At the time of the Nuremberg trials Goering was, of course, off the drugs and he had lost a great deal of his excess weight. At that time he behaved like a new person and exhibited many qualities of leadership and clear-headedness. It was quite a surprising transformation.

METCALF: Was the German failure to execute the cross-channel invasion of England ("Sea Lion") due to your inability to gain command of the air over Britain?

SPEER: Yes. And here again, the need was for a superior fighter capable of knocking down the Royal Air Force, which would have played havoc with our invasion flotilla and our troops on invasion barges during the long passage across the Channel.

METCALF: Was it a mistake to interrupt your campaign against the Royal Air Force, whose fighters were having such telling effects on the Luftwaffe during the Battle of Britain, in order to bomb population centers? That shift in strategy gave the RAF a breather—a chance to recover from the systematic attrition of its fighter forces.

SPEER: Yet, it was. Here again was seen the influence of Adolf Hitler.

EAKER: As I remember, you were charged at the Nuremberg trails with the use and abuse of a so-called slave labor force of some 6,000,000 conquered people.

SPEER: The foreign labor force was guarded, housed, fed, and under the general supervision of Himmler. I only made requisitions and was allotted the labor required in our factories. In hindsight, I should have been more concerned about the treatment of this labor force. My factory managers complained about the training program resulting from the frequent loss of labor, probably due in part to lack of proper housing, feeding, and care.
This labor force had some distinct limitations. As you probably know, the loss of our code machine, which enabled your Ultra process to intercept [and decode] our radio communications, was due to this labor. There were many factory fires that probably were set by the laborers, and continual reports of sabotage. How much wiser you were to bring your women into the labor force. Had we done that initially, as you did, it could well have affected the whole course of the war. We would have found out, as you did, that women were equally effective and, for some skills better than male labor. We never did, despite our hard-

pressed munitions production in the late years of the war, make use of this great potential.

METCALF: Was foreign labor worth the number of occupations troops you had to use to combat local resistance activities that were heightened by taking those workers out of the countries?

SPEER: We had an expression that "Sauckel [Fritz Sauckel, Gauleiter of Thuringia, who was in charge of all foreign labor] was the greatest ally of the French Maquis," whose activities pinned down large numbers of military manpower. On balance, I guess it was not worthwhile. It was also a management problem within our own country to guard these people to prevent sabotage, etc. It was through [Polish workers] that the cryptographic machines for Ultra were handed over to the enemy. No, I don't think the foreign labor program did as much good as it did harm.

EAKER: In your book you refer often to the unity of effort of the whole German people behind Hitler and his war effort.

SPEER: Your premise that the German people were all united behind Hitler I do not believe to be entirely valid. You will recall, there were many attempts to assassinate him. As the dreary war years wound on, there was great disaffection about various phases of his leadership. Undoubtedly Hitler's early successes in the Low Countries and in France gave our people hope that all Germany would again be reunited, that all the territories lost in the First World War would be recovered. Also, as you may remember, we had been suffering great economic depression and deprivation with many people out of work and the tragic depreciation of the mark. With the Second World War, all that changed, of course. This undoubtedly made a tremendous impression on our people, and I can see where you, on the other side, would get the idea of our united effort.
There was great doubt about the wisdom of attacking Russia. I believe most of our military leaders and knowledgeable citizens doubted the wisdom of fighting on two fronts. After 1944, we frequently heard of Churchill's remark that Hitler was the Allies' secret weapon, and that was probably true.

Now I would like to ask some questions about the Allied air effort in World War Two. I have often wondered why you began your bombing attacks with such limited forces. Would it not have been better to have waited until you had several hundred, perhaps a thousand, bombers available?

EAKER: We did not have that option, for several reasons. After Pearl Harbor, there was great pressure, both at the political level and among the military leaders, to send all our bombers against the Japanese. If we had not begun operations against the Nazis, according to our prewar plan, this Pacific deployment would have taken place. The RAF bomber force would then have been left to deal alone with the Luftwaffe and German weapons production. It was only by demonstrating, as early as possible, that the daylight bombing offensive against Germany was feasible and productive that we were able to sustain our bomber buildup for operations out of Britain, as originally planned.

We learned during those limited early operations how to operate bomber forces under the conditions that then prevailed. If we had waited for the arrival of a thousand bombers before making attacks on German-occupied Europe, it probably would have been a tragic disaster. We learned how to deal with the weather, what kind of training we would have to give our combat crews, what types of formations to fly, and what communications we would require. We also learned that significant changes would be required in our aircraft.

Here is another consideration you may not have taken fully into account. Armies and navies have clashed for centuries, and their battles, strategies, and tactics have been recorded, studied, and analyzed by historians and war colleges of many nations. Prior to World War II, airpower had never had similar experience. Although Lord Trenchard of Britain, General Douhet of Italy, and Gen. William Mitchell of the U.S. had prophesied that strategic airpower could exercise a decisive influence on warfare, those theories had never been tested.

The airplane was less than fifty years old. Flying machines with the power and capacity to test the visions of Trenchard, Douhet, and Mitchell had not been developed. For the first time, the U.S. Eighth Air Force, operating out of Britain, and Britain's own Royal Air Force were to be given the resources to test those theories of the use of strategic airpower.

Gen. H.H. Arnold, head of the U.S. Army Air Forces, was a dedicated Mitchell disciple. His instructions to Gen. Carl Spaatz and to me were clear-cut, specific, unmistakable. We were to take the heavy bombers General Arnold would send us and demonstrate what airpower could do. Could it, as he hoped and believed, exercise a decisive influence on warfare by destroying the weapons-making capacity of an industrial nation like Germany?

General Spaatz was diverted from the test temporarily when he was ordered, in October 1942, to accompany General Eisenhower to Africa to conduct the campaign against Rommel and to seize North Africa. I moved up from leading VIII Bomber Command to be Eighth Air Force Commander for six months. This responsibility for the vital test of airpower fell upon us for the next two critical years.

So, during 1942 and '43, this process continued, cooperatively, out of Britain—the RAF by night, the U.S. Eighth Air Force by day.

SPEER: Why did you not attack our sources of electrical power upon which our weapon production so largely depended? We were always apprehensive about the vulnerability of our dams, our transformers, and our electric grid, so essential to continued war production.

EAKER: Our target planners had suggested electric power as one of the critical Nazi targets. However, the operational people, including myself, pointed out that the bomber was not an effective weapon against electric power production and distribution. We had no bombs available of a size and characteristic needed to destroy your water power. Transformers could not be seen at night, or even in daylight from bomber altitudes, and they were much too small to be attacked successfully. The power lines were discernible, but any bomb damage could be quickly repaired, and we realized you undoubtedly had provided for quick repairs of lines and transformers.

You will recall that the British spent a great deal of effort on the development of a bomb large enough to damage your dams. But the work of the dam-busters, though spectacular, did not accomplish decisive results.

As late as the Vietnam War, with the great technical advances that had been made in the meantime, the North Vietnamese power plants, transformers, and electric grid did not become especially lucrative targets until the smart bombs were available. Of course, with nuclear weapons, power sources of the enemy would be productive, perhaps decisive, targets.

SPEER: Why did you not join the British in attacking civilian industrial centers and our labor force?

EAKER: Airpower pioneers, including Lord Trenchard, General Douhet, and General Mitchell, had long believed that bombardment aviation might be able to reduce the will of civilian populations to resist. Our own doctrine held that the way to reduce civilian morale was not by killing people, but by depriving them of the resources for further resistance.
The U.S. airpower doctrine, which covered the employment of the Eighth Air Force out of Britain, never contemplated attack on civilian populations, other than that incidental to attacking munitions factories. A letter I wrote to General Spaatz in 1943 contained this often-quoted observation: "We must never allow the record of this war to convict us of throwing the strategic bomber at the man in the street."
I do not imply any criticism of the Royal Air Force bomber effort. Their position was entirely different. German planes had brutally attacked London, Coventry, and other cities, inflicting heavy loss of life. When the RAF began to retaliate with the limited resources available, all they could do with their night operations was to hit German industrial areas. As the bomber force grew, they were able, as you have said, to effect considerable destruction of your war effort by bombing German industrialized areas.

METCALF: At what time in the war did you feel that the Allied bombing was becoming unbearable to the German people?

SPEER: The best answer I can give is that the gradual buildup of your bombing attacks permitted the German people to become accustomed to and fortified against the great increase in destruction. So it is difficult to say at what point the tolerance of the population may have shown signs of being exceeded. Of course, the fire bombings of Hamburg, Dresden, and the like were great disasters locally. It would have been better if you had been able early in the war to have abruptly increased the size and weight of these bombing raids.

EAKER: I believe you expressed some surprise that there was not closer cooperation between the British night bomber and American daylight operations. It was realized early that the British and American bombers had differing characteristics and limitations and crews with different training and experience. This made it advisable for each to be assigned the distinctive air task that each was best qualified to perform. Occasionally there was close collaboration. The RAF attacked targets we had hit and set afire in daylight, bombing on our fires. We in turn made daylight attacks on installations they had hit at night and which were discernible, even in bad weather, by the fire and smoke. There was close cooperation in the exchange of target data, operational data, and in logistics and communications. This was necessary with so many planes operational in such a limited airspace as the British Isles. I would not want to leave the impression that there was any lack of mutual support and cooperation. Seldom, if ever, have two national military forces cooperated as effectively as did the RAF and the U.S. Eighth Air Force in the war years.

Albert Speer was convicted of war crimes in 1946 at Nuremberg and spent twenty years in prison for his role in Hitler's Third Reich. Within two years after becoming munitions minister in 1942, he almost tripled production of armed vehicles, quadrupled that of large guns, and more than doubled aircraft production.

Speer won a measure of respect at Nuremberg when he alone among those on trial confessed general responsibility for wartime crimes.

Caught in the gravitational pull of the megalomaniac's magnetism, Speer spun in Hitler's orbit until the end. His diaries are a valuable contribution to the knowledge of Nazi Germany and the personalities of the imprisoned top Nazis when stripped of power.

The late Lt. General Ira C. Eaker completed pilot training in 1918. Prior to World War II, he served as Executive Assistant to the Chief of the old Air Corps and participated as a pilot in many pioneering flights, including the "Question Mark" endurance flight and the Pan-American flight of 1926. During the war, he commanded successively VIII Bomber Command, 8th Air Force, and Mediterranean Allied Air Forces. General Eaker flew on the first heavy bombing raid against occupied Europe and the first shuttle bombing mission to bases in Russia.

Dr. Arthur G.B. Metcalf is the Chairman of the Board and President of Electronics Corp. of America, the founder and Chairman of the U.S. Strategic Institute, and Strategic Studies Editor of "Strategic Review." A former faculty member of MIT and Harvard, Dr. Metcalf has been a test pilot and was a pioneer in the field of aircraft control and stability. During World War II, he served as a lieutenant colonel. He is the author of many articles in the fields of mathematics, aerodynamics, and strategy and doctrine.

Despite the Air Force Magazine's claim, General Eaker did not fly on the first heavy bomber raid against Europe. His was the first 8AF raid from England by B-17s on August 17, 1942. The first raid by heavy bombers, B-24s in fact, occurred on June 11, 1942 by 12 "HALPRO" Liberators from Fayid, Egypt, bombing for the first time, Ploesti, Romania.

Unsung People

This is added to honor the millions of persons who shower kindness, help, and counsel to others in need, with little or no recognition. One example that comes to mind is Virginia Lollar, Chico, California, who has, over the 40 years of our friendship, always had a passion to aid others. Fill one need, she finds another.

The Virginias of his world are mostly unrecognized, and to whom I wish to pay respect – and to regret not being blessed with the intense love and care to act for less fortunates.

General Hap Arnold

JOHN E. D. GRUNOW

216 DAVENPORT DRIVE
SOUTHFIELD POINT
STAMFORD, CT 06902

(203) 325-1185 FAX: (203) 961-9511

October 11, 1994

Dear Ralph

This picture of Reichsmarschall Hermann Goering
was taken by a friend of mine who piloted this plane
which transported Goering, Gen'l Keitel, Von Ribbentrop
and others to the Nuremberg trials to be tried for "crimes
against humanity". He committed suicide there.

Goering was #2 Nazi directly under Adolf Hitler, and
he was also chief of the Luftwaffe.

As a former soldier in the Eighth Air Force, this
picture of old Hermann must be especially poignant. (This
picture has never been published.)

My best,

John E.D. Grunow.

Goering

Chapter 6: Mission Stories

The Ballantrae Disaster

Presented by King Schultz, pilot 448th Bomb Group, and their representative to the 2nd Air Division

With the war in Europe having ended in the previous month, in June 1945 the personnel at Seething were making preparations to return home and hand the base back to the RAF. All four squadrons drew lots for those who were to go home by air. Twenty airmen were allocated to each B-24: ten air crew and ten ground crew in each bomber. It was cramped but practicable.

On 10 June the first departures started. The route home was via RAF Valley in Anglesey, then on through either the Azores or Iceland depending upon the route weather. During the following twelve days, 64 bombers of the 448th BG, complete with 640 airmen aboard, took off and days later arrived back safely in the U.S.

The sixty-fifth and very last B-24 departed a little after daybreak on the morning of 12 June, pounding down the 2000 yards of runway 24 for the last time as Capt. Jim Blank eased the 27-ton bomber into the air. His orders were to avoid the RAF Valley route because of poor weather brewing up in the west. He was directed instead to fly via Prestwick, Ayr. So he set course from Seething for Splasher Beacon at Louth in Lincs, and on to Marske Beacon and then Middlesborough, achieving excellent reading on each radio compass. However, as he approached Cheviot Hills on the Scottish border, weather and cloud conditions begin to deteriorate rapidly. Inside the aircraft, the occupants could hear the heavy rain battering the fuselage as the doomed B-24 droned on through the eerie mist towards its destination.

The pilots could no longer get a satisfactory reading on the radio compass. They sensed that the wind had probably backed and that their estimated drift had changed. The navigator, Lt. Bernard F. Pargh, advised that they should continue on course and await improved visibility. Prestwick reported low clouds and rain, with more to come.

The bomber collided with a hillside four miles southeast of Ballantrae whilst making a controlled descent on instruments. Disintegrating as it went, the Liberator slid along on its belly for some 125 yards, scattering debris along the way and throwing some of its packed occupants out onto the moor as it came to an abrupt halt. Only the tail and center bomb bay sections were still recognizable as aircraft components; the rest of the aircraft was totally wrecked.

Of those on board, only four had survived the initial impact, and all were badly injured. After laying unconscious for a considerable period of time, one of the four passengers (all of the aircrew were dead), S/Sgt. John R. May awoke to find a scene of utter devastation. All he could remember was that just prior to impact, someone had yelled, "Hey! There's the ground!" Shortly, in great pain he lapsed into unconsciousness and only recovered that evening. Everyone else had been killed. During the night, one of the survivors, Pfc. George Gaffney, died.

As soon as he could muster the strength, Sgt. May, despite the acute pain he was experiencing from a broken back, attempted to hobble down the hill, tripping and lapsing into a state of unconsciousness after he fell and struck some rocks, which created a gaping hole close to his temple. Eventually he was found by a gamekeeper for the Lagafater Estate. The RAF and police were informed, and ambulance teams were soon on their way. Dick Pokorny and Ken Nelson together with Sgt. May were rescued and taken to Prestwick Hospital. While there, T/Sgt. Pokorny had a visit from an English Land Army girl, returning his wallet which had been found at the crash site, still with his money inside. "Our British allies are very honorable," he remarked. Irony often plays a part in tragedies such as this.

The pilot, Capt. James Blank, prior to takeoff had placed his wife's and baby daughter's photograph above the instrument panel. Then, after his usual request over the intercom of "no smoking in flight," he added, "This is one mission that we want to be perfect." Perhaps the aircraft crashed at the height of only 1400 feet on Pildinny Hill because the waters of Loch Ryan were mistaken for Ayr Bay. The accident report states an occasional sight of water prior to the crash. Perhaps a stronger-than-anticipated tail wind caused an underestimated ETA at Prestwick and they thought they were on the final approach for the airfield.

Whatever the cause, the consequences were tragic, as another seventeen of America's finest lost their lives.

Crew members: Capt. Jim Blank (pilot), Lt. John K. Huber (co-pilot), Lt. Bernard F. Pargh (navigator), Lt. Frank Y. Pollio (bombardier), T/Sgt. Morris L. Kanerak (radio), S/Sgt. Louis Menred (gunner), S/Sgt. Cris C. King (gunner), S/Sgt. John Wildman (gunner), S/Sgt. William T. Harriman (gunner).

Passengers: Ten enlisted men and two officers, Capt. Harold L. Earmant (713th Squadron pilot), Lt. Col. Heber T. Thompson (448th BG Ops Officer, a very experienced top veteran who had come over with the original unit in 1943 as a young 2nd Lieutenant pilot).

(Author's note: "When weather's ahead and you're in doubt, be sure to make a 180 about."

Crossing the U.S. on our way overseas, I obeyed this advice for a safe trip.)

Mission 23: Baumenheim, Germany—19 March, 1945

Mission Diary by Lt. Col. Harld H. Dorfman (448th)

Today's mission was an extremely interesting one from a sightseeing point of view. Again I flew as pilotage navigator. I love that nose turret position, most comfortable seat in the plane. But this time it was really worthwhile. CAVU all the way in, and most of the way out. Flying time 8 hours and 5 minutes.

Takeoff was at 1030 hours. Much too late for a mission of that length. We were to lead the 20th Combat Wing today. Colonel Westover was flying with us as command pilot. Still Lt. Voigt and crew, Lt. Block, the D.R. navigator, was finishing up, so after this I'm to be D.R.

Forming was in Belgium, just south of Brussels. It went over extremely well. We went into Germany somewhere around Strasbourg and headed for the target near Munich, a jet aircraft parts factory.

We bombed visual. Bombs away at 1448 hours, altitude 17,900 feet, temperature -47°F. We really plastered the target.

Coming out we passed north of Frankfurt and then across the Rhine south of Coblenz. Frankfurt was a mess.

Coblenz was leveled, just nothing there, no blip on the radar. You could see north to Cologne and Düsseldorf. One of the two was really burning; at that distance, I couldn't tell which it was. I could see the flashes of the artillery on the west bank of the Rhine and the shells bursting on the east bank. Up at Ramagen, where our troops had crossed the Rhine, you could see the heavy artillery marking the area. We held on the east bank. It looked like hell down there from here. We passed directly over Aachen. That was another pitiful sight. It's beaten to a pulp.

Hit from behind by a jet. Took a picture I would rather forget. From then on the trip was uneventful. I almost went to sleep in that nose turret.

Lt. Block put on quite a flare show in the traffic pattern, celebrating the end of his tour.

That is it for #23.

Duneberg
by Gordon M. Baker, 566th Sqd., 389 B.G.

I thought the Duneberg B April 7, 1945 raid was a closed issue with the March *Newsletter*. But, with the additional two articles in the September *Newsletter,* I thought I might as well add my bit to the confusion.

When the ME-109 was inserted into our box of four aircraft, I was standing with one foot on the raised deck between the seats of the pilot and the co-pilot on the plane flying the slot position in the lead flight. So I had an excellent view (and no duties) of the ME-109 and its destination of two of our aircraft.

When I was first aware of the ME-109, I saw him flying at the same elevation and at the same speed as our element of four planes. He had entered the formation from its rear. The fighter was flying to the left of the tail turret of the lead plane and therefore slightly to the left and ahead of our nose turret. The ME first would fire its guns at the lead plane and then would pull its nose up slightly. Then it would fall back into its level firing position and let off more rounds of ammunition. I have always figured the ME had armor plating on its belly and that the pilot was using this jiggling tactic so as to avail himself of the protection afforded by his armor plating. On the other hand, it may have had something to do with its speed since the ME-109 must have been close to its stalling speed.

It was amazing, considering that at least twelve 50-caliber machine guns were firing at his plane, that the Germans pilot was able to hold his position within our formation as long as he did, which seemed to be minutes, but wasn=t. At any rate, smoke then started to steam from the engine nacelle of the ME and at this point the (wounded?) German pilot must have realized that he had had it. So he accelerated his ME under his left wing of the lead plane and flipped it into the lap of its pilot.

Two things happened next. First, the 3-bladed prop of the ME-109 was detached from its engine and floated directly towards our plane. Luckily, it dropped out of sight before our plane ran into it. I mention this because it had stopped rotating and seemed to be suspended in the air, right in front of us.

The second action involved the engine of the ME-109. It rolled along the top of the right wing of the lead plane and dropped off its end directly onto the deputy lead plane. The German pilot must have wanted to commit suicide, else why would he have flown formation with us, presenting himself as a sitting duck? One German for 20 Americans; one ME for two B-24s.

The bomb damage was quite impressive as viewed through the left blister on the flight deck and through the open bomb bay doors. And the top turret gunner should remember my presence on this flight since I repaired his intercom (a loose wire in his plug-in junction box) and enabled him to claim an enemy plane.

However, I was impressed even more to see a German plane, without any propeller, coming down almost vertically to the right of our formation. This was the first jet aircraft I had ever seen, and it wasn=t one of ours!

I had persuaded the CO to let me fly with the crew as a flight engineer that morning, although my MOS was that of Squadron Engineering Officer. After landing at Hethel, I figured that I was not getting enough (any) flight pay and therefore I would forego any more combat flying; especially after witnessing two B-24s out of four (50%) going down over enemy territory. However, the flight did give me a better outlook on what it was like to fly a mission over Germany.

Unfortunately, after some 40 years I cannot remember our plane designation nor any of the names of the crew. Perhaps someone whom I flew with that morning can tell us.

Duneberg—April 7, 1945
by John B. (Buff) Maguire (389th BG)

My crew also flew that particular mission to Duneberg on April 7, 1945. In fact that target was an ammunition and dynamite dump, and we carried 12-500 lb. GP bombs, and I flew D+ plane that day. This particular mission was my 11th mission, and it was my 3rd mission as a deputy lead pilot. As stated in the Earl Zimmerman article, the 389th BG was leading the entire 2nd Air Division to Duneberg, and the 566th Bomb Squadron was flying the low left position.

This particular mission is still very vivid in my mind—I guess it is because of the importance of our leading the entire 2nd Air Division on the mission that day, and we still are able to completely destroy the target and I had a ringside seat for the action. At the time, and during interrogation, I was never able to figure out how the ME-109 was able to get through the P-51 fighter cover. I remember the ME-109 diving from above at almost a 180 degree angle between our three squadrons in the 389th BG, then pulling up into formation so that it was flying off the right wing of the lead plane and the left wing of the deputy lead plane. The ME-109 just sat there firing its guns until it was put out of commission, at which time it did a roll over and smashed into the cockpit area of the lead plane and then into the deputy lead ship.

The Zimmerman article stated that one of the P-51s was hit by our fire and the pilot bailed out. I remember that. The one thing I was most afraid of during this action was being hit by fire from our own guns, because the ME-109 attacked us at the IP and flew in formation at the beginning of the bomb-run until the ME-109 pilot was apparently killed. We then used the bombardiers of the high right squadron and the low left squadron to still make the bomb run, drop the bombs, and destroy the target.

Even being so close to all of this action, we went over our plane with a fine-toothed comb after landing, and nowhere could we find any holes or hits from any guns. I guess the Old Boy upstairs was looking out for us since we did not even receive a scratch.

Another thing which is very vivid in my memory is the talk or speech that James N. "Jimmy" Stewart gave at our interrogation, telling us what a fine job we did of destroying the target when the lead plane and the deputy lead plane were both lost at the IP commencing the bomb run. At the time, Jimmy Stewart was either a Lieutenant or full Colonel and was the Deputy Wing Commander. I remember that his remarks were just as impressive as any movie I have seen him in.

The article in the March News Letter is accurate. My notes further say that we were also attacked by jet fighters coming down the bomber stream, and that the 389th BG lost two crews and three planes. One of the planes had the crew bail out.

The Zimmerman article stated that he was doing nothing with the waist gun because he was so busy watching all of the action. I just want him to know that my ringside seat was so close to the action, when we returned to base I had to change my underwear.

After The Mission Is Over
by Patrick J. McGuckin

Over the last several years there have been written many stories about the April 7, 1945 raid on Duneburg, and probably each one clouds the story as much as clearing it up. We all see things differently; I remember at debriefing, several gunners lined up to claim the "kill."

The story I want to tell is what happened AFTER the attack, but to review briefly:

I was the left waist gunner on the Kiser crew, in the High Right formation. Saw the German fighter coming in a pursuit curve at about 8 o'clock. I, along with about 60 other gunners, started to fire. Then things really happened in a hurry. The fighter shot out an engine in one plane, forcing it to abort and land at a base near Paris. Then he crashed into the lead plane and bounced off into the deputy lead plane. Both planes were lost. The German just seemed to disintegrate. We lost Col. Herboth in the lead plane.

Now for the story I wish to tell. It's about the pilot on the deputy lead, Lt. Kunkle. I wish I could locate him and have him tell his story, but after checking all the rosters over the years I haven't been able to find him, so here goes.

About a week or so after the mission, it was announced on bulletin boards on base that a survivor of that raid would be in the Aero Club to tell his story. He didn't remember leaving his plane; he only knew that he was in a chute with the ripcord in his hand, and was at about 3000 feet. (He was probably blown out by one of the explosions.) One of his boots and the felt slipper was missing from one foot. He could see three or four other chutes and tried to remember how to pull on the chute cords so he could meet up with the others, but at the last minute it looked like the others were heading for a Stalag, so he quit trying and landed in a forest. He said he was so confused that he ran toward the road instead of going deeper into the woods. It was lucky for him that he did, for at that time some trucks arrived bringing a German search party to look for him. They found his chute and naturally assumed he went deeper into the woods, so that's where they looked while he was hiding under a low branched pine tree. He knew if he was caught he was only obliged to give his name, rank and serial number. He could remember his name and rank, but he was so confused he couldn't remember his serial number.

The Germans didn't find him, so he stayed in the forest trying to think what he would do next. He thought he might make it back if he traveled at night and rested during the day.

That night he heard voices from two men that jumped off a train that went through the woods. Not knowing whether they were friend or foe, he still had his Colt 45 so he confronted them. Seems that one of them was a Lt. in the Russian Army, the other was a young Hulk civilian slave laborer. They had been in Germany for so long that they could speak German, and Kunkle was of German descent, so he could also speak the language.

Lt. Kunkle's bare foot was sore, sprained when leaving the plane, so while traveling that first night they broke into a German farmhouse. The Russians stole food, window drapes (for blankets) and went into the bedroom where the farmer and his wife were sleeping and got boots for Lt. Kunkle. (He said most of the canned food was American.)

On one of the nights they came to a river, with no boats to be had. The Hulk pulled fence posts out of the ground, and with the fence wire they fashioned them into a raft and crossed. When reaching the other side they had no more use for the raft so they let it go down the river, only to find when they had traveled a short distance that they were on an island. While exploring the island for a way off, they found a bombed out bridge. They could travel from girder to girder, but the Hulk couldn't swim, so they had quite a time getting across.

On one of the days they even went into a train depot and bought tickets to get a little closer to home. Another night they were about to bed down for the night when they discovered that there was a German Tank Corps also bedded down in the woods. Needless to say, they went to the next woods.

When they were getting closer to friendly lines one evening, they ran into a German officer and two enlisted men. They thought they were done for, but the Germans were probably deserters, knowing that the war was over as far as Germany was concerned. The officer asked if they had matches; he had cigarettes, but no matches. Kunkle tore off part of the striker and gave it to him. He in turn asked Kunkle if he could do anything for them. Kunkle said they could use some bread or any kind of food. The German left, and a short while later came back with a loaf of white bread. They all bedded down a short distance from each other, and when they awoke the Germans were gone.

Getting closer to the British lines they were crossing a bridge when Kunkle felt a wire with his foot. They all scrambled for a ditch when a very English voice called out, "Who's there?" When they identified themselves they were allowed to cross. It seems that the bridge was zeroed in with two machine guns. If they had tripped the wire the gunners would have to pull the trigger.

I don't know what ever happened to the Russians. Kunkle was held long enough to be identified by American forces, spend a day or two in Paris, and then return to Hethel to tell us his story.

This story may have a twin, because the left waist gunner on the lead plane, Jim Kratoska, and two others from the same crew survived. I don't know if they were the people Lt. Kunkle saw when he was coming down or if there were other survivors.

226

It's been 45 years now since all this happened, yet so much of it is still clear. Only wish I could remember this morning and yesterday.

The Final Flight of the Original "Bird Dog" Crew
by William H. Counts, Sr. (467th)

It would seem our final flight on Thursday, June 29, 1944 was, indeed, jinxed from the beginning. We supposedly were "standing down," but at the last minute were called to fly this mission. At the time we were awakened, around three A.M., none of us were enthusiastic about flying on such short notice. We quickly dressed and rode our bicycles over to the mess hall to eat. After eating, we went to get our flying equipment and dressed for the flight. We were pressed for time, and rather than change into a flying suit, I simply put my electric suit over my dress uniform, and went to mission briefing.

We were one man short because the enlisted men had informed me that Sgt. Thomas Hansbury, our tail gunner, had been on guard duty the night before. The thought of placing a combat crew member on guard duty and then expecting him to fly the next day was irritating to me, and I had the word passed along to Hansbury to remain in the barracks and I would credit him as being on this mission.

Our take-off was to the southwest and we were on instruments almost as soon as we were airborne.

While over the Channel, and before getting over enemy territory, it was customary for each of us to use the "restroom" since we would not be getting out of our seats until we were again back over neutral territory. This was not as simple as it may sound, because of the procedure involved in disconnecting and reconnecting oxygen, electric suit, flak vest and pants, steel helmet, and radio connections, etc. When I sat back down, I reconnected everything except I FORGOT TO FASTEN MY SAFETY BELT AND SHOULDER STRAPS! I had never done this before, and it was to be the major factor later in my not perishing inside the ship.

As we continued inland toward our target, at an altitude of 21,500 feet, I kept eyeing the deputy lead's position, hoping someone would fill that slot. No one did, however, and I waited until almost the last minute before sliding our ship down into that position. This maneuver was accomplished between Wing IP and Group IP. (Wing IP means Wing Initial Point where the Combat Wing breaks up into individual groups and proceeds to that group's target. Group IP means the Initial Point for the individual groups to proceed to their own target.)

As we approached our target, the JU-88 factory at Aschersleben, visibility was good and we could see no flak or fighters in the area. We were not more than 30 seconds from "bombs away" when the first burst was fired, and they hit us with that burst and every ensuing burst. We could hear the flak tearing through the aircraft each time one of the 88mm shells exploded. As I reflect on this, I am amazed that our bombs were not hit in the bomb bay. Just before "bombs away," Sgt. Francis Van Veen, our radio operator, tapped my right shoulder and said, "There's a fire in the bomb bay." I looked back over my shoulder and saw the fire, which appeared to be hydraulic fluid burning. I told Van Veen to try to put it out, and returned to trying to keep the aircraft in formation and clear of other planes. At almost the same time Van Veen reported "fire," I had felt the controls go slack and my oxygen supply was extremely hot. I jerked the oxygen hose loose to avoid inhaling flames, in case that system was on fire—as it is sure death if this happens. Eyewitnesses later reported seeing the men in the back of the plane slump over and fall to the floor, and flames streaking out of the waist windows. It is my belief that they died from breathing the deadly flames from the oxygen system, but there is no way to know this for certain. They could have been hit by flak fragments.

Because of this fact, Sgt. John Murphy may not have been able to get his customary brick thrown out. On every mission he carried one addressed, "to Adolf with love, from Murph," and threw it out somewhere over Germany.

It was Robby's custom to call out "bombs away," and I didn't hear him as I felt the ship rise as the heavy bomb load was released. Our radio was out but I didn't know it at the time. Immediately after bombs away, I fed the two left engines in and cut back the right engines, in order to avoid midair collision with anyone else and clear the formation. As we cleared the formation, in a diving right turn, I fed all four engines back in and the plane began heeling to the left. I felt that we were going to go down, and told the boys on the intercom to abandon the aircraft. I repeated this twice before I realized the radio was out, as I didn't get any "feedback" through my headset. As I reached for the alarm bell to alert the crew to bail out, Lt. Bill Greble, my co-pilot, had risen from his seat and was stepping around the control pedestal, when, it felt to me like the right wing came off. I don't know if the wing did come off then, or there was an explosion, or exactly what happened; but for lack of a better expression—"all hell broke loose." I believe the top turret came loose and crushed Greble and nearly got me, as something grabbed my left leg and held it tight enough to pull my flying boot, electric sock and regular sock completely off.

The aircraft gyrated viciously, with a whipping motion, that I find difficult to accurately describe. I was being tumbled about inside the fuselage like a pea in a rain barrel, and could not maintain any sense of direction, up or down, center of gravity or anything else might think they could do under those circumstances. I had previously thought what I might do if something like this were to happen, but I couldn't even put my hand in front of my face, so violent were the forces. After what seemed an eternity, during this period, I realized I was not going to get out and that I would be smashing lifeless upon striking the ground. I was almost unconscious from the beating I was taking inside the plane, when the violent oscillation suddenly stopped and the plane continued falling with a rolling motion—similar to the rotation of a mixing machine, such as a concrete mixer. After an indeterminate time in this condition, I suddenly felt fresh air blow across my back, and I knew that the next time the plane rotated I would be thrown out—and sure enough, I was thrown out of some hold, like a shot, into cool, fresh air. I estimate the altitude to have been about 2500 feet, and as I got my feet pointed towards earth, I looked down and saw our aircraft fuselage falling below me, rolling over and over, with no wings on it. It appeared to me that the plane had quit burning.

I remember our briefings on being shot down, to delay opening your chute until you could see trees start to spread rapidly and you would miss some ground fire at you. I did this and when I thought it was time, I grasped my "D" ring with my right hand and pulled, but was unable to pull the rip cord. I had injured my right elbow and hadn't realized it until that moment. I then put my left hand over my right hand and pushed, opening the parachute. I swung forward and then backward and started another swing forward when I hit the ground face down in a plowed field, about 100 feet from where the fuselage of our plane hit. I wanted to run over to it, but couldn't because Germans were already coming toward me from across the field.

Thinking of escape, at some later time, I unbuckled my chute and ran about 100 feet into a clump of trees, about the size of a very small house. I quickly broke open my escape kit and hid a tube of condensed milk and an escape compass in my only boot—the right one. My left foot was completely bare. I buried the rest of the kit, containing Germany escape money and other items that I didn't want the Germans to get. As the Germans approached me, I came out of the woods toward them and fell down on my stomach, pretending to be hurt more than I actually was.

The next thing I knew they were standing all around me, both men and women. They looked to be some sort of civilian watch force whose purpose was this very thing. One woman asked me if I had a "pistola." I pretended not to understand. Another one looked at my clothes and asked a man if I was a civilian. He replied, "Nix, officere." They brought my parachute over and the women were feeling the material and looking as though they were thinking of what they could make out of it. They handed it over to some of the men.

They took me over to a road where I sat down. It wasn't until later, when I saw myself in a mirror, that I realized how terrible I must have looked. My head and face were totally covered with blood from head wounds that went to the skull and my face was totally covered in blood; you could see no skin, except for my eyelids. My left foot was also burned and cut, especially on my heel and my right elbow was injured. I was very fortunate, though!

One old man pointed a rifle at me and indicated that he wanted me to start walking down the road, away from the others, and I had no choice but to go. I firmly believed at that time, and do now, that he intended to shoot me when we were out of sight of the others. I made up my mind that I was not going to just walk along and be shot, and I was trying to formulate a plan, in my mind, of how to jump him first, when the regular Wermacht soldiers came down the road in a pick-up truck and put me in the back with two of them. During this time, they were apparently checking the old man out good, which included threatening hand gestures. It was during this trip, where they took me to an airfield we had just bombed, that I saw two B-24s from other groups, on the ground burning and two other plumes of black smoke that I am almost certain were either other aircraft burning, or the wings from our aircraft, which contained the fuel tanks. On the way to the field, as we were passing along a high bluff, someone apparently threw a brick at me from the top of the cliff and it landed in the bed of the truck. One of the young German soldiers drew his pistol and I believe he would have shot at whoever threw the brick if he had located them.

It was at the airport that I saw myself in a mirror. They took me to a room where there were three other American fliers. One of them was named Friend, and he was seriously injured in the back. Another one was named Feldman, who later turned up at Stalag Luft III with me. He was from Tulsa, Oklahoma. If I was told the name of the other flyer, I do not remember it. We were not allowed to speak to one another. I remember that the clocks in the building were stopped at 10:32 from our bombs. They took everything I had away from me, except for my handkerchief, which they must have missed. That handkerchief was really good to have, especially when I was in solitary confinement later. When I went down the corridor to the bathroom, I would wet it and carry it back to my cell and dob it around my face the best I could.

From the room at the airport, I was taken to the local jail, where I was put in a dark room (cell) that had a wooden bunk with nothing but boards on it. It was made to slant upwards for a pillow. (The Germans didn't mollycoddle their outcasts.) Believe it or not, I actually went to sleep, I suppose from a combination of shock and loss of blood. Later that same day, I was transferred to a regular jail at Bernberg, where a German doctor supposedly tended my wounds. He put something on gauze that burned like fire and just scrubbed my head and face wounds with much unnecessary vigor. I decided he was trying to make me show pain, but I was determined to show none, and didn't. I almost fell out though, as when I was standing there everything went slowly black, but I didn't fall. I probably would have if the doctor hadn't stopped scrubbing on my wounds when he did.

I had been asking about any other fliers, hoping some of the crew might have made it, but a German major who interrogated me drew me a picture of the fuselage of our plane, showing the location of the bodies of the crew members that they had recovered. They also told me where Bill Greble and Don

Hudson had been found. Greble hadn't opened his chute, and Hudson was thrown out with no chute on. He was found over half a mile from the fuselage where the others were. They showed me Greble's Zippo cigarette lighter, which was crushed like a wad of tinfoil. They also brought me Don Hudson's left flying boot to wear. I knew Bill and Don didn't make it. But I could not tell, from the information they were giving me, whether it was the truth or not. They were very cunning at obtaining information from downed fliers and we were warned about this. They could not account for the tenth, or missing man from the crew. It puzzled them. They kept asking me if I had a boxer on my crew. I told them no. It seems, as they said, they had shot and killed an airman that day who had tried to fight when they captured him. He took a swing at one of the Germans and was shot to death. I have no way of knowing whether that was the truth or not.

I was kept at Bernberg one night and sent, along with others, to Wetzlar, which seemed to be a distribution center for prisoners. I, along with others, was taken there by train. After a couple of days at Wetzlar, they loaded a whole bunch of us on another train. Those of us in my car were sent to Dulag Luft, the infamous interrogation center at Frankfurt on the Maine. The RAF finally firebombed this place because the Germans were obtaining so much intelligence from captured fliers. It was reported that only one Allied Prisoner of War lost his life in the bombing.

At Dulag Luft, I was placed in solitary confinement, in room 4C. The room was about 5 or 6 feet wide, and about 8 feet long with one barred window that had wooden shutters that were kept closed, making the room quite dark. I never got out of the room except for going to the restroom and to daily interrogation in the mornings.

I was kept in this place a long time, perhaps 10 or 12 days—maybe even 15, as I completely lost track of time. This was in violation of the Geneva Convention, which restricts holding a prisoner in solitary confinement more than 3 days. As I was taken back and forth down the long hall to interrogation, I noticed there was a white card tacked up on my door, where only one or two others along the corridor had them—and even those would disappear after two or three days. One day I asked the guard why the card was on my door and in broken English he replied, "Why don't you speak?" He conveyed to me that they would keep me there until I was too weak to get up off the straw bunk without fainting, if I didn't tell them what they wanted to know. The guard seemed to be trying to warn me and I sensed that he didn't agree with my treatment. They deliberately fed starvation rations to prisoners as that was a part of the breaking-down process.

In the morning I was given a warm cup of ersatz coffee and one piece of black bread, which was thinly spread with some kind of marmalade; at noon they brought me the coffee and a small bowl of warm, watery soup; at night, the coffee with the bread again. Sometimes at night, they would bring two pieces of bread. I saved the hard crusts of the bread to scrub my teeth with, and wash out my mouth with the so-called coffee.

The very next weekend, after I had the talk with the partially friendly guard, I wasn't called in to be interrogated. When I asked why, I was told that my personal interrogator, a German Hauptmann (Captain) was on leave. I then said to the guard, "Why he told me I was going to be released this weekend." To my surprise they believed me!!! They opened my shutters on my window, let me shave and clean up and even gave me a book to read. That very afternoon I was released from Dulag Luft and transferred to Stalag Luft III at Sagan, Germany. I should mention that it was obvious to me the reason they kept me for so long was because they were trying to find out where the tenth man on our crew was. They knew very well there should have been ten men on the airplane as they probably had the papers showing Hansbury as being on the flight.

Before I went outside, another POW handed me a draw string tobacco sack with enough tobacco in it, along with the papers, to roll two or three cigarettes. For the first time since I was captured, I was free to walk from a room, by myself, and go to another location unattended. I sat down by the side of one of the buildings with my cigarette, in the warm sun, and was enjoying my smoke, when I heard a slow, southern drawl beside me, asking, "Can I have a draw off that cigarette?" I handed him the tobacco sack and papers and we struck up a conversation, learning we were both from Arkansas. He was Lt. Roy Dale Thompson, from Clinton, and I was from North Little Rock. We became lifelong friends and were separated only by his death by heart attack in 1984. When Tommy and I returned to the States, his fiancée introduced me to her best friend, and we have now been married for almost 44 years. I feel sure the effects of the war cut his life short some 15 or 20 years, as he came out of prison camp with heart problems and a nerve condition.

For the longest time, after I was in Stalag Luft III, I lived in fear they would discover my absence, when my interrogator returned, and come to Sagan and take me back to Dulag Luft. But they never did. It may be, by that time, the war was so advanced they couldn't keep up with everything. I never gave up hope that some one other than me made it out of our plane that dreadful day, but each time a new group of "Kriegies" (prisoners) came in, I would question them, but never received any hope from anyone I talked with.

Incidentally, while I was at Dulag Luft, one of the threats they used was accusing me of being a spy. I didn't wear my dog tags and they used that as an excuse to tell me that since I had no identification, that anyone could get clothes like my uniform, and therefore they had no way of establishing that I was an American serviceman—so I could be executed for spying.

Before daylight on January 28, 1945, we were marched out of Stalag Luft III because of the advancing Russians from the east. This was a miserable journey of some 2 to 3 weeks in the bitter cold and deep snow. Our German guards (some of them) were in worse shape than we were. There was one old man who got to the point where he couldn't put one foot in front of the other. He would drag his left foot, up to his right, one step at a time. The whites of his eyes were solid red with blood, and I have seen some of our own men carry the old man's rifle for him. We had orders not to escape during the march. These orders were from our own leaders. The reason was that all of Germany had been declared an area that any unauthorized person could be shot as a spy.

We walked from Sagan to Spremberg. During part of this journey, two German intelligence men walked with us. They talked to us about the Russians and made the statement that they had killed 15 million Russians and couldn't whip them—and that we (the Americans) couldn't either. They stated that we would have to team up someday to fight the Russians.

One night on this trip we stayed in a barn, and it was so cold that we stayed up and walked around most of the night to stay warm. We only had one light blanket each that we carried with us. Another night they packed so many of us in a church that the air grew stale, and we all became groggy and some men passed out. We stayed two or three nights in a pottery factory,

234

where we were actually warm inside the building. They had some unique pottery containers there in which a man could crawl inside, and they were said to hold 1,000 liters.

At Halbau, Germany, we were standing in line in the street, with snow on the ground, and it was still snowing. An old German woman kept bringing us hot water, in defiance of a Nazi party member. Each time she went back and forth by him, she would toss her head up. The party member was standing over on a corner, by a post, with his hat brim pulled down over his eyes, like a movie gangster. Out in the country, we were stopped for a rest, and there was a house close to the road. I went over to the house and traded some soap for a bag of potatoes—kartoffels in German. I asked the lady in German if she had any food she would trade me. She said she had some kartoffels and asked me what I would give her for them. I told her soap, and we made a trade. I carried the potatoes all the way to Moosburg, where we had a potato bash. There were many of our men who had varying degrees of frostbitten hands, feet and faces from walking in the bitter cold.

At Spremberg, I traded a cigarette to a German soldier in exchange for his skull and crossbones insignia, which I have to this day. He was in either a storm troop or a panzer unit, I have forgotten which. At Spremberg, we were crowded in boxcars on a long train ride and rode, standing up for the most part, the balance of the way to Moosburg. The only way one could sit down was between the legs of another man, who also needed to rest. For the latter part of our stay in Moosburg, we slept in tents on the ground. It was further south, near Munich, and the snow was off the ground when we got there.

We were liberated by Patton's 14th armored force on April 29, 1945. After we were liberated, we had no food at all. We borrowed rifles, jackets and vehicles from American soldiers in the area, and went out among the German population and obtained our food from them. While this may seem harsh, it was the only way we could get anything to eat. On May 1, 1945, we were flown to Camp Lucky Strike at Le Havre, France, where I obtained leave and had made arrangements to fly out to Rackheath to find out about my crew. But, before I could leave, I became deathly ill with the flu and couldn't make the trip. After I felt better, I did write to the 467th group in England for information and when I arrived home in North Little Rock, I had a letter there from a Lt. Thomas Goodyear, advising me that I was the only survivor of our crew. The last sentence in his letter has often haunted me—"The Group has chalked up a good record *and life at Rackheath has continued just the same as before.*" Just the same as before. Nothing would ever be the same as before to those of us who didn't return to Rackheath from their missions—whether they managed to live through it or not.

There has been much soul-searching and considerable anguish in reliving these events. I will not belabor this account with further details. It is sufficient to say that air crew members had a special camaraderie for each other that is found only under circumstances where they routinely face danger together, time after time, and are dependent upon each other for their safety. To this day, I cannot watch a documentary of aircraft going down in battle without tears coming to my eyes for the gallant, young men riding those machines of war to their deaths. I think of what might have been had the men of my crew been allowed to live and contribute their good minds, talents and enthusiasm to our world. I sometimes think that what we lost was greater than what we won.

My First Trip To Germany, And It Had To Be Berlin
by Louis Loevsky (466th)

On March 22, 1944 the 466th Bomb Group and my crew flew their first mission to Berlin.

Our B-24, "Terry and the Pirates," was hit by flak over Berlin and we lost the #1 propeller. A mid-air collision then ensued, causing "Terry" to also lose props #2 and #3. The other B-24, the "Brand," lost its tail, causing it to go into a tight spin. Len Smith, our bombardier, was trapped in the "Terry" nose turret, and the electrical and manual systems had rendered it inoperable by the crash. The turret would not turn so that its doors could open to let Len out. Len had also sustained substantial injury.

Less than six hours into combat, and here I was, through as a navigator! I remembered when, less than four months before, I had heard the glorious words: "Lt. Louis Loevsky, you are now a navigator!" said my instructor as he pinned the coveted silver wings on me.

But now I had to extricate Len from his predicament, and it was most difficult since he was in shock and kept removing his gloves (at -35□F or below) and oxygen mask (at 23,500 feet). I repeatedly tried putting his mask and gloves back on while trying to spring the nose turret doors open; when I put an arm around his chest and pulled him out, that was quite an achievement. After I got Len out I released the bombs in train. Thirteen of twenty crew members were KIA, five from the "Terry" and eight from the "Brand."

After assisting Len in bailing out, our pilot, Bill Terry, yelled, "Hey, Lou, wait for me!" I waited until he left the control column, then bailed out through the bomb bay. While free falling I saw one parachute open above me, which had to be Terry's. Not trusting the Germans, I realized that with the "H" (Jewish) on my dog tags I risked being shot as a spy if I ripped them off and threw them away... and risked being shot as a Jew if I left them on and fell into the hands of the Gestapo or the SS! I left them on. Still free falling, I thought of the gross of condoms scattered in every pocket of my uniform... "My parents will think they raised a sex fiend!"

When I finally opened my parachute, I found I was being shot at from the ground. Slipping and spilling air, I became an instant expert in maneuvering the chute, despite admonitions to keep our "cotton-picking" hands off the shroud lines. I got away from a small camp where they were shooting at me, toward another small camp where they were not. Selecting a small tree in Berlin, I crossed my legs for posterity, crashed branches off one side of the tree, and with my chute caught on top, my feet whipped over my head and my back injured, I blacked out briefly and then came to with my toes touching the ground. A Home Guard (Volkstrum) had a gun in my ribs, repeating, "Pis-tole? Pis-tole?" Two Wehrmacht troops appeared and took over my custody. While I was getting out of the parachute harness, three SS arrived, apparently from the small camp where they had been shooting at me. The SS argued with the Wehrmacht; they wanted to take custody of me (and since my parents sometimes talked Yiddish, I could understand). Fortunately, the two Wehrmacht troops retained my custody.

As they marched me through the streets of Berlin to their headquarters, the angry civilian mob was yelling in perfect

AMERICAN, "String him up!" "Hang him!" "Lynch him!" They wanted a necktie party. As they were closing in, the Wehrmacht troops had to draw their sidearm to keep the ugly lynching mob at bay. I believe Bill Terry was shot from the ground as he floated down in his parachute.

I became a POW at Stalag Luft III, Sagan, Germany until the Russians got close in January 1945. After that we were evacuated at 2AM in a freezing blizzard. From there we reached Stalag VII A in Moosburg, by marching in sub-zero weather and being crammed into (40 & 8) boxcars. We were improperly clothed and improperly fed; our conditions were unsanitary and inhumane. Imagine hundreds of American officers and enlisted men lined up, evacuating their bowels when the train stopped at a station in full view of German women and children. We were treated like swine!

We were liberated by Gen. George Patton's troops on April 29, 1945. Joel Greenberg, flight engineer of "Terry and the Pirates," folded his wings in early 1993. Fifty-five years after the mid-air collision, the three survivors of both crews are: C. Wayne Beigel, of the "Brand" crew; Len Smith; and me, Louis Loevsky.

"Crunch Landing" at Seething
by Oak Mackey

The date was January 10, 1945, a bad day for the **Jack Clarke** crew of the 392nd Bomb Group of the Second Air Division of the Eighth Air Force. I, **Oak Mackey**, was the copilot; **Brad Eaton**, navigator; **Bob Lowe**, bombardier; **E.C. Brunnette**, engineer; **J.T. Brown**, radio operator; **Ralph Heilman**, nose gunner; **George Peer** and **John Heckman**, waist gunners; and **Kevin Killea**, tail gunner; perhaps the best crew in the 8th AF.

We were awakened at 02:00 a.m. for briefing at 04:30 a.m. The target was Dasburg in the Bastogne area to support our ground troops there. The weather was absolutely atrocious— through the night there had been a combination of freezing rain, sleet, snow showers and fog. The runways and taxiways were covered with a sheet of slippery ice.

At briefing we learned that our usual B-24 was not available and we were assigned the squadron spare. We were a deputy lead crew and would be flying off the right wing of the lead plane of the leading squadron. Upon reaching our assigned airplane, we found it had not been warmed up, the engines were cold and very difficult to start. Only after much cranking, priming and cussing were we able to get them running. We were supposed to be two for takeoff just after the Group lead airplane. By now most of the entire Group had departed.

We made our takeoff, climbed through the overcast to on top of the clouds and had the rest of the Group formation in sight. At this time the #3 engine propeller severely over-speeded, probably because of congealed oil trying to pass through the propeller governor. This is a serious problem—because of the engine over-speed the engine might turn to junk, or the propeller might come off the engine and pass through the fuselage or hit the other engine on that side. Jack told me to shut down the engine and feather the propeller. I reduced power to the engine and pushed the feathering button. It immediately popped out again, for it is its own circuit breaker. Brunnette was sitting between Jack and me on the cockpit jump seat, as all good engineers should. He pushed the feathering button in and held it there, which caused the secondary circuit breaker to pop open, which he immediately held down with his other hand, a risky procedure as it could cause the feathering oil pump motor or associated wiring to catch fire. Oh-so-slowly the prop blades turned to the feathered position and engine rotation stopped.

With one engine out and a loaded airplane there was no way we could stay with the Group. We were now in the vicinity of Great Yarmouth, so we flew out over the North Sea and dumped our bombs. We left the arming safety wires in place so the bombs could not explode.

As we turned to go back to our base, the #2 propeller ran away, compounding our numerous problems. We got the engine shut down and propeller feathered with less trouble than we had with #3. A B-24 cannot maintain airspeed and altitude with two engines out and full fuel tanks, and we gave careful consideration to bailing out but decided to stay with the airplane for a while and conserve altitude as best we could. The weather at our airfield near Wendling had not improved, but we had little choice but to try to return there.

We were about due south of Norwich ten miles or so when we spotted an airport through a hole in the clouds, our first good luck of the day. We descended through the hole in the clouds and had gone through the before-landing checklists, lowered wing flaps to the landing position, extended the landing gear, and were turning to line up with a runway from west of the airport when the thick bullet-resistant windshield and side windows iced up, a common occurrence when descending through a temperature inversion. We could not go around with the landing gear and flaps down with only two engines operating—we were committed to landing.

Jack and I could not see through the iced-up windshields and windows. We had to continue our descent to keep airspeed above stalling. Through a small clear place on my side window I saw men running at full speed, and I also saw that we were about to touch down. I assumed those men were running from a building of some sort and we were lined up to hit it. Without any thought and perhaps with instinct, I pushed full left rudder that caused the airplane to slew around to the left and we touched down in a sideways attitude. The landing gear snapped off, the two outside engine propellers broke off and went cart wheeling across the airfield. We slid sideways on the fuselage for a long way on the ice and snow; it seemed like forever. The fuselage was broken behind the cockpit area and the nose tilted up, which enlarged the window to my right a bit so that I was able to go through it with my backpack parachute on. Likewise, Jack went out the left cockpit window. I ran along the right side of the airplane, stopped at the waist window to look in to see if everyone was out, continued around the tail and there they were, all nine of them and no one had a scratch. We had landed at Seething Airfield, home of the 448th Bomb Group, and we had missed the control tower by only 100 feet or so.

An ambulance pulled up in a few minutes and took us to the base hospital where the doctor looked us over to be certain there were no injuries. For medicinal purposes, someone brought out a bottle of 100-proof rye whiskey. We took our medicine like real men. Someone called our base at Wendling and a truck came for us in an hour or so. So ended a bad day for the Clarke crew. It could have been much worse.

Dessau Was No Picnic!

Submitted by Howard Boldt, Ray Lemons, Jack Knox and Jim Baynham (445th)

The following account occurred on our 3rd mission, Dessau, Germany, August 16, 1944. Lt. Jimmy Baynham, and his Liberator crew somersaulted through flaming wrecks of two other planes high over Germany, and the Texarkana pilot brought 'em back alive.

"With nobody dead—just standing on our heads," that's the newest line of the wing and a prayer thing recently enacted by First Lieutenant James Baynham, of Texarkana and his Liberator crew many miles over flak-flipping Germany. He wrote the details, with military stuff excluded, in a letter to his dad, J. D. Baynham, advertising manager of the *Texarkana Gazette & Daily News*, and it's a thrilling story. Here's the way he tells it:

We got up at 0245 and headed for the mess hall to receive fresh eggs for a change—they really tasted good. Then to briefing where we were told about our mission for that day. It would be a rough one, with plenty of flak, and a good chance for fighters. So, we took off and assembled in our squadron, then group, then wing, then division and finally the whole Air Force, and headed for Germany.

As we looked ahead we could see hundreds of planes stretched for hundreds, it seemed, of miles ahead, and that many more behind us. Then we rumbled across the enemy coast, and we wondered what the people there thought, as day after day, they saw all the heavies slowly go in and then, hours later, come out again, undisturbed, the empty places filled by other ships. They should know that there must be something terrific happening far back in Germany.

As we test-fired our guns, we found we had only one gun working in the nose and one of the tail turret guns ran away, expending a quarter of its ammunition, an unpleasant situation, but not meriting an abort from the mission.

As we flew to the target, we skirted any flak areas that came up, so we didn't get any shots close to us on the way in.

As we hit the I.P. (initial point), and opened our bomb doors, we started getting flak. At first, it was inaccurate, and just as Hec (one of the gunners) said "They're just a bunch of farmers," they closed in on us and really got our number. We were riding through it, however, hearing the flak explode it was so close, and hearing the shrapnel hit the ship, when I looked up and saw a burning ship flying upside down about 100 feet above us. It was going very fast and diving. It looked like a derelict, burning fiercely. Charley, (the copilot) looked up and saw it too, and we both sat spellbound as it dived into the very center of the ship in front of us, not more than 100 feet away. Then we began to act. As I turned the ship to the left, the blast hit us. Both ships had exploded in a great ball of red fire, smoke and debris. As the blast hit us, the force sent us over on our backs, going down and passing through the wreckage.

Instantly Charley and I were on the controls with all we had. The amazing thing was that we were working exactly together, not fighting for the controls. I was sure we were on fire too after flying through that flame, and our only thought at the time was to right it long enough to give everyone a chance to jump.

So as we turned it back over and pulled it up, we looked, and amazingly enough, all our engines were turning. As we had turned over, the bombs had torn loose from their racks and battered the bomb bay roof and sides, then dribbled out as we righted the ship. The inside of our ship was really in a mess. Our equipment was strewn everywhere; some of it had fallen out.

Hec, in the nose turret, released the doors and came tumbling out of the turret backwards, as the explosion occurred. He was weak with the loss of oxygen, so Johnny (another crew member) applied oxygen to him. No injuries in the nose turret. Next, on the flight deck, Charley and I were not affected mentally as were the others because we were busy. Boldt, the engineer, was in the upper turret and was all right. Fields, the radioman, who was under the flight deck at the open bomb bays, was nearly thrown from the ship during the violent maneuvers, but suffered no injuries.

Next, in the waist, Lemons was thrown back towards the tail, with ammunition boxes, chaff and equipment all around him. Byrd, the other waist gunner, was in the same fix. Knox, in the tail turret, seeing the smoke and flames, thought it was our ship that had been hit, and came out of his turret, crawling through the escape hatch, the centrifugal force not permitting him to make much headway. All three were ready to bail out, but the escape hatch was jammed, and by the time they made their way to the waist windows, the plane was in an upright position again, so they realized they were okay. They were all weak from anoxia, so they sat down while regaining their strength, but there were no injuries in the waist.

Then we found we still had one bomb, and the bombardier came back and released it manually. Then we found that the bomb bay doors could not be closed, so we left them until we reached a low altitude. In the meantime, we saw that we had no brake pressure. So when we reached lower levels, I crawled out in the bomb bay and cranked the doors shut, filled the gas gauges at the same time and found we were low on gas.

When we reached the field, we proceeded to come in for a no-brake landing. We were happy when the gear came down, then the flaps also worked, and we put the flap handle down. I noticed that about 700 pounds had been built up on the brake pressure gauges. So when we hit the ground, Boldt hit the flap handle and held it down, giving us some brakes—not enough to use constantly but enough to stop us once we slowed down. So after we slowed down as much as possible, I jammed on the brakes, and as the plane skidded to the side, the throttles kept it straight, and we finally came to a stop, taxied off on the grass and got out to kiss the dear old terra firma.

Upon inspecting the ship, we found the leading edge of the wing between Nos. 1 and 2 engines had been mangled and some more wreckage had hit the right side of the fuselage, bending it. The top of the cockpit had been cracked by more wreckage. Anyway you take it, we were nine very lucky guys that day.

That's the story, Pop. I believe I left out all the censorable stuff—but it's a good story—like a bad dream, no more. I guess the reason it doesn't bother us is that it all happened so fast and was so impersonal when we thought of it afterwards. We find ourselves joking about it and wonder how the hell we do it. I guess we have to be that way.

It's A Small, Small World After All
by Jack D. Pelton, (445th)

It was August 16, 1944, over Dessau, Germany that some lucky flak gunner found the "Sweetest Rose of Texas" at about 20,000 feet, just after bombs away. This wasn't our regularly assigned B-24; our war weary old bird was hanger-bound back at Tibenham and we had been assigned Arnold Nass' "The Rose," as it was affectionately known by its crew. Whoever the gunner was, he really peppered our big-ass bird with 88mm shells until he got lucky and severely damaged our flight control system with a hit that affected our elevator trim tabs in such a way that the elevators were thrown into a full nose-up position. The result was a full hammer head stall out of formation. After dropping rapidly to about 15,000 feet before recovering control, we surveyed our situation. The plane looked like a flying sieve. It had about 150 flak holes, radio knocked out, and severe damage to the flight control system—so bad, in fact, that my co-pilot and I could only maintain level flight by bracing our knees against the wheel and "stiff-arming" it with both arms. Fortunately, we had all four fans running, although No. 3 had a flak hole in the reduction gear housing and had lost all of its oil. Thanks to Mr. Pratt & Mr. Whitney, who made a superb engine, it continued running, without oil, all the way back to England! We made it with an escort of P-51s, Jugs (Thunderbolts), and a covey of P-38s for top cover and set the old girl down on the crash landing strip at Manston (or was it called Woodbridge?) We were afraid we might have flat tires around the wheel wells, so I gently dropped her in from about 100 feet with a 30-degree crab. She rolled to a stop in about 1500 feet. My flight engineer, Ray Pytel, didn't even say "boo" about the heavy landing. He just got out and kissed the ground like the rest of us.

The scene now changes to Hawthorne Municipal Airport in the Los Angels area. It's May of 1993 and I have gone to see the "All American" B-24 and that restored primary trainer, the 909 B-17. I was also responsible for the Second Air Division recruitment booth that day. I noticed a man and his wife carefully examining our display of 1944 Group locations and airfield layouts in England. I approached the couple and asked if they were interested in what they saw, and did they have any questions. He answered, "No, is was on the odder end." I asked what he meant. He replied, "I vass a flak gunner mit de Cherman ground forces in central Chermany." Not only was he a flak gunner, it turned out he was directing the fire over Dessau on August 16, 1944! He remembered knocking two or three Liberators out of the sky on that fateful day. I asked him how he could be so damn accurate with those 88s. He told me they had optics so superior that he would see the waist gunners firing. He was only fourteen years old and had been "recruited" into the Hitler Jugend Corps when there were no more mature men left to man the flak guns. We had an interesting conversation and came to the conclusion that it was likely he had been responsible for our near-demise.

It is, indeed, a small world after all!!

448th's Mission to an Underground Oil Storage Facility
by Jeff Brett

On 25 March 1945, 448th BG crews were awakened early, 1:30, for the briefing. John Stanford was one of the many men listening to the briefing that morning. *"Gentlemen, your target for today is the underground oil storage depot at Buchen. The secondary target will be the marshalling yards at Osnabruk. You will carry twenty 300-pound General Purpose bombs."* Lt. Robinson was the briefing officer and he continued with details of the mission. "He shows us areas where we can expect flak, and says we could come under attack by 100 to 200 single-engine prop fighters and 40 to 50 Me-262 jet fighters. He runs through the order of penetration and other miscellany—code word for the target is 'Hayride'; for the secondary 'Cornsilk'; the recall word 'Coke'; fighter call signs, 'Balance 21 and 22'; weather scout, 'Bootleg Rum'; code word for dropping chaff, 'Black Sheep'; time in the air, 6:40; and time on oxygen, 3:30."

Palm Sunday morning erupted with a roar as the propellers of the Liberators spun to life at Seething. After an uneventful assembly, the formation encountered trouble leaving the English coast. Clouds thickened as they neared the Zuider Zee, making formation flying difficult. The lead squadron elected to fly in a circle in an effort to climb above the clouds. Lt. Elmer Homelvig, flying OLD POP, struggled to stay with his formation as they entered the clouds. *"We did alright for a few seconds. Apparently they increased their turn rate, and it's like snapping a whip, the guy on the tail end always gets the message later, and of course they increase their rate of turn. I lost sight of*

245

Tod (Lt. Fred Tod), and the only thing I could do was gradually increase my turn, hoping I'd catch sight of him before I ran into him. It wasn't more than a few seconds later that I saw a plane coming at me in the opposite direction, coming right at me. After we got on top of the clouds, Stalland was calling out giving his position, and in a few minutes, we found and caught up with him. Stalland had only two airplanes with him; I assumed they were Ray and Wikander. Tod was not with him, or had taken a different position. Stalland kept flying in a circle, and we kept picking up additional airplanes. We finally ended up with eight airplanes." The turn scattered the formation, leaving the 713th BS perilously out of position and lagging behind the remainder of the Group. Despite their scattered state the Group continued with the 713th vainly trying to make up time. By the time they reached the Wing Initial Point, they were still two minutes behind.

Just after 10:00 the sky filled with German fighters. A large force of Me-262s attacked the 448th with deadly results. Sgt. Clair Rowe, a gunner on SONIA, witnessed the jet attacks. He shot one of the attackers down before his aircraft was seriously damaged. *"When he began the attack, I began firing as soon as I thought he was in range. I saw two puffs of smoke when he fired his cannon, which was followed by a loud explosion, and I was blown out of my turret. I immediately got up and put on my chute and opened the escape hatch. We had no communication with anyone up front. Since the waist gunner was lying on the floor, I took over the waist gun. The explosion on the right side of the ship had knocked out our communication system and rudder controls. Our fighter escort then arrived, and we got home without further incident."* When the cannon shell tore into SONIA, the plane dropped 1,500 feet, but the pilots were able to regain the formation. The shrapnel dug into Sgt. Rowe's left leg and foot as well as causing lacerations on his face. With several wounded crew members and a severely damaged plane, the crew of SONIA faced a daunting return trip.

Sgt. Ed Chu fought a raging battle in the tail turret of MY BUDDIE. *"Before the IP, Max, our copilot, called 'Bandits in the area.' I saw three planes approaching out of the sun at six o'clock level. When they got within range, I recognized them as Me-262s. I opened fire at approximately one thousand yards at the closer of the two, the third in trail. I continued firing until he broke away through the squadron toward two o'clock high. I observed no hits or damage to confirm hits, although my tracers appeared to go right into the jet. P-51s boxed one up in front of the squadron and he exploded. Out of the corner of my eye, I could see the plane on our left wing flying the left element, 'Purple Heart Corner,' peel off and in flames. No chutes were observed and the plane was later seen hitting the ground and exploding. We later were told that it was Steffan's crew. Another Me-262 appeared at six o'clock, and this time I opened fire at extreme range. My left gun jammed, the ammo locking up in the booster sprockets. P-51s kept this jet from the formation. 'Bombs were away' and they appeared to have landed in an open field. Four more planes approached from six o'clock level. They looked like jets and I opened fire at extreme range with my one remaining gun, but stopped firing when I recognized them as P-51s. There was a P-47 off to the right being shot at by some other gunners, but luckily they recognized it before it was hit. I recall swearing at those gunners under my breath not to shoot, as it was one of ours. P-51s and P-47s dove by our formation after the jets, one P-47 cutting real close to our tail. I saw a B-24 explode and another one spin down in flames, as jets hit a trailing squadron."* It was the 713th BS still trying to catch the formation.

The first attacks hit the main part of the formation. Lt. Joseph Steffan and crew in TARFU II fell first at 10:17 after Me-262s hit them with cannon fire over Domitz, Germany. The navigator, Lt. Gerald Gottlieb, bailed out of the burning bomber after the interphone was destroyed. *"I suspected the plane exploded after I left it because I was knocked unconscious for a short while and regained consciousness just before hitting the ground."* The last time Lt. Gottlieb heard from his crewmates was during an interphone check two minutes before the attack. Only he survived. The aircraft crashed near Langenhorst, Germany, and was totally destroyed.

After the initial pass, the fighters focused their attention on the straggling low left squadron. Cannon fire exploded in the flight deck of the lead aircraft, 42-50646 at 10:20, mortally wounding the pilot, Lt. Knute Stalland, and the copilot, Lt. Theodore Warner. F/O John Stanford watched from his nearby aircraft. *"The bursts moved up on Stalland's plane, and suddenly he is on fire—bright red-orange flames sweeping back from the left wing inboard fuel tanks. The plane dropped fifty feet or so, recovers, slides off out of formation to the right to about 200 feet, in a shallow climb. Then it pauses and starts to swing back towards the squadron. Someone jumps from the stricken bomber, his chute opening immediately, and boots flying off from the sudden jar. We are at 19,500 feet. It is 10:46."*

Suddenly, the right wing ripped off the fuselage and the plane exploded. The bombardier, Lt. John McHugh, bailed out through the nose wheel door escape hatch. Flames quickly engulfed the B-24 as it started its death spiral. The pilotage navigator, Lt. William Whitson, intended to follow Lt. McHugh but the plane exploded, blowing him clear. Although uninjured, he pulled the ripcord and was captured. The explosion also saved the radio operator, Sgt. Bobbie Glass. The force of the explosion rendered him unconscious just as he buckled his parachute. He fell ten to fifteen thousand feet before regaining consciousness. Amazingly, his parachute dangled from his chest harness by a single clip. He connected it and pulled the ripcord, only to be captured shortly after landing near Schnever-Dingen, Germany. These three men were the only survivors from the crew of twelve. A normal crew complement consisted of nine to ten men, but lead crews routinely carried twelve due to the specialized equipment.

DO BUNNY with Lt. Paul Jones and his crew went down next. On the first pass, Me-262s knocked out their number one engine with 20-millimeter cannon fire despite the curtain of lead from the B-24s fifty caliber machine guns. Subsequent passes by the Me-262 and a JG7 and flown by Luftwaffe ace Lt. Rudolf Rademacher further crippled Lt. Jones' Liberator. Two more engines ceased and numerous holes filled the aluminum skin of the plane. An exploding shell knocked the engineer out of the top turret and the plexiglass tail turret exploded in the face of the tail gunner. Somehow both escaped injury. Fuel and hydraulic fluid from the ruptured lines filled the inside of the aircraft, creating a potentially explosive situation. Also, the electrical system and intercom both failed. To the radio operator, Sgt. Chuck Blaney, the aircraft looked like a sieve from the inside.

"Lt. Jones ordered everyone to bail out, but with no intercom it was obvious that the word did not get out. Also, we were reluctant to jump because intelligence reports suggested that a crew's chances were amplified if capture as the group were at all possible. Single crewmen in the hands of angry German civilians were a poor risk in these times. Our navigator,

Lt. Herman Engel, could see the heavy clouds of smoke caused by our heavy bombing in the Hamburg area. He was able to set a course toward Wesel on the Rhine where British paratroopers had landed just the day before. I guess that we never really expected to make the Rhine, even as we threw everything out of the plane that was not nailed down. Our copilot, Lt. Jim Mucha, kept his eye peeled on a safe place to set DO BUNNY in a soft landing. With minimum power and controllability, our candidate landing sites were always dead ahead. At 11:43 we were at 2,000 feet altitude and sinking fast. One sputtering engine does not provide much power to a B-24 even at minimum loading. The pilots had selected a perfect field to put DO BUNNY down. It was right on the edge of the town of Soltau. We came in wheels-up and all went smooth until one wing dipped and the plane broke up. It was now 11:48 and we had covered all of thirty-six miles of the 180 needed to reach the front lines and freedom. The pilot, copilot, tail and ball gunners were able to get out of the aircraft and were immediately greeted by angry town folks with pitchforks. An SS officer appeared on the scene and arranged to have those crew members already outside of the aircraft run into the town square about 500 yards away. There they were all pinned to a wall across the street from the Mehr Hotel. I was trapped in the wreckage along with the navigator, flight engineer, and nose gunner. We had been pinned there by the top turret that broke away from the aircraft frame and lodged in the flight deck well. The navigator and engineer were unharmed and finally got out after German soldiers axed their way into the wreckage. The nose gunner and I were not so lucky. We were trapped by the top turret and each of us suffered a broken leg. The Soltau Chief of Police joined the German soldiers from the nearby riding academy and after much hard prying and much hack sawing we were freed from the wreckage. They put us on a horse-drawn cart and took us to the town hospital where our legs were set and put in soft casts. We then rejoined the other crew members who were not locked up at the riding academy."

Meanwhile, cannon fire from the four Me-262s tore into EAGER ONE, flown by Lt. Frederick Tod. The damage was severe: Right side flight control cables severed, right flap shot off, right rudder missing, four-foot hole in the left wing, generators out, amplifiers out, main fuel line leaking, upper and tail turrets inoperative, hydraulics gone, radio destroyed, and pilots interphone not working. EAGER ONE immediately fell out of formation and started lagging behind. The B-24 vibrated and shuddered, testifying to the tremendous damage the Liberator endured. Despite the terrific pounding, Lt. Tod and the copilot, Lt. Warren Peterson, kept flying the aircraft. With some difficulty, the bombs were jettisoned and the engineer stopped the fuel leak. Shortly afterwards, a fire started in the number four engine but extinguished itself after they feathered the engine.

The navigator, Lt. Herman James, provided a heading and distance to the nearest emergency airfield, Malmo, Sweden. Lt. Tod ordered everyone to prepare to evacuate the aircraft, as continued flight was uncertain. He advised everyone they could bail out over Germany if they did not want to risk an over-water flight. Everyone remained. With control problems and an engine out, the crew threw all non-essential equipment overboard. Still, they descended while a German Ju-88 followed to witness their demise.

Approaching the southern coast of Sweden, the number three engine started running very erratically and another engine became uncontrollable. Lt. Peterson told everyone to prepare to bail out as soon as they reached the coast. From his position in the nose of the aircraft, Lt. Herman James noticed incredible physical strain on the pilots. Lt. Tod's right leg shook violently from fatigue. They kept the airplane in level flight by sheer strength.

The number three engine abruptly stopped and Lt. Tod issued the bail out order. After Lt. James exited the aircraft, he watched the plane turn away from the village of Falsterbo and head back toward the sea, a selfless act that undoubtedly saved many lives in the village. As the eighth man in the nine-man crew left the plane, the B-24 entered a spin and crashed into the Baltic Sea just off the coast. Obviously, fatigue caught up with the pilots and as Lt. Peterson attempted to bail out, Lt. Tod was not able to fly the crippled plane any longer.

On the ground, numerous people witnessed the life or death struggle. Mr. Herald Anderson and Mr. Lennart Ahlstrom were two men who rushed to the waterfront to help in the rescue. As the parachutes floated earthward, the pursuing German Ju-88 finally caught up with its intended victim, although too late to inflict more damage. Swedish anti-aircraft fire scared them away. The two Swedish men quickly located a boat and set out for the crash site to help anyone in need. Meanwhile, other locals rolled up their pants and waded into the water to help those who landed short of land. One, Sgt. Chester Labus, suffered shrapnel wounds in his leg but managed to make it safely ashore. The wind blew some of the men overland where local residents quickly aided them. Mr. Ahlstrom and Mr. Anderson recovered Lt. Peterson but despite their valiant efforts, Lt. Peterson drowned. Lt. Tod perished in the crash of the B-24. Due to their heroic actions, seven of the crew survived. These two gallant pilots were posthumously awarded the Silver Star for their heroic actions.

After the brutal attacks, the low left squadron fell further behind. However, they dropped their bombs on the target at 10:34, nine minutes after the rest of the 448th. Realizing they would not catch the formation, the decimated squadron took a more direct route back to Seething instead of the intended route flown by the rest of the bombers. With many damaged planes and wounded men, they needed the shortest route home.

While the crew of EAGER ONE fought for their lives, the crew of SONIA held their breath as their plane limped home. A thorough examination of their plane revealed extensive damage. Their hydraulic system was ruptured, rendering it inoperative. The pilot, Lt. William Holden, elected to land at the long emergency runway at Manston. They manually lowered the landing gear and prepared to land without brakes and flaps. Despite missing one rudder, they landed on the long runway without complications. Lt. Douglas Torrance landed short of home. He selected a forward airfield in Belgium to land his shot-up Liberator.

Lt. Ed Anderson struggled to keep his damaged aircraft 42-50590 airborne. With two engines shut down, the crew dumped everything overboard. They even resorted, although unsuccessfully, to using a crash axe in an attempt to jettison the ball turret. With four P-51s providing escort, they received headings from a homing station to a forward airfield. Using maximum braking they stopped the damaged Liberator on the short runway and followed a Jeep to a parking spot. As they parked, the two remaining engines sputtered and shut down as they ran out of fuel.

After taking the shorter route home, the battered remnants of the 713th BS arrived over Seething thirty minutes before the rest of the formation. Red flares indicating wounded on board shot skyward from numerous planes. It was the first indication to the ground crews of the severe beating the Liberators endured.

Damage from the jets was tremendous. Four crews were missing and their friends at Seething wondered about their fates. Thirteen B-24s endured damage but still brought their crews home. Still, numerous men suffered injuries ranging from small lacerations to more severe shrapnel injuries. After a long absence, the Luftwaffe struck back with a mighty blow. Only three other missions flown by the 448th during the entire war suffered more losses. All were early in the war except this one. The new jets attacked with near impunity, as the family escorts were unable to match their tremendous speed. They added a new dimension to the air war and reinstalled the fear of the Lustwaffe in the aircrews.

Half A Mission Gets You
by W. A. Henderson. (392nd)

A person flying combat always takes for granted that it won't happen to him. Then, the day of reckoning comes and you are listed as, "Missing in action." You always wondered what happens when a plane went down, and now you know. Our turn was Gotha—24 Feb. 1944. Our crew was on its 22nd mission.

Just as we turned on the bomb run, six FW 190's came in at 12:00 o'clock level; eight more 2:00 o'clock high. We were hit in #4 engine and the oil pressure zeroed out, so #4 was feathered. Another pass just after bombs away and they got #3 engine and set it on fire. Number 4 engine was un-feathered in hopes we could keep up with the Group, but since it had no oil, it promptly ran away. Johns put the airplane in a steep dive to try to blow out the fire; #4 tachometer had wound around beyond the numbers—screaming away. There was no question—get out and walk! He slowed the aircraft down for bail out—leveling off about 8000 ft.

The bail out was accomplished, but not without a bit of unintended humor. When we rang the bell, "prepare to bail out" the bombardier was locked in the nose turret. He called the navigator to let him out. And what was the navigator doing? Folding maps, putting things away neatly. He finally did open the nose turret door and out tumbled the bombardier. As the navigator was first of the two to bail out, he crouched over the open nose wheel doors, turned to the bombardier and said, "Push me." The #11 shoes did that—post haste.

I made a free fall from about 7500 ft. to about 2000 ft. because we had been told the German fighter pilots might shoot you in your parachute if it looked like you might get away. You never think of the chute not opening while free falling, and mine opened just as it was supposed to. As I was coming down in my chute, I counted the others. Two chutes were missing. We later learned after the war that the graves registration teams had found the graves of waist gunner, Felix Zerangue, and engineer, Jack Indahl. As I neared the ground, our B-24 had made a steep 360° diving spiral and was headed for me when a friendly came between us.

The search party sent out by the Germans had about 8 people in it. They were coming on foot on a road that had a very elongated bend because of a long ridge covered with pine trees about a foot in diameter. I reasoned that it would take some time for them to reach that bend, so after burying my chute in the foot deep snow, I hurried over the hill onto the same road and ran toward them—wanting to be in a position near to them so they would pass me before starting the search. At the bend I got off the road and into the timber and watched them pass by, about 100 ft. away. They had guns, pitch forks, and the like for weapons, not a very friendly reception committee. After they had gone past, I continued through the trees to the road on the far side of the bend; got on it and walked away as if I was one of the search party returning.

I walked across a field in foot deep snow to a railroad to head south, and home. A troop train went by. The soldiers waved and I waved back thinking, "You would be off that train in a hurry if you knew who I was." This gave me confidence in my lack of identity, so I walked down the railroad through a small town, acknowledging greetings with a raise of the hand or a nod of the head, but not speaking. Apparently this was customary of the German populace at the time.

The next town was larger. I could speak very little German, but I could understand it to some degree. I asked a German for a drink of water, but I could not say it like a native. He became suspicious. My ankle was swollen, either badly sprained or broken. He took me to the Mayor of the town, who in turn called the authorities.

Thus ended my missions with the 392nd Bomb Group, and the start of sixteen months of prisoner of war time. Next came the ride to the P.O.W. camp, the interrogations, and the delousing, but those events are another series of stories.

Mission With a Surprise Ending
by Robert W. "Bob" Lambert (453rd)

How many of you old-timers from the 453rd Bomb Group remember a B-24 plane named the "Lonesome Polecat?" As a replacement crew, we inherited this wonderful plane in May 1944. After many successful missions, with a number of close calls, we flew its last mission with Jimmy Woolley as our pilot and I was the radio man. Our crew picture with this plane and some formation missions are in the book *In Search of Peace*.

I am not sure, but I believe this mission was over Hamburg, Germany; if not it was another large city where the sky was black with flak. During our bombing run (bombs dropped) we were hit several times and lost an engine. As we pulled away from the formation, a second engine on the opposite wing began to cough and act up. A short time later, we lost the second engine and gradually began to lose altitude. We stayed aloft, continuing to lose altitude, but since we were over enemy territory our pilot felt it was best to see how far we could go.

After what seemed like an eternity, we finally could see the English Channel. I was immediately told to send an S.O.S., as we probably could not make it across the Channel. I pressed so hard on the key (thinking the signal would go farther) that it broke off; I had to quickly jury-rig an alternative and kept on sending SOS signals until I received a response. Then I continued a signal so they could obtain a fix on our location.

While doing this, the crew was ordered to throw everything out of the plane into the Channel that was not fastened down. Out went the guns, ammunition, equipment, etc. In the excitement even a gunner's parachute was tossed out— what a shock—plans were quickly made that if we were to jump, Barney Feeney (a waist gunner) would take Jack Day with him and the two would go down together on one chute.

Even with the loss of weight, we were still losing altitude and getting closer to the water. Jump or ditch??? As we

254

got even closer to water we prepared to ditch. We then saw the coast of England in the distance and counted our blessings. Maybe we could reach shore and land somewhere on the beach area. However, it was felt that it would be safer to ditch and then swim ashore.

As we were thinking "ditch," our pilot saw a patch of grass he thought he could make and headed for that. We barely cleared the surrounding trees and our pilot was able to land our shot-up B-24 on the grassy area. We all climbed out and kissed the ground. When we looked up, we found we were surrounded by British troops with Tommy-guns and rifles pointed right at us. They stated in English and German that we were under arrest. Naturally we were surprised and spoke to them in English. They paid no attention; ordered us to put our hands behind our heads and marched us to a hidden building. As we did this, we saw many strange planes strategically placed under the umbrella of trees with camouflage netting over some of them. We were ushered into a room and then they asked for the commander of our aircraft. They took our pilot away while we were still being guarded by British troops.

After what seemed like hours, our pilot came in saying that we had landed on a very secret British Royal Air Force experimental aircraft base. They thought we were German spies flying in on a captured American plane. Our 2nd Air Division Headquarters cleared us as Americans returning from a mission.

The British then became friendly and furnished us with tea and crumpets. Later we were led to a waiting bus that returned us to our base at old Buckenham for debriefing, food and bed. We all *counted our blessings*, being very thankful we were all alive and "home."

Not a Happy New Year's Day
by Julian K. Wilson (453rd)

The following is taken from the Station 144 report filed on 4 January 1945. Subject: Mission # 197, 1 January '45, Target: Remagen.

The marshaling was very slow due to the fog. The takeoff was a nightmare. The visibility was never over 100 yards. There were five pots placed on the right side of the runway to assist the copilot in keeping visual contact. The first ship was off a little to the left of the runway as it passed the end. The second ship, Lt. Putman, made a good takeoff. The third ship, Lt. Judd, made a sharp left turn, went through the 732nd hardstand area, took the tail off WHAM-BAM, the wing off another ship, and cracked up just outside the of the 732nd area. The next four ships all went to the left of the runway. Capt. Lutes drug a wing on takeoff and Lt. Stout took over and flew the aircraft off. One aircraft started to take off and when the pilot felt the aircraft running over rough ground he chopped the power and got the aircraft stopped to the left of the runway about 100 yards. The tower controller at the upward end of the runway could neither see nor hear this aircraft although it was not over 100 yards away.

This is an excerpt from a document classified at the time as "Secret":

"Judd leading off in #65 veered left about halfway down the runway. His wheels clipped the tail off WHAM-BAM as the plane started to climb. Even then he might have remained airborne were it not for another ship parked in the path of the oncoming and partially stalled #65. When Judd's wheel hit the wing of the parked plane, #65 flopped over on her back, hurtled forward until a tree stopped the remaining momentum... Two men lived through the disaster miraculously enough: S/Sgt. Walter E. Beck, waist gunner, and Lt. Frank Pitcovich, pilotage navigator. Beck's condition is very serious, while outside of a few broken bones, Pitcovich got out with a bad case of shock. It was a sudden finish of a crew whose average age was 19, and which in the past month had really earned a fine reputation for outstanding ability... Only six ships got off that day—two from the 735th. Schauerman made a normal takeoff while Garrett, on his last mission, left the runway at approximately the same point as Judd. How he managed to stay in the air with a full bomb load will remain one of the unsolved miracles of combat operations."

Garrett has written about the events of January 1, 1945 from the standpoint of what he was doing that day, titling his paper (unpublished to this date) "The Bulge, The Bridge, and Bodenplatte." I have the approval of Bill Garrett to include the direct quotes used in this story taken from his paper.

A number of persons still active in the 453rd Bomb Group Association will recall the events of this day as well. They include the 735th Engineering Officer, Harry Godges.

Harry Godges has maintained a logging of the operational status for each of the aircraft assigned to the the 735th Squadron. Tom Brittan has similarly compiled a record of the history of each specific ASN numbered B-24 assigned to the 453rd.

After the war, Don Olds, the person who must be credited with being the active motivating force in collecting the original nucleus of the members of the 453rd together as an association, collaborated with General Andrew Low to produce the first record of the history of the 453rd outside of the microfilms in which the group history had been imbedded. In order to do this, they had gleaned the official records of daily reports filed during our operational period at Old Buckenham, Station 144. This was supplemented by memoirs held by General Low of his days at Old Buck.

Data from each of the above references are combined in the following story. Fact is the backbone of what could be read as fiction by most any reader.

The following is a recreation of the scene on that morning of January 1, 1945. All quoted text, written by William Garrett, is excerpted out of context.

"At about 0600 we received our first information as to where we were going and what we were to attack. We then picked up our parachutes, emergency kits, maps, and "flimsy" (paper with code words, call signs, colors of the day for flares, control points and radio frequencies and channels for various target and weather information) and catch assigned trucks which carried us to the hardstands where our B-24s were dispersed over the airfield. We would arrive at our respective aircraft at least one hour before takeoff, which was scheduled that day to commence at 0805 hours."

"...The weather was a big problem all through the first few weeks of the Battle of the Bulge, and New Year's Day 1945 was no exception. There was heavy fog at Old Buckenham, with visibility at dawn of a maximum of 100 yards. There was snow on the field, and although the runways had been cleared of it, they were slick. It was a very cold morning. Incidentally, the Allies had converted to British summer time (from British double summer time) on 17 September 1944, and the Germans went back to middle European time on 2 October 1944. As a result, both sides used the same clock time during the entire battle…"

"…After checking out SQUEE-GEE with the crew chief, Master Sergeant Harold H. Fox, and his people, we set up our stations and gathered around the plane awaiting time to be at stations—ready to start engines. We would not have been surprised if the word had come that the mission was delayed or scrubbed because of the miserable visibility conditions. Due to the desperate struggle going on in the battle area, the decision was that we had to go—weather or no."

"… Our load of four M66 2,000 lb bombs on 1 January 1945 was the heaviest bomb load our crew ever carried. Previously we had carried three 2,000 lb bombs on 26 September 1944 when attacking a railway bridge over the Lippe Canal, on 4 November to the railway marshaling yards at Karlsruhe, and on 6 November to the Mitteland Canal Locks at Minden. Since these targets were deeper into Germany than Remagen, we had probably carried 2500-2700 gallons of fuel rather than the 2300 we were carrying to Remagen. This would explain, from a weight standpoint, the additional 2,000 lb bomb on our 1 January 1945 Remagen mission."

"… As we taxied out to the main runway 26 in the fog, I detected what I thought was a bit greater visibility—perhaps more than a football field, a bit greater than when at our hardstand 23 nearby. On the way to takeoff position (we were seventh in line) we were stopped longer than what was normal for such a procedure. It seemed to me—perhaps it was wishful thinking—that visibility was increasing slowly. I thought I might be able to make a visual takeoff. I told my copilot to keep a sharp lookout from his right seat window at the edge of the runway and let me know quickly if we were moving towards or away from it."

"…When I received the green light to go (we were on radio silence as the Luftwaffe Horchdienst, their Y service, was listening), I made a carrier type departure—brakes fully engaged while the throttles were advanced to the stops and the electronic supercharger was set at position 8. This was standard takeoff power with flaps set at 20 degree position. When the engines seemed to be running at full power, with the propellers at high RPM (2700), I released the brakes and we began the takeoff roll."

"…The takeoff made on 1 January 1945 will remain in my memory, vividly, as long as I live. The smaller details, considering it occurred more than fifty years ago, are hazy, though the broader event itself will haunt me as long as I live. I had made a fully instrument takeoff in similar dense fog on 19 December 1944 without any problem. I should have attempted the same on 1 January 1945. I recall SQUEE-GEE, upon release of brakes, rolling forward, slowly at first, but accelerating with alacrity, heading out along the 26 track. Rapidly glancing back and forth, ahead at the directional gyro and saw that the 26 was not centered. As I attempted to bring it back to center, I felt SQUEE-GEE jolt and bounce, which made it clear that she was off the runway to the left. I immediately twisted the electronic turbo control to the "10" position from the standard position of "8" on takeoff. This was "War Emergency Power" which drove the manifold pressure from 48 inches to about 56 inches of mercury. There was an immediate surge of power setting before… this was a power setting for a dire emergency only, that it could be used for five minutes maximum…

SQUEE-GEE was pulled or lifted off the ground with an airspeed of 120-130 miles per hour. We were in dense fog with nothing visible ahead or to the sides. Gear was retracted and we began to gain altitude. In a few minutes we were out of the dense fog and into blinding sunshine."

"…The takeoff was a clear example of the excellence of the designers and builders of SQUEE-GEE, the superb Pratt and Whitney R-1830-65 radial engines, and the dedicated and conscientious maintenance by Master Sergeant Harold H. Fox and his ground crew. These factors and SQUEE-GEE overrode the handicap imposed on her by an impromptu procedure by me and rescued us from the consequences of my mistake."

Upon mission return:

"…When we landed we were met by the usual truck to take us to the standard debriefing procedure. A jeep also arrived, with, I believe, Lt. Col. Edward F. Hubbard, the Air Executive of the 453rd Bomb Group. He may have been accompanied by Lt. Col Van Dowda, who had just become Group Operations Officer. I recall being shown, as they drove me down runway 26, the still visible tracks of B-24 wheels going off the runway to the left (southwest). Some of these tracks were undoubtedly mine. I can't recall now how far from the takeoff position they began to go off to the left, but I believe it was near 4,000 feet down the runway. They identified Judd's tracks in the same area, and we drove to the latter's crash scene..."

"Ellingham, near Attleborough, Norfolk, England... Pat was an 11-year-old schoolboy who lived near our base. He was walking on Abbey Road, along the south perimeter of our airfield, to Old Buckenham School when he came upon the wreckage of a B-24 blocking Abbey Road and his route to school. This was the B-24 piloted by Lt. Alan C. Judd, who had been scheduled to lead the high right squadron on (in which we were to lead the high right element that morning). This location is also verified by reports which state that Judd went off runway 26 to the left on takeoff and into the area of the 732nd Bomb Squadron hardstands which were just south of runway 26 and just north of Abbey Road. In the 732nd area, Judd's B-24 struck the tail of WHAM-BAM (our brightly painted formation and utility B-24D), took the wing off another parked B-24, and then ended up at Abbey Road where Pat Ramm encountered it... This crash was the cause of our delay in getting to takeoff position. Since we were on radio silence, we did not learn of this accident until we returned from the Remagen mission."

This is the end of Garrett's report.

After preparing this material, I felt I had accomplished two things:

(1) A person who had collected bits and pieces of the events involving the crash of her loved one, could now sort out and trash accounts that were not true, plus the true events assembled for her were now identified in their proper sequential series (except for the Station 144 report of 4 January 1945 at the opening of this article).

(2) A remarkable story has been brought to life that would have otherwise gone unpublished. This indeed was the case, and, now practically fifty-five years after the incident and almost five years since its writing, a small portion of the entire story is now seeing daylight!

Over the Rainbow
by William McGinley (392nd)

260

Our crew, commanded by Lt. Stukus, had arrived at Wendling on October 15, 1943 as one of the early replacement crews and had completed eight combat missions when, on January 29th, 1944, we were awakened in the very early hours for our ninth and what eventually turned out to be our last mission.

The primary target was Frankfurt, in central Germany. The misfortune began during the group's assembly over East Anglia when one of our ships, from the 577th Squadron, had a terrible mid air collision, in cloud, with one of the 482nd Group's Pathfinder B-24s with one of our original 392nd crews on board. From the two ships, a total of only three men managed to escape from the tumbling wreckage of the Pathfinder and survive.

Due to those same clouds which extended all along our route, with a few breaks, we lost contact with our group's formation en route to Frankfurt. We decided to turn back when we failed to locate any other B-24s with which we could have joined up and so complete the mission as briefed.

Shortly after turning back, we came under attack by a swarm of German fighters and a running battle ensued for the next 20 minutes or so, in and out of the clouds at high altitude, but as our ship sustained and absorbed more damage we were forced down to 2,000 feet, losing altitude and on fire.

Our navigator and bombardier had been killed during the battle, our gunners were completely out of ammunition, and three German fighters were coming in fast and lining us up in their gun sights, so we survivors had no alternative but to bail out. I scrambled from the tail gun turret, went forward and hauled the ball gunner up from his plexiglass turret. After standing at the open waist exit door for a moment, absolutely terrified as I looked down at the open countryside slowly passing below, I jumped into space. I've never forgotten getting out of that burning bomber.

I had no idea where I was as I floated down and landed clumsily in an open, freshly plowed field. Quickly unbuckling my chute harness, I started running across the field, looking for a hiding place. As I was stumbling my way over the plowed furrows, I saw someone waving at me frantically at me from the edge of the field to get down and stay down.

Little did I know that this was my first contact with the Belgian resistance movement. I immediately flopped forward, face down on the soft soil, and checked my wristwatch. It was 1100 hours. I stayed as still as possible, face down and hugging the cold, damp ground while hearing the distant shouting and yelling from German patrols as they traveled along the surrounding country roads, tracks and through woodland searching for me and the other survivors from our crashed plane.

We'd been told back at Wendling that if we could manage to get through the first 12 hours in enemy-occupied territory without getting caught, there was a reasonable chance that the underground movement would make contact. I was very lucky, because as soon as it began to get dark a resistance member came for me.

I soon learned first hand of the ingenuity, bravado and courage of the resistance organization. They hid me, together with other crew members from our plane, in a small room built with wooden boards and corrugated iron, which had been dug underneath a haystack. The secret hiding place was beneath the closest haystack to the road. Their reasoning was that a very obvious hiding place would be the last one to be thoroughly searched, if at all.

The resistance kept us supplied with sufficient food and drink during our time in the hideout, visiting only after nightfall. Each and every time I heard an unfamiliar sound outside our haystack I had terrifying visions of Nazi soldiers stealthily approaching.

When the resistance decided the time was right for our next move, they made all the necessary arrangements for us to be issued forged documents, civilian clothes, and a guide to take us by train into the large, sprawling city of Brussels, Belgium.

I had just gotten off the train at the railroad station in Brussels and was making my way through the crowds of milling people when I saw a German soldier, in field-grey uniform, walking along the platform towards me. I kept changing direction to avoid him, but clumsily walked right into him. I can only speak English, so there wasn't anything I could say. Luckily, he just laughed. So I laughed and managed to smile. He then said something unintelligible. I could only smile weakly in response and saunter away, my heart beating wildly.

Months later, when I became more accustomed to my behind-the-lines status, I would even ride on the streetcars, occasionally sitting beside German soldiers. If I were captured, I would be sent to a prisoner-of-war camp until the end of the war. What really worried me was that if any of the resistance people, who were hiding me in the city and transferring me to various addresses in Brussels in order to avoid the suspicions of neighbors, were unfortunate enough to be captured, they would either be tortured for information and then shot, or shipped east to face the horrors of a concentration camp where death often came as a blessed relief. For this reason, the percentage of volunteers, especially those with children, involved in the highly dangerous work of the resistance organizations, was very low.

Of course, there were a few exceptions. One of the key members of the underground in Belgium was British-born Anne Brusselmans, a 39-year-old mother of two. I first met Anne in a Brussels basement in February 1944. She played a leading part in looking after us and arranging our moves to different locations. An estimated 130 Allied airmen eventually found their way to freedom because of her efforts. On one occasion the Gestapo managed to infiltrate the resistance network and caught one of her friends harboring downed American airmen. The father of the family was shot and the rest went into concentration camps.

The resistance members in Holland, Belgium and France were truly heroic people and took tremendous risks. Jane, a courageous young woman after whom I subsequently named my daughter, was a typical example.

She had previously been caught and beaten once by the Gestapo, but hadn't cracked under extreme interrogation and was subsequently released after managing to convince them of her innocence. Jane, and two resistance men in German uniforms, would drive towards a specific border point where they tied her up. At the border crossing they'd say she was a prisoner being taken to France for questioning. When they wanted to get back into Belgium they'd use a different border checkpoint and drive through again.

I well remember the Belgian count was also a member of the resistance organization. He spoke fluent German, and, with forged ID documents, would go to an airfield wearing a Gestapo officer's uniform, complete with skull and crossbones insignia, and dine at the officers' mess. In the meantime, Louie, the count's chauffeur/handyman, who was a quite extraordinary character, would wander around the airfield wearing the uniform of a German private and pour sugar in the fuel tanks of their airplanes. They would do anything.

I had given my service number to the underground to notify the International Red Cross authorities, not realizing that

Europeans use a small cross mark on the number 7 and, because of this, an error was made in transmitting my number. Subsequently, all the figure 7s in my number were thought to be 1s, so without any underground or German confirmation of my status, the Red Cross reported me as dead. My mother, at home in Mabelvale, near Little Rock, Arkansas, was notified by our War Department as "missing in action," and then, a little later, as "killed in action." But she adamantly refused to accept that I'd been killed.

During the following weeks and months, I didn't know what was going on. Someone would come to the house where we were hiding and say, "Let's go," and we'd go. We didn't know because we were not supposed to know.

After months of hiding at various locations, I sat in a Belgian café and witnessed the German army in full retreat following the Allied invasion of France. It was really something to see. Thousands of German troops with their equipment (some of the trucks and staff cars were being hauled by horses due to lack of gasoline) jammed the road, barely moving, all heading towards Germany. I felt sorry for the plainly under-nourished horses, but had not the slightest sympathy for the soldiers.

After being reunited with the American forces as the Allies advanced across Europe, I was flown back to England in September 1944, and saw, from the air, the thousands of bomb and shell craters that marked the Allied advance from the Normandy beaches and extended back inland as far as the eye could see.

As we flew over the English Channel and the southern coast of England came into view, I vividly recall seeing one of the biggest and most beautiful rainbows ever created.

Paralyzed With Fear
by Ken Jones (389th)

April 4, 1945—Parchim
German Airfield—Secondary Wesendorf
Aircraft K—567th BS
Flight Time 8:15 hrs.
Bomb Load 12-150 lbs. G.P.

The silver screen—hometown USA—A Sioux War Chief mounts his pony on the run. He gives a blood curdling war cry and shouts, "It's a great way to die."

At briefing we learn we are going to blast the German fighters where they eat their sauerkraut and wienerschnitzel, on the home field in northwestern Germany. Going to meet an ugly "widow maker" in the sunshine.

Flying Lead, Low Left Squadron of 389th Bomb Group. Visual takeoff from base. Some clouds predicted over target. 6/10s to 10/10s in some places.

Unopposed on penetration. A few black smudges of 88s out of range to let us know we are expected. Code word given for primary target visual. We started to uncover to trail the lead squadron at the group IP. While making this slow left turn, I looked down through an opening in the clouds and saw two German fighters taking off from an airfield. Alerted gunners, "Bandits airborne."

One minute or less later, I saw a jet turbine ME 262 coming at us from 9 o'clock level and circling to our rear. I pulled the squadron in close. I don't know why I did it but we were slightly offset to the right of the lead squadron upon completion of the turn. The clock stopped ticking and we braced ourselves for the attack. This twin-jet "bomber destroyer" can punch out 96 lbs of 30 mm canon shells in one three-second burst.

The jet seemed to hesitate and overshot our portside. I think he was going for someone in our low squadron and he misjudged his turn. At a distance he was watching the lead squadron and thought our squadron would come out of the turn in line with the lead. The jet was faster than anything I have ever seen. Joe Walko, left waist gunner, saw him coming all the way and only got off a short burst of 21 rounds of ammo.

Untouched, the jet pulled up, climbing to the lead squadron, his speed falling off. He dropped his flaps, which had holes in them like a navy dive bomber. The Luftwaffe Sturmvogel jet was now flying at formation speed behind #6, B-24 X-, in the three plane element directly behind and below the lead ship. Jerry parked there with his motor running, about 200 yards out.

This action and the following events took place in seconds.

There was no screaming dive to attack with a few short bursts of firepower, followed by a fast, fading breakaway.

Jerry was reckless. He wanted to die—to be out of it. No one tried to help him.

Coming out of nowhere, the German pilot eased up behind X- with his engines idling. Up to this point he hasn't fired a single round of canon shells. The tail gunner and X- spins his turret and lines up his twin fifties and the movement stops. The gunner does not fire his machine guns.

He sits there in disbelief. Time is suspended. Jerry is looking straight down the tail gunner's throat with four 30 mm canons. They stare at each other. The gunner is paralyzed with fear. The last thing the gunner will see is four orange flashes of light from the nose of the jet.

The tail turret shattered. Dissolved. The jet pilot touched his right rudder and fired short bursts. A real ace. The top turret and waist gunners on X- cannot bring their gun sights to bear on the German. Other gunners in the slot or bucket element did not fire their guns, apparently watching in fascination. Damn! I wish I had my squirrel rifle. I can hear someone screaming "Shoot... Shoot" into my oxygen mask.

The right stabilizer came off X- and came sailing down through our squadron, big as a barn door. I could see the impact of canon shell fire striking No. 3 engine and then shifting over to No. 2. Debris was flying off and sailing back into the slipstream. B-24 X- went into a flat spin, trailing smoke.

We were so close, I could see mud splattered on the fuselage of the German plane. The Luftwaffe pilot in the mottled colored jet popped his flaps and dove for the clouds. No shots were fired at him except from our plane on the way in. X- spun into the clouds and no chutes were seen by our gunners.

Like shooting fish in a barrel! I feel nauseated. Half anger and half fear. Maybe mostly fear that "there go I."

Completed bomb run and did not release bombs because clouds obscured the target. Lots of bandit chatter in the air dilutes the threat of flak bursting around us. Going full bore "at a walk" toward the rally point.

Code word given for the secondary target at Wesendorf. Made the IP and uncover from group formation to bomb by squadron. Looking for fighters. The bombardier can see the German airfield and I know we'll get this one visual. Just sitting there. Letting the auto-pilot and bombsight take us on in. Black stuff boiling up to meet us with an explosive welcome.

"Bombs Away" and let's get the hell out of here. Flak moderate to meager. Depends where you are on the dance floor when the band begins to play.

No such thing as an easy mission. If there is only one burst of flak and it gets you, it's a rough mission.

2nd Combat Wing under fighter attacks, off and on for thirty-five minutes. Must be mostly green pilots, they don't seem too aggressive and we don't see anyone else go down. The fighter screen is very effective at keeping Jerry at bay.

Saw many enemy aircraft and dog fights. P-51s diving and climbing all over the sky. The Mustangs better keep their distance—the boys looking over 50 cal. machine guns are a little nervous.

One bomber, another group, had No. 3 on fire. Trailing flame and smoke. A cripple and a straggler. Falling back of his formation. Our navigator, Pat Patterson, praying out loud for them on the intercom. Finally, prayers answered, the fire went out. A straggler will attract lots of attention today.

The war gives you two choices; kill or be killed. Whether you are on the ground in a fox hole or 4 1/2 miles up in the sky, you get him or he gets you. It's impersonal and insane. You must decide ahead of time just how you would react. You can't call a "time out" while you think about it. You just do it.

Sudden death in the cold, rarefied atmosphere of altitude. A tear is shed for ten young men gone in the blinking of an eye and for those who lived to see it happen. The sky has no memory because of gravity. We can't place ten wooden crosses or a granite stone here as a memorial to lost comrades. No marker can be placed to say, "This is where it happened." A scar on the brain and a terse message, "Missing in Action" is all that remains.

Wesel, Germany: D-Day at the Rhine River, 24 March 1945
by Lt. Harold Dorfman 714 Sqdn 448th B.G.

We first learned of this impending mission on the morning of the 22nd. Three crews were taken over to

Headquarters 20th Combat Wing at Hardwick and briefed on the coming event.

We were to form three lead crews in our Group. I was lead DR Navigator, with Lt. Voigt as the lead pilot for 714th squadron flying as high right squadron, 8 planes. General Timberlake briefed us and told us to forget about it until it came off. We learned that the main spearhead of allied troops, commandos, parachutists and glider borne were going to cross the Rhine River just a mile north of Wesel. We were to follow them in at treetop altitude and drop supplies.

The night of the 23rd we were taken in to study the drop area models and maps. Now we knew it was coming off the following day. The route in and out was over friendly territory all the way. We labeled it a milk run, another sightseeing trip. Except for about 5 minutes at the drop area we would never be over enemy territory.

Briefing was at 05:30, take off at 09:30, 26 planes in total (9-9-8). No heavy flying clothing. Just Class B uniform and a light jacket, back parachute and no Mae West. Everything went as briefed right up to the I.P. altitude about 75 feet. All radio homing navigation aids to the target were out of action, visibility down to about 2 miles in the haze. We crossed the Rhine south of course and reached the southern dropping area for American equipment. However, we carried supplies for the British landing area about a mile and a half further north. So we turned north and dropped perfectly on target, the British troops had marked the drop area with a circle of downed gliders. We started a 270 degree right turn out. That's where hell started!

A large bullet hole, the size of a handball appeared in the skin (of the plane) alongside of me, probably a 20mm shell. I dropped to the armored floor between the ammunition cans and landed on Lt. "Shabby" Shabsis the bombardier. Our faces were about 18 inches apart from the nose window and we watched more holes appear in the glass from machine gun fire. We covered ourselves with our flak jackets. I expected a bullet in the face at any moment. I could hear and feel the machine gun bullets raking the bottom of our armor plate that we were laying on. Suddenly there was a loud whine of high pressure being released behind us. We looked back at the nose wheel tire. It had been hit, just about a foot from my rear end. Still the machine guns raked the nose. The hydraulic lines in the wheel housing were hit, red fluid came out over everything, including my chute, which was soaked. A shell exploded between the pilots legs, but mercifully the direction was away from him.

However, the pilots' control cables were shot out. He lost control of the rudder, his controls were crippled. The thing that saved us was their snapping-on the autopilot which continued to work. We were at 50 feet all this time and still to clear 100 feet high electrical wires as we came out of the turn to re-cross Rhine River. By the grace of God did we get over that line of wires and out across to the friendly side of the Rhine. At debriefing, the top turret gunner swore that we went under the wires, if so we had only inches to spare. All this had taken about 5 minutes from drop time on the target to across the Rhine. We were now out.

Col. Heber Thompson riding as Command Pilot alongside Lt. Voigt asked the tail gunner to report on the rest of the squadron. After a long delay, the answer was "Sir, there is nobody behind us." 7 planes vanished.

We had lost the entire squadron, 7 planes, in the turn. This was bad news, later we learned that all 7 had managed to get across to our side of the Rhine River and nobody was seriously wounded.

All our navigation instruments were shot out. No compass, no G Box. But at least we were alive and over friendly territory. We picked our way to Ostend by pilotage. The nose turret Pilotage Navigator got lost en route as we ran completely off his maps. I found our location on my map.

At Ostend, we decided to make for the R.A.F. emergency field at Manston, 2 miles south of Margate on the southeast tip of England. We circled the field, checking our plane for 30 minutes and decided that the airplane was unfit to land. The tires were blown, the wheels wouldn't come down and the manual control cables were out. The autopilot, damaged in the turn out of Germany, would only make left turns and not to the right. The only manual control the pilots had was elevation, up or down. We were at 7000 feet. A case for bailing out or a gear-up landing. The bomb bays were open. I couldn't fit between the bomb racks with a back pack on and I'll be damned if I'd take it off. I grabbed hold of the racks, swung around them and back to the catwalk. Did that twice and then worked through the door down to the waist. Then the word came to "Bail Out" not "Crash Land." I tightened the leg straps on my chute and fastened them.

I knew that my chute was soaked with hydraulic fluid and might not open right away, if at all. It's a hell of a feeling. I was the second man to leave through the camera hatch. Seeing the first man fall clear gave me confidence, his chute opened immediately. I sat down by the hatch, leaned forward and tumbled out. That was something I never thought I could have the nerve to do, but they say if you gotta go, you gotta go.

It's hard to describe those first few seconds out. Tumbling aimlessly through nowhere. I wanted to see that airplane well clear of me before I pulled the ripcord. I looked for it and suddenly saw it well away from me. I was satisfied and pulled the ring. The cable came out about 12 inches and I waited, nothing happened. I was a little panicky, then I pulled it again. The cable came clear out. I waited again, this time for ages. Then it came, a sharp crack in the back of my neck and then a sudden jolt. There she was above me, just so beautiful and white. Not an angel, just a parachute, which at that moment was much better.

The jolt didn't hurt at all and I was comfortably floating. I don't think I have ever heard or rather been conscious of such peaceful quiet. The world was soundless and beautiful. A B-24 passed underneath with a slight hum and then it went quiet again. There is no sensation of falling, just drifting. I tried to remember what I had been taught about jumping and what I should do next.

I remembered that I should land with my back to the wind. I was facing the wrong way, so I reached up, twisted the shroud lines until I faced properly. I looked down and saw that I had quite an audience. I waved to some kids and they waved back. I was swinging badly at the bottom of my chute, but when I landed, luckily enough it was at the right part of the swing and I landed gently.

I don't even remember landing. I landed in a large field, behind a church, fairly smooth, with plenty of room on all sides. I looked up and counted 10 chutes in the air. Everyone out OK. I was first to land. I cussed the loss of my hat when the chute opened. The people saw it come off my head and followed it down. Some kid ran off and got it for me, I gave him my gloves as a gift.

Several women ran toward me from the church obviously to welcome the returning hero, WRONG—they wanted my nylon parachute to make clothing!! I was forced to pull my gun and hold the ladies at gunpoint until an R.A.F. Officer, jeep and driver arrived, collected the chute and explained to the ladies that I would have to pay for the chute if I didn't return it ($300). Then I made the ladies really mad when I showed them that the gun wasn't loaded. I pointed it at the sky and pulled the trigger and all you could hear was a meek "click."

I got R.A.F. transport to Margate, had tea and then with the crew assembled returned to R.A.F. Manston. All crew present and accounted for. Two injured in the jump. Colonel Heber Thompson landed on his face in a field with freshly fertilized manure, "Shabby" landed on his head and Reisinger on his face, but they weren't hurt seriously. Reisinger had swapped chutes with the radio operator, just before the jump because radio had spilled it while checking it. Reisinger jumped successfully with the spilled chute.

At Manston we found our C.O. Col. Westover with Capt. Wilhelmie. They had crash landed. Capt. Wilhelmie was shot in the leg and a gunner shot in the shoulder. Two planes came down from Seething to pick us up. The one that collected us up circled Seething for about 20 minutes and then advised us that we may have to bail out because he was not getting a "gear down" indication. I said "OK" as long as his crew would be kind enough to swap their well packed chutes for our slightly used ones. He managed to land the plane.

We are home, it was 7 pm. It had been a busy day, but it is not over. I took my camera, got on my bike headed for the flight line to photograph the damage on the planes that had returned. The hand brakes on my front wheel jammed. I flew over the wheel, landed on my right face and shoulder in a ditch. They loaded me into an ambulance, took me to the hospital, and with my face covered with bandages, put me to bed with the rest of the crew. Every member had some injury and qualified for the Purple Heart except me. I didn't have a mark on me except for the dumb bicycle accident.

Mission No. 18: "D" Day, June 6, 1944
by Mac Meconis, 466th BG

Of the whole air force our group was to be the second to hit the beach. We had to be at certain places exactly at certain times in order to hit the invasion coast at the precise moment. With thousands of other bombers in the air at the same time, we had to be on schedule. Night flying normally is bad enough for the risks of collision, but this was different—every plane on English soil probably would be up there milling around in the soup. And soup it was before briefing time. It looked like good weather to cancel a mission.

More detailed information of the magnitude of the assault was given us. We learned that the attack by air would cover 25 miles of coast between Cherbourg and Le Havre, and that paratroops would land back of the coastal defense area. Our target secondary was a choke point in a road going through a wood near the coast.

En route we glimpsed something of the tremendous force of planes that were taking part in this assault. Everywhere, no matter in which direction you looked, formations large and small were on their way—all headed south, toward the setting moon. As we passed over the southern coast of England I began straining my eyes to see some of the invasion fleet. A low under cast in patches obscured most of the water, but wherever open spaces permitted I could see the landing craft and large ships on a fairly rough sea. Also below us, just above the clouds, I saw B-26 formations assembling. Didn't see a single friendly fighter, though we were expecting 35 squadrons as cover. They probably were at low altitude, below the clouds, actively aiding the first assault on the coast. We didn't need them.

The invasion coast appeared momentarily; we saw the artillery fire; and seconds later the top cloud layer was directly under us, drawing the white curtain on the show we'd hoped to see from our grandstand seats. PFF ships ahead dropped their bombs, and our bombs were away on their marker trails at 6:12 a.m. We'll never know exactly what we hit

It was daylight, with the sun shining above the clouds in the east, as we turned right to head 270 degrees for 90 miles until we were west of the Cherbourg peninsula. Several bursts of flak came up at a group on our right just after bombs away. Later, as another group passed too close to either Cherbourg or the islands just west of it, a ball of flak like that I'd seen over Brunswick once, came up a them.

Another mission had taken off just before we landed back at base, so we expected to fly sometime in the afternoon. Left all our equipment at the plane and went to breakfast before going back to bed. I had a terrible headache and a gaseous stomach from fatigue and engine noise. Smith had appropriated our radio and newscasts said our troops were ten miles inland already.

When you come back from a mission, you are TIRED.

Photo Gallery

3 B-24s in flight

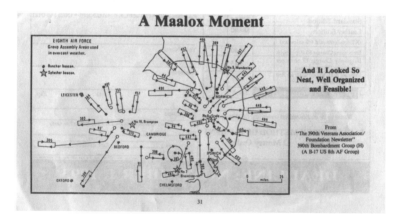

8th AF group assembly

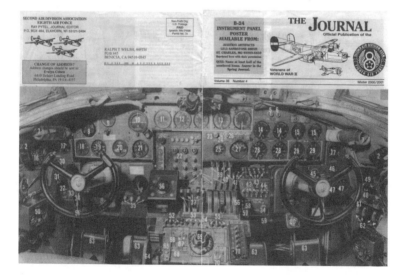

B-24 Instrument Panel

ENGLISH	GERMAN
Minutes	Minuten
Hours	Stunden
Day	Tag
Night	Nacht
Week	Woche
Fortnight	Vierzehn Tage
Month	Monat
O'clock	Uhr
Thank you; please	Danke; Bitte
Yes; No	Ja; Nein
Good morning; Afternoon; Evening	Guten Morgen; Tag; Abend
Good night	Gute Nacht
Out of bounds; Forbidden	Verboten
To; From; Via	Nach; Von; Uber
Train; express; slow	Zug; Schnellzug; Personenzug
Third class	Dritte Klasse
God Bless	Grüss Gott
HEIL HITLER	Heil Hitler
I am in a hurry	Ich habe es eilig

*There is no equivalent in German for "out of bounds". "Verboten"
(forbidden), would be used in most cases.*

*There is no German equivalent for "good afternoon". "Guten Tag"
(good day) is used at any time of the day, and is much more common
than any of the other forms.*

Escape kit: English to French, Belgian, German phrases

Our wedding: Ann and Ralph, 1956

WINDOW IN TIME

JANUARY 5, 1920

THIS IS HOW THE CALENDAR WOULD LOOK ON JANUARY 5, 1920

PRESIDENT OF THE U.S. WAS WOODROW WILSON
    VICE-PRESIDENT WAS THOMAS R. MARSHALL

JANUARY						
S	M	T	W	T	F	S
				1	2	3
4	5	6	7	8	9	10
11	12	13	14	15	16	17
18	19	20	21	22	23	24
25	26	27	28	29	30	31

SOME PRICES IN 1920, COMPARED WITH 1985 ARE:

	1920	1985
A POUND LOAF OF BREAD	$0.11	$0.64
A HALF GALLON OF MILK	$0.33	$1.16
A POUND OF BUTTER	$0.70	$2.63
A POUND OF ROUND STEAK	$0.40	$2.58
TEN POUNDS OF POTATOES	$0.63	$1.69
A NEW FORD AUTOMOBILE	$795.	$8,015.
AVERAGE ANNUAL INCOME	$1,236.	$20,490.

IN 1920 - THE WORLD SERIES WAS WON BY THE CLEVELAND INDIANS (AL)
    BEATING THE BROOKLYN DODGERS (NL)

MOST
POPULAR:
    SONG - TEA FOR TWO
    MOVIE - THE HIGH SIGN
    ACTOR - BUSTER KEATON - "THE HIGH SIGN"
    ACTRESS - GLORIA SWANSON - "SOMETHING TO THINK ABOUT"

SOME STORIES THAT APPEARED IN NEWSPAPERS ON OR NEAR JANUARY 5, 1920 ARE:

1/2   THE BUREAU OF PUBLIC HEALTH ANNOUNCES THAT THE LIFE EXPECTANCY
    IN THE U.S. IS 54.9 YEARS WHICH IS UP FROM 49.2 YEARS IN 1901.

1/12   EUGENE O'NEILL RECEIVES THE PULITZER PRIZE FOR HIS PLAY, "BEYOND
    THE HORIZON."

1/16   CHARLIE CHAPLIN AND A LITTLE BOY NAMED JACKIE COOGAN ARE THE
    STARS OF "THE KID," A MOVING PICTURE RELEASED TODAY.

1/16   THE VOLSTEAD ACT, TO ENFORCE THE 18th AMMENDMENT GOES INTO
    EFFECT. IT PROVIDES FOR THE PROHIBITION OF MANUFACTURE, SALE OR
    TRANSPORTING OF INTOXICATING LIQUORS. NATIONAL PROHIBITION WAS
    ENDED ON 12/5/33.

Window In Time; P.O. Box 53483; San Jose, Ca. 95153

190380

My birthdate, do you doubt inflation?

279

Billings, MT, 1952

Chapter 7: Almost Everything

miscellany, n.: "a collection of writings on various subjects," "a mixture of various things." (Webster's English Dictionary)

Address of John Leary, incoming Gonzaga President:
"Nowadays so many seem alarmed by the travail through which the world suffers, and our efforts seems frighteningly weak. But the only world one can do much about is one's own."

Instruction book for Model T Ford, a 3-1/2" x 6" plain paper instructor, "On receiving your car, and before starting the motor, fill the radiator with clean, fresh water, preferably straining it through muslin or other similar material to prevent foreign matter getting into the small tubes... GO IT EASY—In the flush of enthusiasm, just after receiving your car, remember a new machine should have better care until she "finds herself" than she will need later, when the parts have become better adjusted to each other, limbered up and more thoroughly lubricated by long running." The instructions include how to remove the rear axle, the drive shaft pinion, the large driving gear.

I had included quite a few pilot stories from "Slipping the Surly Bonds" by Dave English; however, I do not want to chance a copyright infringement. But I recommend it for copyright-free old time ditties like "There are old pilots and bold pilots, but no old bold pilots;" and "When weather's ahead and you're in doubt, be sure to make a 180 about."

Same comment as the above for HOW TO TELL A TRUE WAR STORY, by Tim O'Brien,
From Esquire, Oct. 1987, page 208. I'll steal two quotes trusting there's no retribution—"The best things in life are: a good landing; and a good bowel movement. Landing at night on a carrier is one of the few opportunities where you can get to experience both at the same time."

"The three most common expressions (or famous last words) in aviation are: Why is it doing that? Where are we? Oh s—t!!!"

This and That

Something I penned before starting to write some "book stuff"—"I don't date when I write, but make an exception this August 30, 1997. Ann and Lynn left with Brian, who is returning to Dallas to school. They are driving, and Ann and Lynn will rent a car in Dallas and drive through Louisiana, Mississippi, see Savannah and Charleston and return from Atlanta. Over the years I've always had empty feelings when Brian leaves for college. Today, I have three empty feelings..."

"I do not choose to be a common man. It is my right to be uncommon if I can. I seek opportunity, not security. I do not wish to be a kept citizen, humbled and dulled by having the state look after me. I want to take the calculated risk, to dream and to build, to fail and to succeed. I refuse to barter incentive for a dole. I prefer the challenges of life to the guaranteed existence, the thrill of fulfillment to the stale calm of utopia. I will not trade freedom for beneficence, nor my dignity for a handout. I will never cower before any master nor bend to any threat. It is my heritage to stand erect, proud, and unafraid. To think and act for myself, enjoy the benefits of my creations, and to face the world boldly and say, "This I have done..."

IN DAYS GONE BY the San Francisco Chronicle had three excellent columnists—Herb Caen for gossip, Stanton Delaplane for clever, skillful writing, and the not-so-stable philosopher, Charles McCabe. Headings of several columns — Sleep on it, Candide's lesson, No room at the inn, Bye for now, Truths?, Quotes from columns—"I do not believe we can ever prevent the detonation of a nuclear bomb by a lunatic or by a temporarily deranged 'normal' type. Anything that man can do, man will do, somehow. This is perhaps the most cynical of my 'truths' and I hope I am wrong about it..." Man is more good than bad. This is a close one. Its main support is that man, with all his wars and all his perfidiousness, has managed to live
282

together in some form of orderly society…" "I think Leonardo da Vinci was the greatest man who ever lived, excluding Jesus Christ, of course…" "The two books I would like to have on a desert isle are the King James Version of the Bible and the essays of Montaigne. The life of the spirit is covered by both books, but I think Montaigne has the edge in his comprehension of man in all his weaknesses and strengths. Don Quixote would be a close third…" Thanks, Herb, Stanton, and Charles, wherever you are, for good entertainment.

When we lived in the small hamlet of McElroy, Montana in the 1920s, hobos would be riding in and on boxcars, vagrants. They were also associated with the IWW—Independent Workmen of the World. A song to or from them went "Halelulia, I'm a bum, Halelulia, bum again, Halelulia, give us a handout, To revive us again."

And in Lignite, ND during prohibition Lee Dellage was the local bootlegger. He would check into Canada, get a load of gallon cans of pure alcohol, and return by back roads, over railroad tracks, not at the border check points. When the Ford V-8s first came out, Lee bought one as it could outrun the border police. One day he came to town and the V-8 had bullet holes in the trunk, but he outran the border patrol. I remember that on dance nights a friend's father, a cousin of Lee, would sell beer bottles with a mixture of pure alcohol, warm water, butter (melted), and nutmeg for $1. I remember the taste and the result. Okay.

A truck driver stopped at a roadside diner for lunch, and ordered a cheeseburger, coffee, and a slice of apple pie. As he was about to eat, three motorcycles pulled up outside. The bikers came in, and one grabbed the trucker's cheeseburger and took a bite from it. The second one drank the coffee, and the third wolfed down the apple pie. The truck driver didn't say a word. He simply got up, paid the cashier, and left. One of the motorcyclists said, "He ain't much of a man, is he?' "He's not much of a driver, either," the cashier replied. "He just backed his truck over three motorcycles."

The horse and mule live thirty years and never hear of wine or beers; The sheep and goat at twenty die without a taste of scotch or rye; The cow drinks water by the ton and by eighteen is mostly done; The dog at fifteen cashes in without the aid of rum or gin; In healthful milk the kitten soaks and then in twelve short years she croaks; The modest, sober, bone dry hen lays eggs for nogs, then dies at ten; But somehow we outlast them all on coffee, tea, and alcohol; Which proves it sure can't hurt you none, to have yourself a lot of fun.

Note: I clipped this out of The New York Times long ago, and trust that it's okay to print. We did have a Dr. Seuss book or two when our children were growing up. What a rhymer!

"New York—It's diploma season, and across America graduates' eyes glaze over during commencement perorations. Theodor Seuss Geisel, who lives in La Jolla, California, likes to write—he is Dr. Seuss, the author of children's books—but he dislikes making speeches. When Lake Forest College gave him an honorary degree in 1977, he was asked to give a formal speech.
No, he said, I won't but I'll say a few words when you hand me the sheepskin. He indeed meant a few words. The appreciative audience gave him a standing ovation. Here's what he said: "My uncle ordered popovers from the restaurant's bill of fare. And, when they were served, he regarded them with a penetrating stare. Then he spoke great Words of Wisdom as he sat there on that chair: 'To eat these things', said my uncle, 'You must exercise great care. You may swallow down what's solid, But you must spit out the air!' And as you partake of the world's bill of fare, that's darned good advice to follow. Do a lot of spitting out the hot air, and be careful what you swallow."

Robert Frost—"You don't have to deserve your mother's love. You have to deserve your father's. He's more particular." Or—a mother's love is unconditional, a father's, conditional... In peace sons bury their fathers, but in war the fathers bury their sons. Croesus.

Once at a restaurant in northern England a party of two women and a man in an adjoining booth spent the better part of the lunch discussing smells. We thought, how interesting. But smells go with us through life. I still vividly recall the smells of wheat, rye, barley, flax that came into my dad's grain elevator, or roses, pansies, lilacs in bloom, spinach, corn, radishes meats, fresh baked bread, etc… When conversation lags, try it.

The following are messages as published in the Wall Street Journal by United Technologies Corporation, Hartford, Connecticut 06101. 1983. (I have not checked for any copyright for these uplifting messages, 25 years after publication.)

WILL THE REAL YOU PLEASE STAND UP?

Submit to pressure from peers and you move down to their level. Speak up for your own beliefs and you invite them up to your level. If you move with the crowd, you'll get no further than the crowd. When 40 million people believe in a dumb idea, it's still a dumb idea. Simply swimming with the tide leaves you nowhere. So if you believe in something that's good, honest and bright – stand up for it. Maybe your peers will get smart and drift your way.

AIM SO HIGH YOU'LL NEVER BE BORED

The greatest waste of our natural resources is the number of people who never achieve their potential. Get out of that slow lane. Shift into that fast lane. If you think you can't, you won't. If you think you can, there's a good chance you will. Even making the effort will make you feel like a new person. Reputations are made by searching for things that can't be done and doing them. Aim low, boring. Aim high, soaring.

LITTLE THINGS

Most of us miss out on life's big prizes. The Pulitzer. The Nobel. Oscars. Tonys. Emmys. But we're all eligible for life's small pleasures. A pat on the back. A kiss behind the ear. A four-pound bass. A full moon. An empty parking space. A crackling fire. A great meal. A glorious sunset. Hot soup. Cold beer. Don't fret about copping life's grand awards. Enjoy its tiny delights. There are plenty for all of us.

DECISIONS, DECISIONS

Sometimes the decision to do nothing is wise. But you can't make a career of doing nothing.

Freddie Fulcrum weighed everything too carefully. He would say, "On the one hand...but then, on the other," and his arguments weighed out so evenly he never did anything. When Freddie died, they carved a big zero on his tombstone. If you decide to fish – fine. Or, if you decide to cut bait – fine. But if you decide to do nothing, you're not going to have fish for dinner.

DON'T QUIT

Is that what you want to do. Quit? Anybody can do that. Takes no talent. Takes no guts. It's exactly what your adversaries hope you will do. Get your facts straight. Know what you're talking about. And keep going. In the 1948 Presidential election, the nation's leading political reporters all predicted Harry Truman would lose. He won. Winston Churchill said, "Never give in." "Never. Never." Sir Winston stuck his chin out and wouldn't quit. Try sticking out your chin. Don't give up. Ever.

DON'T BE AFRAID TO FAIL

You've failed many times, although you may not remember. You fell down the first time you tried to walk. You almost drowned the first time you tried to swim, didn't you? Did you hit the ball the first time you swung a bat? Heavy hitters, the ones who hit the most home runs, also strike out a lot. R.H. Macy failed seven times before his store in New York caught on. English novelist John Creasey got 753 rejection slips before he published 564 books. Babe Ruth struck out 1,330 times, but he also hit 714 home runs. Don't worry about failure. Worry about the chances you miss when you don't even try.

448th Bomb Group, Office of the Surgeon.
"This is to certify that lst Lt. Ralph T. Welsh, 0-755811 has been examined not more than twenty-four (24) hours prior to departure from this station and found to be free from communicable disease and free from vermin infestation." -Capt. A. Grumper, 11-5-1944.

Two books I liked, "Sweet Agony II, a writing book of sorts," by Gene Olson, about the fun and challenge of writing, but the frustration of trying to get it better, and "The Secret of Santa Vittoria." It's a novel about Germans in WWII taking over this little Italian village, and to protect their wine, the villagers hid it in caves. Well, in December 1996 we're driving around northern Italy and here's a road sign "Santa Vittoria." So up and up we drive to this little hilltop village, that does have caves. Stopping for a cappuccino, fully addicted after a few days in Italy, worker not around, chef called to do the honors. I mentioned we had not as yet had truffles. He took us to his large, beautiful restaurant kitchen and showed us a supply in his refrigerator. He gave us three of them. They were white, as opposed to the more highly prized black variety, and quite small. I had to strongly insist on a gratuity. So that night we mentioned this to our restaurant's owner, with the result of shaved truffles on our pasta. Great! Recalled incidents exemplify the joys of traveling.

"The world is like a book. If you don't travel, you only see a single page."

I have this bad habit of waking up around 4 a.m. and being unable to go back to sleep. However, it is a good time for thinking and my mind seems clearer, so it is productive rather than frustrating time. A couple of early mornings ago I came up with the idea of logging thoughts, impressions, remembrances of various of the states visited. First I recalled a particular stretch of road I had driven that was so pleasant, and then added other tidbits. (Many mornings later I completed the 50)

WYOMING- Why not start with a pretty much unexpected first mention? This state has Yellowstone and the beautiful Rockies, exemplified by the Grand Tetons. My strongest remembrance is the drive through the Wind River Canyon. When canyons have a beautiful winding road along a river, and a train track with the possibility of seeing a choo choo, PLUS notations about the ages of the rock formations, you have a canyon to remember. Not a bad name either. And this drive takes you past the historic South Pass, crossed by thousands of emigrants, and into Lander, which I thought was the most attractive town of those I knew in Wyoming... The other drive I recall with pleasure is from Cody to Yellowstone. Teddy Roosevelt said it was the most scenic 52 miles in America, and who wants to quarrel with Teddy?... Another area I like is the area around Sheridan and Buffalo, in the Bighorn Mountain area,, not too far removed from the Custer debacle... Maybe I put Wyoming first because alphabetically it is last, and with my surname starting with a "W," I have been last or near to it in school and beyond, so here was a way to get a bit of vicarious revenge. And a note for the women—Wyoming was the first government in the world to grant women equal rights! It also was the home of the Sioux, Pawnee, Arapahoe, Pawnee, and several other lesser knowns. The Arapahoe (warriors) and Shoshone (Sacajawea, buried in WY) now live on a large reservation rich in natural gas and oil. That is a lot of history for a state with comparatively few inhabitants. You'll like it when you visit.

My 50th write up "I have saved the best for last, and I'm sure you know that I mean the golden state: CALIFORNIA, our home the last 45 years (51 when I am writing this) being, like most residents, emigrants. etc., etc. It's important to have a curiosity about things and a desire to visit or experience something new. It prolongs the enjoyment of being lucky enough to be alive on this great earth. I think it's a Chinese proverb that says "live for the moment," i.e., enjoy, treasure, every moment you have. Long ago I incorporated that as much as possible into the way I try to think about living. There are so many opportunities in a lifetime. Make them positive, happy. You'll never regret it. I wrote the following at considerable intervals, with no attempt to make them flow together. Like my combat mission write-up, no deleted emotions.

It is Jan 3, 1974. This is the first entry I've ever made in what one might loosely call a diary. We are in a financial bind as my management job does not cover expenses. Fees from my first finder/intermediary activity—the sale of Stevens, Thompson & Runyon of Corvallis, OR to CRS Design Associates of Houston—paid a gross fee of $68 thousand. The firm kept half, so my $34k kept us from problems in 1973. But adversity has been a blessing in that the family has realized, accepted (somewhat), and cohesivized (new word) with the continuing threat.

It is March 3, 1974. As diaries go, one could say this one wheent. But I did not mean it to be a chronicle of daily affairs. It's a means to tell my family after I'm gone how much I appreciate and love them, so they are able to take some confidence from this to lead a richer, fuller life. We are all well, and I am spending my happiest days as an individual. Lots of $ would help—or would it? I mostly want to continue the good feeling we all have together (or I think we have).

5-31-77 Some hiatus in diary. Survival fees are overdone. A couple of small company sales, big help. So far this has been a complaint, or at least an expression, of monetary problems. But the fact that happiness is possible without economic plenty is brought out. (However, Sophie Tucker's "I've been rich and I've been poor, and rich is better" gets no quarrel from me.)

June 24, 1982 Well, after a couple years effort we completed the sale of Kim Products in Clarksville, Arkansas, to Chef Francisco, the frozen food subsidiary of Labatt Breweries, Canada. Fees of $70,000 down, and a note for $100,000 additional, including interest, to be paid Roger and me over the next five years. (NOTE—This was followed up by five more deals, all equal or better than this one. I would locate a profitable company with several million dollars in sales, with a good (preferably proprietary) product, with owner willing to sell at a reasonable price. Getting a fee agreement, I would turn over the selling of the company to one of two fellows I worked with. Both had buying connections, which I didn't. … Sadly, both died in their early fifties. However, our graphic arts mail order company had grown to the point my wife needed more help and I spent full time with it for some twenty years.

Yesterday was our 26th anniversary and Ann and I went to Chez Panisse to a spicy, rich French dinner. Florence is in Alaska, worrying about Mama. Brian started his first college class this week. Kent is in Europe, Clark is fine, as is Lynn.

International Travel

I did not intend to include, in these pages, anything on our travels. But it has been a big and most enjoyable part of our life, so a sketch of it, and maybe a bit more, is forthcoming.

AND—if it can motivate any non-travelers, great. Travelers don't need encouragement to continue. Mexico is so close that it doesn't feel international, and we have been there quite a number of times, covering most of the country. One trip we particularly enjoyed was the Copper Canyon train trip. We have lots of fond Mexican memories… Hawaii is certainly not international, but we have enjoyed probably a half dozen visits over the years. Canada is close, we have visited from British Columbia to Prince Edward Island. The people are friendly and nice, the scenery great. We particularly like Vancouver Island, where we honeymooned, plus our 50th anniversary with our family.

April, 1944: A 4 continent trip flying our new bomber across the U.S., the Caribbean, from South America to Senegal, Africa, and up to Wales.

Oct., 1971: 21 days in rented auto, England, France, Germany, Switzerland. At lunch at Simpsons on the Strand in London, there was Arnold Palmer. I couldn't help but introduce myself, and this gracious man accepted my rude behavior and introduced me to wife Winnie.

1985: 5-1/2 weeks, 6,000 miles, in new Saab picked up in Gothenburg, Sweden, by Ann, me, and 15 year old daughter Lynn, to a dozen or more countries, through communist dominated ones south to Istanbul, then circled back through Greece, Italy, and up to Antwerp where we left our car for shipment to San Francisco. A great trip, very diverse, democratic to state controlled. Purchased a long, wooden fujara, shepherd's horn, in Prague, for son Clark.

November, 1988: We left London, intending to land in Gibraltar, then auto around Spain and Portugal. The runway at Gibraltar was flooded and debris strewn from a storm, so the plane continued on to Casablanca, returning to Gibraltar after the storm. We travel light and often check no bags, so we disembarked, as we had planned to go to Morocco later. We traveled by rail to Meknes, Fez, Tangier, boat to Gibraltar, rented auto, traveled over 2,000 miles in Portugal and Spain, air to London, Edinburgh by train, auto to Aberdeen, Inverness, St. Andrews, Carnoustie, train back to London,

Apr-May, 1989: On our own to Bangkok and Chang Mai (son Kent's family spending few months visiting there, and some months later, we caught up to them again in Ireland.) Seoul, Korea for Rotary International Convention, Tokyo, pleasure and business stop.

May, 1990: London to Kirkeness, Norway (way up and around, healmost in Russia). Took coastal working steamer " Vesteralen" to Bergen, stopping in various towns for commercial or passengers. Very few tourists, more locals, town to town, train to Oslo (great), Copenhagen, Cologne, Berlin, Paris. All on own.

Jan 8-24, 1991: South America Highlites, I think with SmarTours, Rio, Iguasu, B. Aires, Bariloche, Santiago, Lima, Cuzco, Machu Pichu, Lima.

Jan-Feb, 1992: On our own to Australia and New Zealand.

May 5-21, 1995: On own, first and business class to Helsinki, St. Petersburg (recently divulged masterpieces taken from Germans at the Hermitage, and a great, expensive for us, the $230 Astoria, where Hitler intended to celebrate after victory of Russia). Picked up two dohmras for collector son Clark, lugged them rest of way. Miserable sleeper trip to Tallin, drunken porter on what must be the oldest, dirtiest sleeper car in the world, loved Tallin, then Riga on a bus, 2 fellows pulled off for smuggling, boat to Stockholm, could only get one night hotel, busy, but a beautiful like to go back to city, Oslo and the fjord area (Voss, Myrdahl, to Hafslo, where my mother's parents were from, Bergen again, fast boat this time, and same hotel as before. Copenhagen, Hamburg, St. Peter (part of wife's heritage), drive across Schleshwig-Holstein, stayed at Schleshwi (?), old English sailor who keeps boat in area said skip Kiel, visit Lubeck, was good advice. Loved Luxembourg city, Paris for last 5 days. Scandinavia, Russia, smokers!

1996: Probably my favorite place, northern Italy. Rental car, Provence, Genoa, Florence, Siena, hill towns, Rome,Venice, Lake Coma, Milan, Nice. Spent a couple of nights with Orinda, Calif. Wells Fargo retirees who had purchased an eleven acre olive ranch, in Lucignano, restored residence for B & B. (This info retrieved from the most comprehensive, cheap, monthly,

International Travel News, $24/year, 800-486-4968, subscriptions, sample copies.) Then Florence, Orvieto, large, free parking lot, and train to Rome. 5 star Roma was $300, but across the street, Mascagni, 4 star, great, $275 to $160, with bickering. Rome continues wonderful. Back to Orvieto and on to Rick Steves quintessential hill town, Civita di Bagnoregio. There are dozens of hill towns, but this one is unique. Assisi to Venice, lots of trucks. Park in Mestre and train to Grand Canal to save $, rather than the large lot outside Venice. Milan worth visit. Had a truffle experience in Santa Vittoria. Genoa to Nice to New York for a couple of days and "Chicago." Italian autostratas, sedans and coupes instead of minivans, litter free, populace reserved and quiet in buses and subways, almost total lack of obesity. Italy's okay!

Jul 8-23, 1998: Took our older sister along on a trip to Ireland, stayed in the Ashford Castle, Dublin, Belfast, over to my old bomber base in England for a reunion, I returned from Manchester, Ann & Florence, London.

Nov. 1998: Paris, Bordeaux, Gehry Museum, Bilbao, Barcelona, Paris. All train. Returned early to close property purchase in S.F.

Feb. 1999: On own to Panama, rented auto, and a couple days San Blas Islands, bought molas. Panama, okay!

Jan. 2000: Escorted trip China, Bejing, Wall, Xian, Terra Cotta soldiers, Shanghai, Suzhou.

April-May 2000: With our son Clark to Istanbul, Tel Aviv, Jerusalem, Petra in Jordan, Sharm el Sheikh, Luxor, Karnack area, faluja on Nile, Cairo, Alexandria, Tel Aviv, Istanbul, Kusadasi, Samos, Greece, return from Istanbul. Busses, planes, taxis, boat. One of best trips, all on own. (Aquaba?)

Sept, 2000: S. Africa SmarTours. Saw lions, elephants, rhinos, leopards, hyenas, wild dogs, etc. S. Africa coast line, beautiful.

Nov, 2001: France, Spain, Portugal, Salamanca, Spain (visit grandson Tanner, schooled here second year high school), Andorra, Paris.

Dec. 2002: Private car, driver, Quito, Otavalo, Guayaquil, Ecuador. Mistake—no Galapagos.

May 2002: Ann, Ralph, & Clark (could speak some Romanian and Russian, essential, as this was on our own) Frankfurt, Prague, Krakow, Lviv, Ukraine, Romania, Budapest, Slovenia, Trieste City, Opatija, Croatia. , Frankfurt. A few comments— "Good fast train to Krakow, overnight, to Przemysi, then old bus in vicious thunderstorm to Lviv, a wonderful, historic city having picked up cultures, architecture of nationalities who had conquered Ukraine over the centuries. Recommend Hotel George and Natasha tour guide, office in hotel. Honest. Good. Helpful (made reservations for us at next stop). Foreign influences stronger than in Krakow. We liked Lviv... Dirty coach train to Frankivsk, then start of a pattern. Arriving in city, taxi to hotel, driver asks us our next destination, offers to take us, say, 120 miles for $60. From Suceava, taxied to three painted churches, Voronet by far the most impressive. Tried to bus to Moldova, entry refused, visas 2 days off, return to Suceava on bus, Moldovans (poorer than Romanians) occupants smuggling something?. Never knew what, and they hid a couple of bags beneath our feet on overcrowded bus, giving us their seat assuming Romanian border police wouldn't check us. Correct, but they did pull two males off the bus. Most, or all, other passengers were part of this operation. Road was treacherous from lack of repair, bus crawled over rough spots. Dramatic, unsuccessful, trip." (Although Cosescu was strung up in 1989, smarter communists in his administration let him take the heat, still rule. Sad, as we liked Romania and thought it had potential.) Budapest, since l985 trip, sophisticated city. Long train ride to Ljubljana, the small but very nice capital of Slovenia. Great train ride to Trieste.

July, 2003: Supply ship (Amazing Grace) to several sailing ships on the Caribbean. 100 passengers. Embarked in Trinidad, stopped days in a dozen islands, disembark Bahamas.

April, 2006: Rome, Malta, Sicily, Lecce (Italy), Dubrovnik., Montenegro, Croatian coast to Slovenia caves (great) Venice, Rome. Through TravLtips reserved stateroom on 105 passenger MS Andrea for this trip. Due to negative experience in Libya where American passports not allowed in the country for the uncomfortably hot 2 day stay in the harbor, many cancellation for above portion. (The story was that Khadaffi's son was refused a U.S. visa, so retaliation.) Result—on ship with only 3 other couples the first portion of trip, to Dubrovnik. Thereafter, guide and a van, first class hotels and food. No disappointment, and TravLtips refunded us 50% of the $5,756 tour cost, 12 days, Valletta, Malta to Venice.

March-April 2008: Brussels, Viking Sun (195 passengers) embark Antwerp, 15 city tours (included), Antwerp up the Rhine through Belgium, Netherlands, and Germany, to Basel. High water on the Moselle prevented boat trip to Cochem, France. Instead of canceling, Viking River Cruises hired buses for this excursion. Ditto, Basel, again, high water on Rhine prevented upstream travel to intended Basel destination. Disembark Basel, we trained all over Switzerland on 8 day pass, returning from Zurich. Viking Cruises, good quality.

I do not understand the gaps in 2004 & 2005. I may have missed a trip or two, but don't think so. And while we have visited some 70 countries, we don't have many places really experienced travelers have in their dossier. E.g., Singapore, India, Burma, Cambodia, Vietnam, Tierra Del Fuego, the Stans, Antarctica (no desire, prefer people to penguins), but not visiting the Galapagos a mistake, and middle Central America, among unlisted others. Still, traveling gets in your blood and I trust health allows us to add a few more countries to learn and enjoy, and create a good impression of U.S. citizens. My sociology teacher at Gonzaga, who became the university's president, stressed a "one world" outlook, that in 1945.

Fact or Fiction

One of the Spitfires, during the war, had a very odd passenger carried on it. (Not in it). It was common practice to have someone sit on the tailplane whilst the airplane was taxiing along the perimeter track in order to keep the tail on the ground. In this case it was a WAAF (lady airwoman), Margaret Horlton sitting on the fuselage facing backwards, with her legs jammed under the tailplane. The plan was for the pilot to stop at the end of the runway, allowing her to jump off. The pilot forgot she was

294

on there and took off before she could do that. He reported to the tower that he had a very heavy tail trim, and he was instructed to fly low past the tower and they would have a look see. They told him not to panic, but he had a WAAF passenger on the tail. After completing one circuit of the airfield the pilot did land safely and let off a very frightened lady. I met this lady some years ago at an air show. The Spitfire was flown in for her to see, the press and TV were there to cover her reunion with the aircraft. She was invited to sit on the tail again. The aircraft was in the hangar, and she agreed to do so, provided that the hangar doors were closed. I did speak to her about her flight and she said she was terrified, but she seemed to think the pilot was suffering more from the shock than herself." (as reported by Dick Wickham,Dec 2000 Station 146 Tower Assn., Seething Airfield, Norfolk.) Note: I vote fiction.

From the 491st BG Ringmaster's Magazine
Author Unknown

An American soldier, serving in World War II, had just returned from several weeks of intense action on the German front lines. He had finally been granted R&R and was on a train bound for London. The train was very crowded, so the soldier walked the length of the train looking for an empty seat. The only unoccupied seat was directly adjacent to a well-dressed middle-aged lady, and was being used by her little dog. The weary soldier asked, "Please, ma'am, may I sit in that seat?" The woman looked down her nose at the soldier and said, "You Americans. You are such a rude class of people. Can't you see my little Fifi is using that seat?"

The soldier walked away, determined to find a place to rest, but after another trip down to the end of the train found him agaim facing the woman with the dog. "Please, lady. May I sit there? I'm very tired." The English woman wrinkled her nose and snorted, "You Americans! Not only are you rude, you are also arrogant. Imagine!"

The soldier didn't say anything else. He leaned over, picked up the little dog, tossed it out the window of the train and sat down in the empty seat. The woman shrieked and wailed, and demanded someone defend her and chastise the soldier.

An English gentleman sitting across the aisle spoke up: "You know, you Americans do seem to have a particular penchant for doing the wrong thing. You eat holding the fork in the wrong hand. You drive your autos on the wrong side of the road. And now, sir, you've thrown the wrong bitch out the window."

"The greatest editorial writer of this century was Vermont Connecticut Royster. There is no argument about that. With a vigorous mind and a vigorous pen he educated and stimulated readers of The Wall Street Journal from 1946 to 1986. His editorials and columns were polite and persuasive, as he was, and brilliant and charming, as he also was. Each essay was a masterpiece of thinking and of writing." Michael Gartner, Editor, The Des Moines Register. I agree. I hated to see him retire... The Wall Street Journal is a great read, particularly the weekend edition. If you have a negative feeling about the WSJ, you are missing some good journalism on many subjects, including movies, books, sports, international, fashion, you name it. I enjoy Peggy Noonan's thoughtful and entertaining column in the week end edition.

SOME YEARS AGO, I penned "What a dichotomy! The most artistic, subtle, structured, graceful major sport has the least sophisticated and educated, tobacco chewing athletes. (That was more true then than now as many (most?) recruits come from college ranks.) Professional football depends totally on college and university suppliers. But compared to baseball, football does not have the inherent qualities mentioned above. We don't think of tennis as a team sport. I don't follow ice hockey. But in baseball, there are percentage things you do in any conceivable situation. It's a beautiful sport. And kind of boring, waiting for ___ .

When I see spectators waiving anything to distract an opposing free throw shooter, I say, let the athletes, not the spectators, influence the outcome. Same in baseball, some yuk out in center field tries to impair the opposition teams' batter the ability to hit the ball. Football, worse yet. Make so much noise the opposing quarterback can't relay signals to his team. I know of an actual case of a fan throwing out a snowball—in Denver— to distract the punter. It worked. Hooray! I would have ejected the culprit and given the punter a fair chance. Stomping and screaming to the extent it changes the game is accepted. It should not be. The solution? Simple. Let the free throw shooter continue shooting until the distraction ceases. Give the batter ball counts on every pitch until the offender stops. Penalize the home team in five yard increments until the loud roar and stomping ends. However, I do believe fans can and should root for their team— but within reason. After all, if you're the host courtesy to your guest is only proper.

It is amazing the volume of material I have saved. All my army records and orders, records of my 13 corporate finance closings, a check to the Belvedere Ski Club for Kent's trip to the Sugar Bowl. Another check to The Cycle House for shocks for my Bultaco Alpina (I started riding the hills on the Tiburon peninsula on an old Honda, and enjoyed beautiful views). There are checks to Little League, nursery school, baseball cards, Drakes Beach Club. We purchased a half- acre in what became Point Reyes National Park. We planned to build a weekend place on our property, which was about a block up the hill from the ocean. The sandy beach extended for some miles. We were forced to sell to the government. No regrets, it's there now for all to enjoy... Lots of dental and medical bills. The interesting thing is the size of the checks. They are so small compared to today! Inflation may be arrested, but not eradicated.

I have five of the nicely bound B-24 books: flight manual, radio, hydraulics, electrical, and power plant. I thought they were the full set until, some years ago, I saw such a set of probably eight volumes, nicely packaged... My leather flying helmet hangs in the office of osteopath Dickie Hill, my long-time golfing buddy. Still in my possession: my B-4 bag (not in prime condition), A2 leather flight jacket, oxygen mask, E6B circular slide rule, and a 50 mission hat. In addition I have all my military moving orders. As memorabilia I have my March 1931 Boy Scout book, 1936 high school graduation program, hand-made with crepe paper (depression time). I love my Gregg shorthand books, 1920s photos (with model Ts).

CONSOLIDATED
SCHEDULES AND FARES

for # AIR
PASSENGERS

via COMMERCIAL
AIR TRANSPORT LINES

Operating on Regular Schedules
in the
UNITED STATES
and to
FOREIGN AIRPORTS

(Issued by American Air Transport Association, 1610 Bankers Bldg., 105 W. Adams St., Chicago. An organization of twenty companies operating transport planes on established routes over thirty-seven states and to foreign air terminals.)

HAROLD CRARY, *Manager*

Corrected to February 21, 1929

Chapter 8: Other Stories

How We Spent V-E Day
by Ralph Elliott. As printed in the Gilman (Ill.) Star in July 1943

I thought perhaps it might be of some interest to the folks there to hear how several thousand of us in the Eighth Air Force spent V-E Day. (Actually both May 7 and May 8). We had been expecting the end of the war for some time, since our bombing came to an end several days ago. Even then we had to go way down to the Alps to find targets. So we knew the end was coming shortly and were "sweating it out" the same as everyone else.

In the last two and a half years the Eighth has unloaded ton after ton of bombs. In France, after it was liberated, we got to see some of our results. Air fields had been put out of use, refineries burned out, and factories were well wrecked. However, we knew that the devastation still didn't compare with the area along the Rhine River and in the Ruhr Valley.

Then, just before V-E Day, plans came through from higher headquarters to allow us to "tour" the Rhine area with ten ground men per ship as passengers. You can well imagine we were looking forward to it, and it turned out just as planned, only better.

The morning of May 7 found twenty-four skeleton bomber crews—pilot, co-pilot, navigator, engineer and radio operator—plus nearly two hundred and forty officers and enlisted men of our ground personnel, assembled for briefing. Take-off time was 1200 (noon) and as usual we made our times good, thirty seconds between ships off the runway.

I was leading the first three-ship element, and by the time we crossed the coast out of England both of my wing-men (Jones & Ercegovac) were in position. They both flew wide on this trip so that they could show their passengers anything they happened to see of special interest.

We crossed the Belgian coast at Ostend at 1000 feet and, as the weather was beautiful, visibility was perfect. It remained so all day. There were still a few old bomb craters visible, but little damage had been done.

Our route took us over Bruges, Brussels, and Ghent and we went over the center of each. We knew by then it was V-E Day because there were flags on everything; the black, yellow, and red of Belgium, the French Tri-color, the Stars and Stripes, the Union Jack, and half a dozen I couldn't recognize. All the big smoke stacks were covered and store- fronts were a blaze of color. Where all the flags came from I'll never know; maybe they'd been hidden during the occupation.

Our route took us from Ghent and Brussels across the German border near Luxembourg, on down to Mannheim. At the German border we could see the "dragon's teeth" of the Siegfried Line, and every so often we passed burned out tanks and trucks. We could tell where a fight had taken place from the tank tracks in the fields and the holes where the tanks had dug in. Some hills had bomb craters on them where medium or fighter-bombers had helped out—which side they helped we couldn't know. The country across Belgium is quite flat, but as we got into Germany it began to get hilly and proved to be well wooded. There weren't many good roads with the exception of the famous German Autobahns and those are really good. Most of them are 4-lane highways with a wide grass strip down the middle. They seemed to have been little damaged and we saw plenty of traffic (ours) on them.

The first big German city we saw was Mannheim, one of the Eighth AF main targets. The railroad marshalling yards had been largely repaired but the houses near the yards were a mess. Fifty percent of the city will have to be rebuilt, I should guess. Just south of Mannheim lies the old German university city of Heidelberg. We missed it this trip, but I saw it several weeks ago and it is little damaged.

Next "stop" was Hanau, also badly hit. When you remember that this route covered the main industrial area of Western Germany, you get the feeling the "mess" has only begun and our feeling really proved correct. We flew down through a valley from Hanau to Frankfurt, following an autobahn and a railway, and we were hardly prepared for what we saw as we swung in over the city.

The Main River runs through the center of town, but to get from one side to the other must require a bit of swimming, because all of the bridges were down and not even a footbridge was left. Some were completely demolished, and others had just one span blown out at each end. Very likely the Germans had done that. The main railway station was in the center of the city and was as big as any in Chicago. However the resemblance ended there, because this one had no roof on it. We circled at about 500 feet and it all appeared as a blackened mess of steel girders. All of the rail cars were burned out, and even the repair crews couldn't make it look normal again.

This time the whole city was plastered with craters and nearly every house was badly damaged. It rather amazed us to see a big, modern apartment building still standing and in good condition among all the rubble. However, we saw things like that many times and couldn't help but wonder at it. As we followed the Main River up to where it emptied into the Rhine we saw more evidence of heavy bombing, and, from there on up, the Rhine was filled with sunken barges and river steamers. At one place only the two funnels of some tug were out of the water.

We passed Mainz and Wiesbaden past wrecked bridges and factories and turned north at Bingen where hills rose sharply and almost caught me too low. I banked steeply and headed down the river with hills rising on both sides of us, and I soon had to climb several hundred feet to make the bends in the river. That stretch up to Coblenz was the most beautiful I saw all day. The banks were steep and thickly wooded and on either side were old medieval castles. Some were old ruins covered with vines and bushes, but others were well kept. I couldn't help but wish I could land for a few hours and see some of those places closer.

At Coblenz the hills dropped sharply away again to a nearly level plain with factories on both sides of the river. I had seen the city before, but under not nearly so pleasant circumstances. I remembered a certain bridge at Coblenz and took a good look at where it HAD been. The day we went over at 20,000 feet I never expected to go back—or wanted to. In this whole area we saw the flak gun emplacements, and some of the guns were still there with their muzzles pointed upwards. To tell the truth, it almost gave me chills to remember those guns a few months before when I'd seen the muzzle flashes and counted the black puffs as the shells went off—until they got too thick to count and the smell of the black powder floated up into the bomb bays.

Downstream we flew over several prisoner camps, and the men looked like ants against the bare, sandy ground. There were too many to even guess at but there were several thousand of them. They had a few tents for shelter, but most of them looked like they all had were the clothes they wore. We were keeping our eyes open for the Ludendorf Bridge at Remagen as I had a photographer riding in the waist, and he wanted a good picture of it. (Capt. Calvin Horn, head of the camera shop, was the photographer.) I dropped down to treetop level as we saw it coming up, and the picture he got is wonderful. The towers of the bridge at both ends are standing, but appear to have been well blackened by smoke. It gave us a thrill to see the American flag flying off the east end; the German side of the river, and to realize how great an action put it there.

After a sharp turn to avoid the hills above the east end of the bridge, we leveled out almost over Bonn and could see Cologne in the distance. We could pinpoint ourselves by the outline of the cathedral at Cologne, and in a few minutes, we were over the city. The cathedral was pictured in nearly all of the papers back when our troops first took the city. The devastation in the area around there is almost unbelievable. The main railway station stands only a few hundred feet from the cathedral and is completely destroyed. Not a house is left, including the ones just across the street from the cathedral, and yet the cathedral is but slightly damaged. The houses and buildings are just piles of stone, and just pieces of walls are left. Bomb craters are everywhere, and the only paths through the rubble have been cut by bulldozers. Burned out tanks could be seen in the streets, reminders of the fighting that took place there.

I dropped low again and made a steep turn around the cathedral at about fifty feet for a good camera shot. Then we headed on up to Dusseldorf on the south edge of the Ruhr, better known as "happy valley" or "flak alley." Many a bomber went down over the Ruhr, and the Eighth AF will never forget the place—ever. It just wasn't healthy.

Leaving the Ruhr and more bombed out factories, the navigator (Arnold Thompson) gave me a course to Antwerp, Belgium and for 40 or 50 miles we rode the border of Belgium and Holland. Again we saw flags in all the cities we passed, and when we spotted a celebration going on in some little Belgian town we circled back over it low and shot a bunch of yellow-red flares just to celebrate a bit ourselves. The people all waved and were apparently having a wonderful time. We kind of felt good about it all ourselves.

At Antwerp the streets were crowded, and a big parade was in progress so we helped that along too with most of the flares we had left. Then we headed home past Walcheren Island which you may remember hearing of. The Canadians and Germans had a big fight there and the Germans blew the dykes, flooding the entire island. Some of the houses on higher ground were apparently being lived in, but most were clear under water. It was mainly farm land and fields are visible under the water. The trees are dead from the salt water and a hundred years will probably not see the land used again.

Actually, it is hard to imagine the destruction we saw on that trip. But for the boys who had worked on the ground during the war, as well as the ones of us who have been over Germany before, it was a memorable trip. We all agreed that V-E Day wouldn't soon be forgotten by us, and for me it proved to be all the "celebration" that was needed.

Home? Well, I'm hoping just like several million other guys that we'll be there soon.

Ernie Pyle's Column on the St. Lo Air Raid—25 July, 1944

Ernie Pyle was one of the most famous of the war correspondents. His usual reporting site was on or near the front lines. He was in Normandy for the D-Day landings and was with the ground forces on 25 July 1944 when the 8th bombed the front lines. There were 1503 bombers and 561 fighters on this mission. 3395 tons of bombs were dropped by the heavies. This is his account of that mission:

"…A new sound gradually droned in our ears, a sound deep and all-encompassing with no notes in it—just a gigantic faraway surge of doom like sound. It was the heavies. They came from directly behind us.

"At first they were the merest dots in the sky. We could see clots of them against the far heavens, too tiny to count individually. They came on with terrible slowness. They came in flights of twelve, three flights to a group, stretched across the sky. They came in 'families' of about seventy planes each.

"Maybe those gigantic waves were two miles apart, maybe they were ten miles. I don't know. But I do know they came in a constant procession and I thought it would never end. What the Germans must have thought is beyond comprehension.

"The flight across the sky was slow and steady. I've never known a storm, or a machine, or any resolve of man that had about it the aura of such a ghastly restlessness. I had the feeling that had God appeared beseechingly before them in the sky, with palms outstretched to persuade them back, they would not have had within them the power to turn from that irresistible course...

"The first huge flight passed directly overhead and others followed. We spread out our feet trying to look straight up, until our steel helmets fell off... and then the bombs came! They began like a crackle of popcorn and almost instantly swelled into a monstrous fury of noise that seemed surely to destroy all the world ahead of us... the bright day grew slowly dark from it. By now everything was an indescribable caldron of sounds. Individual noises did not exist. The thundering of the motors in the sky and the roar of bombs ahead filled all the space for noise on earth. Our own heavy artillery was crashing all around us, yet we could hardly hear it.

"The Germans began to shoot heavy, high ack-ack. Great black puffs of it by the score speckled the sky, until it was hard to distinguish smoke puffs from planes. And then someone shouted that one of the planes was smoking. Yes, we could all see it. A long faint line of black smoke stretched straight for a mile behind one of them. And as we watched, there was a gigantic sweep of flame over the plane. From nose to tail it disappeared in flame, it slanted slowly down and banked around the sky in great wide curves, this way and that way, as rhythmically and gracefully as in a slow motion waltz... and then, just as slowly it turned over and dived for the earth—a golden spearhead on the straight black shaft of its own creation—and disappeared behind the treetops.

"Before it was down there were more cries of, 'There's another one smoking and there's a a third one now.' Chutes came out of some of the planes. Out of some came no chutes at all. One of white silk caught on the tail of a plane. Men with binoculars could see him fighting to get loose until flames swept over him, and then a tiny black dot fell through space, all alone.

"And all that time the great flat ceiling of the sky was roofed by all the other planes that didn't go down, plowing their way forward as if there were no turmoil in the world. They stalked on, slowly and with a dreadful pall of sound...

"God, how we admired those men up there and were sickened for the ones who fell."

Then, as we know now, the smoke markers began to drift over our own lines. As the smoke drifted back, our planes dropped bombs on our own forces. 102 American soldiers were killed and 380 wounded. Ernie Pyle continues:

"It is possible to become so enthralled by some of the spectacles of war that a man is momentarily captivated away from his own danger. That's what happened to our little group of soldiers as we stood watching the mighty bombing. But that benign state didn't last long. As we watched, the exploding bombs were easing back toward us, flight by flight, instead of gradually forward as the plan called for.

"...An indescribable kind of panic came over us. We stood tensed and muscle and frozen in intellect, watching each flight approach and pass over, feeling trapped and completely helpless. And then all of an instant the universe became filled with a gigantic rattling as of huge ripe seeds in a mammoth dry gourd. I doubt that any of us had heard that sound before, but instinct told us what it was. It was bombs by the hundreds, hurtling down through the air above us.

"Many times I've heard bombs whistle or swish or rustle, but never before had I heard bombs rattle...it is an awful sound...We dived...some got into dugouts...others foxholes, ditches, and some got behind a garden wall—although which side is 'behind' was anybody's guess...I remember hitting the ground flat, all spread out like the cartoons of people flattened by steamrollers, and then squirming like an eel to get under one of the heavy wagons in the shed.

"An officer wriggled in beside me. We stopped...feeling it was hopeless to move farther...we lay with our heads slightly up—like two snakes. I know what was in both our minds and our eyes, asking each other what to do."

Ernie Pyle survived this episode and other narrow escapes in the course of his career as a combat correspondent. Then one day, on an obscure Pacific island—Ie Shima—Ernie Pyle's number finally came up. He was killed by a direct hit from a Japanese mortar in a ditch he had dived into in an attempt to survive.

His description of the bomber stream and the relentless ability of the 8th to continue with its terrible mission of destruction of the German army, is one of the finest of many accounts of the "breakout" from St. Lo.

The 1919 U.S. Army Air Service Flying Regulations

From the Great Memory Book of Ed Wanner (445th)

1 Don't take the machine into the air unless you are satisfied it will fly.
2 Never leave the ground with the motor leaking.
3 Don't turn sharply when taxiing, instead of turning short, have someone lift the tail around.
4 In taking off, look at the ground and the air.
5 Never get out of a machine with the motor running until the pilot relieving you can reach the engine controls.
6 Pilots should carry hankies in a handy position to wipe off goggles.
7 Riding on the steps, wing, or tail of a machine is prohibited.
8 In case the engine fails on takeoff, land straight ahead regardless of obstacles.
9 No man must taxi faster than a man can walk.
10 Do not use altitude instruments.
11 Learn to gauge altitude, especially on landing.
12 If you see another machine near you, get out of its way.

13 No two cadets should ever ride together in the same machine.

14 Never run motor so that blast will blow on other machines.

15 Before you begin a landing glide, see that no machines are under you.

16 Hedge-hopping will not be tolerated.

17 No spins on back or tail slides will be indulged in, as they unnecessarily strain the machine.

18 If flying against the wind, and you wish to turn and fly with the wind, don't make the sharp turn near the ground. You might crash!

19 Motors have been known to stop during a long slide. If pilot wishes to use motor for landing he should open throttle.

20 Don't attempt to force machines onto the ground with more than flying speed. The result is bouncing and ricocheting.

21 Aviators will not wear spurs while flying.

22 Do not use aeronautical gas in cars and motorcycles.

23 You must not take off or land closer than 50 feet to the hangar.

24 Never take a machine into the air until you are familiar with its controls and instruments.

25 If an emergency occurs while flying, land as soon as possible.

26 It is advisable to carry a good pair of pliers in a position where both pilot and passenger can reach them in case of an accident.

27 Joy rides will not be given to civilians.

Tales of the 44th: Return to Kjeller
by Forrest S. Clark

It is imperative that future generations understand the fullest possible perspective on World War II and the kind of forces that opposed each other in the war. The following is meant to give that perspective to *show compassion to the victims and survivors of that terrible war. This is based on an eyewitness account of one of the 8th Air Force bombing raids and contains only the truth as it happened fifty years ago.*

The air raid sirens had sounded that cold snowy November day shortly after 11 AM.

A 14-year-old Norwegian schoolgirl remembered that day fifty years ago.

"I've got to get home. What's happened to my mother?" she said out loud as she rode her bike up the hill toward her home. The year was 1943, the time of the German occupation of Norway, a time of terror and fear. She had huddled in the bomb shelter while the bombs shook the earth.

Smoke was still rising all about her, and huge holes in the ground showed where the bombs had fallen, making the familiar countryside look like "a landscape of the moon." A short time before she had huddled with others of her classmates in a basement air raid shelter as the bombs fell, shaking the ground, sending dust and debris down on the children. They sang as loud as they could to overcome their fear, but they were still shivering with fright.

After school she was so anxious to find her home and her mother amid the confusion that she rode furiously in the direction of her homestead above the airfield. Fires were all about her, but she rode on and on.

She was stopped by German guards on the road to her home. They said she could not pass. They did not want anyone to pass the airfield and see the damage.

"But that's my home up there," she told the guards.

One German guard looked at her very carefully with a stern expression and asked for her identification card. He blocked her way with his gun.

She handed him her card and he looked at it for a long time. Then he turned to another officer standing nearby and said, "Wait."

It was at that time she noted that there was a huge car with flags on it and several officers standing about it. This car was obviously a command car for a German high- ranking officer. Little did she know that Gen. Von Falkenhorst, commander of German forces in Norway, was there that day observing a military exercise of the troops.

In a little while the guard came back and said, "Pass." Out of a corner of one eye the girl saw the officers train their field glasses down on the airfield where huge fires were burning.

Later she was to discover that 29 big bombs had landed around her home and seven unexploded bombs were still buried. But the house was not hit.

"It was as if somebody had held an umbrella above our house," she said. That somebody must have been God, she admitted years later.

Gen. Von Falkenhorst had recently received orders from no less than the German High Command and Hitler to increase security and defense readiness around the Norwegian bases. This was the result of the very recent commando raids and bombing missions against Nazi-occupied Norway. Two days before the Kjeller bomb raid, Allied bombers had struck a blow at the highly important secret operations on Rjukan where heavy water was being processed for experimentation for the atomic bomb. This raid had incensed the German commanders, and word had gone forth to prevent such a surprise attack again.

Here two days later at Kjeller when the first U.S. bombers appeared, the German officers assured Gen. Von Falkenhorst that they were friendly aircraft taking part in the military exercise. However, a tremendous salvo of bombs set off from a few hundred yards downhill from the general's position sent all officers running for cover. The general observed all this and did not have much time to pay attention to the small teenage girl asking permission to proceed up the road to her farmhouse.

The impact of the bombs was particularly frightening because most of Kjeller and the nearby village of Lillestrom were under laid with peat, a substance of jelly-like properties that accentuated the vibrations and prolonged them.

The Norwegians thought they had been forgotten by the Allies and the U.S. Air Force because they had not seen any bombers over their town, only Germans since April of 1940, the date of the German invasion of Norway. Some Norwegians on that November day in 1943 ran outside in the snow and waved at the American bombers. One Norwegian mother shouted, "Those are my boys up there."

The bombing destroyed 85% of the airfield facilities, crippling a major repair depot and German base.

Fifty years later the Americans who bombed the base returned, this time for a friendly reception by the people. Among them was that once teenage girl who had been so frightened and terrorized by the bombing and the German officers.

She is now a mature woman, Sidsel Brun, whose father was commander-in-chief of the Kjeller base before the German occupation. He was a prisoner of war in Germany for nearly the entire war, and returned by some miracle to survive and join his family. Her mother was a prominent woman in Norway, a singer of note and well liked by the people.

This is merely one of the many stories of the survivors of that fearful time, a time when courage was a daily part of living. Courage was also the price of survival.

There is a new American memorial at Kjeller to airmen and Norwegians who lost their lives in World War II. It was dedicated on the 50th anniversary of the Kjeller mission by survivors of that mission. The memorial is a small part of America in the middle of Norway and the Norwegians have promised to honor it and protect it forever.

Norway Remembers Americans' Sacrifice
by Ed Dobson, Jr. (AM, 44th BG)

Lt. Ed Dobson was one of many young men who answered the call to fight in World War II. And like too many others, Lt. Dobson did not come home. After his commissioning as a combat pilot in the Army Air Force, Lt. Dobson served and gave his life in a four engine B-24 Liberator bomber. On May 8, 1995, commemorating the 50th anniversary of the end of the war in Europe, Norwegians dedicated a stone monument with bronze plaque to Lt. Dobson and 62 other American fliers who lost their lives on the mission that began the liberation of Norway.

Lt. Dobson's last mission took him to Norway on November 18, 1943. On the 50th anniversary of that mission in 1993, several men who flew the mission gathered in Norway as guests of the Royal Norwegian Air Force. Over 400 Norwegians filled a church at Lillestrom for the commemorative service. Many had been tortured during the war as members of the resistance.

Lt. Dobson had been assigned to the 8th Air Force as copilot on the crew of Lt. James E. Hill of Midland, TX. They were sent to the 67th Squadron of the 44th Bomb Group, stationed in England, as a replacement crew.

The 67th Squadron was suffering terrible losses, being mathematically entirely wiped out twice by the fall of 1943. On two missions, August 16 and October 1, 1943, while the 67th was on temporary duty based in North Africa, Lt. Dobson's B-24 was the only plane of the squadron that got to the target and returned to base. In October 1943 the remnants of the 67th returned to England. There, Lt. Dobson accomplished the goal of all copilots; promotion to first pilot with his own plane and crew.

Lt. Dobson knew his job, and he knew the odds. At that time in the war, combat crews had to fly 25 missions. The top brass adopted that number based on an expected 4% loss rate per mission. There was some talk of lowering the requirement to 15 missions, but that never happened. The men figured their life expectancy at eight missions. After eight, they figured they were living on borrowed time.

Until the morning of November 16, 1943, when the mission officer first lifted the curtain from the map to expose a target in Norway, none of the B-24 crews in England expected to go there. The trip involved 1400 miles, mostly over the frigid North Sea. A parachute was only short-term help and rescue virtually impossible. But the Germans had a heavy water plant in Norway, a key to their effort to be first with the atomic bomb.

On November 16th, four bomb groups, the 44th, 93rd, 389th, and 392nd, were assigned to the heavy water target. The weather did not cooperate. Most planes, including Lt. Dobson's, were called back. Planes that arrived in Norway could not find the heavy water plant, but a vital chemical plant was destroyed. There was little flak, no enemy aircraft, and no American losses. Later, the heavy water plant and its product were disabled and destroyed by Norwegians on the ground, led by the late Knut Haukelid and now known as the Heroes of Telemark.

On November 18, when the curtain went up to reveal Norway again, the men were more concerned about the long flight over cold weather than about enemy opposition. This time the target was a German fighter repair base outside Oslo. Joseph Stalin was demanding that the Allies open a campaign on the western front to divert Hitler's attention from Russia. D-Day was still half a year away. The Germans' fighter repair base outside Oslo was servicing their fighters from the Russian front. Our bombers would answer Stalin's demands.

107 planes of the same four bomb groups lifted from their bases in the dark of that fogbound and icy morning. In a portent of what was to happen, the 44th was unable to accomplish its formation assembly. Tail-end planes starting late for Norway expected to assemble on the way. Because of this, when the German fighters did come, it was difficult for American flyers to identify their own damaged aircraft.

And come the Germans did. Fighters based in Denmark intercepted the tail of the formation going in, and most of the formation going back, especially the "tail-end Charlies." Lt. Dobson and the rest of the 44th were "tail-end Charlies" that day.

Of the 107 crews from the four groups, three landed in neutral Sweden without loss of life. Only six of the 107 crews were lost. Of those six, four were 44th "Flying Eight-Ball" crews. Three of the four were 67th Squadron crews, and the fourth pilot, Lt. Ed Mitchell, was an original 67th Squadron pilot who had just transferred to another squadron. The 67th's bad luck had struck again.

A report shows that Lt. Dobson made the bomb run and dropped on target, but no one knows what happened to Lt. Dobson and his crew. Two B-24s were positively identified going down in the North Sea on the return, but neither plane was Dobson's. That left two 67th planes unaccounted for and declared missing in action.

One of those two was piloted by Lt. Earl Johnson of Montgomery, Alabama. One 67th crew was reported shot down in the Skagerrak, the sea south of Oslo, prior to the bomb run. That plane must have been Lt. Johnson's. At the end of the war, both crews were declared killed in action. Lt. Dobson is presumed shot down over the North Sea.

The mission was termed a success, as over 70% of our bombs fell within 2,000 feet of the briefed aiming point. Working with the Norwegian Resistance, the Air Force picked a day when the Norwegian work force was on holiday. Only three Norwegians died in the raid. Two half-sisters attending the 50th anniversary in 1993 had lost their father, and one had lost her mother. The two sisters were teens that day, schoolgirls huddled in a bomb shelter.

Later, both women said that they never blamed the Americans for their personal losses that day. They always thought of the Nazis as ultimately responsible for those events.

One of the sisters, Lil Nyheim, invited the Americans to her house the next day for waffles, a traditional Norwegian hospitality meal. On the wall of her living room was a large and beautiful painting with a hole in it. She explained that the hole had been made by a bomb fragment, probably the bomb that killed her parents. Her parents were trying to get away from their house close to the airfield, perhaps thinking that they would be safer in the woods. They suffered a direct hit and died instantly.

Afterwards, as the small party of Americans gathered in their large van, expressing thanks and love to Lil Nyheim, she waved her goodbye with a four-foot Norwegian flag. Lil and other Norwegians are serious about remembering the American airmen who came to help liberate Norway some fifty years ago, especially those like Lt. Ed Dobson who gave their lives. The permanent stone and bronze memorial was dedicated on May 8th at the air base that was their target that day more than fifty years ago. It is a monument to Norwegian-American friendship as well as to the 63 American fliers and three Norwegians lost that day.

In Lt. Ed Dobson's hometown of Merrick, New York, Dobson Avenue is a reminder of his courage and commitment.

Princess' Death Ends Fairy Tale
by Thrity Umrigar Beacon Journal, AKRON, Ohio
August 2, 1993

The princess died in Bucharest, Romania, in May. In Tallmadge, Ohio, a 75-year-old man was overcome with grief. He wasn't the only one. For Clell Riffle and many of the men who served with him in World War II, it was the end of an era.

Princess Catherine Caradja's death may have marked the symbolic end of the most painful period of Riffle's life. But it did not—could not—mark the end of a friendship that began in a cornfield in Brasov/Ploesti, Romania, in 1943.

On August 1, 1943, Riffle was one of the 560 men sent by the U.S. Air Force to bomb the oil fields of Ploesti. Only 110 of the men survived the attack and Riffle was one of them—thanks to the courage of a Romanian princess with a heart of gold.

After they had successfully bombed some of Ploesti's oil refineries, Riffle's plane was shot down. The injured men crash-landed in a cornfield. Riffle himself was hit in the knees and had broken ribs. But his worst nightmare was yet to come.

Within minutes the cornfields parted and Riffle and his comrades were greeted by German and Romanian soldiers. A German officer, not realizing that Riffle was injured, ordered him to get up. As Riffle looked helplessly on, the officer picked up a hand grenade and aimed it at him.

Just then, a handsome, distinguished looking woman strode onto the scene. "Who are you?" she asked the visitors.

"We're Americans."

She turned to the German officer and fixed an imperial gaze upon him. Slowly, the hand holding the grenade lowered.

The fifty-something woman turned out to be Princess Caradja. The cornfield was part of her estate. And although she was limited in what she could do for her American "boys," she continued to help them.

Riffle remembers the first time the princess visited them in the Romanian POW camp he was detained in for 13 months. "I cried," he recalls. Then, he cries again, as if it were 1943 instead of 1993.

The princess would smuggle in wire cutters, glue and other tools to help the Americans escape. When they would thank her, she'd reply, "My dear, I do what I can."

Riffle never got a chance to thank the princess again until 1955. By then, the tables had turned. This time, she was a visitor to his country and it was her fortunes that had come tumbling down. The Communist regime in Romania had stripped her of most of her wealth and she feared for her life. She escaped from her homeland, smuggled out on a vehicle carrying refrigerator coils.

When Riffle spotted the princess on a television talk show in America, he could not believe his eyes. Be he contacted her and four months later, she came to visit the home of one of her boys. For the rest of her life, whenever she wanted a break from the lecture circuit she embarked upon in America, she would visit the Tallmadge home.

Until 1991. With Romania free from its dictatorship, the princess wanted to return to the homeland she had never forgotten.

"My dear," she had once told Riffle, "once these bones are finished, I hope they're buried in Romania to fertilize those beautiful plains."

And now it has come to pass. Princess Catherine Caradja died on May 26 in the Bucharest orphanage she had founded decades ago. She was 100.

Riffle says if he could talk to his beloved princess once more, he'd say: "For what you've contributed to mankind, to the true values that each human must love, I salute you."

Then he falls silent. But his teary eyes write the final eulogy for the aristocrat who had the heart of a lion.

Ed. Note: Clell Riffle was a radio operator aboard the 389th's "Chattanooga Choo Choo" on the August 1, 1943 Ploesti mission.

The Revenge of Corporal Weinberg
by Lt. Samuel W. Taylor, HQ. USSTAF
Reprinted from the Sept. 1945 issue of "Air Force" Magazine

When, in November of 1938, the Gestapo threw a 16-year-old boy into a concentration camp, they didn't dream of the retribution it would entail. He was but one of thousands of boys taken in a roundup following the death of a member of the German legation in Paris named Von Rath who was allegedly killed by a young Jewish boy. The Nazis might well regret that. Despite the brutal treatment they received, he and his family managed to get to America, where Erwin eventually became a corporal in the U.S. Army Air Force.

Corporal Weinberg was never to fly a mission, drop a bomb, or fire a .50 caliber machine gun at the enemy. Yet he was to enlist the enormous might of the 8th Air Force to settle his personal score. He had a very large account to settle with the Gestapo, and now that his people would not suffer any more, his story can be told.

He and his father were arrested and thrown into a boxcar crammed with other Jews. They knew their destination was Buchenwald, a name to be spoken in a whisper even in 1938. At Weimar, they were ordered out, faced against a wall and beaten over the head from behind with rubber truncheons by SS troopers.

"This wasn't the experimentation program," Erwin Weinberg said. "That didn't come until later. The Nazis merely wanted to discourage us and get us out of Germany. We were to be released if we could arrange to get out of the country." Experimentation or not, five hundred Jews died the first month.

The Weinberg family had been trying to get to America since 1936 and their names reached the top of the waiting list in 1940. Erwin arrived in his new country on a Tuesday and went to work Friday morning in a Philadelphia factory making Army uniforms, where he sewed GI blouses and waited.

The British began bombing Germany after they won the Battle of Britain and from that Erwin got the idea of how to settle the score. But he was just one person and he didn't know how to go about doing what he wanted to do. When America entered the war, he couldn't enlist because he was an alien. He wondered whom he could tell his idea to, but it seemed impossible that anyone would listen.

There is something about determination that makes the breaks. He earned his citizenship papers after taking classes at night and that helped a lot.

In June 1943, the Army accepted him for the Air Force and that was just where he wanted to be. The following February he landed in England, again just where he wanted to be. But still, he was only a private at the very bottom of Army channels. What could a lowly private do to convince the Army brass that he had a good idea?

He obtained permission from his 1st Sergeant to speak to an officer. "Sir, I have information that I think is of value to the 8th Air Force. My hometown is Fulda, Germany. Fulda has never been bombed, yet there is a ball bearing factory there, Gebaur and Moller. Gunniwerke Fulda AG is a rubber factory and there is also an enamel factory making war materials. I know the location of all three plants."

The officer listened and suggested that Erwin talk to an intelligence officer. Two days later Pvt. Weinberg was transferred to the U.S. Strategic Air Forces in Europe where he talked with a Major John Simone. Major Simone was more than interested. He called for the target folder on Fulda and learned that a ball bearing plant was known to be there, but its location was unknown. Intelligence was not sure which of the two factories was the rubber plant.

To prove he knew what he was talking about, Weinberg took pencil and paper and drew a sketch showing the two plants in relation to roads and rivers. Satisfied, the major requested air reconnaissance on the target, but the air forces were very busy, at the time, preparing for D-Day and other reconnaissance targets had priority over Fulda.

Erwin was then assigned the job of interpreter and file clerk for reconnaissance photos. As each new batch of photos came in, he hoped one of them would be Fulda. Meanwhile, the attacks on ball bearing plants were discontinued—their purpose of impairing the production of ordnance and aircraft had been achieved. Aren't they ever going to bomb Fulda?

Then one day the major called him in and handed him several reconnaissance photos of Fulda. "Can you pinpoint these three targets?" "Yes Sir, I sure can!" And Private Weinberg proceeded to circle the ball bearing plant, the rubber factory and the factory that had been making enamel.

Finally, in August, the major called him in again and showed him a series of strike photos of bombs exploding on the rubber plant and in the marshaling yards. A photo taken after reconnaissance showed extensive damage to both.

Eighth Air Force heavy bombers struck Fulda twice more in December 1944, again in January 1945 and again in March. To make sure the three plants were completely destroyed, the 9th Air Force sent medium bombers to hit the target one last time in April.

Weinberg's targets were bombed six times on the basis of information he had supplied and he began to collect spare photos of them. The one he likes most of all shows where a bomb fell outside the target area and made a direct hit on his father's house. This was one of the houses the Nazis took without payment. Now they would never be able to use it.

Private Erwin was a little disappointed in the fact that they never sent a lot of bombers over Fulda, never more than 100 in any one raid. However, even that was a pretty fair sized air force for a lowly private. "I think I did all I could for the 8th Air Force," he said.

He is now a corporal, but he doesn't connect his promotion to his contribution towards the destruction of the Fulda target. He says it's just Army T/O.

His one remaining goal is to visit Fulda, after the war, to view the destruction. Considering what he accomplished as a private, no one doubts that he will be able to do just that.

We are the Mustangs, Your "Little Friends" of World War II!

by Robert E. Kuhnert (355th FG)

The 355th Fighter Group has a rich heritage, being descended from perhaps the most illustrious pursuit group in the annals of aerial warfare—the legendary 1st Pursuit Group of World War I, which flew Nieuport 28s, Spads and Sopwith Camels. Capt. Eddie Rickenbacker, America's "ace of aces in WWI," was commanding officer of the 94th (hat-in-ring) Squadron.

In our World War II days we thought of those flimsy WWI fabric-and-wood flying machines as "crates" compared with our mighty all-metal P-47 Thunderbolt and the long-range, highly maneuverable P-51 Mustang, both heavily armed with terrifying multiple 50 caliber machine guns (which fired outside the arc of the propeller). And now our "superior" airplanes seem almost antiquated in the eyes of our young as they watch on TV, sitting in easy chairs at home, present-day jet fighters sending electronically controlled weapons into doorways with surgical precision.

I recall the influx of brand new "gold bar second looies" with shiny silver sings, some of whom commanded 355th Fighter Squadrons and became excellent combat pilots, many of them aces. Sadly, some of them fell in combat and became prisoners of war; too many paid the supreme price of life; happily some evaded capture and returned. It is a gratifying feeling (as one ages) to remember helping "wet-nurse" those young men who distinguished themselves in combat.

The 355th Fighter Group led all fighter groups in the 8th Air Force in the dangerous role of ground strafing, earning the title "Steeple Morden Strafers." Our group emerged from the war in either third or fourth place in combined air/ground victories. There may be a discrepancy in placement. I like to use information released by the 8th Air Force, and printed in the wartime newspaper *Stars and Stripes*. An article from S&S in my scrapbook lists the 355th in third place, showing 356 destroyed in the air, and 504 on the ground, a total of 860; the 355th bested only by the longer-serving 4th Fighter Group (formerly the Eagle Squadrons), and Lt. Col. "Gabby" Gabreski's much-touted 56th Fighter Group.

The 355th can boast having, at one time, the ETO's leading ace, as reported in another *Stars and Stripes* article. Capt. (now retired Colonel) Henry Brown, 354th FS, was the high scorer when Lt. Col. Gabreski went down, Henry having a combined total of 30. He needed only one more to tie Gabreski's record. As fate would have it, we lost our top ace, Henry Brown, to ground fire and POW status. We have him back and have enjoyed him at reunions.

Memorable events are chronicled in the history of our 355th. On April 5, 1944, shortly after switching from P-47s to P-51s, the 355th made a daring and dangerous—and profitable—raid on a German airfield in a raging snowstorm. For that mission the group was awarded the Distinguished Unit Citation (which is often referred to, and is currently listed in *Air Force Magazine* as, the Presidential Unit Citation).

There are interesting, exciting cliff-hanging stories which could fill a book, and there is a book which reviews and relates all missions and events. For those who may not yet be familiar with it, Bill Marshall (son of the late Col. Bert Marshall, one-time C.O. of the 354th FS) has written and published an excellent history of the 355th in WWII. Its appropriate title is *Angels, Bulldogs & Dragons* (nicknames of the three squadrons). We've distributed about 200 copies to members and friends through our 355th PX, and it is available in many bookstores, particularly in the air museums.

A first in WWII was achieved by 355th pilots: the daring "piggyback" rescue of Bert Marshall behind enemy lines by Royce Priest (now a retired Colonel), both returning to Steeple Morden in Priest's P-51. That story received wide publicity, and is told in *Angels, Bulldogs & Dragons*. That morale-building snatch-from-the-jaws-of-capture retrieval took place on August 18, 1944, just a couple hours prior to another fine morale-building event: the great Glenn Miller concert in our Steeple Morden airfield hangar.

Ken Williams (354th FS in WWII, now a retired Lt. Col.) was our 355th pilot to go down in France (26 March 1944), evade and return to Steeple Morden in a very few weeks. Bill Cullerton may well be the only pilot known to survive a bullet from his own .45 going all the way through his body, then to escape, evade, and meet up with friendly forces.

We believe Bill Cullerton (357th FS) was the first pilot in the ETO to destroy eight enemy airplanes in one day. First ace in the 2nd Scouting Force (whose primary mission was not fighting) was Bill Whalen. The 2nd Scouting Force operated out of Steeple Morden airdrome, was supported by the 355th, and is an integral part of our 355th story today).

The second ace of WWII was Carrol McColpin (355th HQ, now retired Major General). He had served with RAF Eagle SQ 133 and the 4th Fighter Group before joining the 355th. Aces-in-a-day (combining both air and ground totals): Henry Brown, Bill Cullerton, John "Moon" Elder, Billy Hovde, Claiborne Kinnard, Halbert Marsh, Jim McElroy, Joe Mellen, Duran Vickery, Bob Woody, and Bob Peters.

Six 355th pilots destroyed the new, mysterious and dreaded ME-262 German jet fighter: Charles Spencer, 354th FS; Wendell Beatty, 358th FS; John Wilkins, 2SF; Charles Redenbaugh, 2SF, and Elmer Riffle, 357th FS. Henry Kirby, 357th FS, shared an ME-262, and Gene Greenwell, 2SF, damaged one.

The 355th flew the last England-Russia-Italy-England shuttle mission, escorting bombers on a mercy mission on 18 September 1944 to drop supplies to beleaguered Polish forces at Warsaw, continuing on to Russia for a refueling stop, then on to Italy and back to England on 22 September.

We cite one more instance of bravery, above and beyond, by ground personnel when, on 1 January 1945, a B-17 from Bassingbourn (91st Bomb Group) crashed on our airdrome, killing all aboard. It destroyed one P-51, damaged several others, and seriously wounded crew chief Bob Marzo (354th FS). C-Flight Chief T/Sgt. Ray Katzensky and crew chief S/Sgt. Morton Braun risked their lives to save Bob Marzo by quickly removing him from the area to the base hospital. Both Ray and Mort were awarded the Soldier's Medal (highest non-combat award) for their bravery and quick action).

All the foregoing is but a "sampler" of 355th "right stuff" quality in bravery, guts, skill, honor, and duty. We can all be proud to have served in the World War II 355th Fighter Group, and to pass on this legacy to our children and grandchildren.

California, One-Way!
by Ralph Elliott (467th)

It's April 29, 1993, and forty-eight years have passed since I landed my B-24 Liberator bomber, 591, at Bradley Field, Connecticut after a seven day flight from England at the close of World War II. Unbelievably, I am again sitting in the pilot's seat, flying the last combat-ready B-24 in existence on a four hour flight from Tucson, Arizona to Santa Monica, California. Slowly, the old skills come back, the altitude settles down on 5000 feet, and the compass heading stays on 270 degrees. Was it always this much work? No power steering here—just the cables from the controls out to the ailerons and back to the elevator and rudders. Trim tabs help to take some of the pressure off the wheel; but then reality sets in—it really was work. I just didn't know it then. The physical difference is in the age, 23 versus 71, but age has done nothing to diminish the thrill of flying the Liberator again.

Only, did they downsize her when she was rebuilt? The catwalk through the bomb bay seems narrower now, and surely four men and all their gear didn't share this little space in the rear with the guns, the flak jackets, the Mae Wests, the parachutes and sand bags. No wonder the bombardier, navigator, and nose turret gunner had a constant fight for room up front, and five men couldn't possibly fit on the flight deck. Even the pilot's seat seems smaller. What does come back are the noise of the engines that make normal conversation impossible, the smell of high-octane gasoline, and the feeling in the pit of the stomach that goes with an air pocket and a "rapid change of altitude."

The desert air is rough at low altitude and the thermals catch me as we go over a low mountain ridge into California. The other two passengers get airsick, and I'm glad I'm doing the flying—not bouncing around in the back. It's drafty back there with the side windows open for the guns, and it was hell for the gunners at 45 below zero, when to touch the guns without gloves meant you'd lose your fingers. Memories ride with me on the flight, and the years fall off in the sights and sounds and smells, but I finally realize that the real wonder is the set of circumstances that have put me up here again after an absence of 48 years.

On April 27, the "All American" arrived at the Avra Valley Airport, north of Tucson, on a cross-country tour sponsored by the College (isn't it Collins?) Foundation of Stow, Massachusetts. During WWII, the B-24 dropped more bombs and flew more missions than any other aircraft; it was the most produced aircraft of all time—over 18,000 planes. The cost to reconstruct the "All American" was over $1,300,000.00, but money can't buy the feelings of nostalgia and the tears the old bomber generates as the veterans stand on the ramp and cheer as she taxis in.

Unbeknownst to me, as a 50th wedding anniversary present (August 28), Yvonne had contacted the organizers of the Avra Valley stop and had made arrangements for me to fly in the plane on the next leg of her flight to California. While the kids joke about "Mom giving Dad a one-way ticket to California for an anniversary present," they were as thrilled as I was about the flight. No surprise in our 50 years together ever topped this one.

France to England in a Life Raft
by Harold Benvenuti (448th)

April 1, 1944 was both my 13th mission and my lucky day. Passing over the French coast on our way to the target we lost our first engine from flak. While making our bomb run, another engine was knocked out. Leaving the target, our third engine ceased to function.

The Pilot, Lt. Jack Black, (our plane was named 'Black's Widow') decided to go on as long as he could knowing that eventually we would have to ditch. We all agreed that ditching was better than a P.O.W. camp for the remainder of the war.

As 'Black's Widow' settled toward the water, we threw out everything that wasn't nailed down, including both waist guns.

The order to prepare to ditch finally came. When we hit the water the ball turret dropped out and water came rushing in. It picked me up and whipped me against the right waist window. Dick Campbell and Wilfred Haschke went out the left waist window and I followed.

When we got to the left wing, the rubber boats were out. I got in one with Dick Campbell, Lt. Burkhartsmeir and Tex Dweaczyk. Lt. Jack Black, Wilfred Haschke, Charles Nissen, Mike Curran and Pete Wermert were in the other. We never did see Joe Pompret, the Co-pilot. We moved away from the plane waiting for it to go under. To our amazement the plane floated for an hour before pointing her nose down, her tail up and going under. When she was gone, we buried Charles Nissen who had died in our arms from serious injuries.

Being only 10 miles off the French Coast (Dunkirk), it was logical to go there and give ourselves up. It was 60 miles to England. We took a vote and paddling to England won. Having made this decision we checked the rafts for survival equipment. Nothing. There wasn't a thing! The only things we had were a few chocolate bars and a couple of compasses. So be it. We set our heading and paddled.

That night the water was really rough, and even though we used a couple of the parachutes to protect us from the wind, everybody was soaked and cold. We could hear planes flying overhead, but without a flashlight there was nothing we could do. Just wish them luck if they were ours and hope they didn't spot us if they were German.

Dawn broke with an overcast sky and all we could see was water in every direction. Lacking food and water we tried not to think about eating. We just continued to scan the water hoping to see land or some boats. After a few hours we did see an object coming toward us, and the closer it got the faster it seemed to be going. It turned out to be one of those buoys with food and a radio inside. I wanted to make a swim for it but I was over-ruled. The current was very fast and it went by us, or we it, before we knew it. It would have been impossible to swim against that current.

As the day went on, we heard airplane motors, but we never saw them as it was still overcast. Night came again with the water still rough and all of us wet and cold. As the night wore on we heard airplane engines, but this time we also saw anti-aircraft flashes and heard bombs exploding. We knew then that we were nearing land.

As it began to get light, a few minesweepers crossed our path off in the distance. We waved but they did not see us. By this time we were certain that the land we were heading towards was England and we began to paddle faster. Finally we came close to some fishing boats and started to yell and wave our arms. It first appeared that they didn't see us either and some of us started cussing as loud as we could.

Suddenly one fishing boat headed our way. The name of the boat was "The Three Brothers," and the crew quickly hauled us aboard. Another boat came along and was sent to shore to notify the authorities. The Captain of our boat told us that we were seen but they thought we were Germans. It wasn't until they heard our cussing that they knew we were "Yanks'.

We came ashore in Folkstone and as soon as we landed, Tex went to his knees and kissed the good old English soil! A waiting ambulance took us to the Folkstone hospital. I was never so glad to get into a bed again and I have no idea how long we slept.

A few days later our new Colonel, Col. Mason, came to see us and told us that a base ambulance would be coming to pick us up. I kind of hated to leave that hospital as they were all so great to us, but it was good to get back to the base again and see familiar faces.

The Mighty Eighth Air Force Heritage Museum

Savannah sparks emotions that surprise you with their intensity. In an era when many view World War II as ancient history and its veterans as relics, this museum brings the hell and the heart of it up-close and very personal, reviving the sheer awe inspired by those who stared down peril in the name of freedom. Activated in Savannah in 1942 and conceived to strike a lethal blow against the Third Reich, the Mighty Eighth Air Force relentlessly bombed strategic German targets in occupied Europe ultimately capable of deploying 2,000 planes every day. Of an estimated 200,000 aviators and crewmen who flew the Eighth, 28,000 became prisoners of war, and 26,000 lost their lives. No other military command suffered a higher percentage of deaths, but not one mission was turned back by the Nazis.

On display among the exhibits are the belongings of pilots, including fleece-lined jackets emblazoned with moral-boosting artwork, and bailout kits containing compasses and syringes for morphine. The Wall of Aces is devoted to the flyers who shot down five or more enemy aircraft. In another section is a replica of the grim interior of a German POW barracks. A nearby video spotlights survivors of a POW camp as a recount their plight. Several images depict the resolve that defined the British during those bleak years.

But the museum's most spellbinding feature is the Mission Experience Theater, which, with authentic film footage, puts you in the center of a bombing raid. Eight screens are filled with terrifying, exhilarating action punctuated by the deafening sounds of air combat. You are there in the aircraft dodging bursts of flak and barreling assaults of the German Luftwaffe, the heavens raining parachutes and airplane fragments. Ultimately locating your target, you drop your explosive payload. At the moment that the bomb bay opens, a whoosh of air sweeps into the theater—a special effect that struck a resounding chord with 1996 visitor Walter Cronkite, who flew with the Eighth as a war correspondent.

Shot Down by the Battleship Archangel
by Earl Zimmerman (389th)

I enjoyed Ken Driscoll's article in the last Journal about the black Libs flying out of Harrington, as I know whereof he writes. I was flying out of Leuchars, Scotland during that time and know the details of the black Lib that was shot down by the Russians near Murmansk. One of the gunners on that crew was from my original crew of the 389th, Lt. Harold L. James, pilot.

The black Libs flying out of Leuchars were assigned to the Ball Project, with Colonel Bernt Balchen as commander. He wore the Medal of Honor and the crews really liked him. I had the privilege of flying with him on two occasions.

On 20 September 1944, Colonel Keith Allen, pilot; Captain Schreiner, copilot; and seven crew members took off from Leuchars on an operational mission to drop supplies to the underground in Norway. After crossing the coastline of Norway, number one engine began to smoke and run rough. This condition existed until they reached the target area and released the containers. The engine then caught fire and was feathered, and the fire extinguished itself. After a short staff meeting on the flight deck it was decided to try for Murmansk, as heading back over the North Sea on three engines was a bit risky.

The plane finally crossed the mouth of Kola inlet as the crew looked for a place to land. Three searchlight cones of three each were turned on, indicating an airfield. In attempting to make a 360 turn, without knowing it the pilot flew over the battleship *Archangel*. During this time, the Russian colors of the day were being fired from the Very pistol; all lights on the plane were turned on, including the landing lights; and calls were being made on the International Distress Frequency.

At this time, the battleship *Archangel* opened fire along with some shore batteries, hitting engine number two which caught fire, shooting off the left rudder and damaging the left wing. With the plane on fire, Col. Allen ordered Capt. Schreiner to bail out the crew, advising that he would follow. Despite the flames, the engineer released two life rafts through the bomb bay. The right waist gunner was hit by flak and bailed out; the navigator escaped through the nose wheel well after destroying all the classified material and making sure the IFF was destroyed.

When his parachute deployed, the navigator looked up and saw his plane explode. When he reached the ground, he threw his gun away and called for the other crew members. His call was answered by machine gun fire. Eventually, he was captured by a Russian lieutenant who took him before Russian engineers for questioning, after which they were convinced of his identity. A Russian staff officer took him to view the plane, which was entirely demolished, and on his return to the Russian quarters he identified the remains of Colonel Allen.

The Russians relinquished control of the crew to Captain S.B. Frankel, USN, who dispatched a message to London. Burial rites for Colonel Allen were conducted by Captain Frankel, in the presence of Russian Admiral Golovko, Commander Morton, Royal Navy and local diplomatic agents, with six of the ambulatory crew members acting as pallbearers. A farewell salute was fired by a Russian Guard of Honor.

All crew members were happy to get out from under the jurisdiction of the Russians as they boarded the HMS Rodnay, which took them to the naval air station at Scapa Flow where they disembarked. Two amphibious aircraft took the crew back to the home base at Leuchars, Scotland.

RAF Leuchars was a strange airfield. Among other units stationed there were the Green Libs, Operation "Sonnie," with civilian markings, flying into Sweden bringing out the American internees; a Canadian outfit flying white Libs on sub patrol; Royal Navy fabric covered biplanes, fitted with torpedoes; strange looking aircraft which were crewed by French, Polish, Norwegians and South Africans, and a few assorted uniforms which could not be distinguished. Our operation was restricted to a small area around a hangar, and we met the other crews at the local pubs but none would reveal their missions.

The Carpetbaggers had missions to Norway, Denmark, Holland, Belgium, Germany and France. Some crews, dressed in civilian clothing, flew across Norway and landed in neutral Sweden to drop off or pick up VIPs. Major William E. Colby, who in later years became director of our Central Intelligence Agency (CIA), was dropped by a Carpetbagger aircraft in France during August 1944 and dropped again in Norway about March, 1945.

In mid-1944, the Carpetbaggers only flew black B-24 type aircraft. As the months went on, they had a few C-47s that they flew and landed behind enemy lines in France. They also flew some modified A-26 aircraft and British Mosquitos to drop agents deep in Germany.

An incident happened one night at Harrington that I have never forgotten. We had been briefed in the afternoon that our drop site was in Belgium and that we would be dropping two agents. As a general rule, air crews did not mingle with the agents to be dropped. I, as pilot, usually introduced myself to them, time permitting, and asked if they had any questions about the flight or drop.

As I approached the two agents, who were standing near the nose of the aircraft just prior to boarding, I noted that one of them was a lady about 20-25 years old. Just before I got to them, I saw their escort hand them some capsules. These capsules contained poison and were to be swallowed by the agents to kill themselves, if they so desired, when they were captured. If captured, they would have been tortured as spies and put to death by the Germans. Seeing this young lady voluntarily embark on such a dangerous mission, knowing the consequences if it failed, has been etched in my memory ever since.

Midnight
by the author

The door opens in our heavily black- out- curtained concrete barracks. Home to a dozen flying officers—3 each pilots, co-pilots, navigators, bombardiers. "BRIEFING AT

ONE" is the unwelcome message. The gut recoils at the prospect of the day. The place is near the city of Norwich, capital of East Anglia, in east central England. It's at U.S. Army Air Forces' B-24 base. I both roll and stumble out of my army cot, along with the three other officers in my crew—along with any other crews who may have been assigned to this mission. We trudge, heavily booted, in the dark to the lavatory. We shave closely in order to get a close fit on our oxygen masks. Then a couple of blocks to the mess where we are often served fresh eggs, but they have been barely warmed in the pan, and the worried stomach can't face them. We know that a couple of cups of coffee, along with the adrenalin we'll muster, will carry us through the next ten hours. We either catch a truck or ride our bikes to operations, and the four officers join the six enlisted men of our crew. We don't feel like a small army, but we are. We're not mad at anybody, but we believe we are preserving our world of freedom of choice and absence of fear, which we wouldn't be if we lose. While we are concerned about winning, we are possessed with survival. A mission is personally successful primarily if we get back safely, and secondarily, if we destroyed our target. Not that it wasn't important. If you didn't, a return trip would be necessary. And you are never more alive than after escaping the alternative. After the general briefing, the non-coms go to our assigned plane to prepare for the flight. The pilots go to a separate briefing room, and the navigator and bombardier to another. Here, intricate details of the flight are covered. It's a big job to put up a thousand or more airplanes in the sky—every day—get them organized and on their way to maybe a dozen or more targets, and coordinate fighter protection. It's a ready-made situation for foul ups, and they occur with regularity.

After these briefings the officers are off to the hardstand where the plane is parked. Pilots check the plane for any visible problem, start the engines at the assigned time, and check them for performance. At briefed signals, we taxi along the perimeter strip to the takeoff runway, plane after plane lined up for takeoff at 30 second intervals. On the runway, hold the brakes and run up the engines before releasing the brakes to give us a kind of slingshot start. We only have 6,000 feet to get 65,000 lbs. or more off the ground, and every little edge helps. Crashing at the end of the runway is very serious business!

The Freckleton Tragedy
by John Threlfall

At 10:30 hours on August 23rd, 1st. Lt. John Bloemendal lifted #291 clear of the runway at Warton. His crew consisted of T/Sgt. Jimmie Parr, acting as copilot, and Gordon Kinney, a Flight Test Aerial Engineer. They were accompanied by a second B-24 flown by 1st Lt. Pete Manaserro and his crew of Dick Pew and Lawrence Smith.

A few minutes into the air tests, things began to go wrong. The control tower at Warton was warned by their counterparts at Burtonwood that a violent storm was approaching from the Warrington area and that any aircraft that were airborne from Warton should be recalled immediately. The message was relayed to the two pilots, who wasted no time in plotting a course for Warton. It was then that the storm hit them.

It was the most violent storm anyone in the area had ever witnessed. People in the village of Freckleton were alarmed by its ferocity. One man stated that the rain battering against his windowpanes was so intense he could not see the houses opposite him. Jane Chestnutwood, an army nurse at the station hospital, was recovering from a bout of flu. She was off duty and resting in her quarters when the storm broke. She later stated that the intensity of the rain and lightning reminded her of the storms she had experienced in her native Indiana. To calm the children in the infant's class in the local school, their teacher was reading them a story.

Meanwhile, Lts. Bloemendal and Manaserro were fighting to control their B-24s. They were being tossed about by the hurricane-force winds in the center of the storm. They also had to contend with pitch-blackness, severe squalls, and lightning. They talked over the radio and decided to head for Scotland. It was the last Lt. Manaserro heard from Lt. Bloemendal. He could not see the other B-24, so he heaved his aircraft onto a new heading and prayed he would be able to find calmer weather conditions.

As nurse Jane Chestnutwood stood staring in the direction of Freckleton, the rain suddenly decreased to a fine drizzle and visibility became clear. It was then that she became the eyewitness of a horrific scene. A B-24 suddenly appeared from the cloudbank some five or six hundred feet above the ground. It was heading in the general direction of Warton. In the next instant it was struck by a huge bolt of lightning, which split the aircraft apart at the wing root. The two parts of the B-24 spiraled to the ground and there followed an enormous explosion. What followed next must have seemed like Armageddon to the villagers of Freckleton.

The front section of the B-24 slammed into the infant's classroom in the village school. The explosion that followed brought the whole building crashing down on the children and their teacher. To make matters worse, the aircraft had a full load of fuel on board when it took off. This fuel, now burning fiercely, covered the debris of the classroom and was also gushing down the main street of Freckleton, causing even more damage by the fires it was starting. Part of the aircraft careened across the road where it demolished a snack bar—The Sad Sack, a popular meeting place for service personnel and villagers. Of all the people who had entered The Sad Sack to shelter from the storm, there were no survivors. In all, the number of people who lost their lives through this dreadful accident was 61. This included 38 children.

The people of Freckleton have been forever grateful to the American Forces and authorities for all the help they received from them, to enable them to come to terms with this tragedy. A great bond of friendship and understanding was forged between them, and is still as strong today as it was 62 years ago when they shared each other's grief.

For the information used in this article I am indebted to Mrs. Margaret Hall, the B.A.D. 2 Association representative in Freckleton. For the photocopied pictures, my thanks go to the staff at the Public Library in Lythan St. Annes.

Oradour sur Glane Saturday, 10th June, 1944

Before D-Day the French Maquis had made many attacks, blowing up roads and railways and generally disrupting communications. These attacks were stepped up in the hours preceding D-Day which was notified to the waiting Maquis by the BBC, the code phrase being two lines from a poem by Verlaine.

After D-Day various reinforcements were rushed by von Runstedt, the German commander, to plug his defenses. The II SS Panzer Division 'Das Reich' reached the Limoges area of France on 6th June.

Fourteen miles north west of Limoges lies Oradour sur Glane. Saturday 10th June was a busy day in the village. Apart from the village population being increased by an influx of refugees, being Saturday, many visitors had come from Limoges and surrounding villages. The village was a typical French village of gray stone houses and narrow streets.

At 2:15 p.m. a large convoy of Waffen SS troops, wearing camouflaged green and yellow denims, drove into the village and parked in two places. The German commander was Heinz Lammerding.

Shortly afterwards the town crier announced that the entire population must assemble with identity cards in the village square. A house-to-house search was carried out to ensure everybody was there including rounding up workers in the fields. The 191 schoolchildren were told to go the church together with all the women and younger children, a group totaling 400. One small boy, Roger Godfrin, aged 8, managed to slip away to the surrounding woods.

The German Commander then announced that they were searching for Maquis arms and accordingly the men were split into six groups and taken to separate barns. Each group was guarded by several soldiers armed with sub-machine guns. Five minutes after they were there a shot was fired in the main square as a signal for the soldiers, who opened fire on the helpless prisoners. After the firing died away the soldiers picked their way between the bodies finishing off with their automatics those who still showed signs of life. The troops then covered the bodies with wood and straw and then set fire to the buildings. Only a handful of the villagers who were hidden by the bodies of their dead compatriots were able to escape.

At 4 p.m. soldiers entered the church where the women and children had been taken, carrying a packing case with fuses attached. These were then lit and the soldiers retired. The case exploded and produced a dense suffocating smoke. Those women that tried to escape the smoke through the chapel door to the churchyard were shot. One woman, Madame Rouffanche, managed to hide behind the altar. Here she found a stepladder and managed to climb up and squeeze through the broken middle window. A woman and child who tried to follow her were machine-gunned.

After destroying and setting fire to the other houses in the village the Germans left.

Later the Germans issued a statement to the effect that in the course of military operations Oradour sur Glane had been destroyed.

The village has been preserved as a memorial to the hundreds that died there. A new Oradour sur Glane has been rebuilt down the road. Signboards mark the location of the six buildings where the men were executed. The church still stands. The window through which Madame Rouffanche escaped is 10 ft. from the ground.

The streets are silent, the tram tracks overgrown, the local garage still full of burnt out cars.

Mike's Flag
Submitted by Walter Mundy (467th), Condensed from a speech by Leo K. Thorness, Recipient of the Congressional Medal of Honor

You've probably seen the bumper sticker somewhere along the road. It depicts an American flag, accompanied by the words "These colors don't run." I'm always glad to see this, because it reminds me of an incident from my confinement in North Vietnam at the Hao Lo POW Camp, or the "Hanoi Hilton," as it became known. Then a Major in the U.S. Air Force, I had been captured and imprisoned from 1967-1973. Our treatment had frequently been brutal. After three years, however, the beatings and torture became less frequent. During the last year, we were allowed out doors most days for a couple of minutes to bathe. We showered by drawing water from a concrete tank with a home- made bucket. One day as we all stood by the tank, stripped of our clothes, a young Navy pilot named Mike Christian found the remnants of a handkerchief in a gutter that ran under the prison wall. Mike managed to sneak the grimy rag into our cell and began fashioning it into a flag. Over time we all loaned him a little soap, and he spent days cleaning the material. We helped by scrounging and stealing bits and pieces of anything he could use. At night, under his mosquito net, Mike worked on the flag. He made red and blue from ground up roof tiles and tiny amounts of ink and painted the colors onto the cloth with watery rice glue. Using thread from his own blanket and a home- made bamboo needle, he sewed on stars. Early in the morning a few days later, when the guards were not alert, he whispered loudly from the back of our cell, "Hey, gang, look here." He proudly held up this tattered piece of cloth, waving it as if in a breeze. If you used your imagination, you could tell it was supposed to be an American flag. When he raised that smudgy fabric, we automatically stood straight and saluted, our chests puffing out, and more than a few eyes had tears. About once a week the guards would strip us, run us outside and go through our clothing. During one of those shakedowns, they found Mike's flag. We all knew what would happen. That night they came for him. Night interrogations were always the worst. They opened the cell door and pulled Mike out. We could hear the beginning of torture even before they had him in the torture cell. They beat him most of the night. About daylight they pushed what was left of him back through the cell door. He was badly broken, even his voice was gone. Within two weeks, despite the danger, Mike scrounged another piece of cloth and began another flag. The Stars and Stripes, our national symbol, was worth the sacrifice for him. Now, whenever I see a flag, I think of Mike and the morning he first waved that tattered emblem of a nation. It was then, thousands of miles from home in a lonely prison cell, that he showed us what it is to be truly free.

The Father Of Aerial Bombardment

His name was Ulysses S. "Sam" Nero. He was born in Phoenixville, PA Before he finished high school, he became a rivet heater in a shipyard and went to night school to earn his high school diploma. On June 13, 1917, he enlisted in the Army and went to New Mexico to chase Pancho Villa with the 13th Cavalry. In World War I, he was in a charge of a wireless station in France with the Aviation Branch of the Signal Corps.

Back in civilian life, he took a job as a heavy equipment operator, attended night school to earn a license as a second-class engineer, and began to invent things. His best invention was a device which he called the "Nero Sight," for aiming bombs from an airplane. It allowed the Air Service to tighten a bombed area from 50-100 acres, to 10 acres. For a while, only Nero was able to use the sight accurately, but he gradually trained others to use it with a fair degree of accuracy.

At this time most of the Army's Signal Corps brass believed that bombs were more likely to hit the target when dropped from a dirigible rather than from a plane. Nero disproved this belief with a two-day test in which he dropped 37 bombs from a plane, 36 of which hit the target. In four months of trying, a dirigible crew missed every time.

In 1923, the U.S. Navy brass were adamant in their opinion that aerial bombardment could not sink a heavily-armed warship. To back up their belief, they provided two obsolete battleships, the USS New Jersey and the USS Virginia, as targets and challenged the Air Service to sink them. The test took place on September 5, 1923. Nero and his pilot, flying a Martin Curtiss NBZS-1, scored two hits on first run, but were grounded because they failed to adhere to the strict guidelines provided by the Navy.

Later in the day, when other pilots had failed to hit the targets, General Billy Mitchell asked Nero if he could do it and the answer was "Yes!" Nero and his pilot took off again and dropped a bomb down one of the New Jersey's funnels. Nothing happened for a few seconds, but then a huge explosion erupted in the bowels of the ship and three minutes later the New Jersey disappeared beneath the waves. Before landing, Nero put a bomb on the deck of the Virginia for good measure.

And so it was that Sam Nero and General Billy Mitchell proved to the embarrassed Navy brass that bombs could sink ships.

(Author unknown)

More On The Luftwaffe Sturmgruppen

After reading "Where Are Our Fighters" in the Winter 2007 *Journal*, I researched a little further and would like to add some information to the fine article from the 361st Fighter Group Newsletter.

I planned to write this by dealing solely with the Sturmgruppen and its formation in the spring of 1944. However, much had transpired in the German Air Force prior to the advent of the Sturmbock, a term formed by combining "sturm" or assault, and "bock," a male goat or ram.

A brief history should begin with the 1936-37 period and the Spanish Civil War when a number of future Luftwaffe leaders were battle-tested and German aircraft including early models of the Bf109 were introduced—an airplane which, incidentally, then soldiered on until the Nazi regime collapsed in May of 1945!

In early September 1939, Germany attacked Poland and unleashed WWII upon the world. The Luftwaffe reigned supreme with the Junkers Ju87 "Stuka" dive bombers, and improved Bf109 fighters and the Heinkel He111 bombers. In the west the "phony war" against England and France continued until the spring of 1940 when Hitler threw his panzer divisions against France and the low countries, defeating them by mid May of 1940. Again, the vaunted Luftwaffe ruled the skies. Eager to invade England, Hitler sent the Luftwaffe against the British Spitfires and Hurricanes in what became known as the Battle of Britain, a time period during which the Luftwaffe received its first bloody nose at the hands of the Royal Air Force.

In its inability to obtain air superiority over the English Channel, many sources believe that this situation prompted Hitler, in his impatience, to attack the Soviet Union, breaking the Hitler-Stalin Pact and creating a two-front war.

By this time, later models of the Bf109 were in service, as well as early models of the Focke-Wulf Fw190.

Even though the Luftwaffe had been stymied by the RAF earlier, their aircraft improved and pilots continued to hone their skills. It was over Russia that many German aces *(experten)* were created. It was not unusual for Luftwaffe pilots to achieve over 100 victories, some over 200 and at least five *experten* with over 300. Erich Hartman was at the top, ending the war with 352 victories. In late 1942 and into 1943, as the Eighth Air Force built its strength, many seasoned pilots from the Eastern Front were brought in to protect Germany's Western border.

As the turbo-supercharged B-24s and B-17s were operating at altitudes of 22,000 to 26,000 feet, both of Germany's top fighters, the Bf-109G and the Fw190, were operating at the upper limits of their performance envelope. This war in the west was a whole new ball game for the Luftwaffe pilots. Some preferred the Eastern Front, in spite of the harsh winter conditions, to this new kind of high altitude air war against heavily armed bombers. In 1943 the attacks were usually two-plane elements firing at the bombers in running battles.

These raging battles took place beyond the range of American escort fighters, therefore, Luftwaffe losses were only to the defensive fire of the bombers.

Many tactics were tried against the four-engine American bombers *(Viermots)*. One method was air-to-air bombing runs against the tight bomber formations. The head-on pass was also used until the "D" model B-24s were superseded by "H&J" models with powered nose turrets. Also, the B-17G chin turret tended to further discourage the head-on pass.

Another device tried on the Fw190, but disliked by the pilots, were time-fused rockets of 21 cm (approximately 8-1/2" diameter) in hopes of breaking up the integrity of the tight formations.

In November 1943, Adolph Galland met with fighter commanders and informed the group that Reich Marshal Herman Goering had ordered the establishment of the Sturmstaffel, organized to fly heavily armed fighters in close formation into the *Viermots*. The attacks, initiated from the rear, aimed to knock out the tail gunner and then use the heavy cannon to destroy the bombers at the closest possible range.

As the Luftwaffe's best hope, the Me262 twin jet fighter, had developmental problems, the Fw190 was being modified for this role.

Firepower increased from the Fw190 A-5 thru the A-6, A-7 and finally the Fw190 A-8, the ultimate Sturmbock! One of the Luftwaffe officers involved with the buildup of the Sturmstaffel and later the Sturmgruppen was Major Gunther von Kornatzki, refining the tactics and modifying the A-8 to carry the Mk108 cannon. The firepower of this A-8 version also included two inboard MG151/20 cannons, but it was the two outboard Mk108s with a 33 mm shell (about 1-1/4" diameter) that made this Sturmbock an awesome weapons platform. As few as three shells striking the inboard engine and the wing root of a B-17 or B-24 would bring it down.

One Luftwaffe pilot stated that although he could shave the wing off a B-17, he believed the B-24 was structurally weaker.

After adding armor plate, bullet-proof windshield and canopy sides (blinkers), the Fw190 A-8 could only carry aloft 55 shells for each of its two Mk109 cannons. These airplanes were no match for the nimble P-51 escorts.

The Sturmgruppen had to rely on Bf109 aircraft to fly top cover, as stated in the 361st Fighter Group newsletter.

It was over Oschersleben on 7 July 1944 that the Sturmgruppen hit the 492nd Bomb Group, wiping out one squadron of eleven B-24s in a little over a minute! The 2nd Air Division lost 28 B-24s that day. The worst attack was against the 445th Bomb Group on 27 September 1944 over Kassel, a mission in which the 491st was close enough for our tail gunner, Burt Blackwell, to describe the scene to the rest of us in the aircraft. We watched the 361st Mustangs fly by us to engage the Luftwaffe, but the 445th lost 25 aircraft over Eisenach.

On 26 November 1944 our own 491st was hit, losing 16 airplanes in less than fifteen minutes. And B-17s were not immune from the carnage wrought on the 8th Air Force, as the 1st and 3rd Air Divisions were also hit hard. However, the constant losses suffered by the Sturmgruppen before the end of 1944 were unsustainable and their effectiveness diminished during the last few months of the war.

Out of one group of storm pilots, ten of thirteen would be killed, one wounded, and only two walked away from their Sturmbock.

How The Nazi Generals Justified Their Defeat

Condensed Excerpts From The Book The War In The Air: A Pictorial History Of WWII Air Forces In Combat, *By Gene Gurney, Major USAF. Submitted By James H. Reeves (HQ)*

GOERING, CHIEF OF LUFTWAFFE:

"I knew first that the Luftwaffe was losing control of the air when the American long-range fighters were able to escort the bombers as far as Hannover. It was not long before they were getting to Berlin. We then knew we must develop the jet planes. Our plan for their early development was unsuccessful only because of your bombing attacks.

"Allied attacks greatly affected our training program, too. For instance, the attacks on oil retarded the training because our pilots couldn't get sufficient training before they were put into the air.

"I am convinced that the jet planes would have won the war for us if we had had only four or five months' more time. Our underground installations were all ready. The factory at Kahla had a capacity of 1,000 to 1,200 jet airplanes a month. Now with 5,000 to 6,000 jets, the outcome would have been quite different.

"We would have trained sufficient pilots for the jet planes despite oil shortage, because we would have had underground factories for oil, producing a sufficient quantity for the jets. The transition to jets was very easy in training. The jet-pilot output was always ahead of the jet-aircraft production.

"Germany could not have been defeated by air power alone, using England as a base, without invasion—because German industry was going underground, and our countermeasures would have kept pace with your bombing. But the point is, that if Germany were attacked in her weakened condition as now, then the air could do it alone. That is, the land invasion meant that so many workers had to be withdrawn from factory production and even from the Luftwaffe.

"We bombed cities in England instead of concentrating on aircraft and engine factories despite my original intention to attack only military targets and factories, because after the British attacked Hamburg our people were angry and I was ordered to attack indiscriminately.

"Allied precision bombing had a greater effect on the defeat of Germany than area bombing, because destroyed cities could be evacuated but destroyed industry was difficult to replace.

"Allied selection of targets was good, particularly in regard to oil. As soon as we started to repair an oil installation, you bombed it again!

"We didn't concentrate on the four-engine Focke-Wulf planes as heavy bombers after the Battle of Britain, because we were developing the He-177 and trying to develop the Me-264, which was designed to go to America and return. Because our production capacity was not so great as America's, we could not produce quickly everything we needed. Moreover, our plants were subject to constant bombing.

"If I had to design the Luftwaffe again, the first airplane I would develop would be the jet fighter—then the jet bomber. It is now a question of fuel. The jet fighter takes so much. The Me-264 awaited only the final solution of the fuel-consumption problem. According to my view the future airplane is one without fuselage (flying wing) equipped with turbine in combination with the jet and propeller.

"Before D-Day, the Allied attacks in northern France hurt us the most because we were not able to rebuild in France as quickly as at home. The attacks on marshalling yards were most effective, next came low-level attacks on troops, then attacks on bridges. The low-flying planes had a terror effect and caused great damage to our communications. Also demoralizing were the umbrella fighters, which after escorting the bombers would swoop down and hit everything, including the jet planes in the process of landing.

"The Allies owe the success of the invasion to the air forces. They prepared the invasion; they made it possible; they carried it through.

"Without the U.S. Air Force the war would still be going on elsewhere, but certainly not on German soil."

GALLAND, CHIEF OF FIGHTERS:

"In my opinion, it was the Allied bombing of our oil industries that had the greatest effect on the German war potential. Even our supplies for training new airmen was severely curtailed—we had plenty of planes from the autumn of 1944 on, and there were enough pilots up to the end of that year, but lack of petrol didn't permit the expansion of proper training to the air force as a whole.

"In the African campaign and in Sicily and Italy, Allied successes were largely due to Allied air superiority. In my opinion, strategic bombing never forced any great change in German strategy and planning until after the opening of the invasion. Then, disorganization of German communications in the West by strategic bombing caused withdrawal to the German frontier. In the last two months of the war, the crippling of the German transport system brought about the final collapse."

KARL GERD VON RUNSTEDT, COMMANDER IN CHIEF IN THE WEST BEFORE THE GERMAN SURRENDER:

"Three factors defeated us in the West where I was in command. First, the unheard of superiority of your air force, which made all movement in daytime impossible. Second, the lack of motor fuel—oil and gas—so that the Panzers and even the remaining Luftwaffe were unable to move. Third, the systematic destruction of all railway communications so that it was impossible to bring one single railroad train across the Rhine. This made impossible the reshuffling of troops and robbed us of all mobility. Our production was also greatly interfered with by the loss of Silesia and bombardments of Saxony, as well as by the loss of oil reserves in Romania."

GEN. VON VIETINGHOFF, SUPREME COMMANDER IN SOUTHWEST (ITALY):

"On the Italian and the Western fronts, all freedom of movement for reserves and tanks was denied during daylight hours. Thus counterattacks were impossible. In isolated instances, when we were successful in assembling troops for a major surprise attack, it could only be done at night, and then the Allies were always in a position to bring their air force into action at any desired spot in a few hours and thus frustrate every German attack."

WAR DIARY OF THE 7TH GERMAN ARMY HIGH COMMAND (GEN. DOLLMAN), JUNE 11, 1944:

"Since the beginning of the Allies' large-scale attack, our transport system has been under constant attack by their air forces. Because of the continuous bombing of the main roads and the constant disruption of the detours, some of which could be kept open for only a few hours, it became evident even after the first three hours that troop movements by rail could not be maintained. Infantry divisions which were being carried by rail, also had to be unloaded because the route was blocked even before they reached the army boundary line.

"Troop movements and all supply traffic by rail to the army sector must be considered as completely cut off. The fact that traffic on the front and in rear areas is under constant attack from Allied air power has led to delays and unavoidable losses in vehicles, which in turn have led to a restriction in the mobility of the numerous Panzer units due to the lack of fuel and the unreliability of the ammunition supply...

"The following information, based on the first few days' experience with the Allied deployment air power, is reported by the German Army Supreme Command:

"1. Rail transport is impossible because the trains are observed and attacked in short order: under these circumstances, the expenditure of fuel and the wear and tear on material in bringing up Panzer units is extremely high.

"2. The movement of units by motor transport is possible only at night, and even then the highways and communication centers are continually bombed. The continual control of the field of battle by Allied air forces makes daylight movement impossible and leads to the destruction from air of our preparations and attacks.

"3. The Army considers it urgently necessary that our own air force be used by day and night in order to neutralize the Allies' now unbearably overwhelming air supremacy."

Chapter 9: Aris A. Mallas

THIS CHAPTER is dedicated to ARIS A. MALLAS, who goes by the very common name of "Bob," but there is nothing ordinary about this rare individual. On only one occasion have I met him, at a gem show in Tucson, about twenty-five years ago, and after a hiatus of some years, we have corresponded frequently. Given the time and energy, Bob could fill up a book like this a dozen times or more about his interesting, unusual experiences and accomplishments—and he is working on it!

Sound far fetched? Take a look at this -

Brief biographical sketch on: Aris A. "Bob" Mallas
Dated April 15, 1990

BORN: April 6, 1926, Galatea, Ohio

MILITARY SERVICE: May 1944 until May 1946

Pfc Combat Infantry; 1st Division and 69th Division; France-Belgium-Germany. Radioman for the special forces of the 69th Division to make first contact with Red Army on the Elbe River in Germany. Was awarded two bronze stars.

Cpl; Sgt; Staff Sgt; Tech Sgt; Sgt Major: Supreme Headquarters, Allied Expeditionary Forces—Europe, Ordnance Section, then with succeeding groups, Hqts. 3rd and 7th Armies, Ordnance Section. Was awarded the Army Commendation Medal.

EDUCATION: September 1946-May 1950
Bachelor of Arts, Cum Laude
Master of Public Administration Degree (Volker fellow)
Doctor of Political Science (Economics)
Advance work at University of Heidelberg, Germany

(Holds the record for shortness of time spent at the respective undergraduate schools in achieving the Bachelors and Masters Degrees.)

PROFESSIONAL: 1950-1964
(Major research only)

Joined the staff of the Detroit Bureau of Governmental Research (non-profit) and was loaned to the Michigan Little Hoover Commission. From May 1950 until May 1953:

Set up the largest child adoptions program in the world at the Michigan Children's Institute.

Developed new reform programs for the State School for Delinquent Boys and for the State School for Delinquent Girls.

Research study of the Michigan National Guard led to the drafting of the State Code of Military Justice, which has become the basis for all National Guard legal systems in all states.

Reorganized state level child care programs and foster care programs. Directed first major study of federally funded Aid to Dependent Children Programs and the impact at state level.

Developed a system of combining into one agency 13 major state promotional agencies.

In 1953 he became Project Director, Texas Research League (non-profit). This organization was set up to provide top-level research services to state agencies upon request, but at no cost to the state. At that time rapidly growing Texas Government needed top quality brainpower, but would not pay to get it. This organization was financed by all the major business and industry organizations of the state.

1953-1955—Designed and directed the largest hospital study ever undertaken in the world.* The 13 volume research study resulted in a constitutional amendment to do away with mandatory jury trial for the mentally ill. (this amendment had failed 4 times before, but we succeeded in getting it passed.) Resulting from the study was also: The Texas Mental Health

Code;** the Texas Mentally Retarded Persons Act;** the T. B. Code, and 27 other less important pieces of reform legislation. The study led to the first in the nation development of local mental health services trying to keep the mentally ill out of state hospitals.

1955-1957—Designed and directed the Texas Board of Control Study. This study resulted in the Model State Purchasing Act** which has since been adopted as basic legislation in most states.

1958-1961—Designed and directed the Texas Welfare Dept. Study.* Led to a 17% caseload drop the first year; developed the first comprehensive program for payment of child support by absent fathers (now widely copied) and receiving worldwide attention was the documentation of the lack of need for federal involvement in indigent medical care services.

1959—Planned for President Eisenhower the part of the 1960 White House Conference on Children and Youth that related to juvenile delinquency.

1961—Wrote nine of the ten President Kennedy's Welfare Reform measures that passed the federal Congress.

1961-1962—Designed and raised money from private sources to establish the Texas Industrial Commission, which became the official state agency in 1963. What made it unique was that public and private industrial development resources were integrated and no tax-funded enticement give-away programs were instituted. (Won the top award for all public and private agencies in this field in 1966.)

1962-1963—Designed and directed the Texas Rehabilitation Study,* which led to a modern program of services that were integrated with all other public and private services.

1963-1964—Developed new programs for the state of Texas in the area of Services to the Blind and Services to the Deaf.

1967-1968—Upon request of the Texas Commissioner of Education, in addition to his business activity, designed and directed the most comprehensive study of special education

344

services ever undertaken. It led to the passage of SB230** that has become the basis of all federal programs in that field, as well as most state programs.

1974—Responding to a request from the National Foundation for the Blind and the Organization of State Commissioners for the Blind, designed the only comprehensive study of nationwide services to the blind. We are still seeing results of that study, which was completed in addition to his deep involvement in personal business activity.

ALL OF THE ABOVE RESEARCH FOR GOVERNMENT WAS PROVIDED AT NO COST TO GOVERNMENT, BUT WERE PAID FOR BY PRIVATE FUNDING.

*indicates this study won the top award for research on government in the United Sates and Canada that year. He is the only person to have won the award three times.
**indicates MAJOR legislation that passed the Texas House and Senate, unanimously. This has happened only five times in the history of the state and four of these legal codes were authored by him.

PRIVATE BUSINESS 1964-1984
(had retired from professional activities)

Major businesses only are listed. (F =Founder; P = President; C = Chairman of the Board; D = Director.)

American Polystyrene Corp. Austin, TX, (chemicals) F,P,C
Kool Kup, Inc., Arlington, VA and El Paso, TX (manufacturing), P, C
Magi Cup Co., San Francisco, CA (mfgr), P,C
Prices, Inc., Houston and Dallas areas, Beaumont, McAllen—all in TX (restaurant chain) P,C
Self Service Foods, Inc., Houston area (wholesale foods), P,C
Management Services Associates, Inc. (research and consultation), New York, NY, Austin TX P,C
Management research International, Inc., Austin (computer soft wear; when sold to Intel became the basis of the Intel-IBM joint venture. F
Canamer, Ltd, Edmonton, Canada (plastic research) , D
Ramada Inns de Mexico, S. A. Mexico City (hotels), F, D

345

Cupples Container Company, Austin and St. Louis (mfgr), F, P, C

Cupples Coiled Pipe, Inc. Austin (mfgr), F,P,C

Precision and Scientific Industries, Inc., Albuquerque NM and Austin (machine tools, etc.) P,C

National Collegiate Marketing Corporation, Austin (marketing), F,P,C

Pacer, Inc., Austin (holding company), F,P,C

Pacer Development Co, Austin (real estate), F,P,C

Pacer Properties, Inc. Austin (real estate), F,P,C

Pacer International, Inc., Austin and Portland, OR (oil technology) F, Executive VP, D

Madrona, Inc., Austin (gems, mining, rare historical items), F,P,C

Madrona Press, Austin (publishing) F,VP, C

Kashan, Inc. (Gem technology, gem marketing), F,P,C

Bennett-Walls, Inc., Rotan, TX (gems, books, rare historical items marketing), F, Treasurer, C

In all, founded 26 successful companies. In 1984, in retirement from his professional life he sold all of his remaining business interests. He devotes his efforts to Bennett-Walls, Inc., which is based on his hobbies, and to his foundation, concerned with multi-handicapped conditions, research, and special functional education projects.

1964-1977—During his business career he served as chief economic consultant to the Capital National Banking Group, and authored their "Bank Correspondent" publication, distributed to approximately 1,400 banks.

1970-1978—Editor, "Tax Correspondent"

OTHER ACTIVITY:

1963-1965—President, Austin Symphony Society (took a bankrupt symphony and operated it in the black for the first time in 25 years and retired 1/3 of its debt.

1958-1968—Director, Austin United Fund and Chairman of its budget committee (1966)

1962-1972—One of the Founders and then a Director of the Goodwill Industries of Austin. When it went bankrupt in 1980 chaired the finance committee to put them back in operation.

1967-1968—Founder of the Austin Community Council.

1958-1969—Trustee of the Professional Committee of the American College of Dentists.

1968-1976—Trustee of the Joint Commission of the American Medical Association and American Hospital Association for CARF.

1978-1980—Trustee of the University of Texas at Dallas

1974-1976—Trustee of the Callier Speech and Hearing Clinic (now part of the U of TX system)

1986-1990—Trustee of the American-Thai University Foundation (we are building a new free-enterprise oriented university about 60 miles north of Bangkok).

1980-)—Founder, past President and now Chairman of the Board of the non-profit foundation "International Research Institute."

Of lesser importance, I have served as a board member or trustee of many national, state and local groups, such as the National Association for Retarded Children. They are not listed since I did not perform a major role or make a major contribution.

Served as advisor to President Eisenhower (1959), President Kennedy (1961), President Nixon (1974-1975), and President Ford (1976-1977). I have served as an advisor to Governors in 16 states, many legislative committees in many states, and to members of Congress and many of their Committees.

Author of the book "40 years in Politics—A Study in Informal Organization," now out of print.

Editor of "Gem Correspondent" and "Gem Connoisseur."

Military Experiences of Bob Mallas

I was drafted into the army as I reached 18, weighed only 104 lbs., but was 5"10" tall. I was knowledgeable of the war and its challenges to our nation and way of life. My father was from an important Greek family and fled to the U.S. when his father, a key Greek government official, was killed when the government was overturned. He loved this country and wanted me to serve. I had 17 weeks of basic training in the infantry, was shipped from Boston in a huge convoy of ships. After 20 days of sub alerts we docked in Cherbourg, loaded onto trucks for a 10 day trip to the 99th Division on the front lines. I had contracted pneumonia, and my foxhole buddy reported my illness and the company commander ordered me back to regiment for medical attention. This was 2 a.m., Dec.15, 1944. Four hours later the 99th and our company was attacked by a major German force. It killed the buddy who was instrumental in saving my life. I was transferred to a medical center some 40 miles behind the front line, a very busy M.D. pronounced me as a goner, but the nurse got permission to give me some new drugs. They were effective, but German troops in the area required the evacuation of the hospital. As all the trucks had left, walking was the only alternative. With a good supply of pills I started down the road to where the Americans were supposed to be, and on 22 Dec. I hooked up with the 69th Division, and was sent to the hospital immediately. So, from Dec. 19 until Jan 3 about all I know is that I ended up about 60 miles from where I started, and with the 69th Division, where I spent the rest of the war. But it was a Christmas season not remembered!

The 69th moved into a defensive position on the Siegfried Line, replacing another division badly mauled during the Bulge. On our left was the remains of another division that had lost two thirds of its men during the Bulge. The Lt. platoon leader came back from company headquarters with a manual on radios, handed it to me, announcing I would be the new radio man. I didn't find this a welcome decision in that all our radiomen had been killed the last three days... If not on patrol I was radioman for an outpost several hundred feet in front of our lines set up to detect any attack. Although the Germans were in retreat, they were contesting every inch. As we neared the Rhine the tension grew since we had heard all the bridges were destroyed and the Germans were prepared to contest any crossing.

On March 8 we reached the west side of the Rhine. On the 9th, word came that a group of engineers had seized a bridge at Remagen, about nine miles to the north, and we had to cross the river and strike north to clear out their front. We crossed in little rubber boats across the wide Rhine, no shooting, the Germans had retreated. We were off to assist our troops at Remagen.

Unfortunately, we had no transportation since tanks and trucks could not get over on temporary bridges for at least another 48-72 hours and we had to immediately attack north to force the Germans away from the bridge. Because about two-thirds of our company were in the early stages of recovering from badly frozen feet, fresh troops were more directly involved in the attack to save the bridgehead. Suddenly the forces to our front collapsed and we had to move up as fast as we could, 76 miles on foot, in three days with full 65 pounds of equipment. One could not drop out since if you did the large number of German soldiers in the forests around us would have killed anyone alone.

Marching distances with full gear presented another problem. With frozen feet one cannot get shoes on right away, so we walked in our overshoes. With the swelling receding, shoes can be worn by cutting open the sides. However, foot bone structure begins to break down, pain increases, until the foot goes numb. Continuing, it feels like you are stepping on your ankles, and then your knees. Stopping, the pain is intense as circulation returns. We were not a good fighting force at the end of those 76 miles, but again luck was on our side. A group of heavy tanks had crossed the Rhine and joined us. We rode them to a key railroad junction, and thousands of displaced persons (slave laborers) lined the road greeting us. The road into town was narrow, I was on the second tank. The first tank was about 30 feet ahead, about ready to make a tight turn when suddenly from a balcony right above the tank a woman drops a chamber pot and its contents down on the tank, spilling on the sergeant in charge. Before we could react she disappeared into the building. The tank stopped, the sergeant barked out an order, the tank backed up about 20 feet and as it went forward it cut into the side of the building, tearing out the first story, causing the second story to collapse. I guess you might say she made her statement, and the sergeant his.

Two mornings later we rode tanks down a road with thick forest on each side. The tank had lost its 50-caliber machine gunner the day before, and the tank commander asked if anyone could fire that gun. Two knew how, myself and a 46 year older whose feet were in very bad condition. I was chosen. Suddenly there was heavy fire. In combat, contrary to the movies, the infantry dismounts and clears out the enemy since the tank is much more valuable. I left the tank and went with the infantry, and the 46 year old took over the gun. He had false teeth. A sniper shot him and the bullet hit him in the lower teeth, curved around, cut his upper lip badly, and came out. The force almost broke his neck. I was stunned to see him running down the center of the road spitting blood and false teeth, firing into the trees to try to find that sniper, and cursing words I had never heard.

Next day we captured a concentration camp which was set up in central Germany for displaced persons who could no longer work, or were sentenced to be killed... A few days later a small group of Germans gave themselves up and told us that our President was dead. We were so far ahead of our supply lines that news (and sometimes rations) did not get to us for days. My radio was effective for only a few miles. Our attitude was "typical Nazi crap." We were stunned when a truck with ammo and food came in the next day and confirmed their story. Major groups of Germans began to surrender. Three elite Hungarian regiments (about 9,000 men) immediately to our front refused to fight U.S. troops. While we had hit and run type action, each day we knew it was just a matter of time until the European war was over.

The next night Sergeant M. handed me a thick letter. He was an outstanding soldier in every respect, and one of the few in our company that, like myself, started at the Seigfried and still survived. He said "I know this sounds silly, but for some time I have known I would not survive the war. Here is my will and a letter to my folks. You will survive! Please get it to them and go see them when you get back to the states." He asked for my promise, and that I gave.

Three nights later we were in a tough house-to-house fight in Colditz—the last remaining link between the Germans in Berlin and those in the south. It also was the location of an old castle that held several hundred top allied prisoners of war, and we were told they were to be killed. To get to the castle we had to cross over a deep stream, with the bridge still intact. In the dark the twisting streets leading to the bridge were death traps. Suddenly, the Germans pulled out and rushed across the bridge. We felt the way was open. We lined up scouts in front, the lieutenant and I next on the left, and Sergeant M on the right. The street took a sharp turn to the right and Sergeant M realized that when the Lt. and I turned the corner we would be most exposed. He motioned for us to change spots.

As we were doing so, a shot from a basement window rang out. I saw Sergeant M. Freeze, and the lieutenant and I fired several shots into the sniper. As I turned around, the sergeant fell into my arms. The shot hit him under the chin and came out the temple. He was dead. I followed his wishes to the letter, but how did he know he would die?

We stopped as we got to the bridge. Too dark and risky. Was the bridge mined? All during the night the guards at the center of the bridge changed every four hours. As soon as they got to the center we would pick them off and they would fall into the water—all except the one who lay on the bridge. Obviously, the Germans were confused and the command structure was breaking down as the regular German units were pulling out.

The next morning we could see the bridge was not mined, and all was quiet. As we went up on the bridge a mother was loading her dead 15 year old son into a little cart. He was the guard that did not fall into the water. The G.I.s helped her.

We got to the castle and liberated the still-alive prisoners of war. At the last minute the SS pulled out and left no instructions for them to be killed, and the prison commander was not about do so now that the end was in sight.

A jeep roared up and the driver said, "Anyone here know how to work the 300 (radio)?" Everyone pointed at me and he said "Get in." He was a lieutenant and wanted to know if I spoke any Russian. I said no, but could speak some French. In a little square were a group of G.I.s of several ranks. All like myself had not bathed or shaved or changed clothes in over four months. Three jeeps, an armored personnel carrier, several types of trucks and tanks began to come in. It turned out there were to be three groups whose mission was to try to rush through the weakly held German lines, about 15-20 miles, to the Elbe River to meet the Russians, who were advancing from the east. Our group rushed headlong toward the Elbe, brushing aside minor resistance. Soon I started picking up a strange language on the radio and our experts identified it as Russian. As morning came, we confirmed they were across the Elbe at Torgau. By the middle of the afternoon we made actual contact. Fortunately, they were even dirtier than we were. It was April 25th—my sister's 23rd birthday. Soon the press was with us taking pictures. As I write this I am looking at the framed front page of the New York Times dated April 28, 1945. Two G.I.s with hands outstretched are greeting four Russian soldiers. The reproductions are poor. I am wearing a helmet that covers part of my face and it is hard for me to see me in the photograph. Much to my surprise a letter from my mother told me my picture had been in Life magazine, the Toledo Blade, and the Cleveland Plain Dealer (the same picture). She recognized me! When I saw the picture I realized that only a mother would ever be able to do that! Only one of the ways mothers are truly remarkable!!!

The Russians shared food , drink, music, dancing and, to the horror of the G.I.s,—kisses. As noted, we were filthy, but they were even worse. They all seemed to have lots of lice and if they were not drinking, they were scratching. Soon, we all were—drinking and scratching.

Since there were no others from my company at this Elbe River meeting with the Russians, it was time to return, and a driver was dispatched to pick me up. He said "You've got a sweet deal. It's guarding Germany's largest ammunition/poison gas dump." So for the first time in months I had a bed (a straw filled mattress cover on the floor), a bath, and clean clothing. All except the officers were quartered in one huge stone room at the center of the ammo dump.

On May 8 all of us—approximately 100 remaining out of full company strength of 186 -except those on guard duty were in that large room, and a BBC new flash came on announcing the ceasefire signing. I looked around the room. In one card game a hand ready to play a card was suspended. No sounds, except the noise of celebration in London, Paris, and New York. Then the arm descended and the card was played. But there was no talking, as each was deep in thoughts. But off to my right I heard a quiet sobbing. Those of us who heard it pretended not to notice. Sitting on his mattress with back to the wall was Sergeant "N," without question the most fearless fighter in the group. He volunteered for every dangerous mission, and had been decorated four times. If he had a fault it was that he never took a prisoner. He loved to kill. The time he could kill and be accepted was gone. With his depression he was sent back for treatment. I hope they could help him, but I often wondered if he ended up as a hit man for organized crime, or a serial killer.

Bear in mind that only one in seventeen in service in WWII had any contact with combat, and only one if fifty were actually part of any group that lost men in combat. This does not mean that their support was any less vital or their contribution less important, but it does mean their viewpoint is different. Often combat veterans do not want to discuss what happened to them.

During the 1950s I did much research on mental illness and mental health programming. The study went on for over two years, and one of the great minds involved had spent time and effort studying battle fatigue cases. He noted that much time and money had been spent on those that combat "broke" mentally, but almost nothing on those who mentally survived. He said that the important thing is what happens mentally if you survive past the statistical point where you should be dead , and realize it. As days go by surviving you make a mental adjustment, and achieve what he called "psychiatric death." The life you were in you have accepted as ended, and you are now in a new life with death no longer a concern.

I feel that the room was so quiet on the announcement of the war's end was that many had achieved fully, or in part, such a mental position. They had tried to end that part by making a mental adjustment.

Three Incidents Relative To Combat Soldiers

Our company was to take a key railroad location. We moved into position, found out the Germans had artillery, and we none. They must have had too few troops for an attack on us, and because we were outgunned it was a standoff. Our artillery didn't get in place until 5 p.m., which caused the German tanks to leave. We were ordered to fire as rapidly as possible as we charged across the farmland into the town, to force any German soldiers to take cover and not fire on us. It turned out they had left with the tanks. We had to search all the houses for hiding enemy soldiers. Near the edge of town was a large, nice looking home. It was not locked and a group of six of us, including the Lieutenant, surrounded it. Instructions were to search all three floors... we knew what to look for... especially booby traps. The search showed no one in any of the three floors, so we relaxed a bit. Suddenly the Lt. pointed to the corner of the living room where we had gathered. Not easily seen was a trapdoor.

The Lt. motioned us into position and guardedly opened the trap door and called down in German "hands overhead." Immediately we could hear movement and all of our weapons were at the ready. One old-time pro suggested we throw a few grenades down into the cellar, and move on. The Lt. said no, let's give them a chance to surrender. Our Sgt., who spoke German, told them to surrender. We could hear movement on the stairs and the first person to come out was a very little girl clutching a doll, followed by a small boy, two children in their early teens, mother, father, and one much older person. I told the Lt. "Just think, 2 grenades would have killed them all!" He replied, "Right, but keep in mind if they tossed two grenades up here we would all have been killed or wounded."

Another happening was at the Siegfried line and word came down that the Germans were preparing to attack. High command wanted the answers to a number of questions, and the only way we could get those was a night patrol into the German lines to capture soldiers. The Lt. was to be the patrol leader, I the radio man, and six others for specific skills, such as mines, language, use of weaponry. "Rich" was chosen because he was the best sharpshooter in the company, and had unlimited skills needed for patrols. He had lied about his age to get in the army, and was only 16 years old. Born in the interior of Alaska of a very poor family almost all the food they ate came from hunting, shooting if they had ammunition money, but mostly from trapping. The family consisted of his parents and a grandmother. None had gone to school, or could read and write. Rich had gone to school a year before the army when they moved to Montana. His dad got a defense job. A retired teacher in the area heard of Rich's needs and taught him to read and write a bit. Rich understood his limitations, was friendly with a great smile, and always listened and tried to be helpful. He was well liked and

ALL understood that when it came to arms, hunting and the out-of-doors, he was the expert in our group. The Lt. asked him for suggestions for our patrol mission. Contrary to a normal setup, Rich suggested one scout in front, another in back, and the Lt. and me in the center with a rifleman. Rich would stay about 6 feet to the rear of the front scout. There were patches of fog and snow falling now and then, with just enough light to see outlines some 20 feet ahead. We had just gotten through the first belt of mines when suddenly Rich stopped and signaled for us to get prone quietly. What seemed like a long time, but probably only a few minutes, he lifted his hand and signaled be VERY QUIET. Another few minutes went by and we could hear someone walking on the snow, and talking quietly.

Quietly Rich got up on one knee and fired three times as rapidly as possible. Each shot killed each German scout, and the officer in charge. A German fired back, and Rich fired once more and that German was dead. The last two Germans surrendered… Our patrol was a success since they quickly gave us the German plans.

We asked Rich later how he knew they were there and he said "I heard them." None of the rest of us did. We had questions as to how could he know how many, the formation they were in and how could he see to fire so quickly. It all boiled down to all those years of outsmarting game so they could eat. He was awarded the Silver Star for that mission,. I understand that he stayed in the army, went to night school, and became a trainer for our special forces, an intelligent use of his skills.

In the third story, we got to a small German town and set up a guard on all sides, sort of like a wagon train preparing to fight Indians. The tank group had its own cook and in the town square, he sat up his kitchen. Small groups of us would come in and eat, while other groups were on guard. The German civilians were very watchful and since we treated them well they grew more relaxed with us. Some of them came out and watched us eat. We noted that a group of children, most under the ages of 10-12, had set up a line near the place we went to dispose of any food left in our mess kits. We understood they were short of food and we were trying to save a bit for them. The children were also interested in the coffee and were standing with a container in each hand… one for the coffee and the other to get any food scraps.

Just before we crossed the Rhine we had gotten a small number of replacements just in from the states. One in particular (his name was Jim) was boastful, never listened, and made few, if any friends. I think we all knew with his attitude he would not last through much combat.

Four of us were walking toward he point where the German children were waiting and three (including Jim) were just ahead of us. Jim was in the lead and when he got to the first child... a five or six year old boy... he poured his hot coffee over the boys' hands saying something like 'take this, you God damn Nazi!" Instantaneously... and I mean faster than any quick draw you will see in a Western movie... the fellow at the head of our group drew his 45 and had it at Jim's temple. None of us moved. We knew that old combat pro could shoot without hesitation.

About 30 seconds went by and with gun in hand he ordered Jim to his knees, threw him a rag, and told him to wipe off the boys' hands. Jim did just as he was told. Fortunately, the coffee was not hot enough to burn the boy. The German children and adults were very carefully watching. My Lt. took Jim to the side and gave him a strict lecture. Jim felt he knew better. As predicted, he was killed a short time later... One can conclude from these three stories that those in combat were very much like men we see each day. They brought to combat the standards and knowledge mostly taught prior to the war.

The Holland Trip... The Reaction of One of Our Allies

In my last military duty in Europe through circumstances I was able to meet and be of value to our General. He repaid me by continuing to add to my stripes as I completed special assignments. One of these was the delivery of secret documents (I did not see them) to a key British General in Holland and, as a personal favor, visiting a nearby military cemetery and take pictures of a grave for the mother of a soldier buried there.

Once again I had a jeep with jeep-trailer to carry gasoline and all supplies, including food for the trip. The driver and I were fully armed since any trip was dangerous in those days. We over-nighted at a base on the edge of our U.S. sector and got everything done the next day.

The cemetery had all the graves indexed and we found the proper grave for photos easily. I was able to find three graves of those I had served with during "The Battle of the Bulge." A sad experience. On the way out to the cemetery along both sides of the road were people carrying flowers. Not just a few, but many—men, women, and children. At the cemetery we saw a vast number of graves with flowers. Cemetery staff told us this was a daily ritual and had been going on even before the war had ended. These people were truly grateful.

The most important display of gratitude happened after we left the cemetery. I could smell something burning. One of the back tires had given way and was slipping on the rim, and smoking. We stopped the jeep and almost immediately one front tire blew out, and the other back tire went flat. We had hit something in the road. There we were in the middle of Holland, in the British Sector, and three flat tires but only one spare.

On the road's opposite side was a little business operation with two men out front looking at us. One young man, not more than 18-19—but tall in size, started across the road toward us. Both the driver and I were armed but the young man was smiling and looked friendly. He saw the problem. I tried to speak to him in English, and then French, but he did not understand either. He put his hand to his ear and motioned to the business place and for us to stay where we were. He went back and phoned, and came back all smiles.

It turned out the U.S. had an MP (military police) station about 40 miles away. It was in the British Sector to help police monitor stolen goods movement. Two weeks before they had seized a stolen jeep and impounded it. When they got the call they understood our need. They took the tires off the jeep for our use... Once they ascertained via our papers we were okay, they gave us the tires and took off. We started to put the tires on but the young man pointed to our uniforms, shook his head, and picked up the tools and started the job. I said to the driver, "Let him do it... he has earned a good fee already."

In record time the tires were replaced. I took out some money and several packages of cigarettes worth around $150 on the black market. When I offered them his face fell and I thought for a moment it was not enough and offered more. He shook his head, stood up very straight, and saluted us! Both of us were stunned. When I recovered I extended my hand and shook his hand and said thank you. I motioned for him to come to the trailer. In it we had some candy bars and other snack goodies. When I handed him a candy bar he looked at it and as I peeled the wrapper off he did so also, but saved the wrapper. I noted he ate two small bites and wrapped the balance up. In looking at him and his reaction to the food I noted that, though tall, he was VERY thin. I got an idea. I told the driver to pick up all the extra food and cigarettes from the trailer, and with our arms full we walked across the road to the door of the business. Inside was an older lady and man, a young girl, and two children 14-16 years of age.

From a quick glance I could see all were very thin. We put the food and over four cartons of cigarettes on a table. (Cigarettes could buy anything, while money usually would not.) We gave a candy bar to each and the driver and I pulled out our partially eaten bar, showing that it was safe to eat. Watching that half starved family enjoy that candy… especially the younger children… is a life-long memory. What was especially meaningful was the young man was doing all that work out of affection for what our troops had done to liberate his country. Later I learned each soldier buried at that cemetery had been adopted by a Dutch family who kept flowers on their grave summers. I noted their name and address before we left. My driver, who talked very little, told me that such an experience of appreciation and gratitude made fighting the war worth while…

The General was impressed when I related the happening to him. He called in his secretary and told her to phone a Colonel and I heard him relate the incident, and how we wanted to help that family. I head the General say "I think 20 cartons will give them enough buying power to last a couple of years… and have that M.P group deliver them in person." Later I asked the secretary who the Colonel was, and she said he headed all the PX (post exchange) operations in the U.S. Sector!

I Leave Europe and Return Home

It was difficult to pack and leave, as many had been of such great value to me. Trying to thank the General was perhaps the hardest. When I finished he took me to the corner of his office and picked up a Mauser rifle and handed it to me. He
358

controlled all the factories that had made German arms so he had made up some from the remaining parts. He told me it would remind me of a part of my life that I would never forget.

I caught a train from Heidelberg to Strausberg. The German part of the trip was comfortable and we were well treated. The French part was dirty, no toilets on the train, and we were treated as enemies... The troop ship going over had some 2,800, now, only 600. It took only 8 days to make the trip to New York. I found myself thinking of home, my family, the events I went through, what I really wanted out of life. I realized that I had changed. It was more than just growing up, as I had done that much earlier than most, but the understanding of strengths and weaknesses, confirmation of the standards installed in me by my parents, family members and educators. The first thing I had to do was get a much better education. I did what my dad had suggested early in life. Face the challenge on one side of a sheet of paper what you plan or want now, and on the other side what you anticipate such will be like at age 40. As we entered New York harbor and I saw the Statue of Liberty for the first time, I was glad the trip was coming to an end. I sincerely hoped that in my lifetime I would never have to repeat it.

The following is one of the writings of Bob Mallas. He wrote it as a foreword to the book EL LOBO AND SPANISH GOLD.

Part l—The Stage is Set:

It was dawn in the valley and the haze hung in light airy patches over our camp. The fire was beginning to blaze up as the Indian cook carefully fed it dry grasses, then small twigs, and finally small limbs. With the snap of the fire and the gradual coming of light, the Indian miners stirred themselves one by one. Throwing wool serapes over their shoulders they squatted over the small fire to warm their hands.

Over the fire was the ever-present kettle of beans, and in the coals a huge coffee pot began to bubble. The cook leaned over and scraped some coals to the side and placed over them a large greased iron skillet. As the grease bean to snap and pop, the cook dropped potato chunks —skins and all—into the skillet. Corn tortillas, made up the night before, were warming on a piece of tin, placed near the fire to reflect the heat. Wood was scarce here in the valley and the Indians had learned long ago to use it sparingly.

The morning was cold and the moist haze added to the chill, but the Indians knew the cool dampness would disappear as the sun rose. By mid-afternoon the temperature would reach 120 degrees and the valley would be brilliantly clear with ever changing patterns of light and shadow as the sun advanced. This was as certain as the rainy season which was two moons away.

Soon the breakfast of beans, potatoes, tortillas and coffee was ready. There was a grace and dignity in the eating ritual, as each took his turn at filling a tin plate, then squatted to eat in a leisurely fashion, talking softly to others nearby.

The Indian miners were short and lean and seemed to move with the grace and swiftness of a cat. Each was dressed in baggy white trousers and shirt, with a hand loomed virgin wool serape over his shoulder, and wore a white straw sweat-stained hat. While the clothing was shabby and worn, it was clean as was hair, face and hands. The work they did was dirty, but they bathed frequently in the river with much boy-like splashing and laughing.

The Indians ranged in age from 18 to 35, although it was hard to tell their ages. There was a certain sameness in their faces—an interesting quality that conveyed a look of shyness, yet good humor. Basically a happy people, they enjoyed their hard life and made the most of it. Hostility and distrust showed only when a Mexican appeared. The hostility stemmed from many years of exploitation, causing the natives to avoid contact with Mexicans. Yet, their animosity and suspicion did not extend to the "gringo" geologists in the camp, who had won their affection and respect.

With the growing light the haze lifted with a rush of cool air, revealing the spectacular scenery of the valley. The camp was in the shadow of a sheer cliff rising more than 4,000 feet. About 50 feet below the camp was the Urique River, in the dry season shallow and sluggish. Within two months it would be a rushing torrent, extending almost to the campsite. Across the valley, about 100 yards, a steep mountain towered more than 5,000 feet and behind it another 3,000 feet higher, then another rising to 9,000 feet. When the sunlight struck the mountain fully, it cast upon it a purple mantle, a reflection of the waist-high grasses. Since the camp was below the plateau, some part of it was in shadow at all times, and thus evening came early. At suppertime darkness always fell on the camp.

As the haze lifted, thousands of green parrots in flocks of 100+ flew up the valley, each screeching constantly. This screeching stopped only when they had reached a point across from the camp, almost halfway up the mountain, where the sparse trees on the hillside produced a bean-like pod. The parrots tore the pods apart with greedy squawks.

The noise of the parrots was the signal for the two gringo geologists to wake up, and in a few minutes they came to the fire from the little grass and mud hut the Indians hadbuilt 30 feet up the trail. The cook dished their breakfast—first a cup of steaming black coffee, then the beans, potatoes and tortillas. As they ate the other Indians disappeared with their personal chores, but not a sound came back to camp. The geologists ate quickly, discussing the work detail for the day, and suddenly, as if by magic, the Indians appeared for work. No one looked at a watch—it was 8 am.

A young Indian named Tito came forward. He, like the others, was a Tarahumara, and there was intelligence and pride in his demeanor. He obviously was a leader. Tito spoke to the geologists in Spanish and then issued their instructions to the other Indians in Tarahumara. The language is hard and guttural. Tito added emphasis by shaking his head. As a baby Tito had been abandoned by his parents because they were starving—a not unusual means to survival among the Tarahumara. He was found by a Mexican mule skinner who reared him as one of his family. The Indians never lost track of him, however, and he learned both languages and customs. This wilderness canyon was his home and these were his people, little touched by civilization hours away by rail, but blocked by mountains.

Mexicans call his home Barranca de Cobre (Copper Canyon) and since they first explored it in the 1690s, they have recognized it as one of the great mineralized area of the world. The powerful attraction of gold, silver, copper, lead and zinc brought first the Spanish and then the Mexicans to this wild, rugged area. With them came disease and slavery and thus the fear of the Indian has its roots in the greed of the exploiters.

That afternoon, as the cliff shadows lengthened and the heat began to dissipate the miners returned to camp, washed off the dirt of the day's labor by splashing in the river, and then carried up to the campsite four large jugs that had been cooling in the stream. Tin cups were passed around and filled with tesquino—a corn beer. Thus began a ritual, repeated daily in the mining camp. The geologists, offered a cup, accept it as a token of respect and friendship. In turn, the geologists pass out cigarettes and each Indian takes one and lights it, completing the friendship cycle. The beer flows freely and the Indians begin their story telling, punctuating their language with much arm, hand and head motion, since story telling to them is more than mere conversation.

An hour before sunset, darkness was already falling in the valley. The cooking fire once again provided a circle of light. Suddenly, without sound another Indian stood at the edge of the flickering circle, waiting to be invited to join the group. The geologists were startled, but no surprise shows on the faces of the Indian miners. They had heard the man coming for some time. In his arms the man held a small boy, clad only in torn and baggy trousers. The man spoke rapidly and with great emphasis to the miners. Tito, instantly at the man's side, spoke rapidly to the geologists in Spanish.: "boy hurt... fell of cliff and cut head... blood will not stop... need white man. Will white man help?

Without a word one geologist spread his coat before the fire and ran to get a medicine kit and blankets while the other motioned for the father to come near the fire and lay the boy on the coat. The father hesitated, as the boy was bleeding badly, but the geologist took the youth gently and placed him on the coat. The boy, having lost a lot of blood, was in a state of shock and already cool to the touch.

Every mining geologist has to know more than just basic first aid, as accidents are frequent in mining. He must be prepared to tend broken bones, fevers and the normal range of infections and mining injuries. Both geologists worked quickly and in a few minutes the bleeding was stopped and the wound sewed up. The boy was wrapped in blankets near the fire. Warm rocks were placed at his feet, color began to return to his face, and soon he was able to drink some coffee. The geologist produced some silver coins and Tito sent one of the miners to the nearest hut to buy a chicken.

During this process the Indians were quiet, watching every movement of the white men, not missing the concern for the life of one of them, they noted that the white man used his silver to buy food for the boy, then he used his own coat and blanket—and the boy's father did not even work for them! Such points were discussed in many ways. These strange white men—so confusing!

The days went by, and the boy grew stronger. Each meal he had meat, a luxury for the Indian. The geologist told Tito that by the next day the boy would be ready to go home. When Tito informed the boy's father, he was silent—an indication of respect for the white man's decision. Tito knew the father was concerned because the white man had done him a favor. How could he repay it when they owned everything? It was a difficult problem for the father, whose code did not permit taking without giving. But what had he to give? He sat quietly by the fire until long after the miners had gone to sleep. Then without a sound he crawled under his son's blanket to add his warmth to that of the blanket and fire. It is December 23, 1970.

Part Two—The Surprise!
(Part 2 tells how the act of Christian charity in Part One led to the last major silver discovery in North America)

The next morning the father took Tito aside and told him he must pay his debt to the white man but, since he was very poor, all he had to give was his labor. He would take his son home and return to work for the white men without pay as long as Tito thought proper. Tito turned away and looked into the morning mist that still hung in patches over the river. He was silent for a long time, but the father waited because Tito understood these strange white men, and would know if his offer was proper.

Finally Tito turned back to face him and said "You offer what is good and fair, but it can not help the white men, since they must leave. They search for the bright shiny rock, and they have not found enough of it. In two days we will all have no work. It is sad for all of us." The father, saying nothing, went to wake his son. After breakfast he and his son disappeared into the brush.

Early that evening the father appeared again at the edge of the firelight and awaited an invitation to join the group. Tito invited him, but his offer of food was politely declined. The man sat rigidly near the fire. All the Indians watched him as they hurriedly finished their meal. They sensed something important was going to happen. When the first Indian had finished eating, Tito sent him to he river to bring jugs of tesquino. Coffee was tossed out of the cups and the beer was poured. A cup was offered the visitor, but he declined with a shake of his head and reached into his rolled blanket for a drinking gourd. Beer was poured into the gourd and he joined in the drinking. When the geologist passed out cigarettes, he took one and smoked it.

Tonight there was no story telling, no chatter among the Indians. Even the geologists sensed an omen. Hours went by and the beer drinking continued. Tito placed himself near the father, who had become the center of attention. Suddenly a torrent of words from the father shattered the silence. While he spoke words the white man could not understand, he looked at each of them directly.

Suddenly, there was quiet and the geologist asked Tito "What in the hell is all that?" Tito stood and faced the white men and translated with great dignity. The faces of the other Indians gave no hint they had understood what the father said. They awaited the reaction of the white men. There was a debt of honor that must be paid properly; what would these strange men consider proper?

Tito knew he was the center of attention and his Spanish words were slow and carefully spoken, without emotion or emphasis: "He says he owes you for saving the life of his son, but he is a poor man and you are very, very rich and own the world, so he can not give you what you do not have except to work for you for no silver coin, but you have no work to do so he can not repay his debt." Tito paused for breath, then he continued, "I know the white men look for the bright shining rock and I know where there is much such rock and I will show the white men and then I can repay my debt."

At this point Tito sat down and the eyes of the Indians carefully searched the faces of the white men. One geologist leaped to his feet. "Where does he say it is, Tito?" Tito put the question to the father, who walked with great dignity to the edge of the firelight and pointed across the valley to the huge mountain on the other side. He uttered a few words, raised his hands to indicate length, walked back to the fire and rolled up his blanket and went to sleep.

Tito translated: "It is there on the side of the mountain. Covered up, but it has this much bright shining rock in it (his hands were placed about one foot apart) and I will take you there with the light."

The geologists talked with each other, the Indians studying their faces intently. One felt it was a waste of time since the geology of that mountain was not right for silver and he had looked it over several times. The other wanted to see what the Indian had to offer. Tito was asked his opinion but all he would venture was that there were many old Spanish mines and some Indians had found them, but they would not tell the white man for fear it would bring the Mexicans.

These mine entrances remained carefully hidden.

Next morning the father, Tito, the geologists and three miners set out to explore the side of the huge mountain. Hours passed, and everyone except the father became discouraged. The day was hot and there was little shade. Soon all the water was gone. One geologist would have liked to give up, but the father would not. About two o'clock he let out a yell and all rushed to his side. But what he indicated appeared to be no more than a snake or gopher hole.

The father spoke excitedly to Tito who translated to the geologists: Here was the hidden mine, closed since the Indians had driven out the Spaniards (in the 1700s), but during WWII he and some other Indians had gone in and found the bright shiny metal. They had taken a quantity of the ore by pack mule to the smelter 350 miles away. When the Mexicans saw the rich ore, they tried to find the mine; but the Indians closed it again and it has not been touched since.

The geologists had the miners dig out the entrance and, indeed, there was an old mine. It was partially filled with mud and rotted timber, but it definitely was an old Spanish mine. They would have to check with those who were financing the venture.

A report was duly made to the three investors at a meeting in Chihuahua, but while one of the geologists believed an attempt should be made to explore the find, the other remained skeptical. The Mexican investor declined to put up any more money, since the rich vein the project had started out to explore had pinched out.

Still the *norteamericanos* who had invested in the project believed the old mine worth checking out. They returned to the U.S., the geologists returned to the mine, distanced by a day's train ride and another day by mule back.

Two weeks were spent in moving the equipment and campsite across the river and up onto the site of the mountain. While this was being done, largely by hand because of the difficult terrain, other Indian miners were mucking out the old mine. It was slow going, since rotted timber, small rocks and mud had gradually built up in the shaft, but there was progress each day. On the third day a broken pick of the type used in Spanish mines was found. The sixth day more old hand tools were uncovered. Suddenly the mine branched out into drifts leading from the main shaft. It was a bigger mine than the geologist had expected, but they feared it had been worked out. (Later the geologist would compute that it probably had taken the Spaniards forty years, with the tools of that period, to mine such a large area.) On the fourteenth day a number of skeletons were uncovered and, just below them, the bottom of the mine. It appeared someone had discovered the mine but had not lived to work it.

The Indians climbed out to tell the gringo geologists they had reached the bottom. With his hand torch one geologist crawled in, and then down into the mine. Each step on the ladder was slippery and dangerous and the dank smell of the rotting wood and stagnant water was almost stifling. Finally he reached the bottom and shined his light in all directions, but saw nothing of value. Searching the bottom carefully, he still found nothing. Then straight ahead the wall was caked with mud. He picked away at the face of it, and suddenly metal gleamed. Before him was a vein of rich silver and zinc ore eleven inches wide. The Indian father had remembered correctly. It would not take an assay to show this was very rich ore. It was without question a major silver discovery.

EPILOGUE: This event is not fiction, but took place around Christmas 1970 into early 1971. The key geologist on site was Bill Belk who was, for seventeen years, an Executive Vice President of our mining/gem companies, and an outstanding authority in those fields. Bill made the discovery, helped save the boy's life, and recommended trying to reopen the mine. I was the investor who agreed to do so. This event was related to me by Bill. The mine produced such rich ore that the value of the lead and zinc paid the mining and transportation costs so each ton produced a net profit of $10,000. Due to its location we had to develop the largest number of mule teams ever used in Mexico. The transportation logistics were very complicated and, due to the high value, very dangerous.

As loads of such rich ore reached the smelter, word came to us via the ex-mistress of a President of Mexico that the state was going to seize the mine. Mexico has a long history of this type of abuse so the warning was taken seriously. Quickly the mine was traded for assets in the U.S. and the new Mexican owners warned. Unconcerned, they felt they could "handle," i.e., pay off, the Governor. We know only general details of what happened next. The Governor seized the property and brought in Mexican miners. No ore was ever shipped. Quickly the Mexican miners hid all the equipment and traces of the mine. Word was passed out not to try to come into that area to mine. So today in one of the remote and beautiful areas of Mexico there is a huge canyon as big as our Grand Canyon, surrounded by many steep mountains. On the side of one mountain, carefully hidden, is a tiny opening that leads to a huge fortune. Christian charity led to its rediscovery and greed to its closing. I hope in time it will benefit those Indians who guard it so carefully.

Chapter 10: Flying Stories (Mostly)

My B-24 Experience
by Hazel Hohn, WASP (from Bomber Legends)

I think maybe the only thing interesting about my flying B-24 Liberators during World War II is that I was a female pilot. I don't think there too many of them, so I will write about it. After graduating from Avenger Field, Sweetwater, Texas in May, 1944, as a WASP (Women's Airforce Service Pilot). I was assigned to the Air Transport Command in Romulus, Michigan, hoping to become a fighter (pursuit) pilot. First we checked out In UC78s and Norduyne Norsemans and after one flight around the field in the nose of a 24, I went directly to the co-pilot seat on ferry trips. We picked up the 24s from the factory at Willow Run. I understand they were putting out a 24 every hour and there were usually no test or other flights before we got them. Hence, we were actually production test pilots, though I never thought of us as such until long after the war. I remember that often the autopilot would not work.

My first trip was the pilot's 2nd trip, and he was so nervous he actually shook. Here he gets a totally inexperienced WASP as co-pilot. If it weren't for the flight engineer I don't think we would have gotten to our destination. Actually, we started to land at the wrong base, and the engineer called our attention to it. From there, we picked up other 24s to deliver to other bases, and by the time we finished we knew what we were doing.

I had a different left seat pilot each time, so had to adjust to their expectations of me. But usually as soon as we got to altitude and synchronized our engines, he and the engineer would go back somewhere and play cards. I would slide over to the left seat and fly the plane to the destination. This made me feel pretty proud—all that horsepower, when I had been flying Cubs a short time before. It was also amusing to see men's faces when we would land at a base and I'd come out of that big plane.

One thing that made my flying 24s unique is that when they were shipped to Europe to bomb Germany, underneath were my future husband and in-laws, who were German nationals during the war. The men all fought on the Eastern front, as far as

I know, and one was captured and sent to Siberia. My husband was in the Hitler Youth, and he said he would lie in bed wondering "Why are they doing this to me? I'm just an innocent kid." Little did he know the plane might have been delivered by his future wife. I heard about this from time to time. My sister in law's father, a Luftwaffe fighter pilot, was shot down and killed by an American fighter. Such is war. It seemed strange at first to visit the former "enemy" but that didn't last long. However, visiting my sister in law on the North Sea (Husum) which was always foggy, I would think of those bombers and the fog on those raids which I had heard so much about during the war.

From "Before I say Adieu"
by Earl E. Wassom, 466tlh, Past President

The B-24 was a great airplane, but we lost many of them. A typical bomber lasted only 147 days. The Eighth Air Force logged 6,537 heavy bombers lost and 3,337 fighter aircraft destroyed. The B-24 brought many, but not all of us, home.

When the conflict ended in 1945, almost 7,000 of our Second Air Division had made the ultimate sacrifice. Thousands more had become prisoners of war. But when the victory celebration finally came, our Eighth Air Force commander, in addressing his British hosts, said this: "We hope that after we are gone, you'll be happy we came."

The American Eagle Squadrons

In the early days of World War II, 244 American pilots made their way to England and volunteered to fly for the Royal Air Force. They played significant rolls in the Battle of Britain during the months of August and September 1940, and subsequent action against the Luftwaffe.

In 1940 and 1941 three fighter squadrons were created within the RAF specifically for the Americans; these units became known as the American Eagle Squadrons. A number of Eagles became aces by shooting down five or more enemy planes. The RAF awarded 40 decorations to 31 Eagles. In 18 months of operations with the RAF, the Eagle pilots shot down more than 73 enemy aircraft. Each squadron at some point led in total scoring throughout the RAF for a given month.

In September 1942 the three Eagle units were formally transferred to the United States Army Air Forces, where they became part of the 4th Fighter Group of the 8th Air force.

The 4th, in turn, profiting from the combat experiences of the former Eagle pilots, eventually became the highest-scoring U.S. fighter group of World War II.

The Eagles individual and collective experiences have been chronicled in three books by Vern Haugland, a veteran Associated Press war correspondent and later AP's aviation/space editor. The first two books, "The Eagle Squadrons: Yanks in the RAF, 1940-1942" and "The Eagles' War: The Saga of the Eagle Squadron Pilots, 1940-1945" were published some decades ago. A third book, "Caged Eagles: Downed American Fighter Pilots, 1940-1945," was completed just before Mr. Haugland's death in 1984. It was not published until early 1992 when his widow, Tess, was successful in finding a publisher for all three books in a set. These three paperback books are published by TAB Books, Blue Ridge Summit, PA, 17294, and sold at many bookstores. In Canada they are available through McGraw-Hill Ryerson, 300 Water Street, Whitby, Ontario L1N 9B6.

On May 12, 1986, the Eagle Squadron Memorial was unveiled in London in Grosvenor Square, directly across from the statue of Franklin D. Roosevelt.

YOU MAY RECALL earlier remarks regarding my first combat mission, to Brunswick. I found these comments, with no author or publication noted—"Rough is the title of the mission for today, May 19, 1944. We went to Brunswick, Germany for the second time this month, but it was much rougher this time. Our bombs were dropped on the southern part of the city, after making three bomb runs. I don't know who was leading us over that blasted place so many times, but I could have given him a big kick. The flak was something awful over the target. Fighters also attacked us. We were under attack for about an hour, but it seemed like days. They came in forty and fifty at a time."

Some Stats on WWII Era Aircraft Losses

Taken from THE TIN GOOSE, a information letter of the Aviation History Club, POB 940445, Doraville, GA 30340

Military aircraft losses, 1939-1945: Germany, 95,000; U.S., 59,295; Japan, 49,485; Great Britain. 33.090; Australia, 7,160; Italy, 4,000; Canada, 2,389; France, 2,400; New Zealand, 684; and India, 527. (Russian losses were extremely high, but unreported by the Soviet government.) Also included in the article were ladder scale listing of numbers of aircraft produced. 16,188 B-24s, 12,677 B-17a, 9,846 B-25Js, 7,385 A-20s, 5,157 B-26Es, 3,000 B-29s, and 1,355 A-26 Invaders. From Crosshairs Dec. 1989

My Shortest Mission
by John F. Fay, 466th

Standing behind the pilot and copilot, I looked out the window and saw the No. 2 engine and part of the wing on fire. I tapped the pilot on the shoulder and pointed to the flame. He immediately turned toward land and I started to crawl through the tunnel to the nose to get my chute. I was the navigator, and my chest pack was at the navigator's position in the nose... My position during takeoff was standing between the pilot and copilot, calling out the airspeeds. After takeoff, I remained on the flight deck as we were heading out over the North Sea. It was only ten to fifteen minutes after takeoff that the fire was first noticed... It was February 17, 1945, and we set out on a mission to Magdeburg loaded with RDX bombs. I recall that before takeoff, the crew chief was working on the No. 2 engine until just before we started the engines, but no one envisioned the problems we would soon encounter... Robinson, the nose gunner, met me head on in the tunnel, dragging his chest pack. I prevailed on him to back up so I could get my chute, and we then started toward the waist because the camera hatch was a better bailout opportunity than the nose wheel hatch. Going past the flight deck we saw Eclov (radio operator) and Curly (engineer) attempting to buckle on their chute straps... By this time, the situation was getting desperate because the wing was fully enveloped in flames and it was loaded with gasoline. Upon reaching the waist, three of the gunners waived goodbye and bailed out, although we were still over the North Sea and the bail out signal had not been given...

Robinson and I positioned ourselves at the camera hatch and waited for the bail-out signal as the plane started down. As we crossed the shoreline, the pilot gave the signal and Robinson and I bailed out at less than 1,000 feet. The bailout was witnessed by personnel at the British Air Sea Rescue field at Langham, where we landed. The plane crashed on the other side of the field, killing the pilot, copilot, engineer, radio operator, and an Italian POW on the ground. British planes and rescue boats immediately attempted to rescue the men in the water, but it was too late. Unfortunately, the three gunners who bailed out over the North Sea perished due to the temperature of the water, although they were equipped with Mae Wests. Robinson and I were the only survivors. The whole trip lasted no more than an hour—short mission indeed!

The "Liberalization" of the Soviet Air Forces
Reprinted from the 446th BG's "Beachbell Echo"

As Soviet forces proceeded westward, more and more American crews chose to land their damaged aircraft in Soviet-held territory. Saving these machines for the Soviet AF was not an easy task. Some aircraft were damaged or destroyed by anti-Soviet partisans. Some were robbed by Soviet soldiers of everything which could be sold, and even guarding the aircraft did not always help. So, many aircraft were useful only for spare parts.

The first task in adopting B-24s and B-17s to Soviet service was replacing white stars with red ones. It was decided that Soviet airmen could not fly in machines with naked girls and other things painted on them, so orders were issued to get rid of all nose art.

The Liberator was not liked by Soviet crews due to her low aerodynamics. With reduced engines the speed dropped quickly; take-off and landing were difficult. These reasons may explain why the only American aircraft crashed was a B-24 (#42-94800). This machine lost one engine at take-off and broke in two parts during emergency landing. All crew in the tail part perished.

In the beginning of October 1945, the 203rd Air Regiment had 21 B-24s in flying condition. The B-17s were used in the Soviet AF to the summer of 1947; the B-24s served longer due to their more durable engines. The main reason for a B-24 to be put out of service was lack of pneumatic parts for nose wheels. B-24s were used for crew training since they were the only type aircraft equipped with a nose wheel. The last Liberators in Soviet service could be found still in 1950…

Russian Excursion—World War II Style
As told to David Paterson by his 445th BG crew members.
Reprinted from the 2ADA Journal. Chapter II (In Chapter I, a 445th crew on a mission to Zossen, German, made an emergency landing in Russia.)

The second evening we were there the base C.O., a Russian Colonel, had a party for us.

In addition to our crew of 8, there were about 15 Russian AF officers. Our crew was all seated at the Colonel's end of the table. We were served a borscht-type soup, thick with vegetables, some strange fresh-cooked meat, black bread, and real butter. Empty water glasses were at each place; pitchers of water and "soda-pop" looking bottles of clear liquid were placed up and down the table. The Colonel poured his glass half full of the clear liquid, and filled up the glass with water. As everyone else in the room did the same, we obediently followed suit. The Colonel stood up. "Stalin, Roosevelt, Churchill!" All glasses were raised, and all went bottom up. Wow! Did that burn! The "pop" was pure 100% alcohol!

As the evening progressed, the Russians got delight and laughs at our incapability to keep up with their drinking. Toast after toast was proposed, with all possible combinations of Churchill, Roosevelt, Stalin, Zukov, Eisenhower, Patton, etc. etc. etc.

After dinner we staggered, while the Russians walked, up the outside stairs into a big upstairs room. There, with the music being furnished by two or three of the group who played guitars and the like, a dancing party concluded the evening. The dancing was Cossack style, men with men partners. We were wheedled into joining, which created great merriment not only because we had no idea of the dance steps required but because of the vast quantities of vodka we had consumed.

The next few days gave us insight into several things. Despite our constant pleas to have our plight communicated to U.S. forces, it was obvious nothing was done in this regard. ….Emergency facilities were minimal at this base. We saw a Yak come in to land, tail too high. He hit the brakes, and finally skidded to a halt with the nose in the dirt, tail up in the air. From an old rickety shed across the field came the sound of someone trying to crank-start an engine. This failed, then several men pushed, by hand, out of the shed an old square-built ambulance, World War I vintage. With one man steering, and three to four pushing, they pushed this "emergency vehicle" over to the wrecked plane. They dragged the pilot out, put him in the ambulance, and again hand-pushed it, this time to the hospital. Fortunately, the pilot was no worse than bruised and shaken up. We never saw any medical equipment in the "hospital." We assumed a few bandages and lots of vodka solved all problems.

One morning, after about a week of what was becoming more and more obvious confinement, lo and behold a C-47 with U.S. markings circled the field, landed, and taxied up. ATC, the pilot said, made a practice of touring every week or so up and down these areas, looking for downed crews. They saw our B-24, and came in for us. Little more was said, we hurriedly got our stuff together and climbed aboard. We didn't wait to say goodbye to the Russians, because we weren't sure we'd get away if they got wind of our intended departure. (In all fairness to the Russians, they were a combat unit, flying daily combat from a few miles behind the front lines; they had more pressing matters to attend to than providing us with the immediate service we desired. But we weren't about to let this opportunity go!)

The C-47 took us to Poltava, Russia, a U.S. shuttle base. There we were washed, deloused, and issued clean Class B uniforms. We were issued orders marked "Secret" directing us to proceed by the best and most direct military means possible to the 8th AF HQ in England.

Our return trip was interesting. It included stops at Teheran, Cairo, Libya, Athens, Rome, Naples, Marseilles, Paris, and finally London, and then our base at Tibenham, all of this courtesy of U.S. Air Transport Command. Because of ATC flight schedules, we stayed over at several of these places, sometimes several days each and, whenever we had time, were able to sightsee by borrowed Jeep or tour vehicle, courtesy of the USAAF.

(Sightseeing in Paris, by the way, included such sights as all-night nightclubs, etc.!)…

Upon our return to our base at Tibenham, we first rescued our belongings (the items which hadn't mysteriously disappeared, that is!) from the MIA (missing in action) storage room, then got new quarters assignments, and reported for operational duty. We resumed bombing flights shortly thereafter, almost a month to the day of the Zossen raid.

OSS Code Name: Carpetbagger
by Jim Hanford, reprinted from "Yankee Wings"

Liberators assigned to "Carpetbagger" operations had to be modified. The ball turret was removed, and in its location a metal-shrouded circular hatch, called a "Joe Hole," was provided for the agents to drop through. At just under sixteen tons, the Liberator was too heavy to land on the improvised landing strips in occupied Europe. The nose turret, if installed, was also removed. In its place a greenhouse provided a good view of the drop zone, and enabled the bombardier to assist the navigator in pilotage. Additional navigation equipment included the British radio navigation aid, GEE, a U.S. Navy homing system which was effective up to 100 miles; and a radar altimeter of extreme accuracy for use in making drops. Blister windows were installed to improve the pilot's visibility, and flame dampers were added to suppress engine exhaust flames. Waist guns were also removed, and black-out curtains covered the waist windows. Finally, the entire exterior was painted non-glare black. With the aircraft blacked out in flight, a "Carpetbagger" B-24 was practically undetectable at night. All operations over enemy territory were conducted during total darkness. As a result, the crews of four officers and four airmen began briefings at 1:00 p.m. Afterward, the crews drew up their own flight plans. Routes normally consisted of dog-legs, no longer than 30 miles each, to avoid known anti-aircraft guns and to discourage interceptions by night fighters. At least ten minute intervals were allowed between planes entering the same area. Most offloading operations were coordinated with lights or fires on the ground. The final approach was made at slow speed and 400 feet altitude (600 feet if "Joes" were dropped).

Such missions were fraught with danger. One Liberator returned to Harrington with over 1,000 bullet holes, resulting from a tangle with two night fighters. On April 27, 1944, 1st Lt. George Ambrose was flying "The Worry Bird" on a mission over France. While pushing a package through the "Joe" hole Jim Monier, who was on his first "Carpetbagger" mission, slipped and tumbled through the opening. It is believed he rode the package parachute down, for although he was badly injured, he survived the fall, and the war, as a POW. The next night "The Worry Bird" was shot down with only two survivors... The "Carpetbaggers" dropped 100 three-man teams, composed of two officers and a radio operator, just prior to and after D-Day, and their effect was significant... During the period January to May 1944, 25 Liberators were lost on "Carpetbagger" operations, and another eight were so severely damaged by ground fire that they were scrapped. By the war's end, some 4,500 tons of material and hundreds of "Joes" had been dropped. There were other operations mounted with B-24s to assist the Underground in Scandinavia, but that is another story.

Recovery Team Gets First Glimpse of B-24 Crash Site in China
Xing'an, China (AP), Jan. 14, 1997

The two farmers were nine hours by foot from the nearest village, searching for herbs on south China's tallest mountain, when they spotted an airplane wing jutting up from a cliff. It turned out to be the shreds of an American B-24 that crashed with a crew of 10 men during World War II, missing for 52 years. U.S. officials from the POW/MIA office in Washington got their first chance Monday to examine remains and wreckage that local officials had retrieved from the crash site. The U.S. team was scheduled to hike to the crash site today. It is only the second time that remains of airmen missing from World War II have been recovered in China, said Jay Liotta, deputy director of the POW/MIA office and a member of the mission. The other recovery was from a glacier in Tibet in 1994.

The farmers in Guangxi, on the border with Vietnam, discovered the wreckage on Oct. 2nd. Within weeks, local officials mobilized 500 workers, including museum experts, to bring back human bones and parts of the plane. The U.S. officials found the remains carefully placed on a long table. Beside them were eye glasses in a case, the dog tags of five men, coins from India, two pocket watches, and a fountain pen. On the floor nearby were twisted chunks of the plane, some with the U.S. military star still visible.

Jiang Jun, 29, one of the farmers who found the wreckage, said he and his friend Pan Qiwen were looking for a path when they spotted the wing. After a steep climb of more than 3000 feet, they reached the wreckage scattered on a cliff. Jiang said he had never seen an airplane, except on television. The two immediately reported the find and will be rewarded with $6,000, a county official said.

The bomber lost on Mao'er mountain set out from Liuzhou on August 31st, 1944, and bombed Japanese ships around Taiwan. Warned by radio not to return to Liuzhou because Japanese bombers were attacking the base, it headed back in bad weather at night to Guilin. It crashed 990 feet below the summit of the 7,068 foot mountain.

Stevens and Holm—Ditching With Nose Turret Shot Off

On June 20, 1944, Lt. Charles Sevens and his copilot, Lt. Bill Holm, did an outstanding job with their aircraft when they ditched their plane #42-95171 with the nose turret shot off. One flak burst had shot away the entire nose section, instantly killing the navigator, Lt. Harold R. Meng, and the bombardier, Lt. William F. Weck. The plane left the target with two engines out, and a third engine was lost over the English Channel. The remaining engine was losing power as they ditched just off Dover. Two other crew members parachuted and were lost. Bill Holm reported than an Englishman on shore was trying to wave him back into the water. When he finally made shore, the man

377

told him: "You're lucky, Yank—the area's mined and a Typhoon pilot was blown to bits following your path yesterday."

Lt. Stevens returned to combat Nov. 26, 1944, only to be blown clear of his aircraft over Misburg. He finished the war in a POW camp. He remained in the Air Force after WWII and was killed flying fighters in the Korean War. Bill Holm, retired from NASA, continues to fly his own plane today.

On The Trail of "Wabbit Tracks"

On 6 March 1944 the 8th Air Force completed its first mission to Berlin amid heavy flak, fighters, and cloud cover up to 29,000 feet. A formation of 658 heavies took part in this raid, and 69 of the bombers didn't return—the highest number ever lost on a single day. The 458th dispatched twenty-seven B-24s for the sortie, and five failed to return. This would be their highest total of losses on any mission for the remainder of its tour.

One of the wounded 458th Libs that limped away from the German capital was #41-29286-T, better known as "Wabbit Tracks." Just over the Dutch border and approaching Amsterdam, the crew saw that their "bunny" could go no farther and bailed out. Capt. Jack Bogusch, the pilot, was killed on this mission. The ship crashed in a field and was demolished... In October, 1995, Robert Swift, the bombardier, and Robert Robinson, waist gunner, and his three sons visited the crash site of the ship at Tubbergen, Holland. With the help of a local historian and metal detectors, they located the exact spot of Wabbit Tracks' demise. They recovered small bits and pieces of the plane along with some .50 caliber ammo. The historian, Martin Klaassan, had salvaged a 36" x 14" section of a wing after the crash and gave it to Bob, who carried it home for mounting on the wall behind his easy chair.

Over the past 52 years, this is only the second known case of 458th crewmen going back to the site of their plane's crash. The other was when the late Richard Eselgroth, navigator, went to an area southeast of Frankfurt, Germany in 1974 and recovered parts of 44-10491, "The Iron Duke," shot down 22 Feb. 1945... George Reynolds (458th}, 4009 Saddle Run Circle, Pelham, AL 35124.

378

(Author unknown)

Lest We Forget
by Myron Keilman.

On 16 November 1943 eighteen B-2s of he 392nd took off on a nine and a half hour mission to bomb the Germany heavy water plant at Rjuken, Norway. Lt. Harold (Doc) Weiland was the lead bombardier. Major Lawrence Gilbert, our group operations officer, was the command pilot. At the time, none of us were aware of the strategic importance of heavy water (ordinary hydrogen replaced by an isotope of twice the atomic weight called deuterium) being used in the production of the first atomic bombs. The Norsk Hydro hydrogen electrolysis plant near Rjuken was the only plant available to the Germans capable of manufacturing heavy-water in significant quantity. The plant was a large six-story concrete and steel structure, situated like a fortress on a mountain cliff. British Intelligence, early in 1942, made Prime Minister Churchill aware of its strategic importance. On 18 Oct. 1942 and 18 Feb. 1943 small teams of British and Norwegian commandos parachuted into isolated areas. On 27 Feb. 1943 they linked up 18 miles from the plant. At midnight 28 February they performed one of the most daring raids ever, and destroyed the high concentration heavy-water tanks.

By midnight April 1943 the plant was repaired—and security greatly strengthened against further sabotage. Consequently—with British and atomic bomb research and development trailing—Winston Churchill and President Roosevelt made the decision to launch a heavy bomber attack. On Nov. 1943 the Second and Third Divisions of the Eight Air Force struck the plant with 160 B-24s and B-17s. The heavy water plant was put out of commission—never to operate again. The salvaged heavy water was sabotaged en route to Germany.

Dr. Joseph Carter, Professor of Nuclear Engineering, University of Kentucky, having served in the research and development of the atomic bomb under General Leslie Groves of the Manhattan Project, stated in Nov. 1988, "The bomber run of 16 Nov. 1943 and the subsequent destruction of nuclear laboratories at Peenemundi was a major contribution to winning World War II."

Think! What would the world be like today had the Nazi Regime been able to perfect and deploy the atomic bomb?!

From BOMBER LEGENDS—Dear Editor
(The Beacon), Nov. 25, 1998.

In your September 1997 issue here was something that sent up the "red flag," and I was disturbed by it. You listed the names of World War II and Vietnam veterans who gave their lives for their country. What about Korea?

Korea is called "the forgotten war," but one cannot understand why. It was very much a war. I was there. I know that one Francis Eugene Holland was the first Eagle Rock casualty and there may be others. I believe you should honor the Korean War as a war and a tablet should be mounted on the wall of the auditorium with the others.

Here are some facts. 8,177 men are still missing in action. 389 men are still listed as prisoners of war. 54,262 of the military force did not make it back. Also, it should be noted, that in the 3 years, 1 month and 2 days of the Korean conflict almost as many men were lost as compared with the 58,202 who died in the Vietnam war, which lasted 11 years and 9 months. Military historians now agree that Korea was one of the bloodiest wars in the history of this country.

Thank you for giving this letter your attention.

Sincerely, Don Sutherland

Impact of Air Combat
by Carl H. Albright. From the 446th BG, Flixton-Bungay Update.

Flight surgeons determined who was to fly and who was grounded. They voluntarily flew combat missions searching for answers to questions such as: What would be the psychological impact of aerial combat on young men in their teens and early twenties? How would they stand the rigors of attacks from the ground and air, flying five miles high? Would they be able to fire machine guns in subzero temperatures, with flak so heavy that some crews said: "It was so thick you could walk on it." How would they react to seeing a plane explode in a ball of flame and men jumping with chutes on fire? How would they react when their buddy's bed next to theirs was empty? A flight surgeon once invited medical officers to consider the role of the combat flyer. He asked them to consider if they could manage 130 controls, switches, levers, dials and gauges of a bomber cockpit from the comfort of their swivel chairs. The flight surgeon continued:

"Cut your office to the size of a five-foot cube—engulf it in the roar of four 1,000 horsepower engines—increase your height above the ground to four or five miles—reduce the atmospheric pressure by one-half to two-thirds, and lower the outside temperature 40 degrees to 50 degrees below zero. That will give you an idea of the normal conditions under which pilots, engineers, navigators and bombardiers must work out mathematical relations of engine revolutions, manifold and fuel pressure, aerodynamics, barometric pressure, wind drift, air speed, ground speed, position, direction and plane attitude. As a final touch to their picture of concentration, ADD THE FEAR OF DEATH."

You just gotta "hand it" to this guy!
Reprinted from "Stars and Stripes"

A Liberator base, May 19, 1944 (Brunswick??)
Without a parachute, Lt. Edward M. Gibbens, of Mountain Home, Idaho, hung precariously by one hand in the open belly of a bomber high over the Channel for almost five minutes, then pulled himself up to safety. Gibbens, bombardier on the Liberator named "Sweating It Out," fell out on the way home from a raid after "chopping" bombs off the damaged rack with a fire axe.

The bomber ran into terrific flak over a French airfield and was shot up so badly that the bombs wouldn't release. It had 87 holes in the framework, all four engines were damaged, and the hydraulic system was shot out, meaning no brakes and an inevitable explosion in the event of a crash landing. While the pilot, Lt. Robert T. Hall, of Wayne, IN, struggled to keep the plane up, Gibbens shed his parachute, took the fire axe, and squeezed into the narrow catwalk to knock the bombs loose. The first one burst the bomb bay doors wide.

Bracing himself against a 100 mile per hour gale, Gibbons knocked the rest free, one by one. As the last one came free, Gibbens slipped on the catwalk, slippery with hydraulic fluid. He grabbed the bomb rack with one hand, holding the axe in the other. One slip of his fingers meant he'd go hurtling thousands of feet to death in the Channel. Slowly, he pulled himself back up to where he could regain his footing. Realizing he'd accomplished the feat with just one hand, Gibbens first words were, "And I didn't lose the axe…" (Bombardiers weren't just the guys who let the bombs go. They were the armament officer and the above was one of their jobs. Doing it, no room on the narrow catwalk for your chest parachute, so if Gibbens let go, he was a goner. If this has to be done at altitude, it was necessary to have a carry-on oxygen supply. Freezing cold, breezy, terrible job. I was always very appreciative of Phil Goplen, our bombardier, who had the not infrequent task of getting rid of unreleased bombs Sometimes the bottom ones wouldn't release, usually with smaller bombs, and higher ones would, so there was a pileup.)

Pilot dead, 2 others injured, nose battered, B-24 returns.
Reprinted from Stars and Stripes, 27 Nov. 1944— 445th BG

With the pilot dead, two other crew members injured, and its flight instruments useless, a Liberator returned safely from a mission over Misburg on November 26, 1944—quick thinking and teamwork doing the trick. Several minutes before bombs away, the formation was attacked by enemy fighters. Lt. Vincent Mazza, copilot from Naperville, Illinois, fought to keep the bomber from swerving into other bombers after the pilot, killed by a 20mm shell which penetrated his flak suit, slumped over the controls. A second wave of German fighters lobbed shells into the Lib's nose, shrapnel wounding Lt. John C. Christiansen, of Plymouth, Michigan, who was manning the nose guns. Lt. Leo J. Lewis, bombardier from Clayton, Missouri, also was hit. The bombs were salvoed by the navigator, Lt. Frank W. Federici of Chicago, who remained at his post in the nose.

When the enemy fighters departed, S/Sgt. Eddie W. Goodgion, right waist gunner from Lubbock, Texas, and T/Sgt. Carl E. Bally, radio operator from Ashland, Ohio, came to the aid of the dazed bombardier, whose helmet and oxygen mask had been torn off.

T/Sgt. Herbert A. Krieg, engineer from Atlantic City, NJ went to the cockpit and pulled the dead pilot clear of the controls. Christiansen made his way back from the nose turret to the waist, where his wounded leg was treated by S/Sgt. Kenneth J. Brass, left waist gunner.

At the channel, Mazza left the formation and headed for England alone. His maps blown away by the terrific wind which swept through the gaping hole in he nose, Federici directed the copilot back to base by recalling landmarks along the way. The radio and interphone went dead, making communication with the ground and other planes impossible. The tail gunner, S/Sgt. Charles lW. Bickett of New Richmond, Ohio, had been cut off from communication with other crew members. Neither altimeter nor air-speed indicator were functioning. Massa circled the field behind another B-24 to get his proper landing speed, Krieg behind him to handle the throttles. The landing was fast, but smooth..,. Some of the most dramatic reminiscences were about brushes with death. Bob recalled having been assigned a plane on one particular mission that had just had bulletproof glass installed in it. The planes they normally flew did not have this feature. As they were flying, a fragment from flak hit the windows directly beside the pilot's position. On returning to base, they found it lacked a fraction of an inch from coming all the way through the glass. Both Bob and Marty agreed that had there been regular glass on the plane that day, Bob would not be here to tell the story...WHEN I read this I said, hey, this is pretty close to my experience with the thick glass that was only installed when the plane went to the repair depot with damage not fixable at the base. In my case, recounted elsewhere, the flak did get through the glass, plus the metal frame of the glass, and hit me at an angle which would have had my heart in the way. All I received was a sore black and blue mark. Of course, my body was not as resilient as two panes of the thick glass plus the frame, so it was literally a life- saver. I still have the piece of flak with glass embedded, and elsewhere include my picture with the two shattered panes of glass.

Drama Over Cologne, 14 October 1944

On 14 Oct. 1944, B-24J, S/N 42-50864, "Jolly Roger," with a crew of ten was the lead plane of the 458th Bomb Group, 755th Squadron, to bomb marshalling yards at Cologne, Germany. Immediately after bombs away, "Jolly Roger" was hit by three bursts of flak, knocking out the #3 engine and injuring several crew members, the most severe was MC Miller who was struck by shrapnel in the head and face. Lt. Robert Ferrel and Lt. Ernest Sands pulled Lt. Miller from the nose turret and administered first aid. The "Jolly Roger" was on fire and going down. Pilot Lt. William Klusmeyer ordered everyone to bail out. Sands attached a line to Miller's parachute ripcord and pushed him out the camera hatch, immediately followed by S/Sgt. Joseph Pohler.

Lt. Sands left the ship via the nose wheel doors and pulled his ripcord after passing through several cloud layers. After landing, Lt. Sands hid himself in a depression till after dark, and then started walking west. The nine other crew members had been captured by German soldiers. Lt. Sands evaded capture for seven days but was caught and beaten by German civilians as he was trying to cross a river to get to Belgium. Sands ended up in Stalag Luft III and on January 27, 1945, was marched west during a blizzard, eventually ending up in Stalag VIIA at Mooseburg in the spring of 1945. On April 29, 1945, an American tank burst through the front gate at Mooseburg with a force led by General Patton. It was one day before Sands' 24th birthday.

Ernie Sands always wondered what had happened to MC Miller. The last he had seen him was when he had parachuted from the plane. Had he survived? Many years later, after the war, Ernie received a phone call—it was MC Miller. He had tracked Ernie down to thank him for helping save his life. Miller had survived after being treated by German doctors and had fully recovered in a POW camp.

Ernest Sands served as North Dakota's Lt. Governor from 1981 to 1984… (Noted elsewhere is mention of my cadet friend Donald Nutter who lived through the war as a pilot, and

384

died in a National Guard plane crash when serving as governor of Montana.)

Note: Artist proofs of Drama over Cologne, signed by bombardier Ernest Sands, are available from Scott Nelson, 6705 CR 82, Solen, ND 58570, 701-597-3525, www.scottnelsonart.com.

Buzz Bombs: D-Day Was Too Late
by Graham Heathcote, Associated Press

(The writer, a schoolboy at the time, was there when the German V-1s and V-2s began falling. These are his memories.)

LONDON—In the early morning darkness of June 13, 1944, we heard a noise different from anything we had known though five years of air battles and bombs.

A far off rumbling in the sky became louder and louder, turning into a roar that shook the house in Kent and filled the fields with shattering sound. With a deafening rattle, whatever it was passed low over the house. The reflections of a red flame climbed up the bedroom wall and across the ceiling. Then the roar became a rumbling again, dying away as the thing flew on in the direction of London. I lay in bed petrified! My mother ran into my room in her nightdress crying, "Graham, Graham, what is it?"

The government did not tell us immediately, but the assault of Hitler's secret weapon had begun with the V-1 flying bomb. Just one week earlier, the allies had invaded Normandy, giving us confidence that peace in the air would come. It did not happen. The third of the four LV-1s on that first night killed three people in London's Bethnal Green area. On September 8, another secret weapon arrived. The first supersonic rocket killed three people in Chiswick, west London. The V-2 was more terrifying because it could not be seen or detected.

In the closing months of World War II, Britain became the first nation to suffer attack by ballistic missiles from beyond its borders. The bombardment lasted nine months. The target was London, but the flying bombs and rockets fell all over southeast England, where American GIs waited to ship out to the continent. General Dwight D. Eisenhower, the supreme Allied commander, ordered more bombing of the launch sites in France and the Netherlands. By March 1945 when the attacks ended, 5,823 flying bombs and 1,054 rockets had fallen on England, killing 8,300 people badly wounding at least twice that number, destroying 23,000 homes and damaging many more. Another 2,771 people were killed in Belgium and France and 2,900 Allied airmen died in raids on launch sites and production plants. Both V-1 and V-2 were brilliant scientific and engineering achievements that might have enabled Germany to defeat Britain if they had come earlier. But after D-Day, they were militarily irrelevant.

Together, the flying bomb and the rocket created terror in London, which still bears scars from the attacks. One million people fled the capital to seek safety in the countryside. Another 250,000 mothers and children were evacuated by the government. Despite the terror, Britons managed a joke: They called the flying bombs "doodle bugs."

Chapter 11: Non-Flying Stories

USAAF Air Transport Command
Excerpt from the Book: "Official Pictorial History of the USAAF"

The Army's great aerial transportation agency was the Air Transport Command. Whenever men, planes and supplies had to be delivered in a hurry or whenever there was no other means of getting them where they were needed, the Air Transport Command took on the job. Under wartime conditions transport or combat planes crossed the Atlantic on an average of one every 13 minutes, the broader Pacific, every hour and a half; and, in one year, more than a billion pounds of high priority cargo, passengers, and mail were carried to war theaters around the globe.

The ATC began as the Air Corps Ferrying Command on May 29, 1941 with two officers, one civilian, a world map posted in a Washington office, and an assignment to assist in delivering military aircraft to the countries then fighting for democracy. Within a year, airfields, isolated stations, and lonely weather and communications outposts had been built on deserts, tropical islands, and arctic wastes. The first ferry delivery reached Montreal on June 9, 1941. The first transatlantic flight—from Washington to Prestwick—departed on July 1. A trip to Cairo was undertaken in September, followed by a round-the-world journey touching Washington, Prestwick, Moscow and Singapore. From the first contract in August 1941, fullest use was made of the skill and experience of the commercial airlines flying under contract to the War Department and dependent for control upon the ATC.

After America entered the war, many civilian transport pilots were commissioned as officers to ferry military aircraft. Experienced commercial airline executives donned uniforms to serve on the staff of veteran flyer Lt. Gen. Harold L. George, who had assumed command of the Ferrying Command on April 1, 1942.

By June 1942, ATC routes touched all six continents. Routes were inaugurated to Alaska in April 1942, and in June, when the ATC took its present name, B-17s were delivered on short notice to participate in the Battle of Midway, and personnel and munitions were rushed to Dutch harbor to check the Japanese in the Aleutians. In July the first plane landed at Ascension Island base on the South Atlantic route, P-38s were flown to the United Kingdom in August, and A-20s to North Africa with the U.S. landings in November. In December the ATC took over the route from Assam to China, flown since April 1942 by the 1st Ferrying Group of the Tenth Air Force.

By 1945 the ATC, with more than 20,000 members in uniform, was flying with clockwise regularity routes that were considered un-flyable before the war. To supply the Fourteenth Air Force and the XX Bomber Command, it carried fuel, bombs, jeeps, five-ton trucks, and 12 ½ -ton road scrapers over the towering Himalayas, achieving during July 1945 an average of one plane every 1.3 minutes over the Hump. By the war's end, ATC operated 11 divisions, delivering at airplane speed to every front the critically needed items on which global victory was to hinge.

B-47 Stratojet

NOTE: My B-24 bombardier, Phil Goplen of Zumbrota, Minnesota, was recalled after his WWII discharge, and subsequently spent a dozen years as navigator on a B-47 crew. He has interesting stories about the Cuban missile crisis and how the 47s were prepared to bomb Moscow… I communicated with and had personal contacts with four members of my crew over the years after the war. They are, sadly, all gone. I learned of the death of the twin brother Snyders of Boston through Ken's widow. I never could find the radio operator or ball turret gunner, or Phil, bombardier. But last year he contacted Pat Everson, historian par excellence for our 448th Bomb Group, who has tons of records, to ask about any information of his WWII crew. SO—that's 8 of the 10 accounted for. It was lonely until Phil and I connected. As far as we know, we're the last two…

The B-47 was the first pure jet strategic bomber whose many unique features included six jet engines; a two-engine, pylon-mounted pod under each wing near the fuselage; and a single-engine pod further outboard. The wings were attached high on he fuselage and swept 35 degrees. The design incorporated revolutionary bicycle-type, retractable main landing gear with single, two-wheel struts on the forward and aft fuselage. Outrigger wheels added lateral stability and retracted into the two-engine pod cowling. The B-47 was 107 feet long, 28 feet high at the tail, and had a wing- span of 116 feet. The crew consisted of an aircraft commander pilot, pilot, and navigator... With a maximum gross weight of about 225,000 pounds, it used rocket assist on takeoff. They carried 17,554 gallons of fuel, which included two drop- tanks, 1,700 gallons each. Maximum landing weight, 125,000 pounds. A tail chute was used to slow down the aircraft during landings.

Although heavier than the heaviest World War II bomber, the B-47 was designed to be a medium-range penetrator with approximately a 3,500 nautical mile range. This was not a problem in the early 1950s since forward basing was available in the United Kingdom, Spain, Morocco, Guam, and Alaska. In addition, the B-47 was equipped with an air refueling capability and, on several occasions, 36-hour missions were flown.

The aircraft's payload capacity was limited to 20,000 pounds internally. Since nuclear weapons were large in the early 1950s, the bomb bay was limited to one or two of high yield. This lack of payload capacity was compensated for by the large numbers of B-47s, which resulted in an acceptable overall weapon delivery capacity. By 1956, B-47 deployment reached its peak with over 1,300 assigned to SAC (Strategic Air Command). Subsequently, phase out of the B-47 took place in the 1960s. It coincided with the rapid build up of ICBM and SLBM deployment by the U.S.

In summary, the B-47 was a technological innovation in bomber aircraft design with swept wings, jet engines, the ability to be air-refueled, and an operational envelope equal to the fighter aircraft of the early 1950s.

Some statistics: Takeoff ground run, at sea level, 10,400', jet assisted, 7,350', over 50' obstacle, 12,000', jet assisted, 8,800'. Maximum speed, 600 mph; combat speed, 557 mph at 38,500', 435 mph, average. Rate of climb, Sea level,

1,850' per minute, combat rate with maximum power, 4,350' per minute. Combat radius, 2,050 nautical miles. Tail guns, two .20mm cannons in remote tail turret. (With near-fighter speed and a higher altitude ceiling they could only be successfully intercepted from the rear.)

Bits and Pieces of a Tour
by Frank A. Reed (448th)

With the 50th anniversary of what went on back in the 8th, many of us naturally attempt to recall the times and events that we lived through. I have read many accounts in the *Journal* of those involved where they told in great detail what transpired on a particular eventful mission they flew. Although my crew flew a few that would make an interesting story, it is beyond me to do the same. First of all, I didn't keep a diary to refer to. Second, I flew my missions in the tail, and as a result I didn't always know what was going on in the waist, much less what transpired up front. Third, after fifty years, even if I had known all the facts to tell a good story, with Mr. Senility creeping in on me, I would be hard pressed to detail any one mission. I do recall, however, as many of the readers probably do, many varied and isolated events, both in and out of the plane, that pop into my mind, with no recollection of what transpired just prior to or after the event; such as:

Still being awake at 3 AM before my first mission when someone from operations came to wake me up.

My first mission, and knowing this was "for keeps" when I saw one of our group go down.

My first real fighter attack near Brunswick, when we lost three planes.

Taxiing out to the runway to take off and seeing the English civilian workers give us a "thumbs up" salute. I liked that.

Twice seeing a 24 in our formation, while flying through a heavy flak field, suddenly disappear in a large ball of fire.

Going to a movie on the base one night, when the lights dimmed and the credits came on, "starring Jimmy Stewart," then seeing a pilot get up and walk out, saying, "I've seen this one, and it's not a very good picture."

390

In formation over the North Sea, at some 18,000 feet, just before entering the continent—icing up and falling out of control, finally getting control at 1,000 feet.

The *night* we returned from a *day* mission and the Jerrys followed us back, in our formation—the Jerrys shooting at us, we at them, the British ack-ack shooting at both of us. Everybody shouting, being strafed while landing, etc., etc. God, what an ugly ending for a beautiful (?) day.

The time the plexiglass three inches above my head was shattered by flak.

Seeing a fellow tail gunner sailing right past me in his turret when it had been shot away from his plane during a fierce fighter attack.

The night on leave in London during the mini-blitz, staying at the Russell Square Hotel when the Jerrys came over and hit the hotel, setting it on fire with incendiary bombs.

Escorting a P-38, under our right wing, home from a mission after he had lost an engine and probably had other difficulties.

The time our pilot, during a five abreast head-on attack near Tutow, caught a .303mm slug square in his chest, but survived because he was wearing two flak vests.

The time my left gun barrel was hit and left dangling at a 90 degree angle.

Seeing my copilot, flying next to us, shot down on his first mission after getting his own crew.

That memorable night at the Strand Palace Hotel—with Ann.

The only "make-up" mission I had with a strange crew, flying a new silver plane on its maiden flight to the Ruhr Valley, returning home with some 300 holes from flak and being dubbed thereafter "Patches."

Always the fear of running out of ammunition.

The time during a particular fierce fighter attack when we salvoed a load of fragmentation bombs on one of our own planes, which while doing severe evasive action, slid right under us.

Waking up in the middle of the night in our barracks and seeing the glow of half a dozen cigarettes in the dark.

The day after 19 missions (over which we had lost 55 planes) when we were told that since things were getting easier, we would no longer do 25 missions, but 30.

Seeing the three double bunks right next to me emptied three times by crews shot down.

Seeing our right waist gunner, who had left our crew after a falling-out with our pilot, bail out with his new crew on his first mission with them, over the heart of Berlin.

The time on our next-to-the-last mission when #3 engine blew, caught fire, and we dropped out of formation to return home alone across Germany and France.

During a fighter attack seeing a group member who had bailed out going down right past me with his chute on fire.

Seeing a fellow crew member, late in our tour and after a particularly rough fighter attack, completely break down, never to fly again.

The best five days in almost a year, which I spent in England at a "flak shack" near Oxford where a cute little English girl would wake me up each morning in my big double bed with a tray of orange juice.

Yes, bits and pieces of the past that I will never forget.

Journal Editor Visits with "Hump" Fliers

Ray Pytel, editor of the 2ADA *Journal* was invited to a reunion to outline the procedures used in collecting funds for the Bronze B-24 exhibit at the U.S. Air Force Academy.

The China-Burma-India Hump Pilots and Crewmen Association held its 56th Annual Reunion August 21-26, 2001 in Washington, DC. The members of the Hump Fliers Association are considering a C-46 cargo replica for the Academy's Court of Honor. The Hump Fliers flew C-47's (also known as DC-3's), the Liberator Cargo Versions C-87's and C-109's, and the roomy Curtiss 'Commando' C-46.

The Association is composed of nearly 3,500 air crew members and support personnel who were engaged in the China-Burma-India Theater of Operations during WWII. A major portion of the flying provided the entire supplies for the American and Chinese Armies and Air Forces in China—the first time such a massive airlift was ever attempted. The November 19, 1945 issue of *TIME* magazine reported on page 26: "Unofficial estimates were that 3,000 Allied transport and tactical aircraft had been lost among those jagged peaks (Himalaya Mountains). But for this price, the U.S. had backed

China, and U.S. units in China, with invaluable aid: 78,000 tons went over the Hump in the peak month of July." These downed aircraft made an "aluminum trail" over the "Hump," as the Himalayas were called. The terrible weather and rugged terrain posed constant danger as did the Japanese fighters and bombers.

A four-volume set of books, CHINA AIRLIFT—THE HUMP records a first-hand "history" of the CBI Theater during WWII and was compiled by the members. HPA placed two memorials to those who flew the "Hump." One is located at the Air Force Museum, Wright Patterson Air Force Base, Dayton, Ohio. The other was placed at the Air Force Academy in Colorado Springs. The Museum of Aviation, Warner-Robins Air Force Base, Warner-Robins, Georgia, houses an extensive exhibit of the China-Burma-India Theater, and displays for future generations what was accomplished by these veterans. A new C-17 P-62 #90062 was dedicated in June 2000 to the memory of the Hump Operation. This aircraft is presently stationed at McChord AFB, near Tacoma, Washington.

The Hump Operation was made necessary by the loss of the famed Burma Road to the Japanese early in the war. With no other access a bad situation in China became desperate. Loss of an important ally seemed imminent. The legendary Flying Tigers were the first to suffer, for without fuel, bombs and ammunitions these heroic volunteers were helpless. The Chinese National Airways Corporation (CNAC) did what it could to fill the gap flying pre-war, DC-2/DC-3 aircraft over the southern India-China route.

It was soon apparent that CNAC alone couldn't bear the burden. Chinese General Chiang Kai Shek finally convinced a harried U.S. War Department of the gravity of the situation. As a result, a few planes, crews and support personnel were sent to India to start an aerial bridge over the mighty Himalayas to China. Active enemy air opposition, primitive airfields and lack of navigational aids hindered the operation at every turn. But the worst obstacle was the weather, which was always a factor, either on the ground, in flight, or both. Little was written or said about the Hump during its operation, which gave rise to the CBI's reputation as "The Forgotten Theatre." Losses were as great as any other WWII air operation and higher than most.

Once established with sufficient manning and equipment, the airlift kept China in the war until victory was achieved. Many Humpsters were coincidently supporting ground forces in winning the battle of Burma. HPA members point with pride to today's awesome airlift forces as their descendents.

Let's Play Tag!!!
by Clayton K. Gross, 355th FG

In a thousand flights, including 105 combat missions in my two fighter tours, I remember this one as vividly as any, and man, would I like to meet the pilot of the Liberator that day!

My crew chief, Smitty, came to our Ops office in the early dawn to tell me that "Live Bait" was back in commission with a new engine and needed "slow time." I scheduled the sixteen mission pilots and with their two spares, and saw them off with the group for a deep escort mission. Then after another coffee with the Ops gang, I leisurely proceeded to GQ-I and after a proper pre-flight, lifted it into the broken clouds over Boxted.

There are few things I would rather do than fly a beautiful fighter plane, but nothing more boring than flying it straight and level when it was capable of doing so much. I leveled off just below the 3500 foot ceiling and decided on a sightseeing tour. First, I went south to the Thames, then turned West toward the barrage balloon fields of London. Before long on that course, I found company in the form of a B-24 cruising at the same altitude and crossing my course, left to right. Since it looked like something to do, I banked right and pulled along his right side. I really didn't want to frighten the bomber crew, so I sat—oh, maybe 50 feet off his wing tip, throttling back a little to match air speed. I could clearly see pilot and co-pilot not frightened, but grinning ear to ear. They beckoned me in, and now I grinned—they were speaking my language.

I moved in tight—like 10 feet—but they weren't satisfied. With more waving and what I thought might have been a mouthed word "coward," they asked for it! I tucked Live Bait in under the Lib wing, careful only that their #3 and #4 engines did not slice through my canopy. The co-pilots gave me the universal "OK—Alright!" sign, and I smiled—not ready for what happened next. That bomber broke hard left and up like a fighter who suddenly discovered a covey of 109's on his tail. Blessed with pretty good reflexes which I honed in two years of flying fighters, I tucked back in quickly after the initial move left me just slightly behind.

For the next five minutes I went for a ride following that guy in maneuvers I had **no** idea a B-24 could do! I knew several things for sure—they had to be empty and the pilot was no beginner! After five minutes or so, which left me in a fair sweat, they leveled off and, still grinning, waved me forward. I couldn't believe it, but he tucked in on me. Probably I could have lost him if I really wanted to, but I didn't. I took them through the rest of the maneuvers the Liberator tech manual said they couldn't do— and they did them! If I hadn't been having so much fun in the air, I would have wished to be on the ground to watch the show—unbelievable!

When I finally leveled out, my big friend was firmly on my wing, still grinning. He then motioned me to follow and, leading our tight formation, flew north for 15 minutes. We gradually started a letdown until I could see trees at our level from the corner of my eye. Then we skipped over the last tree patch and let down to ground level—down a runway I found was a B-24 base. I mean, we beat that field up the full length of the runway and then chandelled left and up. I thought he would make a fighter approach and land from that position, but he leveled out again and signaled me to lead the same kind of buzz job. I sincerely hope he was the Group C.O. of that outfit because what we were doing was my favorite pastime, and one that notoriously had me in trouble in my 355th Fighter Squadron. I didn't want them to suffer the same fate. In the meantime, I had the reputation of all fighter aviation to uphold, so from a mile or so out, I got my wingman in position—silently wished him well because I needed my concentration and would not be watching out for him. I gave that field a pass that may well have set a USAAF record for buzz jobs in which the participants survived. I know I cut grass and raised dust, and in the pullout, my friend was still there as always. This time he did roll out, gave me a giant wing waggle and made an approach and landing that would have made any fighter pilot proud. After his landing I made one more pass—rocking wings in farewell.

If I knew the markings of that aircraft, I have long since forgotten them. If I knew which of the Liberator bases we beat up, I have forgotten that also, but I do know that everybody at that station was out to watch the show and someone must remember it.

Landing in "Neutral" Switzerland
Reprinted From Wisconsin Badger News

In WWII, most of the 166 U.S. aircraft that landed in Switzerland did so out of necessity. It was either that or risk a crash landing in occupied France, or worse, running out of fuel long before reaching English shores. Only about five to ten percent of the crews landed there deliberately to escape the rest of the war. A large number of Americans escaped from the Swiss interment camps and made their way back to England. Of the 1,740 internees and evadees, 947 tried to escape. Of these, 184 attempts failed and the airmen were sent to brutal prison camps that were worse than the Stalag Luft camps in Germany.

The first airmen to arrive in Switzerland did not land there. They had been shot down over France or Germany and managed to make their way across the Swiss border. These men were considered "evadees" rather than internees. According to Swiss laws dating back to medieval times, they were entitled to sanctuary and some were free to leave like tourists. They were kept in separate camps from the internees who landed or parachuted into Switzerland.

A popular saying at that time was, "The Swiss are working for the Germans six days a week and praying for the Allies on the seventh!" However, the alliance between Switzerland and Germany was mostly an economic one. Looking at it from another perspective, if the Swiss had not cooperated with Germany, they would most likely have been annexed and occupied by German forces. Probably 95% of the Swiss people were openly pro-Allies.

The first foreign aircraft to land in Switzerland was a Luftwaffe Dornier Do-17Z-3 on 21 April 1940. The crew mistook Basel-Biresfelden airfield for a German field and landed. They were interned by the Swiss, but were later released due to pressure from the German government.

Until the summer of 1942, all landings or crashes of foreign aircraft on Swiss soil were made by Axis planes. A number of Me-110s and He-111s were shot down by Swiss fighters and a number of Luftwaffe training aircraft landed in error. Some of the German crews were allowed to return to Germany.

The first landing of an Allied aircraft was made by a British Mosquito in August of 1942. The pilot and copilot were returning from a recon mission to Venice when an engine overheated and they were forced to land at the Berne-Belp airfield. The two-man crew tried to destroy the plane, but they failed in the attempt. The aircraft was repaired by the Swiss and later saw service in the Swiss Air Force. Both pilot and copilot were returned to England and paired with two German pilots sent back to Germany.

The first U.S. aircraft to land on Swiss soil was a B-24D named "Death Dealer." It was from the 93rd Bomb Group and had taken part in a raid on the Messerschmitt factory at Weiner-Neustadt. The plane was set on fire and destroyed by the crew. In an almost unbelievable coincidence, the first B-24 to land in Sweden was also from the 93rd Bomb Group and it too was named "Death Dealer."

The first B-17 to put down in Switzerland was from the 100th Bomb Group. They crash landed with #3 feathered, #2 shot up with the prop wind milling and the landing gear up. They had just left Schweinfurt on 17 August 1943. The second B-17 to land was from the 390th Bomb Group and had also been on the Schweinfurt mission. They bellied in near Berne on the 17th with two engines shot out. The last arrival landed on 20 April 1945. It was a B-17G from the 15th Air Force.

Of the 166 U.S. aircraft that landed, 74 were B-17s and 82 were B-24s. The rest were fighters and recon aircraft. A record of 16 U.S. aircraft landed in one day on 18 March 1944. Twelve were B-24s and four were B-17s. Six of the twelve B-24s were from the 44th Bomb Group alone. Some landings were highly questionable, such as when a B-24D from the 93rd Bomb Group, a veteran of the famous Ploesti raid, landed at Dubendorf on 16 March 1944. The Swiss noted , "The aircraft was virtually undamaged and contained enough fuel to get them back to England."

From August to October of 1945, 30 B-17s and 41 B-24s were flown back to Burtonwood in the U.K. The rest were scrapped in Switzerland. Ironically, those that were flown to England arrived too late to be flown back to the U.S. and so were scrapped at Burtonwood. Other items, such as aircraft equipment, bombs, flight clothing, etc. were hauled out of Switzerland by trucks to Munich-Erding, Germany where they were destroyed or burned.

Lest We Forget: "The Black March"

by John Frisbee & George Gudderly.
Reprinted from "AIR FORCE" Magazine, Vol. 80, No. 9, September
1997

*This article by John Frisbee, co-authored by Col. George Gudderly,
chronicles the Black March and its casualties. Col. Gudderly survived
the march and went on to a successful career in the Air Force.
Instrumental in the effort to place a monument at the location of Luft
IV, he regularly writes and lectures on the subject.*

During the winter of 1944-45, 6,000 Air Force noncoms
took part in an event of mass heroism that has been neglected by
history. Most Americans know, in a general way, about the
Bataan Death March that took place in the Philippines during
April 1942. Few have even heard of an equally grim march of
Allied POWs in Northern Germany, during the winter of 1945
(the most severe winter Europe had suffered in many years). The
march started at Stalag Luft IV in German Pomerania (now part
of Poland), a POW camp for U.S. and British aircrew men.

Early in 1945, as the Soviet forces continued to advance
after their breakout at Leningrad, the Germans decided to
evacuate Stalag Luft IV. Some 1500 of the POWs, who were not
physically able to walk, were sent by train to Stalag Luft I...On
February 6, with little notice, more than 6,000 U.S. and British
airmen began a forced march to the west in subzero weather, for
which they were not adequately clothed or shod.

Conditions on the march were shocking. There was a
total lack of sanitary facilities. Coupled with that was a
completely inadequate diet of about 700 calories per day,
contrasted to the 3,500 provided by the U.S. military services.
Red Cross food parcels added additional calories when and if the
Germans decided to distribute them. As a result of the unsanitary
conditions and a near starvation diet, disease became rampant;
typhus fever spread by body lice, dysentery that was suffered in
some degree by everyone, pneumonia, diphtheria, pellagra, and
other diseases. A major problem was frostbite that in many cases
resulted in the amputation of extremities. At night, the men slept
on frozen ground or, where available, in barns or any other
shelter that could be found.

The five Allied doctors on the march were provided
almost no medicines or help by the Germans. Those doctors, and

a British chaplain, stood high in the ranks of the many heroes of the march. After walking all day with frequent pauses to care for stragglers, they spent the night caring for the ill, and then marched again the next day. When no medication was available, their encouragement and good humor helped many a man who was on the verge of giving up.

Acts of heroism were virtually universal. The stronger helped the weaker. Those fortunate enough to have a coat shared it with others. Sometimes the Germans provided farm wagons for those unable to walk. There seldom were horses available, so teams of POWs pulled the wagons through the snow. Capt. (Dr.) Caplan, in his testimony to the War Crimes Commission, described it was "a domain of heroes."

The range of talents and experience among the men was almost unlimited. Those with medical experience helped the doctors. Others proved to be talented traders, swapping the contents of Red Cross parcels with local civilians for eggs and other food. The price for being caught at this was instant death on both sides of the deal. A few less Nazified guards could be bribed with cigarettes to round up small amounts of local food.

In a few instances, when Allied air attacks killed a cow or horse in the fields, the animal was butchered expertly to supplement the meager rations. In every way possible, the men took care of each other in an almost universal display of compassion. Accounts of personal heroism are legend.

Because of war damage, the inadequacy of the roads, and the flow of battle, not all the POWs followed the same route west. It became a meandering passage over the northern part of Germany. As winter grew to a close, suffering from the cold abated. When the sound of Allied artillery grew closer, the German guards were less harsh in their treatment of POWs.

The march finally came to an end when the main element of the column encountered Allied forces east of Hamburg on May 2, 1945. They had covered more than 600 miles in 87 never-to-be-forgotten days. Of those who started on the march, about 1,500 perished from disease, starvation, or at the hands of German guards while attempting to escape. In terms of percentage of mortality, it comes very close to the Bataan Death March. The heroism of these men stands as a legacy to Air Force crewmen and deserves to be recognized.

In 1992, the American survivors of the march funded and dedicated a memorial at the former site of Stalag Luft IV in

Poland, the starting place of a march that is an important part of Air Force history. It should be widely recognized and its many heroes honored for their valor.

Excerpt from Chris Christiansen's book: Seven Years Among Prisoners of War; Ohio University Press, Athens, Ohio (1944):

As early as March 1944, the camp commandments had received instructions that in case of imminent invasion all POWs were to be evacuated from the border areas and the invasion zones. From September 1944 onward this evacuation claimed an incredible number of victims. And the closer the Allied armed forces came to the German boarders, the more chaotic and undisciplined was the evacuation. I do not know just how many Allied POWs were killed in the process, but the number of British and Americans alone might be an indication; during the period from September 1944 through January 1945, the evacuations had claimed 1,987 victims, but during the last three months of the war that number increased to a total of 8,438. With so many dead among those who were relatively well treated and who—much more importantly, received Red Cross parcels with food for their daily meals, it can be assumed that the number of dead among the Russian POWs must have been considerably higher. About one hundred thousand POWS from the camps in Silesia were evacuated and marched through Saxony to Bavaria and Austria. Transportation by train had been planned, but had proved impossible because of the rapid Russian advance. Lack of winter clothes, food and quarters claimed many victims. Over-excited party members and nervous home guard (members of the "Volkssturm") decided the fate of the POWs in these last weeks of the war. The German High Command wanted to keep the POWs at any cost, to be able to negotiate more favorable peace terms, and it was therefore necessary to evacuate them under these most inhumane conditions instead of just leaving them to await the advancing Allied armies.

The Tempelhof Experience 1949-1951
by William E. Hendrix, Jr. (466th)

THE NORTHERN LIGHTS

Night missions on the Berlin Airlift were particularly difficult and nerve-wracking. We never knew what to expect in the darkness. (Barrage balloons trailing 1,000 feet long steel cables were a Soviet favorite. The steel cables would saw into our aluminum wings—possibly causing us to crash.) Light was usually non-existent except for the "black" light on the aircraft instrument panel. This night in January 1949—our first encounter with the Aurora Borealis—was a new experience. The Aurora was low in the northern sky and widespread across the horizon. It hung in the sky like icicles but was irregular in size and shape. Adding to the eeriness of the Aurora was Saint Elmo's fire! Comparatively dim greenish yellow static electricity "played" along the top of the instrument panel and the outer edges of the windshield. Large halos of fire were formed in the arcs around the tips of the propeller blades. Fascinating! We saw the Aurora "fires" many times during the winter nights. Thankfully, they were harmless, but sometimes caused static electricity, together with minor shocks and noisy static in our radios.

THE BLUE LIGHT SPECIAL

Most of our landings and takeoffs on the Berlin Airlift were to the west. On this day, however, the GCA controllers had us landing to the east at the airfield (Tempelhof) in Berlin. This route placed us very low over a large rail yard just prior to touchdown. At the western edge of Tempelhof runway was a concrete wall about 8 feet high and 100 feet from the end of the runway. The top of this wall was the rail yard, about 100 yards wide to the west. Situated in the approximate center of the yard was a "farm style" blue light mounted on top of a 50-foot high telephone pole. I was the copilot on this trip. The pilot was my roommate and good friend Jack Thornton. Jack was a tall, lanky Texan (Denis, TX) and a superb pilot. As usual, the fog was thick and low. According to the rules, if we could not see the runway when we were down to 200 feet altitude, we were to abort the landing and return to our home base (Rhein Main). We

401

are now on the final approach to landing. We had already passed 200 feet—now down to about 100 feet and thinking of aborting the landing. Suddenly, from the dirty, gray "soup" came a quick glimpse of a bright blue light. I yelled to Jack, "Keep going, I know where we are!" Within seconds, the runway became visible straight in front of us. We were now down to less than 50 feet. We landed without incident and unloaded 10 tons of cargo (food, flour, coal, etc.) for Berlin. To my knowledge, we were the only aircraft to land in Berlin that day—all because of a blue light on top of a telephone pole. Also, I was recently informed that as of February 1999, the blue light is still there. Apparently it is there to provide light for the rail yard during darkness. On this day, it lighted our path into Tempelhof Airfield.

THE FOG UND SMOG CLUB

The 1807th Army Airways Communications Service (AACS) issued a 2.5 x 4 inch card for membership into the Fog Und Smoggers by use of the GCA controllers and was coveted by Berlin Airlift pilots. My tour of 125 missions on the airlift contained some 60-65 GCA landings. These were landings in heavy, dense fog which could *not* have been made without the ground controllers guiding us in by use of radar. The Berlin Airlift itself would have been impossible without the talent of the controllers and their radar—which was in its infancy! Yet, never once in all my GCA landings was I given erroneous guidance. On 12 January 1949, I was approaching Rhein Main on completion of a mission to Berlin. As usual, the clouds and fog were thick and dangerous. After the landing, I was awarded a card which read 400 feet, visibility 2.5 miles. These measurements were incorrect because regulations would have been broken otherwise. The actual numbers were ceiling 75 feet, visibility 1/16th mile (528 feet). Looking back today, I think they should have been ceiling 25-30 feet, visibility 100 feet. Even then, I could only see the runway by looking down, not ahead. Landing was without incident thanks to the GCA controllers. However, I had difficulty seeing where to taxi to the parking area. This one was great fun!

PLAYING IN THE SAND

The runways at Tempelhof Airfield were built for German ME-109 fighters. No one ever dreamed that one day they would have to bear the weight and impact of four engine aircraft of almost *35 tons*. It wasn't very long before the most used runway was pounded into rubble. Someone came up with the idea to cover the runway with *sand* while another was being built. The sand was available in large quantity from several large lakes around Berlin. The sand was trucked into the airfield and spread over the west runway to a depth of one foot. This made an excellent landing pad for a very soft touchdown which required almost no braking to stop the aircraft. It was generally necessary to apply power to get off the runway. Needless to say, the C-54s left deep ruts in the sand when landing. Solving this problem was a stroke of genius! Hundreds of Germans and displaced persons had made their way into the Allied zone (American) and could be utilized for labor. So, numerous persons were dispersed along both sides of the runway and provided with shovels, rakes or brooms. As soon as a landing aircraft passed by, they would swarm onto the runway and smooth out the ruts! They had to work swiftly because there was always another aircraft just about to touch down. Believe it or not, this worked quite well for some time. New runways were built in short order, and the Airlift wasn't even slowed down.

A HAIL OF A DEAL

On a flight out of Tempelhof to Rhein Main this particular day, we are in the western corridor toward Hamburg. As usual, high, thick clouds and bad visibility. We began running into rain which soon turned into hail—lots of hail. The noise of the hail striking the aircraft windshield was absolutely *deafening*, even with headsets tightly covering both ears. Airspeed was usually 170 mph, but because of the hail I slowed to 150 for about three minutes. (Interval today was 5 minutes because of weather.) Shortly, I began to break out of the weather and resumed 170 mph. At about the same time I spotted what appeared to be a British C-47, according to the markings on the fuselage. It seemed to me that something wasn't quite right with the aircraft. Suddenly, I realized that there was a *jet engine* exhaust nozzle protruding from the bottom of the fuselage! I overcame the C-47 fairly rapidly and got a good look when— whoosh—it pulled away from me in short order. The pilot also dropped down into the clouds and it was gone. To this day, I have no idea what that bird really was or what country it belonged to. My main concern now was what damage the hail might have done to the aircraft. Good fortune was ours, and in spite of extreme noise, there was no visible damage. It was the worst hail I have ever encountered.

Reflections on Tonopah Lights and Delights
by George A. Reynolds (458th)

Tonopah, Nevada, a small town near the California border, population 1600, was a training base for the 458th Bomb Group from about September 1943 to early January 1944. Based on clippings sent to me by historian Allen Metscher, it's apparent that the troops left this area—rich in history—to make some of their own with the Mighty Eighth thousands of miles away. A cartoon included in the clippings shows a milepost with distances to other places from the TAAF, and it tells quite a story in itself. It reads: Ely 176, Tonopah 7, Reno 240, Las Vegas 210, and Hell 0.

Perhaps the last minute reading alludes in part to Metschwer's research of the area since 1986. He has documented at least 26 crashes of B-24s and 110 deaths, and from the crash sites he still retrieves dog tags, engines, bombs, machine guns, gauges, wheels, and the like. He and other volunteers for the Central Nevada Museum have erected 12 markers at the crash sites, and they will complete work on the remainder as time allows. Surviving air crews labeled the base as decidedly jinxed!

There are, however, *some* pleasant memories relating to TAAF for those who served there, albeit living in tent cities while tussling with Army life at the time. Wong's cafe, featuring American/Chinese dishes, was a popular pit stop for the troops. Check these menu prices, with the trimmings: T-bone steak $1.50, sirloin $1.20, coffee or tea .10, chow mein $1.00, and chop suey .75.

The base opened in July, 1942, and pilots were training to fly the Bell P-39 Aircobra. But there were so many crashes that the fighter jocks moved out, and then came the Libs. It continued as a training field until closing in August '45. The airport still serves Tonopah-Goldfield, but little remains of TAAF.

The most prominent landmark in Tonopah was the five-story Mizpah Hotel. It's now 90 years old, and has hosted many celebrities over the years. Jack Dempsey was a barkeep and bouncer there before he found his niche in the boxing ring. Lawman-gunslinger Wyatt Earp stayed there quite regularly while chasing claim jumpers in nearby Goldfield. Howard Hughes married actress Jean Peters at the Mizpah. Kay Kyser, his band and gorgeous Georgia Carroll were guests while entertaining the TAAF troops. Finally, it is said that a lady of the evening was decapitated inside during the '40s and her ghost still haunts the facility.

The name Mizpah itself is rather intriguing. This Hebrew word, in an area known mostly for Indian folklore, was taken from the Bible's Old Testament in asking God to keep watch over travelers. Perhaps this is why Col. Valain R. Woodward chose it as a nickname for his B-24 when he left TAAF and joined the 458th at Horsham St. Faith. History confirms that it was a wise choice. Col. Woodward completed 25 missions, then was reassigned to HQ and eventually rotated to the States. Later he returned to the 458th and flew 35 more missions as C.O. of the 755th lead crew squadron until the war's end. "Mizpah," under the expert care of M/Sgt. John Miligan, completed 70 missions without ever failing to be ready when called upon, and then returned to the… ZI in June '45.

One of the local prodigies was Taxscine Ornclas, the owner of a bar frequented by TAAF airmen, and she became endeared to all of her customers. It was said that she never refused anyone in financial need and regularly collected small donations from the patrons in a "kitty" jug placed on the bar. These funds were used for various causes such as aiding the school in buying a badly needed bus, the cancer society, the Red Cross, et al. She also included the TAAF stockade, and the tenants said of "the Little Desert Mother," "If everyone had the kind of heart you do, this would be a different world to live in."

Taxscine died in 1954 at age 54 of a hemorrhage, but some say it was more likely a broken heart. A lady of the evening, her friend and a fixture in the bar, was murdered and the killer never apprehended. Authorities then closed Taxscine's bar and wouldn't allow it to reopen. She went into seclusion thereafter and died all alone.

Col. Woodward flew back to Tonopah in December '96. The flight was a birthday gift from his brother, and it would be interesting to have a recap of his memories after 50+ years. From several others who were stationed there, the comments are usually, "Most of us don't want to remember Tonopah—the cold, heat, isolation and wind. But there is one thing for sure—if you were there in 1943, you can't ever forget it!" The Central Nevada Historical Society is trying very hard to ensure that very thing. They continue to build their museum with artifacts from the war years as well as marking crash and historical sites, mostly with individuals' own time, efforts and funds... (Author's Note: In the late 1930s and early 40s, Lucky Strike cigarettes had an ad, LSMFT, translated as "Lucky Strike Means Fine Tobacco." Air crews about to be deployed to training bases had a different translation—"Lord, save me from Tonopah.")

Chivalry In Adversity
by General Andy Low

Graduates of Service Academies have, for more than one hundred and fifty years, worn finger rings to commemorate their alma mater. In earlier years, before the advent of a gummed envelope, these commemorative rings served the useful purpose of imprinting the sealing wax on letters—even serving as an exterior identifier of the author. Many collegians of other institutions did a similar rite of passage. However, many of these collegians owed a closer allegiance to Greek-letter fraternities to which they belonged. Often their rings reflected this latter allegiance.

Since 1897, rings of West Point have reflected on the motto "Duty, Honor, Country" and the Academy Crest on one side of the ring, and a class-adopted crest on the other. During the third year, great activity by each class member marks the arrival of class rings.

Because of the closeness of the Academy experience—living in barracks, meals in a common mess, formations for all phases of daily life—the class ring is a ready manifestation of this closeness. Most graduates wear their rings much of the time—and certainly at activities associated with the Academy experience.

And thus, I was one who wore my class ring most of the time. In combat, in Europe, in early 1944, we were required to wear our issue name plates ("dog tags") at all times, but were discouraged from carrying other identification which might be "of aid and/or comfort to the enemy."

On 31 July 1944, there was some confusion on the assignment from our Group for the Combat Air Commander. He would command the Second Combat Wing, and the Second Air Division, which the Wing would lead. As Group Operations Officer, I had been up all night during mission preparations, and thus was most familiar with targeting, routes, communications, and the myriad of detail to get over four hundred Liberator bombers to the target—Ludwigshaven, and the IG Farben Chemical Works. So, I took the assignment.

In a last minute rush, I changed into my flying gear and proceeded by jeep to Wing headquarters, some ten miles down the road.

Briefing, take-off, form-up, coast-out, tight formation— all went well until we began our bombing run. We were at 24,000 feet, the highest I had ever flown on an attack. We encountered heavy flak at our altitude, and took random hits with no personnel injuries up to "Bomb Doors Open." Just as the bombardier announced "Bombs Away" we took a burst just under our bomb-bay which set our hydraulic lines and reservoir on fire—a raging fire.

The crew fought the fire but warned we were in serious condition, with a chance of an explosion of the gasoline tanks above the bomb bay.

Quickly, the aircraft commander and I decided we had to leave the formation, dive to attempt to blow out the fire—and to clear the target area. I told the Deputy to take over the formation and we dove sharply in a sweeping arc away from the target.

The Flight Engineer in the bomb-bay reported that the structure was catching fire. We knew we had to jump, and the aircraft commander sounded the "Stand-by to bail" on the alarm, and "Jump" almost immediately.

We were three on the flight deck, the Pathfinder Navigator, the Aircraft Commander, and me. The Navigator attempted to open our normal egress through the bomb-bay. The fire was just too much of a blazing inferno. I had shed my harness, and stood up as he was re-closing the door. Over my head was a hatch used on the ground during taxiing, but was not an authorized egress in the air. It was forward of the top turret, and could be blocked by guns. It was forward of the propellers—but both number two and number three engines had been feathered. There were two vertical stabilizers on the B-24J, but we found out we had already lost one in the dive.

I bent down, grabbed the Navigator around his legs, and shoved him through the hatch. I followed quickly, and the Aircraft Commander was right behind me. We cleared the aircraft, pulled our ripcords—and the plane blew up.

I was alone as I floated out of the clouds close to the ground, and could see I was headed for farm land outside a village. As I neared the ground and prepared to land, I realized I was headed right at two military figures with rifles—and the longest fixed bayonets I had ever seen.

I touched down, collapsed my chute, and the German soldiers were not twenty yards from me, rifles at ready.

"Haben sie pistole?"

I did not understand what they said, but guessed. I shook my head and raised my arms, and then I realized I was really hurt. My flying suit was still smoldering. The Germans put down their guns and helped me beat out the embers. That done, they picked up their rifles, and began to search me. I was told to take off my watch by their motions. Then they emptied my pockets, found my dog tags but did not take them, and then helped me pull off my burned gloves.

And there it was—my West Point 1942 Class Ring. They motioned me to take it off, and it was dropped into a pack one soldier carried.

As they motioned me to march, I suddenly realized how scared I really was—and fearful of what was going to happen next.

We were taken to the village jail—all nine of us who made the jump. Two crewmen in the rear of the aircraft did not get out. We had all been quickly rounded up by the militia-type soldiers who had been turned out to look for downed men.

From the civilian jail, we were taken to a German Air Force airfield. We were given some medical treatment, wrapped with paper bandages, and readied for a trip to the Interrogation Center.

At the Interrogation Center, I was put in a plain, small solitary cell. I had told them my name, my rank and my serial number. I was bandaged so that I had to have someone feed me, and help with trips to the personal facilities.

My first session with the Interrogator was brief. I repeated my name, my rank, and my serial number. He called me major, but said he needed to know more. As he remarked, they did not give medical treatment to spies. I hurt terribly, and was not sure what was happening under the bandages. But, I had endured West Point, and I knew they weren't going to be any tougher.

The second morning was a repeat, giving only name, rank, and serial number, and back I was sent to my cell. Still hurting.

As I thought over my situation, and what was happening to the others whom I had not seen, I realized I had been riding with a 458th Bomb Group aircrew, transferred to the 389th as a lead crew. The aircraft wreckage would have 389th insignia. I deduced therefore they were not too sure who I was.

The third day session was another repeat. But the interrogator said I was foolish, as they would find me out. No medical treatment until they did. Back to my cell.

It was a warm August evening, but from my cell I could see nothing, and hear very little. Time dragged.

Suddenly, the guard was opening my cell, and in came a German flying officer. His left arm was mangled, and heavily bandaged. The guard locked him in, and went away.

In excellent English, with a British accent, he asked if I wanted a cigarette. I told him I did not smoke, so that ended that entrée. I really hurt and the bandage reeked, so I was angry enough to be rude.

He asked if I would like something to read—*Life*, maybe. I replied I could not handle a book with my bandages.

He said he was sorry for me as an airplane pilot, for me the war was over. But he added he would never fly again either. We warmed to each other—a little.

He asked about my family.

I told him I had a daughter I had never seen. He told me about his family. There was more small talk, and then he arose to leave. He walked to the door, and then came back to me. His good hand was in his pocket. He pulled it out and dropped my Class Ring inside my clothes.

Simply he said, "I am sure this means something to you, and it means nothing to them. Hide it, and do not wear it until you are free!"

With that, he turned quickly and left me alone—with my thoughts.

Can there be such chivalry among such obvious adversity? For me, there was.

How Did My Brother Die?

The story begins in England, on the misty morning of Wednesday, September 27, 1944. The 8th U.S. Army Air Force left its bases for targets in central Germany. Copilot Newell Brainard's 445th Bomb Group was assigned to the Henschel locomotive factory in Kassel, which was believed to be building tanks and cannons.

At the point where the groups split into separate bombing runs, amid cloudy skies and poor visibility, the leader of the 445th deviated 30 degrees from his route.

"That Mickey man (the radar navigator) in the lead ship has screwed up," one navigator said over his intercom. "We shouldn't have turned yet."

In moments, the planes were separated from the other bombers—and their protective fighter escorts.

The bombers of the 445th mistakenly flew to the town of Goettingen and dropped their bombs with no casualties or significant damage. Then the lumbering, vulnerable bombers followed the planned route back—50 miles behind the other planes, which had made a successful raid on Kassel. Veterans say the leader may have actually thought he was still on course and had bombed Kassel.

"It was a complete fiasco," recalls battle veteran George M. Collar.

The Germans, pursuing the main convoy, launched ME-109 Messerschmidtt fighter planes—designed to distract American fighters—and slower, more deadly Focke Wulf 190 storm fighters especially built to pick off bombers.

About 45 miles southeast of Kassel, the 150 German fighters instead came upon the lagging 445th. Within three minutes 25 American bombers were spiraling down in flames. Five more later crashed trying to get home or returned so

410

damaged that they were declared total losses. It was the greatest loss of bombers for any individual group of the 8th Air Force.

During the battle, gunners aboard the bombers and several late-arriving American P-51 fighters managed to down 29 German fighters.

From their B-24, nicknamed "Patches," Newell Brainard and his pilot, Lt. Raphael Carrow, saw the plane in front of them burst into flames. Newell pounded on Carrow's arm—an engine was afire and Germans were bearing down. "Patches" tail assembly had been all but destroyed. A fire spread and the crew was bailing out.

"Brainard was trying to get out, (but) the bomb bay was a roaring inferno," Carrow later wrote a companion. Carrow finally made it to the bomb bay but found only blue sky—the plane had split in two. He had no choice but to leap into the abyss.

Carrow, one of 121 Americans taken as prisoners of war, knew when he bailed out that Newell Brainard was no longer in the plane. But he never learned his copilot's fate. He believed, as did most, that Newell was one of the 118 Americans killed that day as their planes fell in a 20 mile circle around the small town of Bad Hersfeld.

On the ground, a 12-year old boy watched in awe as the explosions formed black clouds in the sky and airmen parachuted to earth. His name was Walter Hassenpflug.

Back in West Palm Beach, Florida, the Brainard family learned that Newell was missing in action.

In November 1944, Kay (who had been secretary to the commander at The Breakers hotel, which had been converted to Ream military hospital) joined the American Red Cross and went to Europe. But there was no further word about her brother.

In September 1945, after he had been missing one year, the army declared Newell Brainard KIA—"killed in action." The family never held a memorial ceremony.

A September 1947 report identifies Newell. He had been buried in March 1946 at the American military cemetery at St. Avold, France, as un-known soldier X-1535. The military used dental records, physical characteristics, and the name "Brainard" found on a wool undershirt on the body to identify him.

It wasn't until April of 1948 that the American military told the family of the identification. They gave no indication that the cause of death was any different from that given earlier—shot down over Germany.

Newell's mother opted to have him remain buried with his comrades.

In later years, Kay became an assistant to actor and part-time Palm Beach resident Douglas Fairbanks, Jr. In the early 1980s, she was a volunteer historian for the 8th Air Force. That led her to Walter Hassenpflug.

The day of the Kassel raid, Hassenpflug and fellow members of the Bad Hersfeld Hitler Youth had scattered into adjoining fields, gathering and burning leaflets and ration cards dropped by the American planes.

Two months later, during an American raid a bomb struck his house, killing his parents.

The drama of the Kassel battle intrigued him in later years, especially when veterans from both sides began visiting the area. He began gathering everything he could about it—interviewing townspeople and contacting veterans groups and archives from both countries. His efforts intensified in the 1980s with the launching of a project to build a battle memorial.

In April of 1987, Kay Hutchins got a letter from Kassel veteran George Collar, who had seen in a newsletter a note from her asking for details of her brother's death.

Collar attached a copy of the March 1987 letter to him from Walter Hassenpflug in Germany. Kay saw her brother's name.

"It is possible that he landed with his chute near the village of Nentershausen and was one of the five airmen who were shot to death there," Hassenpflug wrote.

"I was horrified," Kay says now. "I owed it to myself to find out."

In March of 1990, Kay was in New York working with Fairbanks. She decided to board a train for the National Archives center near Washington. After spending an entire day in the 8th Air Force files, she was unable to find the report about the Kassel mission. A researcher told her it had been missing since 1970.

As a dejected Kay prepared to leave, the researcher stopped her. He told her that what she really wanted was her brother's burial file. He would find it and send her copies. About a month later, 129 pages arrived.

"Nobody had ever looked past the first page of his file," she says now. "It wasn't until I reached page 80 that the story began to gel."

The September 17, 1947 burial report—the one that identified Newell Brainard as the body that had been discovered in a mass grave—was a poor copy, but one word on it could be clearly read: "Murdered."

For the Germans, nothing inspired more hate, or glee at the opportunity for vengeance, than a loving, downed American airman.

With American GIs fighting Germans far off at the front, it was the U.S. bombers alone who the Germans saw destroying their factories and towns. And it was the airmen alone whom people could punish when they fell from the sky. But the first Germans to encounter Newell Brainard presented only compassion. They found him lying amid his parachute in a field, suffering a head wound, and they took him to a nearby village, where a Red Cross nurse treated him.

In the next town, the German government ran an *ostarbeitslager*—a labor camp where citizens of eastern European countries were forced to mine copper. Its commanders—under orders to pick up any downed American airmen and hold them for military authorities—quickly learned that some had been captured nearby.

"They were supposed to detain them," says Gunter Lemke, Hassenpflug's interpreter and associate on much of the Kassel battle research. "They took it on their own to murder these people."

One pilot was shot in town; the other four, including Newell, were taken to the labor camp. There, the fliers were interrogated and beaten. Finally, they were led outside and shot with pistols. All five were thrown into a single grave in the town cemetery.

Even as the atrocities were taking place, the labor camp's days were numbered. That week the Russians were in the Baltics, Bulgaria and Yugoslavia; the Allies were marching through the Netherlands. Within months, the war was over, the German Reich destroyed.

Soon after setting up an occupation force, Americans began asking residents about any downed airmen. The townspeople led them to the grave. A February 28, 1945 report on Newell's as-yet-unidentified body said he had been clubbed, then shot. According to reports, the remains had been found in a mattress cover in a box, two bullet holes in his head.

Residents identified suspects. Seven were rounded up; an eighth had committed suicide on the last day of the war.

The Americans set up a war crimes trial that began in June, 1947, in the town of Dachau, site of the infamous concentration camp. The military court ruled that all but one of the seven defendants were eager principals in the beatings or killings and not merely curious bystanders, as each of the accused contended he was.

Three were hanged, one was sentenced to death but had already been hanged for another crime, and the other three were given jail terms.

The camp commanders would have shared all Germans' hatred for airmen, and most were put in such jobs specifically because they were fanatics and were especially cruel, say Hassenpflug and Lemke. But it would be pure speculation to try to place a firm motive on the slayings, the two say.

Kay Hutchins says her brother's murderers were "just mean, I think."

Newell Brainard's mother died in 1957, never knowing how her son really died. There's no way to know after all these years why or how the military never told Brainard's family the circumstances of his death, says Doug Howard, mortuary programs specialist for the U.S. Army. Howard notes that the military did not have the communications setup it does now, but says it would be pure speculation to blame the omission on bureaucracy. There's no evidence that the military had a policy of withholding such details from families, he says.

Kay Hutchins knows her brother's killers paid for their crimes. She also knows that atrocities were committed on both sides: An American soldier admitted to her that he machine-gunned five German prisoners because one called him a swine.

On August 1, 1990, Kay and nearly 80 other Americans traveled to a site deep in the Hesse State Forest in central Germany. On three granite stones, markers detailed the battle of Kassel and listed the 25 German and 118 American airmen who died.

Five hundred Germans joined the Americans for a solemn ceremony. A German Air Force trumpeter played taps. Former enemies shook hands. Prayers were offered.

Kay Hutchins finally met Walter Hassenpflug. Through an interpreter, the two shared the stories of how each had lost loved ones to the war.

The following day, as church bells tolled, Kay Hutchins would see where her brother's plane crashed, where he parachuted down, and the house where a Red Cross nurse had performed an act of mercy later fouled by an act of evil.

But for a moment, there in front of the stark stones, she reached out to touch the brass plate and run her finger over her brother's name.

Editor's Note: The preceding article, slightly condensed here, originally appeared in The Palm Beach Post on May 31, 1992, written by Post Staff Writer Eliot Kleinberg. George Collar, referred to in the article, was a bombardier on the crew of James Schaen, whose B-24 was also shot down. Collar became a POW, but before he was taken away, Collar was forced to collect all the American dead and wounded in the area. (His story appeared in the Spring 1995 issue of the Journal, page 21).

Of the nine men who were on the crew of Raphael Carrow, five perished either on the plane or upon capture, including the murdered copilot Newell Brainard. Four survived the capture and the war. Since then, all but Carrow have died.

Aside from Newell Brainard, the four additional 445th airmen murdered on that fateful day were John Donahue, of Oliver Elder's crew, and John Cowgill, Hector Scala and James Fields, all of James Baynhams's crew.

Taps—Do You Know the Whole Story?
Reprinted from The Santa Ana Cadet, Costa Mesa Historical Society

It all began in 1862 during the Civil War, when Union Army Captain Robert Ellicombe was with his men near Harrison's Landing in Virginia. The Confederate Army was on the other side of the narrow strip of land. During the night, Captain Ellicombe heard the moans of a soldier who lay mortally wounded on the field. Not knowing if it was a Union or Confederate soldier, the Captain decided to risk his life and bring the stricken man back for medical attention.

Crawling on his stomach through the gunfire, the Captain reached the stricken soldier and began pulling him toward his encampment. When the Captain finally reached his own lines, he discovered it was actually a Confederate soldier but the soldier was dead.

The Captain lit a lantern and suddenly caught his breath and went numb with shock. In the dim light, he saw the face of the soldier. It was his own son. The boy had been studying music in the South when the war broke out. Without telling his father, he enlisted in the Confederate Army.

The following morning, heartbroken, the father asked permission of his superiors to give his son a full military burial despite his enemy status. His request was only partially granted. The Captain had asked if he could have a group of Army band members play a funeral dirge for his son at the funeral. The request was turned down since the soldier was a Confederate but out of respect for the father, they did say they could give him one musician.

The Captain chose a bugler. He asked the bugler to play a series of musical notes he had found on a piece of paper in the pocket of the dead youth's uniform. This wish was granted. The haunting melody we now know as "Taps" used at military funerals was born.

Auf Wiedersehen
by Ken "Deacon" Jones (389th)

Letter orders of the 389th Bombardment Group (H) set up the first Trolley Mission the group flew on 3 May 1945.

These tours were a belated recognition of the vital and invaluable services provided by ground support personnel in bringing the war to a successful conclusion.

The pre-dawn briefing held that morning revealed this first aerial tour of war-torn Germany would get to land on the German border at Y-55, an advance base at Venlo, Holland. Army trucks would transport visitors to the heavily bombed cities of Cologne and Dusseldorf for walking tours.

The sightseeing bombers would fly individually. We were one minimum flight crew of four, with 16 ground support people as passengers. Nazi fanatics were still active. We were issued helmets, firearms, K-rations, canteens and two blankets. The .45 cal. pistol in a shoulder holster was the deodorant prescribed by the Army Air Force for some of us and others had carbines.

The weather set the overall mood for this special flight—cold, dreary, and bleak.

I noted that although the war was not officially over, the 8th A.F. ran out of targets in April. The Allied ground forces were busy rounding up the last remnants of the Wehrmacht armies in now mostly occupied Germany.

No one could have adequately prepared us for the big picture we were going to see—the massive destruction of aerial bombing and hundreds of thousands of German prisoners behind barbed wire fences without shelter of any kind.

The sameness of the scenery of sunken barges, collapsed bridges, including the Ludendorf Bridge at Remagen, the shredded devastation of a torn landscape littered with burned-out military vehicles and the shocking view of leveled cities became monotonous as we became immune to the savagery of war. You knew what the next town would look like before you came to it.

Going south, we passed over Duren, Germany on the way out. Another pulverized town. No roofs or ceilings intact; only jagged walls. We left behind the ruin that was Germany and turned west to Liege, Belgium and the coast. A silence came over the occupants of a front line military bomber called "The Liberator."

The feeling of a door closing behind you came as the coastal city of Ostende went astern for the last time. We pointed the nose across the Channel for England, flying smoothly under a low ceiling and leaden skies, into dim light and home. We landed at Hethel, in the quiet of the evening, at 18:00 hours.

Chapter 12: Me Again

Biography 1945-2008

Gonzaga U., operated by the Jesuits, was indeed a serious place of learning. For me it opened up new ideas but also filled in and explained things that were in my mind but not settled. The class I remember with the greatest clarity was one in sociology, taught by a mister (priest in training), John Leary— This guy was brilliant. I was so impressed that I said to myself that if I ever got married, he was the one to officiate at my wedding. Well, he did, also became the university's president, and in addition, was the founder of two other colleges, one each in San Francisco and Reno. Like many my age, he's no longer with us.

I attended Gonzaga for two years, and my classification was pre-law. A terrible choice as time proved, but I didn't have much if any guidance or idea of what I wanted to do other than become better educated. I applied for law school at Stanford and was accepted. It was such a nice campus, I worked so hard, but in the end of two quarters it was apparent to me that law was not my bag. The assistant dean, Professor Thurman, re-read my Torts exam and said that while I did not explain in the depth I should have, I understood the concepts and should continue in law school. Truthfully, what they were talking about in Private Property was a mystery, and while I might have been able to get a C in Contracts, it would have taken a lot of work. Many of the law students had degrees from the likes of Yale and Harvard, and they were better prepared for law school than I, and it was a good decision to leave the suing to them. However, I was determined to get a Stanford degree, and switched to economics.

After law, it was quite simple. In order to get a degree in two quarters, it required taking something like 23 hours, but with one exception I got A grades. I had two very good professors - Shaw, in Money and Banking, and Anatol Mazur, Russian History.

Upon finishing my fourth quarter at Stanford, I had enough credits for a B.A. This, with only 2 years at Gonzaga, a pretty much blown first two quarters at Stanford which brought in something like only 3 or 4 hours. Because I had received some credit for my training in the service, particularly in math and science (physics of flying), I did not have one single college credit in either of those two essential areas. I may be the only recipient of a BA from a quality institution without credits in either of these. I completed what was necessary to get a Stanford degree the fall quarter of 1948, but am listed as a graduate of the class of 1949. I never seriously considered getting an MBA because the GI Bill did not cover enough of my expenses, and I felt I should be able to make a living with an undergraduate degree. So I returned to Spokane, after turning down a Stanford generated job with the Chamber of Commerce in Yreka, CA, and not being hired by Thompson Aircraft Tire Company, in Oakland.

I am now 29 years of age as of Jan. 5, 1949, with no clear idea of what to do or where I am going. I did not have an urge to get married, although I must admit that I truly loved the opposite sex. My parents must have thought good heavens, we're going to have him on our necks again. Mostly, I had been gone from home since I was 18. 29 is too old to move back with the folks. But I did, but now, thinking like a parent faced with this situation, I realize that maturity doesn't necessarily come in with sufficient force just because one has lived for three decades. I have to give my wonderful parents credit for graciously accepting a fact which was not entirely to their liking, I suspect.

I went to work for the local chapter of the American Auto Association, the Inland Auto Association. I was a salesman, selling club memberships which offered maps and trip information, emergency road service, a bit of accident insurance, etc. Additionally, we sold auto insurance. We worked totally on commission, and for someone who was willing to work, perfect. Salaries make you beholden to the salary giver. Working for commission means that you set your income by your willingness to work and your intelligence. In relatively short order, I became the leading salesman of the 30 or so such employed. I went to the office early, prepared for the calls I would make, and worked several hours. Then I would take time off to begin a game which is addictive, enjoyable, and has a measure of class when played by the rules. It is golf. I met a lot of people out beating the bushes to sell memberships and insurance, and one was a Pat

Clarke. He introduced me to the game at Downriver golf course in Spokane. My first set of clubs was purchased from Al Mengert, a local pro. Pat and I played with the Funseth brothers. Rod became a successful PGA tour player—not a great name on the tour, but, because he was such an unbelievably nice guy, fondly remembered by his peers. He died from cancer in his early 50s. A really great loss. The first tee at Downriver has a commemorative plaque dedicated to this fine man.

I am content to make a good living, to enjoy life, which meant good food and good booze and lovely females. I wasn't preparing for anything in particular other than enjoying life. This didn't change in any material way when I was recalled during the Korean conflict. I had maintained my commission by signing up for the reserves. I was assigned as Operations Officer to a filter center in Billings, Montana. It was as far as I could tell a psychological attempt to get the populace worked up about the Russian threat to bomb the U.S. We were pretty paranoid about Communism in the 50s and subsequently for at least two more decades. We were to enlist civilians who would serve in lookout posts over a quite extensive geographic area. Their duty was to report by phone to a central location, called a filter center. Here, other civilians would plot the intruders on a large location board and report to the military for defensive action. It was a pleasant assignment in a nice town, I got to travel over much of eastern. Montana. I requested release after seventeen months, resigned my commission, and became a civilian again... There are two items I'd like to mention. First, I was assigned to serve as an instructor at Tyndall Air Force Base in Panama City, Florida. I drove there in my red Chrysler convertible, and traveled the area. I particularly enjoyed going down the Gulf Coast for Apalachicola oysters, and boat trips in the Gulf. Second, I met a girl who was from Panama. I believe her father was in the diplomatic corps. She had lost her mother and was living with her aunt's family. I met her at a young person's club because I could do a couple of Latin dances and she became my No. 1 girl friend in Billings. She gave me two books, inscribed with the comment they were given to me because they were her prized possessions. In later life, I have made three professional attempts to locate her, to no avail. So if you know of a Kathleen Carroll Donaldson, who married a Dr. Charles Donaldson Chapman, in

Montreal in 1953 or 1954, I'd very much appreciate the opportunity to return the books and say hello to this great girl.

I am now 33 years of age and it was time to be serious about a career. I was interested in the stock market. I had no social standing in the relatively small city of Spokane and realized San Francisco would be a better location. I lived in a guest house, along with a couple dozen other young people, and found a job with an investment manager who had a branch office in San Francisco. However, the home office was in Portland, and I was offered the job as administrative assistant to the founder and president, which I accepted. I enjoyed the Portland area, and rented a small cabin at pleasant Lake Oswego as one of my residences in my two and half years in Portland. And it produced the best and most momentous thing in my life—I met and married Ann Boe, a teacher at a Portland school, a one room schooler like me, who grew up in the country of eastern Colorado, and I in the sparsely settled area of northeastern Montana... I had returned from a skiing trip at Sun Valley, and a girl I knew went the following week. I contacted her by phone upon her return, and Ann happened to be at the same location. She reports that she heard my voice and was interested in meeting this guy. And voila, we were on the phone together. I suggested my friend and I come to the apartment she shared with another girl for a game of bridge. I am over 6', and my friend Jim Smith a couple of inches taller. Ann reports "what have I done?" But Jim and I are harmless. I first asked her room mate for a date, but no spark, and we started dating in April. I had liked girls before, but this was different. We were engaged in May, and married in June. All in 1956. Hearing this bit of history, our children were shocked. As I write this, we are 52 years married. It's great to have a wife who is your very best friend. And she pays me what I consider a great compliment when she tells someone we have been married so many years, and "I've never been bored".

Well, marriage was great. We rented a cabin at a lake some 35 miles out of Spokane, Loon Lake. I learned to water ski on one ski. We were friendly with the neighbors, and went to country dances. To backtrack, we went to Vancouver Island for our honeymoon, and returned with our family for our 50th, in 2006. Vancouver Island has the nicest people, great scenery, and the famous Empress Hotel, where we stayed on our honeymoon before heading north to see more of this interesting island… However, I was not happy or successful at the Spokane office of my employer. I had been too much of an insider and recognized the shortcomings in their investment philosophy. They had begun to rely, by necessity, on professional analysts such as my friend Jim Smith, but the founder was a strong headed person who wouldn't hesitate to put his ideas in a preferential position. So I knew it was time to make a big jump. Ann and I saved our money. She was teaching. However, Spokane was a small town and Ann did not particularly like it. And I knew I had to get to a bigger place for a securities career.

When Ann finished the school year teaching in Spokane, we took off for San Francisco. Object—she to get a teaching job, so we could survive until I found something. The first day in the Bay Area I took Ann to the East Bay, next day, the Peninsula, and I was saving what I considered the best for last, Marin. She agreed. She got a position teaching in Mill Valley at the Strawberry Point elementary. Now we did just a bit more sight seeing, getting down a bit into Baja. I resigned my position in Spokane, and we took off in our new 1957 black Ford station wagon. We had saved enough money to pay cash for it. It was our bed, our kitchen, and our traveling vehicle for something like six weeks. We went thousands of miles and visited something like 36 states and several Canadian provinces. We were on a tight budget but stayed in a motel about every third night so we could bathe. We visited the Ford manufacturing plant in Detroit and saw station wagons just like ours coming off the assembly line. We parked in Chicago overnight and the most intensive rain and lightning storm I've encountered was very scary. I only hoped we were on high ground so that we wouldn't be flooded. Although lightning is beautiful and dramatic it frightens me but I do have a bit more secure feeling in an auto. We visited Niagra Falls, Montreal, Toronto, Quebec, Trois Riviers, New England, Manhattan, etc..We even stopped off at my one room school house in McElroy, MT. Near the end we were getting pretty tired of traveling, and we visited Ann's parents, me for the first time, in Otis, Colorado. They had not been able to attend our wedding. Her father, Louis, and I had a pleasant and easy relationship. Unfortunately, her mother died an untimely death some few years after our marriage. We visited my folks in Spokane, and

Ann's in Otis, almost on a yearly basis when our children were young.

Back to Spokane to pack our belongings and start a new life. We had an Oldsmobile coupe. Ann drove it, and I pulled a trailer with the station wagon. Ann had not had too much experience driving and it was trying for her. The first night we stopped at a campground in Bend, Oregon. While I was preparing our dinner, Ann was so tired she went to sleep. The next day we got as far as Castle Crags, California, through a windy road that today is freeway. Again, we camped. We arrived in Mill Valley and rented an apartment on Miller Avenue.

I began applying for a stockbroker job in San Francisco. In that I had a college education and selling experience, I had my pick. The best known local firm that was a member of the New York Stock Exchange—anything less was really not desirable— was Schwabacher & Company. It had a good San Francisco reputation with a prominent family name. The training was almost nil. We were given information to study, and I passed the necessary test to enable me to inflict my lack of knowledge on clients. But it was a good market, and one could learn a lot in a short time. I was a hard worker, and would "cold turkey" business owners in the area. At that time the current Golden Gateway and Rockefeller buildings were pretty much a produce area of low buildings. It did not take long to get off the meager salary and get on commission. This was fun. I opened hundreds of accounts, and became one of the better producers. Good enough that when there was stock available upon a merger with another firm, Blair & Co., I was one of four who was offered this "opportunity." Also, when we got a new manager, Dave Brazil, I was offered the job of assistant manager. He was a very good manager, concerned with helping his account executives. I asked him what he wanted as a detailed description of my duties, and he told me to write it up. I did. He didn't change a word. We understood each other... Later, becoming qualified in a managerial license with the NYSE stood me in very good stead. But I'm ahead in my story.

Ann taught in Strawberry that first year. Marin was, and is, a pleasant place. But the inevitable happened, and we were to become parents. We found a little house in Strawberry. Over the fourth of July weekend I repainted the entire inside of the house. It only had two bedrooms, and was pretty old. It did have a little view of San Francisco. At that time I suppose it was worth $10,000. Last I heard, several hundred thousand!... Our son Clark was born July 11. If there's a greater thrill than your first born, I don't know what it is.

We were friendly with the other Schwabacher brokers who lived in the area. We would drink and barbecue together. And at lunch time I shamefully admit that I would have two or three martinis, and shake bull dice. What a waste of time. Obviously, I had some distance to go in the maturity department. We found a place in Corte Madera, called Marin Estates. They were new 4 bedroom tract houses, and we purchased one for $19,500. Our payments, including principal, taxes, and interest, were something like $150 per month. The down payment was very small. It was a GI loan, reasonable. And shortly after we moved in, our second son, Kent, was born, December 27, 1958. If it were possible to return to a previous time of one's life, I believe I would choose this time. I was making decent money, we had our own home and the beginnings of a fine family. I didn't fully realize the demands on a wife, which only became greater as our family grew.

Clark and Kent were born just 17 months apart. Pretty close. And we didn't even think of superman (Clark Kent) when we were doing the name choosing. And then there were Kent cigarettes too. But because my name of Ralph was clumsy when connected to my last name, we made sure to name our children without that drawback. And after a hiatus of some 4-1/2 years, our son Brian was born, May 1, 1964. Another joy. Ann's letters to her parents, saved by them and in our possession, tell of the activities of these guys.

A digression—I have been diagnosed as having cancer of the colon and am slated to have 40% of it removed on November 19, 1997, which is less than two weeks hence. Naturally one hopes and believes in the best, but if not, I want to get on with this anthology... (The best happened.)

I thoroughly enjoyed my time as a Schwabacher stockbroker as long as the market was positive and I could make

424

people money. But when it goes the other way, and you are pressed to continue to make a living, which means generating commissions, sometimes a bit of rationalization is necessary. I like to generate sayings, and mine to explain this is "I don't have enough larceny in my heart to be a successful stockbroker through bad markets."

Schwabacher had by far the biggest stock board in town. Two marker girls would enter stock sales prices with chalk. In those days, the prices could easily be 15 or more minutes old. But it was a way to show the prices of a lot of stocks, I would guess three or four hundred. In the trading section where I was there would always be a crowd of onlookers. In addition to the board, there was the tape. I never was much of a tape watcher as some of the brokers were... In the back section were the "investment" brokers. Basically, they did the same thing we did, except that they could not see the NY and American trades on tape. We also used the Dow Jones news ticker, which hammered away all day with business news and stock information.

There were any number of characters at Schwabacher. These were older days in the business, and when I started out we were expected to wear a hat. I will mention several sad incidents. One of our brokers was a pleasant, quiet fellow, well liked. One day while commuting to SF on the train, he either fell or jumped off and was killed. It then came out that he had not paid his income taxes for a number of years. I have to hand it to him, because it couldn't be proven that it was a suicide so his family collected his life insurance... Another fellow, a corporate finance guy, jumped from an 18 story hotel while on a business trip. An unbelievably handsome fellow, who was our sales manager for a time, put a pistol to his mouth and pulled the trigger... Another married a semi-socialite and it was said he had other girl friends, but died at a young age of a heart attack. Quite a few were wealthy socialites who had their own clique... And equally interesting were the clients. In that I had, over the course of my stock career, several thousand different clients, there were all kinds. People are interesting, and fun.

After I had been with Schwabacher about a dozen years I could see that they were making serious mistakes. I believed that they could become bankrupt. An English fellow, Reg Kennedy, a partner in a Los Angeles based NYSE member firm, used to drop into my little cubicle and pitch me in joining his firm. I did not consider making a lateral move, or in this case, a downside move from assistant manager to plain old broker again. But the managership opened up as I was searching my way out of what I considered a losing situation—even with my investment in the firm. I became manager of Morgan, Olmstead, Kennedy & Gardner's San Francisco office. And Schwabacher/Blair did not survive as an entity.

Here again I must retract a bit. While we were living at 26 Sonora Way in Corte Madera an innovative school was built. No longer were students stuck in one classroom with one teacher. The physical layout was changed at Granada School. Clark and Kent were attending, and Ann and I were involved in various activities with the school and parent groups. We were invited to a gathering ostensibly to pass judgment on the purchase of some video equipment. I noted a couple of strangers when we arrived at the complex. Then coffee was served, and I was asked my opinion of it. My wife points out that, to be gallant to the lady, exclaimed its virtues in my strong voice. When leaving that evening we were told by the strangers that this was a surprised Sanka coffee taping, and that if they used our comments we would be paid $1, and who was I. I suggested that they knew me at school, and left it at that. However, I was sent a release to sign by Young & Ribicam, a national advertising agency, as to my comments. I signed, and shortly thereafter a couple of 30 seconds spots and another for a minute, with my comments, were shown on television. To make a long story short, I would come home and here would be several hundred dollars in pink colored checks from Y & R as residuals.

And Ann got into the act, remembering that she had said one word in response. Actually, she said that one word twice, but it was worth something like $1,000. Our joint take totaled something like $12,000. All because of a resonant, loud voice. So we bought a half acre on a hillside in Tiburon. It had a marvelous view of San Francisco, Angel Island, Alcatraz, the Golden Gate Bridge, and the first couple of sections of the Bay Bridge. In addition it had a stream running through the middle of the property that ran about 6 months of the year as drainage from the west side of Mount Tiburon. And when it rained, it was a torrent. We thought the architect, Jim Leverson, would build the garage on one side of this creek and the house on the other. But he did the even more dramatic, and built the house over the creek, in sort of two sections, with a connecting inside bridge. It's there, at 270 Round Hill Road. We had purchased the lot from Jim Smith, and he was our building contractor. A lad from Nebraska whose family moved to Bonners Ferry, Idaho area, and as good a building contractor as has been born… Anyway, we built a 4,100 square foot house with a detached garage and a San Francisco view as you go to press the doorbell. Again, we moved in just days before another stupendous event in our lives, the birth of our one and only daughter, Lynn, on August 13, 1969. Mommy and I cried when she was born, we were so happy. And like the three before, she was born in Marin General Hospital. All within probably 100 feet of each other… These were the days when you chose your doctor and paid for what you needed when you needed it. We were fortunate. Ann's obstetrician for our children was Dr. Guthrie, who died from hand cancer at a young age. Pediatrician, Dr. Manson. My doctor died from a heart attack when putting on snow chains while on a trip to Tahoe. Here were three fine men who we were intimately connected with our family needs, and two died at an early age.

My dad had died in 1964, just a couple of months before our son Brian was born. My mother would spend the winters with us, a great help for Ann with the children. She had left Spokane a year or so after my fathers' death and moved in with my sister Florence, who had purchased a home in Seattle. Another reason why I always feel indebted to my older sister.

Here I am, manager of a branch office of a brokerage firm. I had a moderate salary, and with the limited amount of commission I generated, afforded a decent living. I was a stockholder. I worked at hiring new brokers. Morgan Olmstead Kennedy & Gardner paid high commissions on unlisted issues, and had a number of big producers. I was able to bring in a number of registered reps, but most of them were, well, marginal. Kennedy was the only big producer in our office. He had institutional clients in Britain, and would visit them a couple of times a year. When their analysts and execs would visit the U.S. and Reg was in England, I was the one who would take them down to Pebble Beach to lunch. It was not a bad life. Although I was branch manager, Kennedy's name was on the door and he was actually the real boss. I had to work with the men and the clerks and secretaries. I enjoyed it for the first few years. I had extra time, and secretarial help. I had always been interested in business owners, and had made them a cornerstone of my stock business. Successful business owners had two great qualities—they had money, they understood risk and reward... I started to contact likely businesses regarding their interest in selling. I spun a lot of wheels, became totally immersed in the activity, but the results on any continuous basis were slow in coming. It was suggested I devote more time to selling stocks and less to merger activity, but it fell on deaf ears. I loved what I was doing. So it cost me the managership, I really didn't care. I had some smaller successes while still at MOKG. My first closed deal of any consequence was the sale of a sanitary engineering firm, Stevens, Thompson and Runyon in Corvallis, Oregon to an architectural firm in Houston, CRS Design Associates. The fee earned was $68,000, which was split with the firm. It was pleasant working with these two factual professional organizations... After that, a few small situations that paid little, but I was happy and learning. But it was the only one of any size, thus the managership loss. I wasn't about to spend full time selling stocks, I was now a finder/intermediary in the sale of profitable companies.

What had happened is that inflation had hit. I was still making almost $40,000 a year, which had been comfortable. But we had a family of four children, and the area we lived had become pretty upscale. Our neighbors had not only a swimming pool, but could afford to spend a few hundred thousand to build a tennis court in this rocky hillside area, and in our adjoining neighbor, a separate cottage overlooking the court. Our big house was a burden for Ann, our yard demanding in the time it took to maintain, and we with no housekeeper or gardener as others in the area. Our two oldest were gone. It was time to sell. The Iranians were buying in the area, and we sold for $335,000, which offered a very good profit from the approximately $75,000 cost. Our lot had cost $14,500, but the area's appreciation had brought this up to the $200,000 area. By 1990 it had reached $750,000. Our home sold in the early 90s for over $900,000. (Now, in 2008, the owner says it would sell for approximately $2 million.) However, it was the liberator which got us into our business, which ultimately became a totally satisfying and profitable venture—thanks to one Ann Welsh.

The next period, when I am not employed, have the proceeds from the sale of our Tiburon home, and need to make decisions of where we are going, was, in retrospect, and probably then, a frustrating time. First on the agenda was our desire to purchase a business which would make us a living. I wrote to business brokers, no good leads. I wrote to manufacturers' reps, figuring that a couple about ready to retire would welcome some help and payment. We were prepared to pay at least $75,000 down on a business, and a total purchase price of something like $250,000 to $300,000. We looked at a lot of businesses for sale! We did not want retail and the necessity to work with the sometimes disagreeable general public. We looked at a bottler of Dr. Brown's sodas, a favorite in Brooklyn. However, while it was a profitable company, the owner had built a new building, intending to use the income from its rental for a part of his retirement. This made it marginal and unacceptable. We looked at a office supply company in Sebastopol, a glass company in San Leandro that could pocket cash sales thus reducing their tax. We got a response from a C.C. Ray, who had lived in Japan for many years as a representative of a national office machines company. C.C. had married a Japanese woman, had saved his money, knew the printing products Riso company , and decided that introducing their simplified screen printing products in the U.S. would be a profitable venture. He had attended not many, maybe just one or two, teacher conventions showing this simplified silk screen. He had a number of unfilled orders, as he had concluded this was not the growth item for him, and had found something else. I contacted the 22 teachers who had purchased the product with an easy questionnaire, and received I believe it was 18 responses, every one positive, even some raving, about this innovative screen. Although it obviously wasn't something that was the company that would support us, Ann and Clark liked the idea. I dickered for it and purchased which wasn't much more than an idea that seemed attractive for the great sum of $11,500. So we were in business in a non-heated warehouse in an industrial park in Ignacio, CA. We decided to incorporate as a C corporation. We could not get any of the preferred names, so we settled on the ingenious name of Welsh Products, Inc.

It was difficult to consider leaving Marin County, our home ever since coming to California. We rented an apartment and looked for places to buy. Marin real estate was getting expensive. In the East Bay, we found a lot for sale that had a beautiful view of the Sacramento River from the Carquinez bridge to the Benicia-Martinez bridge, and the price was a very affordable $35,000. Il didn't have anything to do, why not act as my own contractor, about which I knew absolutely nothing, to build our residence? It was a totally enjoyable experience. Our next door neighbor, Harry Gray, retired, about 80, knew a lot about construction. He loved to offer his suggestions. I would advertise for the contractor needed, and then check his references. This was effective and there was a minimum of disappointments. My problem was in knowing the next stage of construction, and Harry was helpful in this. The house was finished and while it was not as large and grand as our former residence in Tiburon it was comfortable with this great view of ships and trains. Also, it was close to good schools for Brian and Lynn.

We have a home, totally paid for. I am out of cash. I join Dean Witter as a stockbroker. Although I had not been licensed for some years, I was re-licensed as a NYSE operative. It was a different world. I can't come up with the exact word to define my fellow brokers, but it wouldn't be laudatory. I had never worked for a large national firm. They expected me to sell their loaded packaged products. I was a stock and bond broker who chose specific investments for my clients. To make a disagreeable story short, I rebelled and was fired. Frankly, it's a very profit oriented world.

I subsidized Welsh Products, Inc., a graphic arts mail order company from fees earned acting as finder, intermediary, and seller—sometimes sharing fees 50-50 with two separate fellows who had buying contacts. The last six completions, out of a total of eleven company sales, were all worth fees of $150,000 or more—one was $210,000. That was real money in the 1980s. Four of the buyers of these last six were Chef Francisco, a subsidiary of Labatt Breweries; Weetabix, in England; Schreiber Foods, in Green Bay, WI; and H. J. Heinz.
    ...The real turning point had come after I left MOKG. A fellow I knew through my finder/intermediary activity was aware

of a firm in Clarksville, Arkansas that made portion-controlled sweet potato patties for the food service industry that was for sale. He never did divulge his source, but I visited the company and got a written fee agreement. The first year, bad crop, not enough profit to justify the five million asking price. Next year, great crop, not enough freezer capacity, trucked product all over Arkansas to rented facilities, tough on profits. Next year, it all worked out. A subsidiary of a Canadian brewer, Labatt, name of Chef Francisco, Labatt's frozen food division, bought it. My partner and I split $150,000. This was in 1981, when $75,000 went quite a ways further than now. In a relatively short time we were able to sell three other food companies. I'd find them, get the fee agreement and follow up with them and my partner would find a buyer. My partners' name in the four food company sales was Roger Morf, wealthy, a perfect match of his capabilities and mine, we had such an enjoyable time in our successful endeavors. Roger died of a heart attack in his early 50s. Like my 8 year older sister Florence, both were powerful positive influences in my life. I miss both of them… The two water meter companies I located and represented along with Jim Mahoney, the author of a monthly merger activity letter who located the buyers, were both California companies, one in Hemet, the other Porterville. And Jim died of a brain tumor, again, early 50s. End of my most enjoyable and challenging business venture.

Our company had grown to the extent my involvement was necessary. But—I have to mention just one more fun deal…

Our business was in its infancy. Ann went to Chico, California to a teacher conference to show our products. I went to the Chamber of Commerce for a copy of their business and industrial directory. Oftentimes no company in town would be worth following up. But in Chico, I spotted a company that had enough employees to indicate their sales would be in the range of several million and had a product that looked promising. The name of the company was Chico San, a manufacturer of rice cakes, then a fairly new commodity, with only one other national competitor. They had a retail outlet and upon seeing the product, I was motivated to meet the president. Normally I would send a letter. I was not successful in obtaining an interview, but started correspondence. It turned out that the president and principal owner had a verbal agreement with a large food company relative to some future association. I contacted him at reasonable intervals. It was interesting in that he had been a studio musician in New York City, a trumpet player, who had moved to Chico because he and friends figured it was the least likely place that Russia would drop an atomic bomb... Some year or so later he said there had been a change in the head of the food section of the possible buyer of Chico San. Quickly I set up an appointment for Roger and me. We walked away with a fee agreement and an approved draft of a letter to send to prospective purchasers. My shorthand and typing skills came in handy that day... H. J. Heinz responded and visited with a staff of four or five. When it seemed there was an impasse, Roger's skills prevented their leaving without signing a letter of intent, and the deal closed some five months later. Easy, and it generated a fee of $215,000... However, none were really easy. They would look ready to close, some hitch would come up, and I'd get it back together or they would, so it was touch and go until the closing actually occurred. There's a story that two owners were at the closing and the buyer sat in the seller's chair, trying it out, as it was in a very nice office with a view. The seller was incensed, and told the buyer to get out of my chair, you S.O.B., it's not yours yet. Killed deal. The fact is, deals are killed at the last minute for trivial matters. So we can use Yogi Berra's "it's not over till it's over."

Although it took quite a few years and the dedicated and intelligent effort of Ann and subsidization from my company sales activity, it has turned out to be a very successful and enjoyable venture selling to schools. We worked with teachers, who are generally very pleasant individuals. But this would all have been naught if we did not have quality products. Teachers were overjoyed with the results they achieved from introducing our screen and safe water-based products to their students. And we took care of our customers, giving them timely service, friendly advice, and reasonable prices. With good products and service, and marketing, which we accomplished by exhibiting at some thirty teacher conferences a year. Only one result, and that's success. We're thankful. It's given us the opportunity to travel extensively throughout the U.S., and with the success of the business, a lot of world travel.

Clark realized that his future lay outside WPI and give him credit, he worked hard and went to S.F. State and then on to the Univ. of CA at Berkeley, and graduated as an optometrist. Kent also graduated from Berkeley, and went on to get a masters in religion and philosophy from another institution. Brian got his B.A. from Berklee, a music school in Boston, and his masters' from the Univ. of Texas at Denton. All three had and have strong musical leanings and capability. Lynn is a graduate of Chico State. She has a good business head. All four are our very good friends, our job…Not that I can say I have been, or am, a perfect parent. I read to them and spent enjoyable time with them. I know I wasn't a bad parent, but could have been a better one.

We lived in Benicia from 1981 to 2007, immersed in our business. We purchased a historic two story brick building built by the army in 1909 for a mule barn. It was comfortable and charming with a view of the river and ships. We did a lot of renovating, and the upstairs was improved to the point we sold our house and moved in. As we were married to the business, it made life easier. But after a number of years it was time to move on to something new and different. We turned our business over to our son Kent in 2007, sold the Benicia property, and moved into the San Francisco home we had purchased jointly with our son Clark some ten years previously, which we used as a week-end retreat away from our time-demanding business. So, at ages 87 and 74 we are at last, retired. But – we loved our business, but now, our discretion on how to use our time is even better. And used to get this effort to a printer, late in 2008. Viva la WOW!

another institution. Brian got his B.A. from Berklee, a music school in Boston, and his master's from the Univ. of Texas at Denton. All three had and have strong musical leanings and capability. Lynn is a graduate of Chico State. She has a good business head. All four are our very good friends, our joy… Not that I can say I have been, or am, a perfect parent. I read to them and spent enjoyable time with them. I know I wasn't a bad parent, but I could have been a better one.

We lived in Benicia from 1981 to 2007, immersed in our business. We purchased a historic two story brick building built by the army in 1909 for a mule barn. It was comfortable and charming with a view of the river and ships. We did a lot of renovating, and the upstairs was improved to the point that we sold our house and moved in. As we were married to the business, it made life easier. But after a number of years it was time to move on to something new and different. We turned our business over to our son Kent in 2007, sold the Benicia property, and moved into the San Francisco home we had purchased jointly with son Clark some ten years previously, which we had used as a week-end retreat away from our time- demanding business. So, at ages 87 and 74 we are, at last, retired. But—we loved our business, but now, our discretion on how to use our time is even better. And used to get the first edition to the printer early in 2009, and then demand for a second printing, late 2009. We sincerely thank you   Viva la WOW!

By Ralph T. Welsh

SPEAKING OUT

WHY WALL STREET ISN'T ALL BAD FOR SMALL BUSINESS

I n "Why Wall Street is Bad for Small Business" (Speaking Out, July 1979), Ray Dirks laments the current trend among investment banking firms of promoting mergers over public offerings. But is it really true, as Dirks suggests, that Wall Street therefore is bad for small business? I suggest it's not. Wall Street capital brokers don't create trends. They react to the market.

Dirks is right on one count. Government intervention has pared Wall Street's profit margins on new issue underwritings. If this action makes mergers more profitable than underwritings for firms on the Street, they can hardly be faulted for changing their tactics.

Furthermore, it's important to remember that Wall Street has two constituencies—buyers and sellers. While the Street can be innovative in devising and applying new techniques for raising corporate capital, it is not the trendsetter it should be because of its other role as adviser and broker to corporate, individual, and institutional investors.

As a dramatic example of the Street's failure to show real leadership on either side of the investment banking relationship—to companies seeking to raise capital or to investors seeking a return—consider 1969. Wall Street brought out a record 1,298 initial public offerings. Many companies with questionable chances for survival were underwritten by investment bankers at least in part to promote the underwriter's prestige and profit. Many of those deals had nothing to do with responsibly raising equity capital for deserving companies to finance sound growth prospects. They were marketed to eager but often unsophisticated speculators, many of whom watched their high-fliers crash in bankruptcy.

In the span of a few years during the public's acceptance of speculative offerings, the firm I was then with managed underwritings for nine issues. Three of these companies went bankrupt and no

Ralph T. Welsh upholds Wall Street's right to favor mergers over underwritings.

longer exist; two, no longer publicly traded, have offered to repurchase their shares at a fraction of the original offering price. The stock of the remaining three companies, though marketable, trades at less than the offering price.

The majority—or possibly all—of these companies should have remained private, to limp along or die, or, better still, they should have been merged with larger, stronger corporations. By merging into companies with substantial capital and management resources, these young firms might have become profitable operating divisions instead of foundering under inadequate management and competitive pressures too great to overcome.

But it is the capital markets, not Wall Street investment bankers, that have given the push to mergers. Individual investors, badly bruised by the beatings they took in the early 1970s, deserted the equity market and left the way clear for larger firms to expand by acquisition. Wall Street didn't have to encourage them. They saw the opportunities for investment in the capital needs of young, growing companies.

If Wall Street did anything to encourage the current high pace of mergers, it was to promote questionable stock

issues to a too-willing and unsophisticated public 10 years ago.

Let's look at what has happened more recently as rising interest rates have reinforced investor disenchantment with new issues. Amdahl, Avantek, Evans & Sutherland, Four-Phase, Harper Group, Rolm, Tandem Computers, Verbatim, and Xidex—to mention a few companies—have managed to raise capital via a public offering. These companies had to pay more for capital, selling at lower-than-usual price/earnings ratios—a reflection of conditions in the total money market, not only the new issue market. But they were able to raise funds because they were capable of standing up under hard-nosed investor scrutiny. If a company can prove it is a proper recipient of other people's money to be used in financing expansion and growth, the funds will be forthcoming.

The capital may not be furnished at the cheapest price, but it will be available at a rate competitive with other alternatives in the marketplace. An investor able to earn 10% in a low-risk situation must believe that the return from an untested new issue will pay considerably greater rewards, or he won't buy it. The door is not, and has not been, closed to those seeking funds for a well-managed, growing company with a good idea or product. It should never have been opened wide for companies lacking these strengths.

Mergers provide an alternative opportunity: to strengthen a business by adding the resources of a larger company, while liquidating the owner's interest in the business. Indeed, many entrepreneurs reach a point in their companies' development where the best move they could make is to turn the increasingly complex management problems over to managers. Few owner-founders enjoy dealing with the demands of stockholders, the financial community, and government that public companies face. Fewer yet handle these demands well.

So, is the shortage of capital Wall Street's fault, because it favors mergers over underwritings? I think not. And the fact is that for many small companies looking for the resources they need to grow, a merger is not a bad deal. □

R. T. WELSH & ASSOCIATES, INC.

P.O. BOX 246

BENICIA, CA 94510

435

MRS. HENRY H. ARNOLD
EL RANCHO FELIZ
SONOMA, CALIFORNIA

July 23rd.
'65

Dear Clark :—

Thank you for your card from the Air Academy. I wish you could see a Parade when the whole Regiment is there. It is an inspiring sight.

The enclosed is a replica of the tracking ship the USATS "Gen. H.H. Arnold" + has taken part in the latest space flights. My boys use these pins as tie pins but you could pin it on that wonderful blouse of yours. Please give my regards to the family and thanks again—

Sincerely Eleanor P. Arnold
Mrs. "Hap" Arnold.

Mrs. Hap Arnold letter to our son Clark at age 7

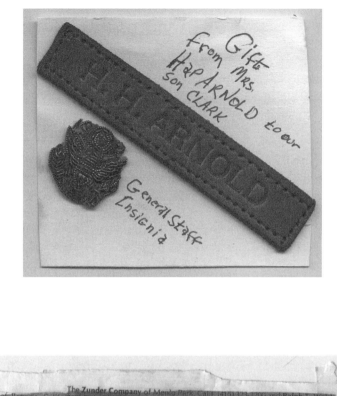

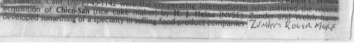

Zunder-RTW-Chico San from Corporate Acquisitions Newsletter

Epilogue

When I first thought about an epilogue, I wondered what it should contain. By this time you realize I'm not an expert in anything, but have a multitude of curiosities, and the principal one is people. No two the same, all have something interesting to tell.

What made my life pleasant and happy: wonderful parents and sisters; growing up on the prairie; being a pilot; college; falling in love with Ann; having four rewarding children; the challenge and success in finder/intermediary activity; starting and managing a family business and growing it to a sizeable, profitable, fun enterprise; traveling extensively, U.S. and abroad; and retirement at age 87 and the time to formulate this effort.

Have I made the world a better place? It's not worse because of me. I recognize that's not enough. I have day dreamed that, if I were immensely wealthy, I would devise a test for impoverished people, everywhere, to determine where their innate abilities lie. Everyone can be good at something. Give them training to succeed. The world would be a better, happier place.

I've discovered that the writings are never finished. You think of passages to improve, and delete others that don't sound as good when written. But—at some point it must go to the printer, short of what you consider your best effort.

Even with a few aches, pains, and maladies, living is a gift. BE POSITIVE AND ENJOY IT!